D1746912

Antonio Citterio. Architecture and Design

Alba Cappellieri

Antonio Citterio

Architecture and Design

SKIRA

Cover
Villasimius, Sardinia
Photo Leo Torri

Back Cover
Antonio Citterio
Photo Wolfgang Sheppe

Design
Marcello Francone

Editorial Coordination
Elena Carotti

Editing
Emily Ligniti

Layout
Alessandro Banfi, Antonio Citterio and Partners

Translations
Robert Burns for
Language Consulting Congressi srl, Milan

First published in Italy in 2007 by
Skira editore S.p.A.
Palazzo Casati Stampa
Via Torino 61
20123 Milan
Italy
www.skira.net

© 2007 Skira editore, Milano

All rights reserved under international copyright conventions.
No part of this book may be reproduced or utilized in any form or by any means, electronic or mechanical, including photocopying, recording, or any information storage and retrieval system, without permission in writing from the publisher.

Printed and bound in Italy. First edition

ISBN-13: 978-88-7624-647-0

Distributed in North America by Rizzoli International Publications, Inc., 300 Park Avenue South, New York, NY 10010, USA.
Distributed elsewhere in the world by Thames and Hudson Ltd., 181a High Holborn, London WC1V 7QX, United Kingdom.

Photo Credits
Aldo Ballo, p. 69
Simone Barberis, p. 284
Gabriele Basilico, pp. 33, 46, 47, 69, 90, 92, 93, 104 (top), 170, 171, 172 (right), 173 (bottom), 212 (bottom), 213 (left, bottom), 251
Fabrizio Bergamo, pp. 32, 34, 35, 70, 71, 72, 73, 122, 124, 125, 127, 234, 235
Hans Georg Esch, p. 249
Piero Fasanotto, pp. 244, 246
Ramak Fazel, pp. 286, 287
Klaus Frahm, pp. 80, 81, 82, 83, 175, 176, 177, 210, 211, 212 (top), 213 (top; right, bottom)
Hans Hansen, pp. 158, 160, 161
Rio Helmi, pp. 52, 53, 54, 55
Marc Hillesheim, pp. 30, 31
Marco Introini, p. 98
Enrico Pellegrini, pp. 100, 104 (bottom), 105, 106, 107, 172 (left, top and bottom), 173 (top), 252, 253, 254, 255, 270, 275
Pesarini & Michetti, pp. 238, 239, 240, 241
Francesco Radino, p. 91
Leo Torri, pp. 38, 39, 40, 41, 48, 49, 50, 51, 142, 143, 144, 145, 148, 149, 150, 151, 153, 154, 155, 156, 157, 186, 187, 188, 189, 190, 191, 192, 193, 194, 195, 206, 207, 214, 215, 230, 231, 232, 233, 256, 257, 259, 285
Studio Frea, p. 147
Studio IKB - Carlo Gessaga, Bruno Vezzoli, pp. 74, 75, 196, 197
Studio On time, p. 146
Gionata Xerra, pp. 282, 283

Courtesy 2x4 New York, p. 159
Courtesy Albatros, pp. 208, 209
Courtesy Ansorg, pp. 248, 249
Courtesy Antonio Citterio and Partners, pp. 102, 103
Courtesy Aubrilam, p. 301
Courtesy Arclinea, pp. 136, 137, 138, 139
Courtesy B&B Italia, p. 234
Courtesy Flos, pp. 244, 247
Courtesy Hansgrohe, pp. 141, 201, 202, 203
Courtesy Iittala, pp. 76, 77
Courtesy Inda, pp. 204, 205
Courtesy Kartell, pp. 236, 237
Courtesy Pozzi Ginori, pp. 206, 207
Courtesy Skantherm, pp. 78, 79
Courtesy Tre Più, p. 128
Courtesy Vitra, pp. 42, 43, 94, 95, 96, 97, 161

The iconographic material was provided by Antonio Citterio and Partners

Contents

9 Foreword
  Rolf Fehlbaum

13 Introduction
  Alba Cappellieri

23 History.1
31 Cene, Bergamo
32 B&B Italia: Eileen
   Xilitalia-B&B Italia: Quadrante
34 Maxalto: AC Collection
36 Busto Arsizio, Varese
39 Palazzo dell'Orologio of Clusone, Bergamo
42 Vitra: Spatio
45 Deutsche Schule, Milan
46 Bulgari Hotel, Milan
53 Bulgari Hotel, Bali
56 Jubilee, Rome

59 Comfort.2
69 B&B Italia: Diesis
71 B&B Italia: Freetime
   B&B Italia: Harry
   B&B Italia: Charles
   B&B Italia: Arne
73 B&B Italia: Mart
   B&B Italia: J.J.
74 Flexform: Air
   Flexform: Timeless
   Flexform: ABC
76 Iittala: Decanter
77 Iittala: Collective Tools
79 Skantherm: Shaker
81 Switzerland
85 Comparto Te Brunetti, Mantua
89 Eden, Bormio
90 Esprit, Milan
94 Vitra: Mobile Elements
98 Rozzano, Milan
100 Vighizzolo, Cantù
101 Metalco: Sedis
102 Piazza Cordusio, Milan
104 Underground, Milan
108 Ravenna Marina

111 Utility.3
120 Citterio-Dwan House, Milan
128 Tre Più: Planus
130 House in Sagaponack
137 Arclinea: Convivium
141 Hansgrohe: Axor Citterio Kitchen
143 Guzzini: My Table
145 Guzzini: Square
146 Fusital: K2
   Fusital: AC3
149 Lecce
151 Multinational Pharmaceutical Company, Verona
154 B&B Italia, Novedrate
158 Vitra: Ad One
   Vitra: Ad Hoc
161 Vitra: Ad Wall
163 Technogym, Cesena
170 Antonio Citterio and Partners, Milan
175 Neuer Wall, Hamburg

179 Structure.4
187 Villasimius, Sardinia
191 Colda, Sondrio
193 Sondrio
196 Flexform: Lightpiece
   Flexform: Vic
197 Flexform: Infinity
199 Hansgrohe: Axor Citterio
205 Inda: H2O
207 Pozzi Ginori, Bathroom Collections
209 Albatros: Cube
211 Edel Music, Hamburg
215 Aspesi, Milan
216 Convention Centre, Palma de Mallorca

221 Technology.5
231 Technogym: Kinesis Personal
235 B&B Italia: Otto Chair
236 Kartell: Battista
237 Kartell: Mobil
   Kartell: Dolly
239 Kartell: Glossy
   Kartell: Flip
240 Kartell: Spoon Chair
   Kartell: Spoon
243 Simon Urmet: Nea
   Simon Urmet: Folio
244 Flos: Lastra
245 Flos: Kelvin
248 Ansorg: Elettra
249 Ansorg: Brick
   Ansorg: Camera
250 Esprit, Amsterdam
253 Ermenegildo Zegna, Milan
256 Company Day-care Centre, Verona

261 Economy.6
271 Assago Milanofiori, Milan
272 Mercury Hotel in Barvikha, Moscow
277 Fairgrounds Hotels, Milan / Sviluppo Sistema Fiera
280 Varesine, Milan
282 Fausto Santini, Düsseldorf
284 De Beers, Los Angeles
285 De Beers, London
286 Flos: U Beam
287 Flos: H Beam
288 Shinsaibashi, Osaka
293 Brooktorkai Hafencity, Hamburg
294 Wettbewerb Brooktorkai Hafencity, Hamburg
296 Former Tobacco Works, Verona / Palladium
298 Wall: Mon bijou
301 Aubrilam: Alba
302 Historical Milan fairgrounds / Greenway Exposition Park
304 Neubau ABC Strasse / Hochfiel http
307 Palazzo Toro, Milan / CB Richard Ellis Limited
309 Former Martinelli Morbegno, Sondrio

311 Client.7
319 Biography Antonio Citterio and Partners
321 Architecture
322 Interiors
323 Design Products
326 Competitions
327 Selected Bibliography: Books
328 Selected Bibliography: Periodicals

"He who does not search the unsearchable
will not find ways in what is trackless and unsolved."
Heraclitus

Acknowledgements

Special thanks to

Antonio Citterio and Patricia Viel
For the attention, patience and precious food for thought they gave me during our many encounters and long discussions. Their generosity, willingness to help and hospitality went well beyond what a critic might hope for. You have my most heartfelt gratitude.

Emanuela Russo, Alessandro Banfi and especially Alessandra Noto of the Antonio Citterio and Partners studio
For the information and materials they provided. Their support and extraordinary efficiency were a fundamental asset in researching this book.

Nerio Alessandri, Andrea Branzi, Giorgio Busnelli, Aldo Cibic, Rolf Fehlbaum, Piero Gandini, Fulvio Irace, Italo Lupi, Cristina Morozzi, Vanni Pasca, Ettore Sottsass and Anna Zegna
The wealth of their stories helped me see Antonio Citterio's work from a variety of perspectives, and offered unexpected glimpses into his work.

Arturo Dell'Acqua Bellavitis, Alfonso Gambardella and Benedetto Gravagnuolo
Their guidance and advice provided me with invaluable tools for approaching the complexity of the critical process.

Silvana Annicchiarico, Federico Bucci, Flaviano Celaschi, Luca Molinari and Marco Romanelli
For their suggestions which, like their precious friendship, lightened and brightened the years dedicated to this work.

This book is dedicated to Marco,
who has given me the peace
of mind to complete this and many
other endeavours

Foreword

Rolf Fehlbaum

"Style reflects one's idiosyncrasies. Your personality is apt to show more to the degree that you did not solve the problem than to the degree you did."
Charles Eames

There are many ways to be a designer today, and Italian Design has been instrumental in creating this diversity. Alessandro Mendini and Antonio Citterio are both Italian designers, but how much overlap is there in their work?

And how are these types of work judged by the gatekeepers of the cultural archives: the curators, writers, collectors?

The answer seems easy: there is work which is rewarded by the market and work which is rewarded by entering design history. Is this mutually exclusive? And if so, do the gatekeepers miss an important point?

It is in the nature of cultural institutions like museums and collections that they select the radical for entry into the archives, the product or concept which breaks with the past, the solution which solves one aspect of a problem brilliantly and spectacularly at the expense of other aspects of the problem.

Contrary to the general expectations it is not the "timeless" which enters the archives, but the "fashionable" which uniquely and strongly expresses a time (Boris Groys, *Über das Neue*). The appropriate, even if it is innovative, has no place there. It becomes absorbed by everyday life. Its innovative aspects are so obviously useful that they are copied by the industry and become part of a new standard.

The gatekeepers as a rule are not aware of these innovations. That is why these innovations and their authors rarely appear in exhibitions on contemporary design. The gatekeepers usually look at design through the eyes of an art historian or an architect. These eyes see what is strong in expression or surprising in concept. These eyes look for something which can be grasped and reproduced in an image.

However, the eyes of the industry, the competitors of the producer who presents a new progressive product or designers who work in the same field see the strength of these innovations immediately, and without much comment or concern are integrating them in their own product.

Of course I make this point in order to emphasise Antonio Citterio's contribution to design, but before I do this in more detail, I want to draw attention to the fame of the American designer George Nelson. He is remembered for his expressive 1950s designs, the *Coconut* chair, the *Marshmallow Sofa* and the marvellous clocks. However, his contribution to the development of new typologies for workstations, modular seating and modular storage are only known by a few specialists. The reason is that after awhile almost all workstations looked like the one originally designed by George Nelson, and every manufacturer had a modular storage system in the spirit of the one developed by George Nelson. So his contribution to design is not fully understood, as it has become part of the vocabulary of a time, an element of evolution, which a historian of design may find difficult to isolate.

Antonio Citterio also realised a number of iconic designs. The fact that he is one of the most influential contemporary designers, however, is mostly due to his innovations in typology. Almost every producer of office furniture today has a system which is derived from Citterio's *Ad Hoc* system, and the sofa industry has received numerous inspirations from the work he did with B&B. Every industry insider knows this. But who else?

For the permanent renewal of design the iconic innovation is of course important, but so are the typological ones and the many small steps that are made to improve a product, to make it more usable, more pleasant. Antonio Citterio is the master of the good compromise. In the design process, he listens to all the needs and constraints of program (issues of beauty, technology, price, ecology, ergonomics, distribution, etc.) and in a time-consuming trial and error process, he proceeds until an appropriate solution is found.

He says that the project has a mother and a father, the couple being the designer and the producer. He sees the result as a common result, the result of the meeting of two minds, two sets of expertise, two wills which want to achieve the best solution together.

I have worked constantly with Antonio Citterio for twenty-four years, longer than with any other designer. There are never more than three weeks between meetings. In our discussions, we have no set roles. Sometimes he thinks like a producer and I think like a designer. He cares for Vitra in a generous way, not just as an instrument for the development and production of his own products. He is eminently generous and trusting and all of us at Vitra trust him. Nobody understands the full cycle of the product from development through manufacturing and distribution to the customer better than he does. We discuss not only products, but also the market, the business model, the role of design in our society.

In the course of this collaboration, memorable and highly successful chairs, office chairs and systems, storage programs and tables were developed. They form a crucial part of the Vitra offer.

Are we always aware of the importance of his contribution? Sometimes we get swept away by the spectacular project of another designer. And Antonio may feel that while he is responsible for the bread and butter lines, eccentric stuff gets more attention. But what is more important than providing bread and butter? Especially when they come in such delightful form.

Introduction

[1] Antonio Citterio, conversation with the author, November 2005.

"Are you sure you're an architect? Architects usually don't understand real estate."[1] The Californian magnate's puzzlement is not surprising. Antonio Citterio does understand real estate, and to make things worse, he lacks the *physique du rôle* of an architect. He does not adhere to the monasticism of the New York intellectual-in-black, nor does he have the allure of the British gentleman. He does not like the extravagancies of the archistars or the worldly-cultural lobbies. He is neither Narcissus nor Peter Pan. He does not start friendships to cinch contracts, but chooses his friends carefully, and his clients well.

He is a discreet and informal man. He spends most of his time in his houses and his studios. His point of reference is his family. His passion is his work. He has few friends, but he always seeks out the opinions of his partners and collaborators.

Rigour and an ethical vision of his work characterise Citterio's private and professional life and career, which has conceded nothing to excess or ostentation. His works are a crystallisation of discreetness and determination, two traits which have otherwise been summarily pushed aside in the "age of spectacle" as amounting to nothing more than lukewarm expressivity. Instead, by agency of his extraordinary ability to observe the settings in which people live and their newly evolving consumption patterns, Antonio Citterio has quietly ushered in innovations that have changed not only our perception of the objects around us – such as upholstered furniture and chairs – but also the makeup of certain domestic spaces – such as the bathrooms and kitchens that have emerged from his unquenchable penchant for exploration.

The objects created by Citterio acquire their ingenious and efficacious forms by taking their cues, as do those of Achille Castiglioni, from everyday behaviours and gestures. Antonio Citterio represents the excellence of Italian design in its contemporary version: quality, discreetness, lightness, but also the ability to dialogue with industry. He is *Homo faber*, offspring of the Milanese architectural culture founded by such masters as Ponti, Caccia Dominioni, Albini, Gardella and Magistretti, for whom the compositional gesture is never ostentatious, and architecture, interior design and interior decoration respond to a unitary vision of the project.

The Discreet Charm of Homo Faber

Antonio Citterio was born in Meda (Milan) in 1950. These geographical and temporal coordinates may appear insignificant, but in fact they mark his destiny, binding him inexorably to the universe of furniture and furniture makers, to the art of crafting and shaping. He moves within a discerning equilibrium between artisanship and industry, between conceiving with the mind and crafting with the hand, a capability which has made Brianza the world's premier industrial district for furnishings and interior design.

The industriousness of the *Brianzoli* runs in Citterio's blood. He is a prolific and generous architect and designer who states modestly: "I have never done anything else in my life, and I don't think I could." Planning and designing have been the stuff of his daily life ever since, at the age of eleven, he started working in his father's workshop. At the age of thirteen, he went to study at the Istituto d'Arte of Cantù, "a sort of school of arts and professions where you worked eight hours in a row, designing things down to the last detail." The diploma he earned there was his ticket into the School of Architecture at the Politecnico in Milan. At the age of eighteen, he won his first industrial design contest, and at twenty, in 1970, he opened his first studio, or as he puts it, "a small workshop", and returned, in the garb of an instructor, to the Istituto d'Arte of Cantù.

His burning desire to awaken the soul of his materials and seek out the best technique for expressing them in form, something which has characterised all of his work, dates back to his years of training. He had the "old-fashioned" kind of training as an apprentice, one that concentrated more on the pleasures of knowledge than on the richness of expression. "I would study during winter and spend the summer with my teacher," recalls Citterio. "He, with his grey coveralls, was a classic sculptor. I, with my yellow paper and tripod, would spend hours watching him sculpt."

Those were the years of the birth of Italian Design, and all its "founding fathers" passed through Meda, generating great upheaval, but also an effervescent climate among the methodical *Brianzolo* furniture makers, who found themselves transforming their workshops into "little factories". Citterio felt the ferment of an epochal shift, he sensed the innovative charge, and took his stand: "Gio Ponti was producing his *Superleggera* in the house next door to my parents', where my father designed and built period furniture. That marked the beginning of the conflict with my father on the meaning of modernity. My friends and I carried on the debate about the project, about design and about style; but it was a really fierce clash."

During his university years, Citterio concentrated mainly on design, and with a group of friends he began generating everyday household objects. His first works date back to 1972 for B&B. They were objects produced in his "studio-workshop, where I worked with my hands, which have always been for me an indispensable tool for gaining knowledge. Working with my hands helps me understand the materials, and it is through my hands that the project takes form." Probing manually the soul of a material in order to give it life was, to put it mildly, an unusual vocation within the architectural ferment of the 1970s, animated by the "new dimension" of development of the territory more than by actual architectural experimentation.

Citterio graduated from university in 1976, a period when, as he himself recalls, "total chaos reigned in the School of Architecture. It was forbidden to talk about architecture, with the result being that you no longer had an idea of what architecture was, much less aesthetics or creativity. I think this seriously penalised our generation, it created a deep void." In opposition to the void, Citterio and his friends – Michele De Lucchi, Aldo Cibic and Marco Zanini, to name just a few – found a vigorous *point d'appui* in Ettore Sottsass, a brilliant interpreter and soul of that euphoria that would sweep over the Milan of fashion and design in the 1980s. But Memphis did not touch Citterio. His well-rooted point of reference remained the modern movement. Citterio absorbed the formal rigour of the early masters of the modern, "the aesthetic of functionality", the sculptural abstraction of volume. Mies van der Rohe was foremost among them. This was demonstrated in Citterio's first sofa, *Diesis*, created in 1980, but so austere that it would still sell twenty years later, and by the Piero della Francesca gallery in the Pinacoteca di Brera, created with Vittorio Gregotti in 1983. The process of reduction in design was accompanied by exploration of structure in architecture. The lesson of Louis Kahn is clearly evident, and all of Citterio's work may be read as a variation on the theme of the wall and of the skin, lying along the borderline that marks contact with the outside world, like in the buildings of the 1980s, or a skin which, conversely, opens transparently to welcome in the surrounding landscape through a process of osmosis, as in the projects for the Deutsche Schule Mailand or the Fiera di Milano. Citterio's silent yet obstinate consistency and his preference for the industrial scale over the limited edition (hence his use of non-opulent, non-precious materials) inspired none other than Sottsass to mention him to Esprit, who were looking for someone to design their Italian quarters. This invaluable experience marked an important professional turning point for Citterio. Esprit recruited him and sent him to San Francisco, Hong Kong and Tokyo to meet their consultants: Norman Foster, Tadao Ando and Shiro Kuramata, thus allowing him to participate in that *esprit de corps* based on creativity and the *joie de vivre* that characterise the brand. In 1985, Citterio designed Esprit's Milanese quarters, in 1987 the one in Amsterdam and Antwerp and in 1990 the stores in Paris, Madrid and Lisbon.

"The real fortune for a professional is to meet exceptional clients," states Citterio. "In this regard, I can say I have been very fortunate. Doug Tompkins, Rolf Fehlbaum and the Busnelli have been very important clients for my professional growth. In the 1980s, design oscillated between the pragmatism of the American school, which would not give up the numbers made possible by industry, and the aesthetics of the Radical movement, which was opposed to industry. Personally, I think industry offers a great opportunity. Design is an integral part of the generative substrate of industry and narrates, especially in the Italian case, the history of industry. Italian design grew out of an ambiguous situation. Italian industrialists were artisans who could afford to make prototypes and thus forego industrial numbers. This openness to experimentation favoured collaboration with architects and designers, and was what marked the birth of Italian Design."

Citterio's professional career was nourished by industrial clients: Esprit, Vitra, B&B Italia, Zegna, Flos, Technogym, Kartell, Flexform, Maxalto, Arclinea, Hansgrohe and still many others. Citterio established a privileged relationship with them. He designed their offices, the decor of their stores and their products, always displaying the same meticulousness and almost maniacal attention to detail, without any vain protagonism or ostentatious display.

This overall approach to the project won him a number of recognitions: the Compasso d'Oro in 1987 for his *Sity* chairs for B&B Italia, and in 1995 for the *Mobil* trolleys for Kartell. These trolleys, along with the *Battista* trolley, are part of the permanent collections of the New York Museum of Modern Art. *Mobil* and *Battista*, along with the *Oxo* trolley, the small table *Gastone* and the *Dolly* folding chairs are also part of the permanent collections of the Centre Georges Pompidou in Paris. The *Collective Tools* tableware collection designed for Iittala is part of the permanent design collection of the Chicago Athenaeum Museum of Architecture and Design.

The professional associations he has established over time have been of fundamental importance: Paolo Nava at the beginning, then Terry Dwan, the Californian architect who would become his wife, and Patricia Viel, a partner in his studio and reference point for architecture, while Glen Oliver Löw, until 2000, and later Toan Nguyen, collaborated with him on design projects.

Design, interior design and architecture intermingle into a unity of arts that was proper to the masters of the Milanese school, but that is very little practised nowadays. "My principal clients are foreign," comments Citterio. "I believe I am better known abroad than in Italy. This is probably due to a sort of completely Italian resistance to the mixture of my work as an architect with that as a designer. I see no schism or crisis between architecture and design. Architecture differs from design in its locations and scales, however, the production process is the same. Personally, I always start with the ground plan. I am, as Caccia Dominioni used to say, a 'plannist' in the sense that my projects always start from the ground plan and the emotions aroused in me by the location." This approach characterises works such as the above-mentioned Milanese quarters of Esprit, along with more recent works such as the Edel Music building in Hamburg, the buildings

[2] Alba Cappellieri, "Antonio Citterio", in Silvana Annicchiarico, ed., *Maestri. Design Italiano*, Permanent Collection of the Triennale di Milano, Europalia, Hornu, 2003, pp. 144–149.

[3] Conversation with the author, February 2006.

and day care centre for GlaxoSmithKline in Verona, the Ravenna pier and Bulgari Hotels.

One might be surprised by Citterio's polite cordiality, his gentle humility. He smiles in his Milanese retreat on Via Cerva, decorated with drawings by Scarpa and models by Eames, he smiles and comments mockingly on the future: "If Milan had had its Frank Gehry, it would have been a different city, perhaps even revolutionary. I cannot think of doing things like Gehry would have because these things do not belong to me. It is a question of limits. I am a conservative, I stand still while others move and I do not believe in revolutions."[2]

The Designer as Knowledge Broker

"What is the role of the designer? The designer is a person who is part of a team and has to work with a host of other players who might be engineers, technicians and so on. As long as there is industry, there will be designers." Citterio fully displays the capacity to act as a liaison between the company and the production chain: from the supplier, through marketing and advertising, all the way to the consumer. "Designing fundamentally means resolving a problem," affirms Rolf Fehlbaum. "A designer has to have a good grasp of production processes and an equally good grasp of company identity. Good designers are problem solvers. They work with an aesthetic sensitivity to resolve ergonomic, formal or ecological problems. Citterio is an excellent problem solver."[3]

Citterio is more than a problem solver: he is a knowledge broker, a knowledge catalyst, a designer who does not merely propose a product concept, but also a method for producing it, a designer who directs knowledge and brings people into contact. Within a conception of design as a process where what counts is not just the creative act, but above all being part of a system, Citterio is one of the few designers capable of directing the entire process that stretches from the producer to the consumer. And in a system like the Italian one, where debate continues as to whether design has to be industrial or artistic and artisanal, this capacity is unquestionably a highly novel element.

Innovation in Citterio's work comes from his silent yet tenacious exploration of form and materials, and his encounters with other creative experiences. He never misses a tradeshow; he scrutinises all types of objects to find solutions that cut across borderlines. His architecture, offices, decor and objects all contribute to a company's experimental quest, as we see, for instance, in the upholstered furniture for B&B Italia, in the *Lastra* lamp, in the chairs for Vitra or his *Kinesis Personal* for Technogym. They also contribute to the improvement of habitats, as in his exploration of the kitchen system for Arclinea or the bathroom system for Hansgrohe. His *Ad Hoc* and *Vademecum* projects for Vitra enhance the office space, while his decor for Malvestio embellishes healthcare facilities.

But he moves across a broad range of scales, expanding to a territorial vocation as exemplified by his work for Technogym, or moving to enrich the urban context, as we see in the Ravenna pier, his urban fixtures, his piazza in Rozzano, the Clusone town hall and the project he submitted to the design contest for the Brooktorhafen bridge in Hamburg.

Vittorio Gregotti quite correctly points out the "professional" stamp of architecture, understood as "the completion of a job that has, beyond its subjective ends, a collective purpose as a product of art associated with a social condition and its prospects for transformation."[4]

I believe this is particularly true in Antonio Citterio's case, where the guiding thread of the knowledge that circulates in his work follows a very sinuous path, nourished by the many changes of scale that characterise the designer's work: from his knives to the Wellness Valley, from his lamps to his office systems and from his armchairs to his hotels. The practice of architecture and design, shaped according to the work ethic, implies a functional, formal, semantic and aesthetic review of the project, understood as a service to the community and not as an instance of self-celebration. Indicative in this regard is Bruno Munari's definition of a designer as "a planner with an aesthetic sensibility who works for the community."[5] Citterio revolutionises the concept of domestic space. He rethinks kitchen and bathroom environments, integrating architecture, interior design and decor. He meditates on the evolution of the individual functions, and is thus able to eliminate the barriers between the different types. And so we find office tables that look like household tables, and offices with all the warmth and comfort of home. "It is very important to be an architect if you are going to design offices," he affirms. "It is only through a study of layouts that you can understand exactly what the needs of the users are. We were among the first to think that a worktop did not necessarily have to be a canonical table. We began to talk about flexibility and went on to develop products based on this concept. By knowing how an office works we are able to design objects that resolve various issues."[6]

The office systems created for Vitra are characterised by their combinational flexibility. They can be customised depending on the dimensions of the space and the type of furnishings required. But above all, they highlight Citterio's ability to view design as a system, where the single elements – tables, chairs, cabinets, storage units – are conceived both as individual objects and as components of a habitat.

Antonio Citterio understood well ahead of the rest that the products of design would be integrated into the rationale of the global market, and he thus falls into that small number of Italian professionals whose products range in a continuum from small to

[4] Vittorio Gregotti, "L'architettura come lavoro", in *Architettura, tecnica, finalità*. Rome–Bari: Editori Laterza, 2002, p. 110.

[5] Bruno Munari, *Artista e Designer*. Rome–Bari: Editori Laterza, 1971, p. 28.

[6] Conversation with the author, April 2007.

[7] Philip Johnson, "The Seven Crutches of Modern Architecture", *Perspecta 3*, 1955, pp. 40–44, based on the Italian translation "I sette puntelli dell'architettura moderna", in Philip Johnson, *Verso il Postmoderno. Genesi di una deregulation creativa*. Genoa: Costa&Nolan, 1985, p. 100.

[8] After his famous lecture at Harvard, in a 1962 speech at the Annual Northeast Regional Conference of the American Institute of Architects, Johnson stated his position and replaced the crutch of beautiful drawing with technology.

[9] Philip Johnson, *Op. cit.*, p. 112.

large dimensions without losing any of their power and effectiveness. Seemingly coincident, architecture and design are actually distinct realms that are governed by sets of conceptions, aesthetics and management approaches which are convergent yet distinct. This is clearly shown by the projects for Vitra and B&B, where Citterio is called upon not only to design the container, but also the contents, paying equal attention to issues involving aesthetics and economics.

This attention to the economic factors in the compositional process, seeking to fill in the space between the intimate world of the project and the disenchanted reality of production, installation and use, runs through and represents one of the distinctive characteristics of all of Antonio Citterio's works. As he sees it, you do not achieve contemporary works by using colours and forms that are in fashion at the moment: contemporary works are the outcome of harmony between design and production, in the sense that all elements have to be easily manufactured, packaged, transported and stored. They must have low investment costs, "which does not mean lowering the quality; it means controlling the process," explains Citterio.

Right from his first buildings – Esprit in Milan or the Antonio Fusco facility in Corsico – Citterio has demonstrated the unusual quality of being able to see normal things in a different way. His secret lies precisely in this work of elevating normalcy to the ranks of exceptionality. It is work that focuses on details, materials, finishings, the organisation of function, integration of technology and performance. This is what determines the utility of use of a building, but also the utility of context, in the sense that it improves the urban setting without invading it. In this dual expressive register, we see the filigree of the culture of a city – Milan – which holds design and production together, and that has historically preferred the discreet quality of the contents over the ostentatious display of form.

The "Seven Crutches"

On 7 December 1954, Philip Johnson gave a lecture at the Harvard School of Architectural Design titled "The Seven Crutches of Modern Architecture", ironically echoing John Ruskin's "Seven Lamps of Architecture". Johnson said that he was there to fight the seven props of architecture. Some are happy to use them as crutches, convinced that walking on two legs is a sort of handicap.[7] The seven props are history, beautiful drawings (soon to be replaced by technology[8]), structure, utility, economy, comfort and the client. They are considered to be seven crutches, seven touchstones, seven catchwords that architects use every day to excuse themselves and defend themselves before the world.[9] Johnson's seven crutches still represent an interesting interpretive key for the planning and design process, and this is why they are proposed for a critical interpretation of Citterio's work, being preferred to the more usual diachronic and typological reading.

The seven crutches were elaborated in a period that was profoundly different from the current era, and in the cultural climate of Harvard University, which, under the guidance of Gropius, had become the frontier post of functionalism and *existenz minimum*. As Peter Eisenman commented, much of what Johnson said was considered pure heresy by the instructors, and perhaps even by the students. And yet this conversation represented the most intelligent contribution to architecture in a pluralistic society. When Eisenman read those pages for the first time as a budding architecture student, he was an instant convert. Johnson had said all that needed to be said against the pseudo rules that a first-year student learns by heart.[10]

Thus the clarity of Johnson's *j'accuse* is stunning when he asked what it was that wasn't working in the art of building and ventured that no one had any clear ideas about it. Why was it that the architect's art in one of the most affluent societies that the earth had ever seen was not the greatest that had ever existed? In ancient times, architecture was the mother of all arts. Even though Michelangelo and Bernini were both sculptors and architects, there is no doubt as to which one was the principal art of their age.[11]

Stated this way and so charged with meaning, Johnson's crutches have given excellent results in the critical reading of Citterio's works. In certain cases, they served to support the fallaciousness of the props, but in others they have shown how a crutch may at times transform itself into a foot and become a foundational element of the language of planning and design. "Economy", for example, can be a constraint, but also a project stimulus – as happens in Citterio's work – that brings together different fields and enriches the overall project. Or take "comfort", which may certainly passively condition a form to the detriment of beauty, but may also represent an objective to attain through ease and wellbeing: environments and objects that make home and work spaces comfortable, structures that enhance the usability of the city and its urban spaces and so on.

These pages seek to initiate a discussion about the work of Antonio Citterio, architect and designer, with the goal of acknowledging his influence on the international design culture. The detailed monographs dedicated to the work of Citterio[12] evidence a certain discontinuity of language in favour of a uniformity of method. Personally, I feel that this extraordinary output of buildings and objects, on the contrary, exhibits a well-defined coherence and a linguistic uniformity. Sure, the buildings of the 1980s are profoundly different from their contemporary counterparts, but the structural tension, the work with the surface, the interpenetration of planes and the interaction between outside and inside all appear to represent instances of unvarying semantics. On the Italian scene,

[10] Ibid., p. 99.

[11] Ibid., pp. 105–106.

[12] Luigi Prestinenza Puglisi, *Antonio Citterio*. Rome: Edilstampa, 2005; Alberto Bassi, *Antonio Citterio. Industrial Design*. Milan: Electa, 2004; Pippo Ciorra, Vanni Pasca, *Antonio Citterio, Terry Dwan: Ten Years of Architecture and Design*. Basel: Birkhäuser, 1995; Pippo Ciorra, Brigitte Fitoussi, Vanni Pasca, *Antonio Citterio & Terry Dwan. Architecture & Design. 1992–1979*. Zurich: Artemis, 1993.

[13] Enzo Mari, *Progetto e Passione*. Turin: Bollati Boringhieri, 2001, p. 52.

Citterio is among those who stay the course, albeit making whatever adjustments are necessary. The ultimate objective for both architecture and design is the quest for form, but it is the method and not the scale of the work that provides continuity among the different areas.

From this perspective, it would be baseless to classify his work by type, utility or as a chronological catalogue. This book does not set out to highlight his successes, but rather to analyse the context that produced them and the measure of innovation that they have introduced into the complex pathway, because, as Enzo Mari used to say, "the quality of a project depends on the degree, however small, of cultural change that it sparks."[13]

"Be Here Now"

Antonio Citterio is among the few who in the 1980s did not jump on the postmodern addition bandwagon, but instead worked with subtraction, with the legacy of Mies van der Rohe, adhering to an aesthetic – the aesthetic of reduction – that would soon rise to the stature of one of the new paradigms of international architectural culture.

His architecture stands as a backdrop to changes in society. His interiors mark the shift from the bourgeois house of the 1950s to the contemporary house, while his objects anticipate the new rites of intangible luxury. The masters of Milanese architecture taught him that there is no innovation without tradition . . . and no tradition without innovation. Tradition has to be renewed by culture, but at the same time there can be no creativity without tradition. Citterio interprets tradition by choosing modernity as the object of mimesis. His expressive coherence derives partially from this choice of field. Memphis did not sway him, nor was he touched by postmodernism as translated by Paolo Portoghesi in his famous *Strada Novissima*. "I was fascinated by a Charles Jencks conference I attended," recounts Citterio, "and when I came out I felt even more *modern*, if one may say so, in the sense that modernity seemed more alive than ever to me and my reference points were still well-rooted in the masters of the modern movement: Le Corbusier, Louis Kahn and Mies van der Rohe."

Antonio Citterio is, and always will be, profoundly "modern". His is a modernity that is admittedly stripped of the ideologies of its pioneers, but faithful to the principles of regularity, to the emphasis of volume, to the intrinsic elegance of materials, to the correspondence between form and context. It is a modernity, in the words of Giorgio Busnelli, that "suffers without straying off course", that does not veer off stylistically or respond to the winds of fashion. It is a modernity understood as a coherent way of life, whose meaning was well captured in John Lennon's response to a journalist who asked him what rock was: "Being here now."

HISTORY.1

On 5 February 1959, Philip Johnson held a lecture at Yale where he affirmed that his direction was clear and that it was traditionalism. His was not an academic revival; in his work, there were neither classical orders nor gothic spires. He took what he liked from history, but stated that "we cannot not know history".[1] But thirty years later in Chicago, the political economist and philosopher Francis Fukuyama would write his brilliant and provocatory essay, "The End of History?".[2] The apocalyptical title was based on a searching analysis of the driving forces behind the process of history, which Fukuyama later identifies as the part of the human soul that Plato (and Hegel) referred to as *thymòs*. While Plato's meaning is perhaps best translated as *spiritedness*, Fukuyama takes it to mean *desire for recognition*, with all the sentiments of indignation, shame and pride attendant to this explosion of *amour-propre*. Once this desire for recognition has been satisfied, as happens to varying extents in liberal democracies, Fukuyama believes that the process of history will reach its end, and its new protagonist can only be a "last man" stripped of aspirations and the willingness to struggle.

Let us use this fine distillate of political science to observe the events of the past architectural century. Anthony Vidler says that futurist-trained modern architects sought to eliminate all traces of history from their work in an attempt to liberate culture from what Henry James referred to as an oppressive sense of the past. Their haste to free themselves of history was part of a therapeutic programme dedicated to the elimination of nineteenth-century squalor in all its forms.[3] The "battle for modern architecture", as it was called by its pioneers, pushed the art of building ahead with great strides from the avant-garde's heroic season to the recent empire of its more or less orthodox interpretations, which had grown up in the shadow of a struggle whose will was now broken. However, if we set aside the debate over the "end of architecture" and limit ourselves to thinking about how *thymòs* has been expressed by twentieth-century architects, we will see that in the desire for recognition of the fathers, sons and grandsons of the so-called "modern movement", forays into history have played a fundamental role. In a twist, the history that Gropius banished from Bauhaus programmes and that Johnson over-emphasised with the postmodern, had actually become the secret weapon for defeating the foes of modernity. Gio Ponti, in his *In Praise of Architecture*, wrote that the past does not exist, everything is simultaneous in our culture. The only thing that exists is the present in the representation that we make for ourselves of the past and in our intuitions about the future.[4]

But in Italian architectural culture, the debate on "tradition" and "preexisting environmental elements" that began in the 1950s in the pages of *Casabella-continuità* opened a new way for the pioneers and epigones of Italian rationalism. In Milan and Rome, the Italian masters — from Albini, the BBPR, Gardella, Figini and Pollini to Quaroni and Ridolfi — used history to revitalise the language of modern architecture, even at the cost of international excommunication.[5]

It would be a new language, one which approached history and tradition with restraint and rigour. As Calvino put it in his criticism of Vittorini, it was a language that chose to speak of "means of production", while ignoring "consumer goods". Unfortunately, we hear this language spoken less and less. The courageous vessel of Italian architecture has begun a slow, but inexorable shipwreck, hit by rampant speculation, by ruination of a landscape and an architectural heritage that is increasingly

[1] Philip Johnson, in a lecture on non-Miesian trends held at Yale University, 5 February 1959, published in Philip Johnson, *Writings*. Oxford: Oxford University Press, 1979. The excerpt here is based on the Italian translation, Philip Johnson, *Verso il Postmoderno. Genesi di una deregulation creativa*. Genoa: Costa&Nolan, 1985, p. 202.

[2] Francis Fukuyama, "The End of History?", *National Interest*, 1989.

[3] Anthony Vidler, *The Architectural Uncanny*. Cambridge, Massachusetts: MIT Press, 1992.

[4] Gio Ponti, *Amate l'architettura*. Genoa: Editrice Vitali e Ghianda, 1957, p. 93. Published in English as *In Praise of Architecture*.

[5] See Manfredo Tafuri, *Storia dell'architettura italiana 1944-1985*. Turin: Einaudi, 2002.

[6] A point of view well expressed in Francesco Dal Co, ed., *Storia dell'architettura italiana. Il secondo Novecento (1945-1996)*. Milan: Electa, 1997.

[7] Ernesto Nathan Rogers, "Il passo da fare", *Casabella-continuità*, May 1961, no. 251, p. 2.

[8] Ibid.

[9] See Ernesto Nathan Rogers, *Esperienza dell'architettura*. Milan: Skira, 1997.

overcrowded and defenceless against incursion. The daring ventures of Italian architects, ready to express themselves with coarse words if that was what it took to be understood by all, were emasculated by insidious traps and the sirenic allure of the economic "miracle".

Starting in the 1960s, the so-called "new dimension" of the Italian territory gained numerous proselytes ready for whatever balancing act was necessary to get them the job of building several thousand cubic metres devoid of history, where they could concentrate all those who were not to have access to the "heart" of the city, to the government of the country. Without a doubt, many erred in good faith, but ingenuous accomplices to deceit were few in number as compared to those many architects who consciously and willingly appended their names to irreparable damage. In general, the few pieces of quality work in the past fifty years testify to the drama of lost illusions, the tragedy of a fighting "mood" reduced to silence by the distressing sight of a horribly disfigured landscape.[6]

In reality, this is the chronicle of a foretold disaster. In 1961, Ernesto Nathan Rogers, Editor-in-Chief of *Casabella-continuità*, opened the special edition of the magazine dedicated to "Fifteen Years of Italian Architecture" as follows: "We have to admit that even here in Italy, in spite of a greater desire to communicate, architecture has not succeeded in breaking through to the elite and has failed to permeate society. The living works are scattered islands in a sea of speculators and embalmers: the economic boom, which had the effect of multiplying the number of work sites, has not been accompanied by a widespread architectural culture."[7]

But Rogers also indicated a way out: "The thing to do is to study history until — as paradoxical as it may sound — we forget it. If we achieve perfect combustion of tradition there will be no residue left behind and all the energy will go into a new flame."[8] Rogers was not talking about consigning history to oblivion, but rather about all that we believe we have assimilated, "forgotten", but that is necessary for the achievement of a creative act, similar to the way that when we write or speak we "forget" the rules of grammar and spelling that we have absorbed.

At the Milan Faculty of Architecture in the 1950s and 1960s, Ernesto Nathan Rogers was the spearhead of a bona fide "pedagogic revolution" based on a way of reading the history of modern architecture in relation to the planning and design process, and on whose coattails — staying within the confines of the Milanese school — we find pupils such as Vittorio Gregotti, Aldo Rossi, Guido Canella and Giorgio Grassi. The pages of *Casabella-continuità*, which Rogers directed from 1953 to 1965, were the training ground for developing the close interweave of history and design.

Rogers's history was an "operative history" and he had his young pupils studying Van de Velde and the nineteenth century in Lombardy, Loos and German expressionism, the Amsterdam school and Soviet architecture so that they could apply these pioneering quests to a critical "continuity" with the modern movement. For Rogers, the "sense of history" was not just the key for interpreting and getting beyond the teachings of the masters — Gropius above all — on modern European architecture, but it was also a way to relate to the new realities of life.[9]

Antonio Citterio, graduating from the School of Architecture of the Politecnico in Milan in 1976, has developed this particular aspect of Rogers's lesson and now numbers among the Italian designers who are most sensitive to an "operative history" based on the continuity of a tradition reinterpreted through contemporary eyes. The rigour of the Milanese school – as exemplified by Caccia Dominioni, Albini and Gardella in particular – is well represented in his work, as is the lightness of the modern masters – Mies van der Rohe, Le Corbusier and Aalto – where the integration of architecture, interior design and interior decoration is the goal to be pursued.

History for the Home

Private residence, Cene; B&B Italia: Eileen*; Xilitalia-B&B Italia:* Quadrante*; Maxalto:* AC Collection

Antonio Citterio's first works date back to the 1980s, the postmodern season, when the use of historicist elements, previously limited to the theoretical matrix of the work, was now also extended to the form of the buildings and their ornamentation. Citterio has no patience for or interest in rehashing the ornamental or decorative album of history – he already demonstrated this with Memphis – and the object of his mimesis is always the "modern". His modernist rigour accepts experimentation with traditional materials, whose membership in the local tradition, thus to the history of places, is the only reference he tolerates. In his house in Cene, for example, the geometrical purity of the volumes combined with the stone face-work recalls the villa that Le Corbusier designed for Hélène de Mandrot. As in Le Corbusier's work, while on the one hand the stonework violates the functionalist dictum *nihil addi* (add nothing), on the other it refers to a culture associated with a place, the *genius loci* of Norberg Schulz, to which Citterio often refers. The austere rigour of the base unit with its narrow light-modulating slits is tempered by the materiality of the stone and harmonises nicely with the surrounding landscape.

The interest in using materials deriving from local traditions is also seen in his design objects. This is the case for the *Compagnia delle Filippine* collection for B&B Italia, while for other objects he designed for them Citterio moved away from furniture designs proper to the Italian tradition. We see this, for example, in the *Quadrante* and *Eileen* collections. The choice of the name *Quadrante* – the legendary architecture magazine founded by Bardi and Bontempi in 1933 – is a reference to the design culture of the 1930s and 1940s and to the furniture by Asnago and Vender exhibited at the sixth edition of the Triennale in 1936. They are a series of low, lacquered cabinets emphasising the expanded horizontality of the internal space, creating an effect of depth. "The architectural aspect of this project lies in its structural work," states Citterio, "in addressing the concept of bearing and borne elements, in emphasising the horizontal elements, the frame members, the joints, where each piece has a functional definition."[10] Citterio carries out experiments within the rationalist tradition, thus innovating it. The focus on structure of the masters of the modern movement is exalted and sublimed in the delicacy of the bearing elements counterpoised by the horizontal gravity of the piece of furniture.

The same design principle is later reelaborated to achieve its expressive acme in 2003 in the *AC Collection* for Maxalto (part of the B&B Group). Tables and cabinets appear suspended on nearly invisible frames, the lines are clean and crisp and the structural clarity is evident throughout. Here the rationale of the single piece becomes part of a system of logic. "I think that a furniture project consists of designing an environment in which the object, via its uses and its relations with other objects, participates in the ritual qualities of the domestic components. The rituality represents the

[10] Ibid., p. 45.

[11] Ibid., p. 126.

[12] Giorgio Busnelli, conversation with the author, June 2005.

[13] Ibid., p. 94.

essence of the middle class culture of the home."[11] Citterio has contributed to defining the new rites of dwelling that draw from deep reaching roots of tradition. His relationship with the Busnelli family has developed to the point where the client participates directly in the experimentation, as Giorgio Busnelli relates: "The relationship between Citterio and B&B began when my father commissioned Antonio to design the *Baia* sofa in 1975. I then took over the house division of B&B in the early 1990s. Antonio became the prime designer for the company with me. He was born in Meda, just like us. My father had a liking for him because he had, and still has, a strong yet flexible personality, but he is also very witty and fun to be with. But what my father liked best about Antonio was his determination, the clear sighted vision he had of his career. In spite of the fact that he needed to work, he suffered without straying off into C-series products. He wanted to work with B&B, and with tenacity and determination he succeeded. He is someone who breaks things down and analyses them. He is almost always with me, he supports me, he encourages me, and I do the same for him, because there is no one in the last thirty years who has innovated products the way he has. All the upholstered furniture of the last twenty years owes something to him. Antonio has brought us contemporary culture without forgetting – or worse, betraying – our tradition."[12]

History for the Workplace

New pedestrian piazza in Busto Arsizio, project; Palazzo dell'Orologio, Clusone; Vitra: Spatio

While in many works in Milan one can read the tradition of elegant architecture that characterised postwar Milan, Citterio's choice in two works affecting the historical urban fabric of Busto Arsizio and Clusone reflects a precise way of approaching Rogers's theme of "preexisting environmental elements" via the interpretation of the local tradition of building, elaborated in a contemporary key and making no concessions to the "picturesque".

In the new pedestrian piazza in Busto Arsizio, the design choice reestablishes the continuity of the historical built fabric of the city through a row of buildings with peaked roofs and vertical windows, forming a backdrop to a series of new public pedestrian areas. As opposed to Citterio's piazza in Rozzano, here the bond with the built fabric of the city is represented by the historical vocation of the buildings facing the piazza.

In Clusone, on the other hand, the restoration of the town hall offices was resolved primarily by reproposing elements from the local architectural tradition, such as wood and stone, to create particularly elegant and functional interiors. Architecture and internal architecture integrate harmoniously and the decor becomes the space-arranging element, facilitating office work through flexible, modular systems.

Among the most versatile and functional office systems, paradigm of a new concept of furnishing the work space, is the *Spatio* system designed for Vitra, where "we were among the first to think that a worktop did not necessarily have to be a canonical table," explains Citterio. "We began to talk about flexibility and went on to develop products based on this concept. By knowing how an office works we are able to design objects that resolve various issues."[13] With the unveiling of this collection in 1992, the office furniture paradigm was overturned with apparent simplicity. The workstation was born – a composite system: table, drawer unit, cabinet and bookcase that for the first time were conceived so as to be freely combinable to create environments that are able to adapt to transforming work styles. Traditional materials such as wood are associated with lightweight, simple steel and aluminium frames into an overall image that is at once familiar and innovative. Citterio proves that he knows his history and has assimilated it to the point of being able to get beyond it because, as Apollinaire used to say, "only those who know the rules are able to break them".

History for the City and Territory

Deutsche Schule, Milan, competition project; Bulgari Hotels, Milan and Bali

In a period when architectural styles are reacquiring an autonomous urban identity through the power of the figure, Citterio confirms an ethical vision of the project process founded on the values of discretion and integration. Lightness, elegance and irony are the characteristics of the work of the Antonio Citterio and Partners studio, where the lessons of the masters of the modern movement have a strong presence, but without ever driving the studio to resort to the ornamental album of history.

Citterio is well aware of the context in which he works, and he shows it clearly as much in the project for the Deutsche Schule Mailand as in the Bulgari hotels, for example, by demonstrating just how much the relationship to the place represents the complexity of the exercises of the project.

In the design contest for the Deutsche Schule Mailand in 2004, Antonio Citterio succeeded in carving out a tree-filled green space in the heart of Milan and integrating it into a multifunctional structure that includes a nursery school with seven sections, a refectory and a number of gymnasiums. A bridge connects the new building to the preexisting one, which houses the offices of the principal and staff. One of the characteristics of the project is the mimetic neutrality of the façade, which reflects the cityscape and the monumental qualities of the setting in wood and glass façades. The glass is tinted in different nuances of green depending on the different requirements of prospect. On the inside, materials were chosen with a concern for maintenance, safety and cleanliness. The grey PVC floor enhances both the colours of the service blocks and the qualities of the wood partitions. The lightness of the work strongly characterises the space, freeing it of Milanese gravity and exalting, in the transparency of the green glass and the reflections of the surrounding trees, the sense of cosiness and warmth becoming to a nursery school.

In the Bulgari Hotel in Milan, created in the former convent for Augustinian nuns of Santa Chiara and overlooking the Botanical Garden of the Accademia di Brera, the architect had to address a number of important historical elements. There was a fragment of the eighteenth-century façade of the convent, which he framed in bronze on the new façade of the building. And he chose to recompose the historical urban fabric by building a continuous wall along the road. But it is especially in the expression of the relationship between interior and exterior that Citterio demonstrates his ability to interpret the tradition of the history of Milanese architecture via a series of refined and discerning references. The elegant façades, with their polished white stucco, are resolved with a geometrical series of full height apertures – windows, loggias and French doors – that create a sober and rigorous composition that is highly connoted.

The constructional pattern is clearly visible in the alternating sequence of solid and void spaces: in the base, with the entrance foyer, the doors appear oversized. The *piano nobile* is embellished with a broad loggia, as is the top floor; the three floors of the central section are cadenced by the rhythmic alternation of windows of different widths, aligned along one side, but out of line with the pillars of the loggias.

In its overall appearance, the building reminds one of Caccia Dominioni's house in Piazza Sant'Ambrogio in Milan. The full height windows are a homage to Gardella, while the arrangement of the windows, cut cleanly into the white surface of the façade (with fine, slightly protruding black granite edging), is a clear tribute to the two-dimensional compositions of Asnago and Vender.

It is a large leap from Lombardy to Indonesia, but Citterio's method has now acquired a particular ability to relate to the history of its place. The Bulgari Resort in Bali is incorporated into an area that has been landscaped with a series of terraces built using a local stone known as *bukit*. This stone is initially white, but becomes black as it absorbs moisture to blend in with the dark grey rocky landscape of hewn stone and lava. This evocative panorama surrounds the sixty rooms, which are bona fide independent villas laid out around a swimming pool and a tropical garden. The hotel-village structures have traditional *alang alang* roofs (a coconut leaf thatch), and the frames, doors, windows and floors are made of *bangkiray*, a Javanese mahogany with an intense reddish hue.

Here we see a particular characteristic of Citterio's architecture in its way of relating to a historical reality that must neither be dominated nor erased by imposing arbitrary forms. The local reality with which the architect must establish a relationship is to become acquainted with and to shape through the planning and design process guided by an idea of the necessary qualities of living space. Citterio thus appears to stand outside of a formal vernacular tradition. The difficulty in identifying the origin of his architectural grammar lies in the fact that the material with which the architect works is the history of the place and of those who live in it. Looking at these works, one might even go so far as to affirm that the "sense of history" for Citterio lies in an unusual capacity to represent the aspects of the reality of the place where he is working, in diametric contrast to the spectacular plastic expressivity and characteristic alienation of much of today's architecture. Here, mimesis (from the Greek μιμεσισ, "imitation, representation") is to be understood in the Aristotelian sense of "pleasure of recognition". It does not mean copying or repeating, much less duplicating, the objects of life. Mimesis has an expressive – not a reproductive – power, and this is why true mimesis brings recognition. It is recognition that is sparked by an analogic-creative imitation that ends up producing something different from what it imitates: the "pleasure of recognition" lies in the act of giving life back to the model, as if it were being created anew.

HISTORY

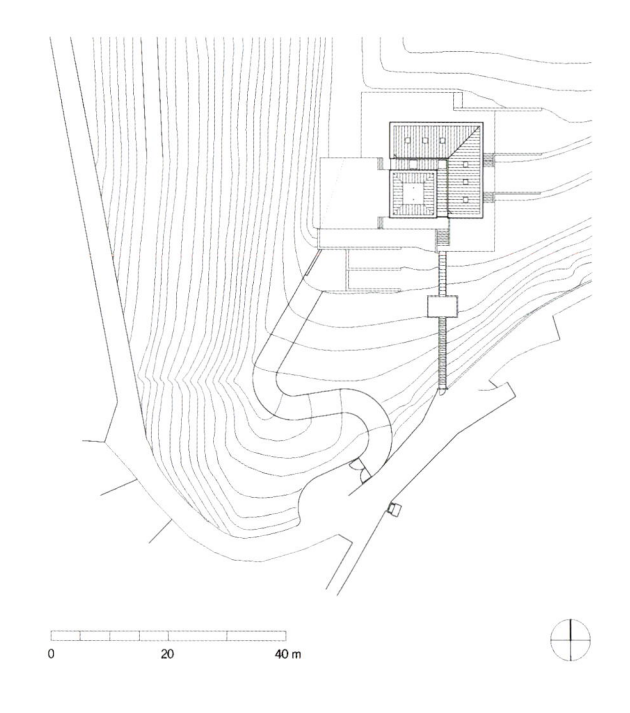

Antonio Citterio numbers among the Italian designers who are most sensitive to an "operative history" based on the continuity of a tradition reinterpreted through contemporary eyes. The rigour of the Milanese school – as exemplified by Caccia Dominioni, Albini and Gardella in particular – is well represented in his work, as is the lightness of the modern masters – Mies van der Rohe, Le Corbusier and Aalto – where the integration of architecture, interior design and interior decoration is the goal to be pursued.

1993–1995 Cene, Bergamo

Private residence
415 sq. m

The austere rigour of the base unit with its narrow light-modulating slits is tempered by the materiality of the stone and harmonises nicely with the surrounding landscape.

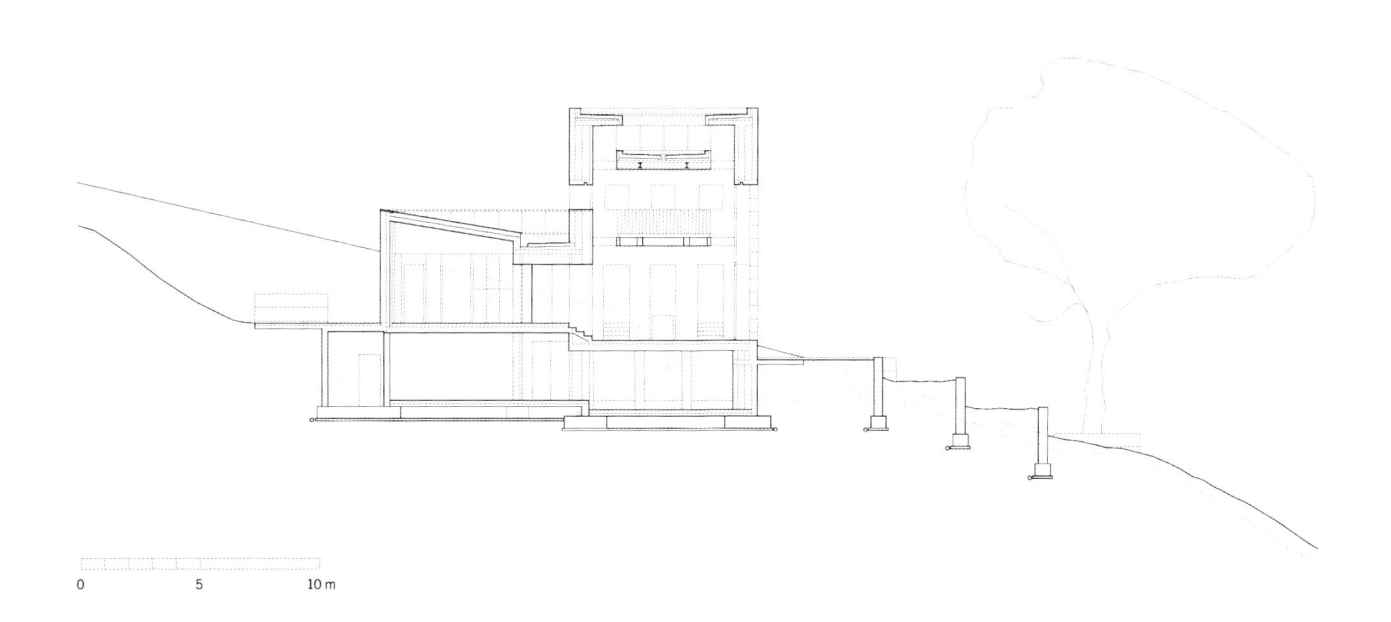

HISTORY

< 2003 Eileen, B&B Italia

> 1981, Quadrante, Xilitalia-B&B Italia

Antonio Citterio and Paolo Nava

The choice of the name *Quadrante* – the legendary architecture magazine founded by Bardi and Bontempi in 1933 – is a reference to the design culture of the 1930s and 1940s and to the furniture by Asnago and Vender exhibited at the sixth edition of the Triennale in 1936. They are a series of low, lacquered cabinets emphasising the expanded horizontality of the internal space, creating an effect of depth.
"The architectural aspect of this project lies in its structural work, in addressing the concept of bearing and borne elements, in emphasising the horizontal elements, the frame members, the joints, where each piece has a functional definition." Antonio Citterio

HISTORY

33

2003 AC Collection, Maxalto

Tables and cabinets appear suspended on nearly invisible frames, the lines are clean and crisp and the structural clarity is evident throughout. Here the rationale of the single piece becomes part of a system.

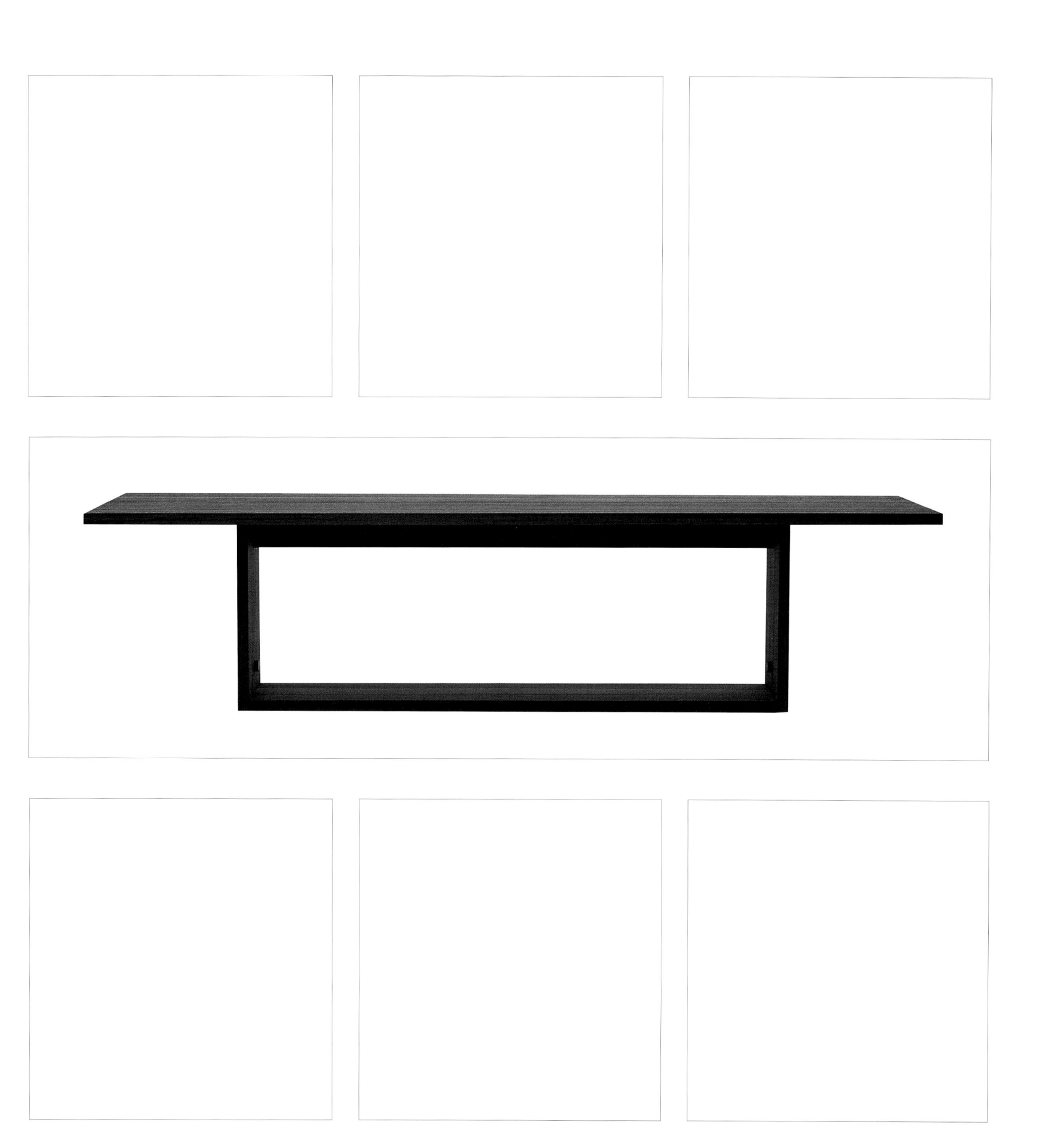

HISTORY

HISTORY

2004–2006 Busto Arsizio, Varese

with Studio Locati
Integrated programme for residential area
7,000 sq. m

In the new pedestrian piazza in Busto Arsizio, the design choice reestablishes the continuity of the historical built fabric of the city through a row of buildings with peaked roofs and vertical windows, forming a backdrop to numerous new public pedestrian areas.

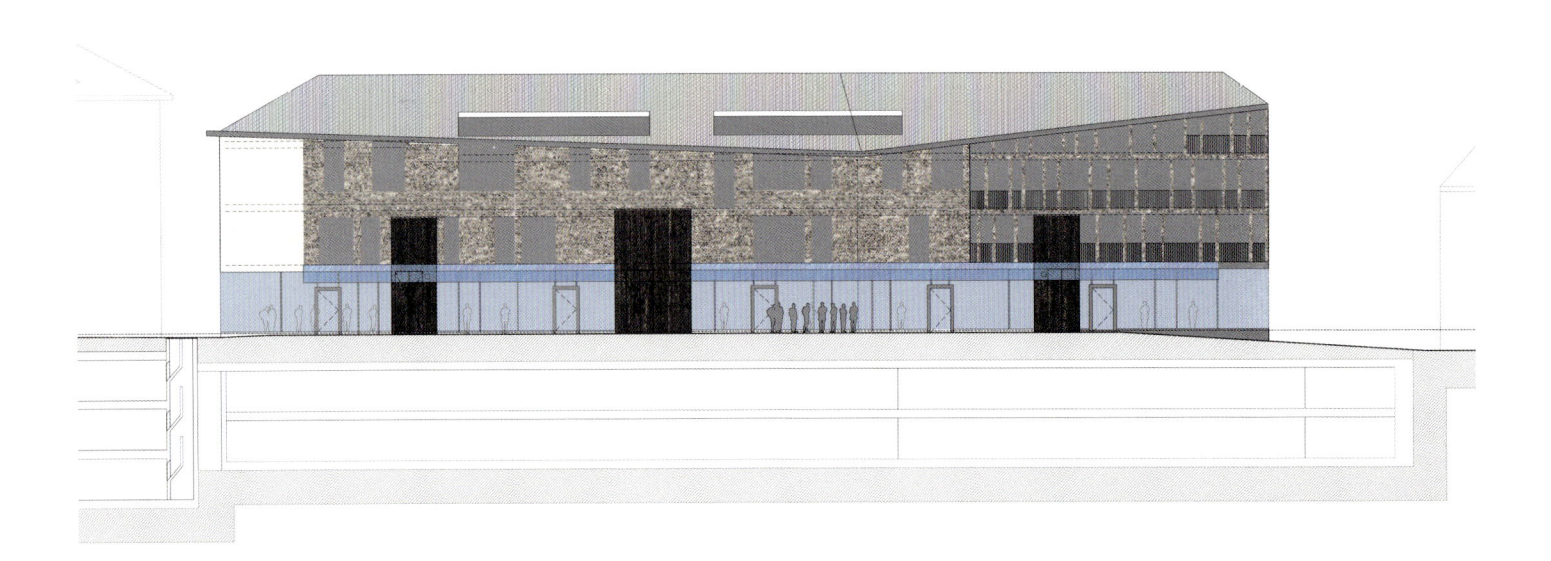

HISTORY

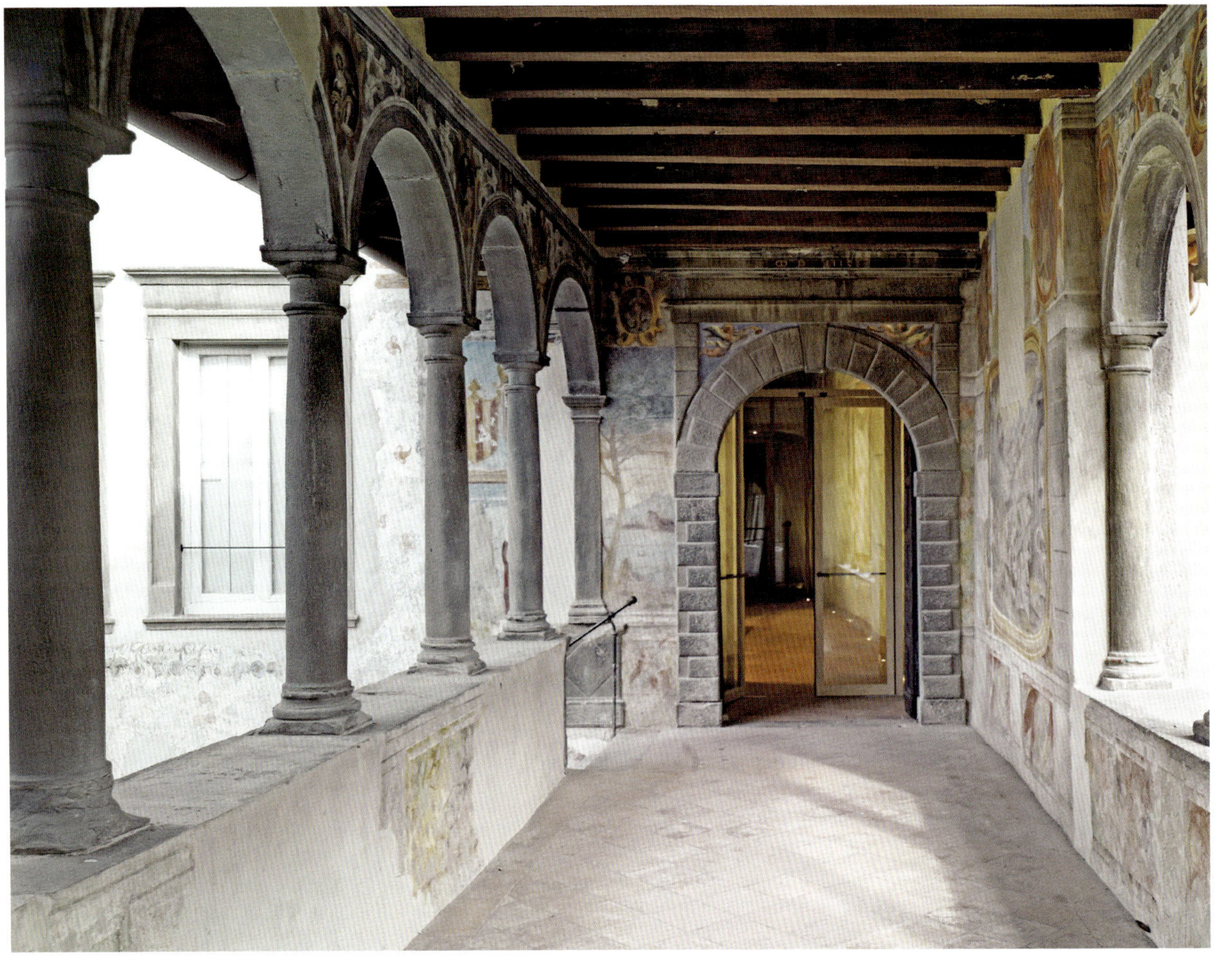

2005 Palazzo dell'Orologio of Clusone, Bergamo

with Bonicelli e Percassi Architetti Associati
Requalification of town hall offices
1,200 sq. m

The restoration of the town hall offices was resolved by reproposing elements from the local architectural tradition, such as wood and stone, to create particularly elegant and functional interiors.

HISTORY

40

Architecture and internal architecture integrate harmoniously and the decor becomes the space-arranging element, facilitating office work through flexible, modular systems.

HISTORY

1992–2006 Spatio, Vitra

"We were among the first to think that a worktop did not necessarily have to be a canonical table; we began to talk about flexibility and went on to develop products based on this concept. By knowing how an office works we are able to design objects that resolve various issues." Antonio Citterio

HISTORY

PROSPETTO SUL CORTILE

PIANTA scala 1:100

SEZIONE TRASVERSALE

2004 Deutsche Schule, Milan

Design competition
2,512 sq. m

One of the characteristics of the project is the mimetic neutrality of the façade, which reflects the cityscape and the monumental qualities of the setting in wood and glass façades. The glass is tinted in different nuances of green depending on the different requirements of prospect.

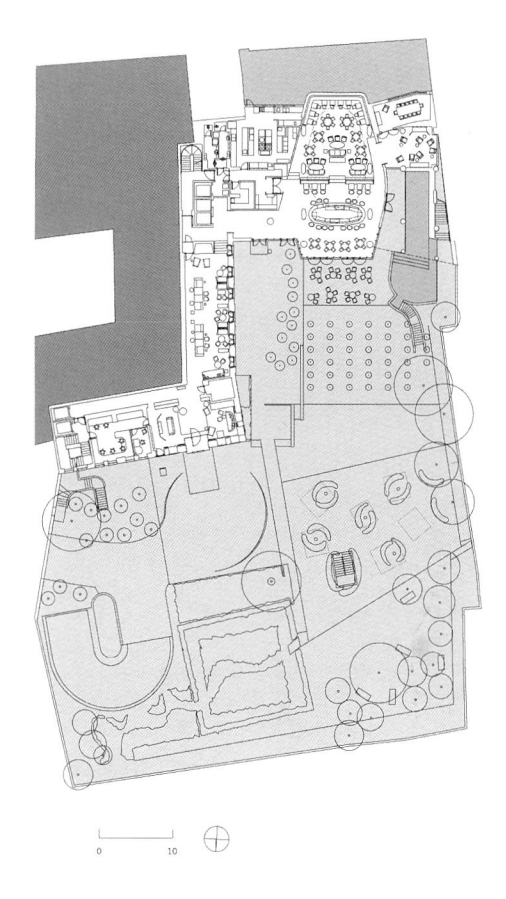

HISTORY

2001–2003 Bulgari Hotel, Milan

7,000 sq. m with 4,000 sq. m of private garden

In a period when architectural styles are reacquiring an autonomous urban identity through the power of the figure, Citterio confirms an ethical vision of the project process founded on the values of discretion and integration.

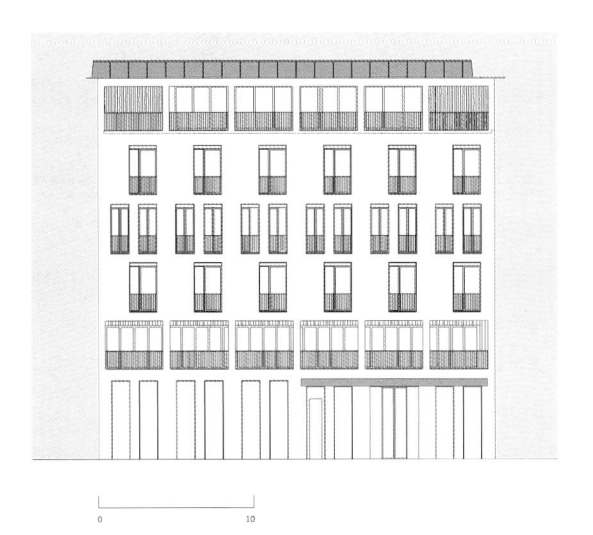

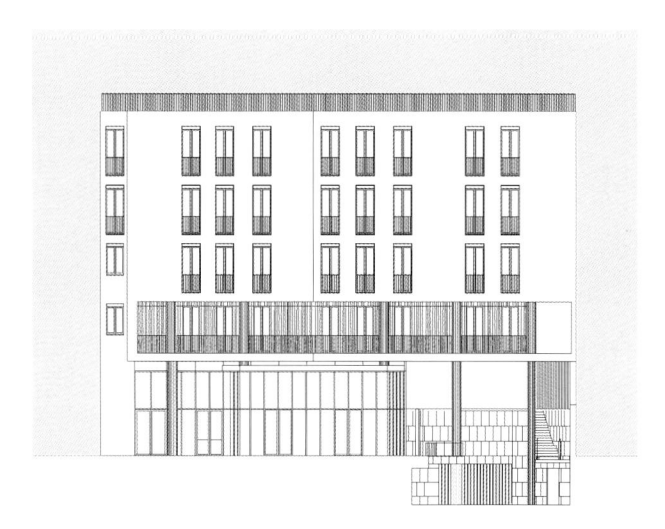

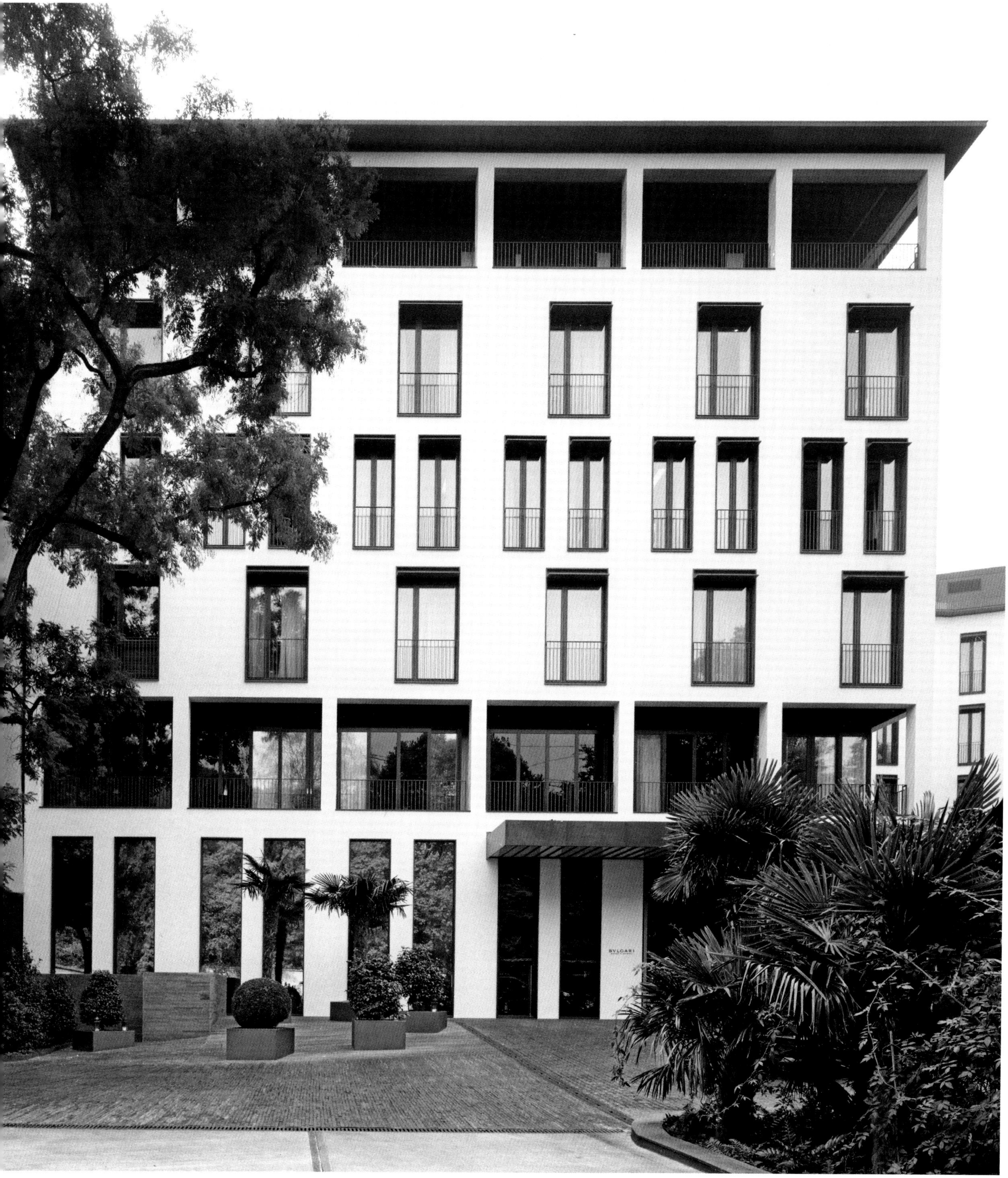
BVLGARI

HISTORY

HISTORY

HISTORY

HISTORY

HISTORY

HISTORY

2004–2006 Bulgari Hotel, Bali

28,000 sq. m
Team leader: Ella Dinoi

The "sense of history" for Citterio lies in an unusual capacity to represent the aspects of the reality of the place where he is working.

HISTORY

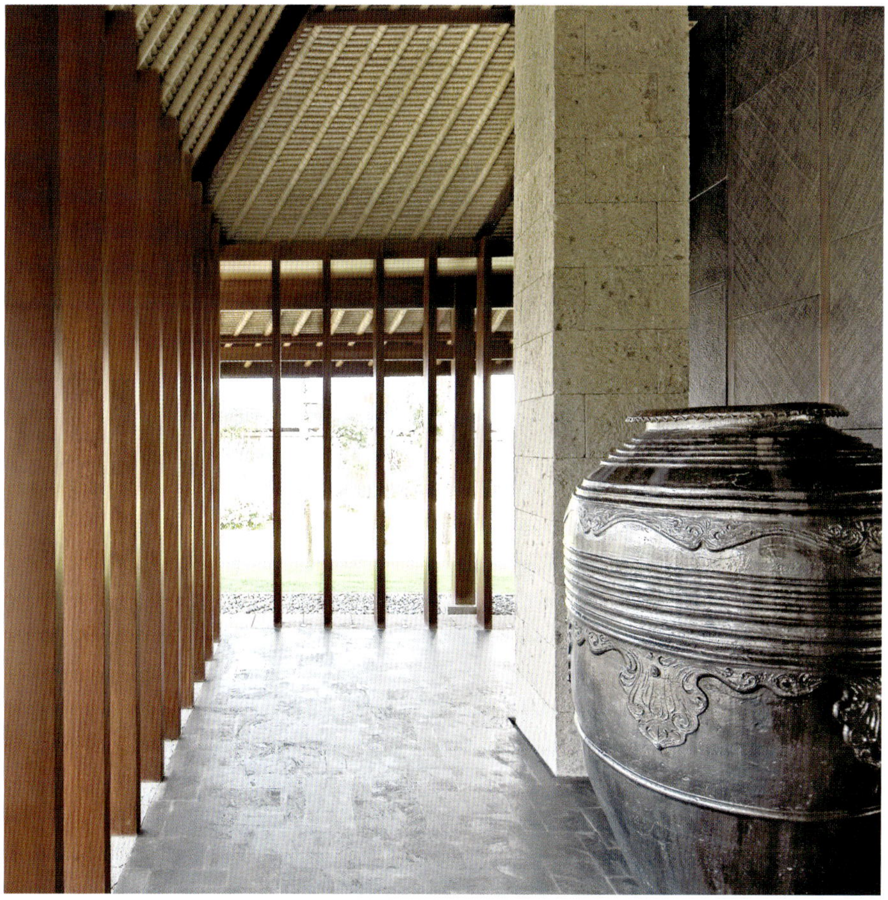

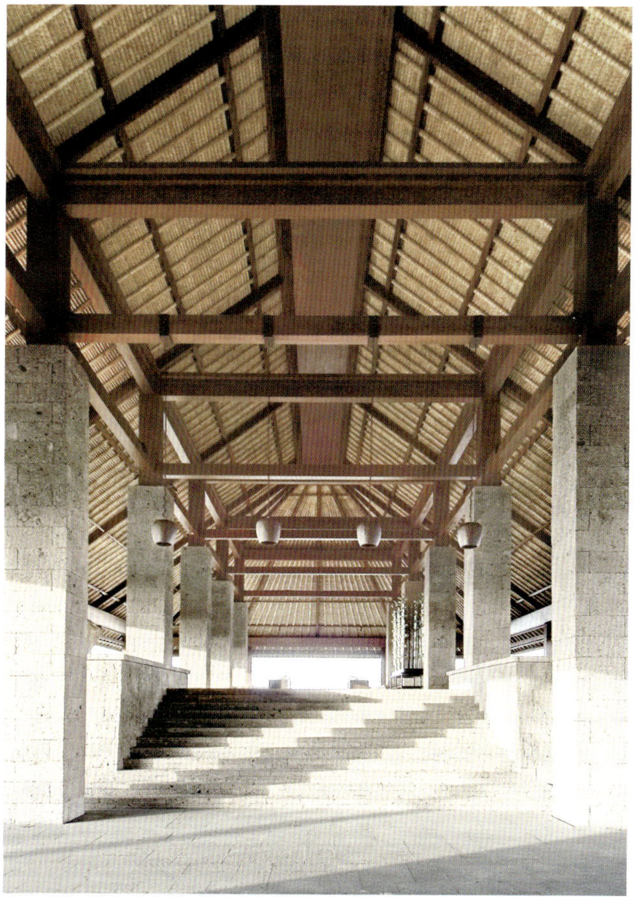

HISTORY

1999 Jubilee, Rome

Project for temporary structures, graphic design and signs
5,000 sq. m

Temporary structures made of wooden slats set up in Rome near the Basilica of Saint Peter and Saint John, near the Vatican Museums, and in the Church of Santa Maria Maggiore, Saint Paul's Basilica and Piazza Santa Croce in Gerusalemme, providing facilities for events associated with the Jubilee.

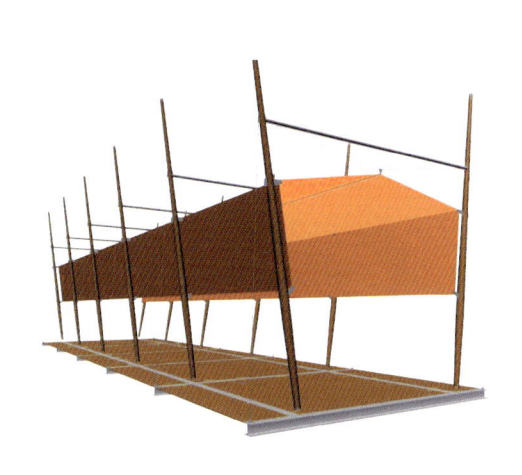

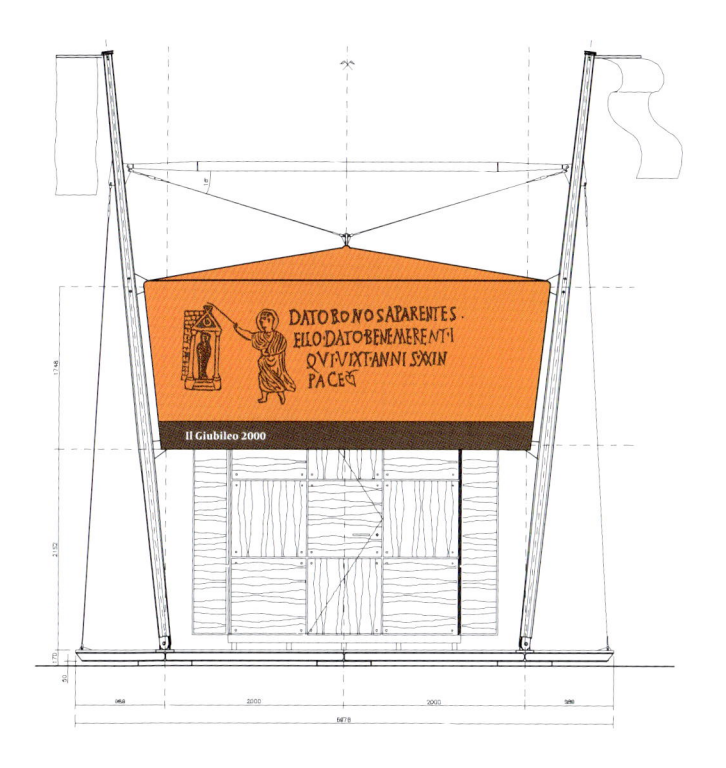

HISTORY

57

COMFORT.2

A very broad term deriving from Old French, comfort is that which brings ease and well-being. In our context, it refers to spaces and objects that permit convenience and ease in the workplace, or structures that enhance the "usability" of the city and its urban environments. Philip Johnson commented that many people think that a nice-looking chair must also be comfortable, although he personally saw no relation between comfort and beauty. He had had some chairs by Mies van der Rohe that he had been moving around with him for twenty-five years to every house he lived in. They were not very comfortable, but everyone who saw them commented on their beauty. When they sat down on them they also tended to exclaim that they were also comfortable.[1]

Comfort is often associated with "practicality", which often represents a crutch for the absence of beauty, although Johnson insinuates that in many people's minds, comfort is an intrinsic virtue of beauty, understood as the correspondence between form and function. But the American architect left the question open and his humanistic background,[2] strongly permeated with classical culture, oriented him toward a union between form and beauty, while avoiding the functionalist dispute.

Form is thus not a "condition" of function; nor is function a condition of form. As Gio Ponti observed, function is independent of form; you can sit on any chair, even an ugly one.[3] And, we might add, you can also sit on an uncomfortable one. It follows that comfort is neither an aesthetic nor a functional attribute of the object, but belongs rather to the requisites of good design, which, while not synonymous with beauty, certainly optimises the practicality and performance of an object, along with the way it is used, whether this object is found in the home or in an urban setting. All the objects around us are premised upon a need that gives them their justification[4] and their form, because, as Le Corbusier saw it, searching for the human level, the human function, means identifying human needs, and these needs are standard.[5]

Comfort ends up representing the contemporary status of "standard" needs, whose satisfaction takes priority over an ideal aesthetic quality. The new rites of dwelling or working, the new urban rites, now demand objects that are comfortable, but whose comfort does not interfere with their intended functions. On the contrary, it must provide support for them without being ostentatious. The protagonist in this case is not the object – or the designer – but the harmonious relationship established between the person and the object and between the object and its setting. If the art of the twentieth century has among its characteristic traits a constant attention towards everyday objects then, as Umberto Eco has observed, "the reduction of every object to a commodity and the gradual disappearance of its use-related value in a world governed exclusively by exchange value radically modify the nature of everyday objects: the object has to be useful, comfortable, relatively economical, appeal to popular taste and produced in series."[6] This means that in the commodity circuit, the qualitative aspects of beauty are transformed into quantities: function is what determines the enjoyment of an object, and the more mass produced objects there are in the world, the greater the function and enjoyment. The object loses the requisites of uniqueness that defined its beauty in Johnson's sense of the word. "The new beauty is reproducible, but also transitory and perishable. It has to induce the consumer, whether by consumption or disaffection, to replace it quickly in order not to stop the exponential growth of the cycle of production, distribution and consumption of goods."[7]

[1] Philip Johnson, "The Seven Crutches of Modern Architecture", *Perspecta 3*, 1955, pp. 40–44, based on the Italian translation, "I sette puntelli dell'architettura moderna", in Philip Johnson, *Verso il Postmoderno. Genesi di una deregulation creativa*. Genoa: Costa&Nolan, 1985, p. 102.

[2] The ancient Greeks recognised the unity of form and beauty, but it was with Humanism that beauty became harmony, proportion and correspondence between form and function in accordance with Leon Battista Alberti's conclusive definition of *concinnitas*. In his *De Re aedificatoria*, Alberti relates the need for beauty to the development of civilisation. See Paolo Portoghesi, *L'angelo della storia*. Rome–Bari: Laterza, 1982, p. 25.

[3] Gio Ponti, *Amate l'architettura*. Genoa: Editrice Vitali e Ghianda, 1957, p. 186. Published in English as *In Praise of Architecture*.

[4] George Kubler, *La forma del tempo*. Turin: Einaudi, 1976, p. 76: "Beyond the ties between needs and things, there are also ties between things and things. It is as if things generated other things in their image by the interposed agency of human beings fascinated by the possibilities of sequences and progressions."

[5] Le Corbusier, *Arte Decorativa e Design*. Rome–Bari: Laterza, 1973, p. 69.

[6] Umberto Eco, ed., *Storia della Bellezza*. Milan: Bompiani, 2004, p. 376.

[7] Ibid., p. 377.

[8] See Guy Debord, *La società dello spettacolo*. Milan: Baldini e Castoldi, 1997.

[9] Antonio Citterio, conversation with the author, June 2005.

[10] Philip Johnson, *Op. cit.*, p. 102.

This is truer than ever in design, whose mimesis with respect to the processes of fashion is mainly oriented toward the spectacularisation of the object[8] and its transitoriness. Citterio is thus going against the current when he chooses to dedicate attention to comfort and to technology that can extend an object's life cycle. From his chairs to his covered walkways, his kitchens to his nursery schools, Antonio Citterio seeks comfort on different scales because "for me, comfort is like technology. In the design phase, I try to ignore them, but there's no way around it. They always crop up. I can't manage to forget that an object has to function and also be comfortable at the same time. I have a maid's syndrome: I always ask myself what will have become of that object after three years. Many focus on the image and don't concern themselves with durability. It is difficult to be both spectacular and comfortable at the same time. Only the great masters have succeeded."[9]

Comfort for the Home
B&B Italia: Diesis, Arne, Harry, Charles, Freetime; *B&B Italia:* Mart; *Flexform:* ABC; *Iittala:* Decanter, Collective Tools; *Skantherm:* Shaker; *Private residence Switzerland; Residential complex in Mantua, competition project; Residential complex in Bormio, project*

Philip Johnson affirmed that we are all descendants of John Stuart Mill. After all, what is the architecture of a building if not the comfort of those living in it?[10] Johnson's faux naïveté conceals the trap of associating comfort with utility and making it coincide with the object's intended function. Actually, the American architect asks us to think about comfort as the yardstick for the usability of spaces and objects. In this reading, it represents a fundamental element for architects like Citterio who consider comfort to be an expression of quality and a stimulus for innovation. "Comfort is a mania for me," affirms Antonio Citterio. "My projects get their spark from comfort and convenience. With my chairs, for example, comfort becomes a stimulus for innovation. All my chairs grow out of the idea of comfort; my design efforts involve disarticulating the seat, and figuring out how to make the back move in a certain way becomes the inspirational motif. I keep at them until they are comfortable. There are certain objects that are comfortable by their very nature, such as down pillows, for example. But they cannot guarantee the comfort of a chair, which is one of the most difficult aspects in the overall comfort of the project."

In his search for comfort, Citterio has inexorably modified the form and perception of upholstered furniture. He has ushered in a new concept of comfort starting with his *Diesis* for B&B in 1979. Here he pioneered a longer, wider and higher sofa stripped of its textile and metal decorations with an enlarged emphasis on its role as a seat. The structural lightness and modularity of his *Arne* system, for example, are made possible by the constructional technology of its component elements. It has a steel frame immersed in injection-moulded polyurethane, die-cast aluminium supports and polyester fibre upholstery. In Citterio's design approach, the sofa is a foundational element of an interior that modifies the way space is used and also its very meaning. "Among the projects that Antonio has done for B&B, the *Arne* and especially the *Diesis* are the ones I like best," states Giorgio Busnelli, "because they required the greatest pains. The *Diesis* was so tremendously essential for the years in which it was produced that it was still selling twenty years later. But time has vindicated Antonio. He was the first to understand that people's habits had changed, and that the living room was no longer the showcase of the bourgeois household, but had become a place for people to relax or entertain their friends. Antonio does not consider himself an innovator, but he's wrong. His works are silent, but inexhaustible innovations. And there is no turning back." *Diesis* introduced a light and inconspicuous metal frame supporting thick, regularly shaped cushions. It represents the paradigm of the comfortable sofa: a broad, soft, cosy and informal "island" that invites you to lie down more than sit and that gently responds to your desire to relax without giving up its distinct identity within the domestic space. It is an object that has nothing more of the neutrality – in terms of form and style – of the traditional sofa, but one that nevertheless reinterprets the typically Italian tradition of details. "My sofas seem very simple, but they're not."[11] And in Citterio's statement, simplicity takes on the characteristic features of their constructive makeup rather than their formal choices. The structure of *Diesis* is then reinterpreted in various ways to create new types. From the traditional form of *Harry* (1995) to the curves of *Arne*, which are so well suited to home theatre, and from the chaise lounge to the angular solution of *Charles* (1998) and the reclining cushion of *Freetime* (1999), Citterio's aptitude for designing a flexible system that can satisfy different formal and compositional needs is clearly demonstrated. If the tubular metal frame is a reference to the masters of the modern movement (the reference to Le Corbusier[12] is especially evident), Citterio's references oscillate yet again between the lightness of the Milanese school (represented by the floating foot of Marco Zanuso's *Triennale* sofa (1951), the mass of the cushions of BBPR's *Elettra* (1953), the support of Franco Albini's *Fiorenza* (1952) or the ergonomics of Castiglioni's *San Luca* armchair (1960)) and the quest for comfort of the American school (the softness of the objects designed by Eames or the sinuosity of George Nelson's *Kangaroo*). "I always think of the Eames in my design projects,"[13] states Citterio, who reproposes the ability to create furnishings having the "familiar look of a soft, well-used baseball glove", as Charles Eames described his legendary *Lounge Chair*. The armchairs *Mart* for B&B and *ABC* for Flexform, for example, have a familiar yet elegant allure, where the simplicity of their constituent elements disguises their constructional complexity. This allure recalls the experiment of Italian Design, caught between the comfort of upholstered pieces with enwrapping forms à la Jacobsen, the new materials of Saarinen, Panton's one-piece bodies and the visible frames of the Eames. "I bring family sofas back to life; I reuse them," comments Citterio. "You just have to change their scale, add new elements, combine different pieces: in a word, it is the recovery of memory associated more with use than with form."[14] And so on a par with the masterpieces of the masters of Italian Design, Antonio Citterio's seats interpret innovative technologies and materials in the familiar forms of tradition. *ABC* in particular represents an icon of contemporary design not merely for the grace of its form, but also for the comfort of its seat, which reclines and stretches out to follow the anatomy of the body's movements.

Citterio's work on the object as the representation of a gesture is clearly seen also in pieces not traditionally associated with comfort. This is the case, among others, in *Decanter* and in the *Collective Tools* collection created for Iittala, where the hollow in the decanter's handle provides a comfortable and natural grip. The Finnish company's pursuit found a happy point of correspondence in that of the Milanese de-

[11] Conversation with the author, March 2006.

[12] It is no coincidence that the famous *LC2*, designed by Le Corbusier in 1928, was called *Grand Confort*.

[13] Conversation with the author, February 2005.

[14] Ibid.

[15] Enzo Mari, *Progetto e passione*. Turin: Bollati Boringhieri, 2001, p. 52.

[16] Gio Ponti, *Op. cit.*, p. 107.

signer, when the technologies proper to the company culture were interpreted in a design key. Similarly, the *Shaker* wood-burning fireplace-stove, designed for the German firm Skantherm unites the Euclidean simplicity of the stove with a sophisticated space-optimising technology. The fire becomes a furnishing element, sitting atop a small table that breaks up the stove's vertical lines and gives it a vase-like feeling of lightness. "I design objects for myself," explains Citterio, "and not in response to market demands. I came up with many of my objects because I was looking for something like them, but they did not yet exist. And I would never go on developing something that I wouldn't want to have in my own house. I can't force things. If something doesn't work, I don't make it. It's that simple."

Citterio is a testament to an ethical vision of the project, where comfort reflects new lifestyles and thus new uses of the home environment. Starting in the 1990s the house is experienced as a place for emotional experiences, a generator of wellbeing, a chrysalis in which one can regenerate oneself and welcome in others. How else can we explain the extraordinary success of home theatre, bathtubs, kitchen implements and all those accessories that indicate a way of living that is characterised by slowness and fullness? Time spent at home expands to become an expression of care for oneself and cultivation of one's affections. The project for the domestic environment changes: kitchens are larger so that the pleasure of cooking becomes blended with that of receiving guests; bathrooms expand to contain bookcases, armchairs and chaise lounges for relaxing and meditating.

This is why houses designed by Citterio are "true" homes, homes that are fully inhabitable, comfortable and custom designed for the client and his or her needs. If Enzo Mari's dictum is true that "the quality of a project depends on the degree, however small, of cultural change that it sparks",[15] then comfort in the home becomes an innovative element. Citterio claims not to be a revolutionary, and yet his work in both architecture and design has radically changed the organisation of the home and its furnishings.

"The historical Italian house is without complications, both inside and out. It contains objects and beautiful art and wants to keep them in order and separated in space. It does not want crowding and mixing," declared Gio Ponti. "Its wealth is based on grandeur and simplicity, not on preciosity. Its design does not derive exclusively from the material needs of life. Comfort is not found in the Italian-style house only as a response to necessity, to needs, to our life's ease and to the organisation of services. This comfort is in something higher: it is in providing us with a measure for our thoughts through architecture, in giving us with its simplicity a salute to our lifestyles, in giving us with its open receptivity the feeling of a confident and abundant life and lastly, it is found in the invitation that the Italian-style house offers to our spirit to recreate itself in relaxing visions of peace, in sunny nature. This, in the full sense of the Italian word *conforto*, is what it means."[16]

Citterio explores the theme of dwelling by considering both the contents and the container. He has applied a consistent methodology right from his earliest houses, from the experimental one in Kumamoto City (1991) to the ones in Cene (1993–1995) and in Lugano Marinone (1994–1995). The integration of the interiors expresses his unitary vision of the design project, a project that is not affected by changes in scale. The designer proves he can control perfectly both the architectural envelope and the furnishing element, as is clearly seen in his single-family dwelling in Switzerland (2006). Designed for a young family showing little inclination for the bourgeois rites of dwelling, this house was built around the children, whose rhythms determine the metric of the domestic spaces. Instead of hiding it, the project emphasises the presence of the children both in its spatial arrangements and in its relationship with the outdoors through an internal court that regulates circulation flows and acts as an interconnection node between the spaces. The social space of the house is completely glassed in and looks out onto the garden. This transparency distinguishes the first floor sleeping areas from the base, which contains the kitchen, other utility areas and the fitness room. The two-storey house is raised on pilotis in a structural and architectural reference to Le Corbusier's Ville Savoye. The rigour of the structure in unfinished cement is interrupted by the coloured shutters that slide to create unexpected chromatic superimpositions and graphic effects. Colour also distinguishes the interiors and creates, along with the large windows, a fluidity of space, which is achieved through the elimination of vertical partitions and expands outward, amplified by the windows, into the courtyard. It is a house arranged in terms of openings and vistas rather than in terms of enclosed spaces, where decor follows function and not vice versa.

Yet again, Citterio proves himself to be an extraordinary interpreter of the culture of household comfort inaugurated by Gio Ponti. He responds to the manifesto-house with the liveable house, the expression of the needs of the people who live in it. The same trait is found in his multifamily dwellings, such as the residential complex in Mantua, and the Eden residence in Bormio. We find residential units crafted in natural materials such as stone and wood and integrated into their natural surroundings, with shared facilities to enhance the "happiness" (to use Gio Ponti's term) of those who live there. With different structural types corresponding to different types of users, his building complexes seek integration with their surrounding environment, adhering to a principle of maintaining a discreet presence in the environment, one of the typical traits of Citterio's language. In Bormio, for example, the built volume is fragmented into small wood-faced, peaked-roof structures that are noteworthy for the cadenced alternation of openings in their walls, but remain unobtrusive in the valley both dimensionally and as marks. The façades present a tight rhythm of solids and voids in the loggias and gently hug the sloping side of the valley, while the construction technology was chosen to optimise passive thermal exchange by means of insulating elements in the outer walls. Tradition and innovation are brought together with the usual elegance of a language marked by convenience and comfort.

Comfort for the Workplace
Esprit Headquarters, Milan; Vitra: Mobile Elements

"The success of my products also depends on comfort," says Citterio. "I have a very *normal* approach to design. Unlike Italian Design, which considers comfort to be an incidental aspect, I do not look at comfort as an exception. For me, it means facilitating the use of an object. If you want to use a lamp, you have to be able to regulate the lighting, not burn yourself. This principle generates a very complex process, and becomes a way of designing, a work method. Comfort is like technology, it is an intrinsic element in the design process."[17]

Citterio has designed numerous office

[17] Conversation with the author, January 2006.

[18] Conversation with the author, March 2006.

[19] Ettore Sottsass, conversation with the author, May 2005.

[20] See the chapter "Clients" in this volume.

[21] Alberto Bassi, *Antonio Citterio, Industrial Design*. Milan: Electa, 2004, p. 164.

buildings and their ease of use represents a common thread uniting his works from the Esprit facility in 1984 to the GlaxoSmithKline facility in Verona in 2005. The arrangement of space, like the organisation of the furnishings, is determined on the basis of the coordinates of comfort and technology, which are considered, as stated above, intrinsic conditions of the project. In the Milan offices of Esprit (1984–1988), Citterio restores the industrial spirit of the building, a former torrefaction works, through the use of materials such as hot-dip galvanised steel for the stairs, coated cement floors and visible ductwork. Industrial archaeology had not yet found an echo in the media, and structural "honesty" was a design choice which was, to say the least, unusual. The Esprit Italia headquarters marked a fundamental milestone in the Milanese architect's career. It brought him international recognition and the chance to measure himself against internationally famous luminaries. "But that's not all. Esprit allowed me to do architecture in a period when most of my work was in industrial design. I missed working on the large scale, and then suddenly they called me from San Francisco and sent me on a tour of the world, to Hong Kong and Tokyo, to meet the other architects they worked with: Tadao Ando, Kuramata . . . It was a fundamental experience on both the professional and the human level; it was a one-of-a-kind relationship with a client. I was fascinated by the Esprit philosophy, looking at the project in terms of creativity and *joie de vivre*. It was no coincidence that their image was in the hands of Oliviero Toscani, who did a great job of translating the company culture."[18]

Citterio had been suggested to Doug Tompkins by Ettore Sottsass, who had done the showrooms in Hamburg, Düsseldorf and Zurich, but at that time was not interested in doing the Italian branch. Although Citterio was not very close to Memphis, Sottsass chose him because "I had been thinking about a structure in cement, and he seemed the right one to do it."[19] One Sunday morning, Aldo Cibic phoned Citterio to tell him about Sottsass's choice. That call would mark the professional turning point for our architect. The formal propriety and expositional clarity of the Esprit building bear out the wisdom of Sottsass's choice. Esprit crystallised a new way of interpreting work, oriented along the lines of Tompkin's[20] hedonistic vision, by which you could and should have fun working. Citterio's work ethic is ideologically distant from this position, but that did not prevent him from giving architectural form to the experimentation of Esprit's founder. The new business model, oriented toward comfort and leisure, found an accurate response in Citterio's designs for the offices, the workshops and the showroom, where all the elements, from the circulation paths to the natural lighting, contribute to creating a functional and harmonious space.

His interpretive sensitivity for the workspace found further confirmation in furnishing elements that Citterio has considered with an eye for comfort. The *Mobile Elements* designed for Vitra are a crystalline example of this. As has been observed, "in Citterio's research for Vitra into workplaces, *Mobile Elements* represents a novel approach to this theme. The main element of the system is its flexibility of arrangement, one that is not strictly confined to the office, but also quite suitable in the home or in auxiliary facilities."[21] A few white, lightweight, flexible elements provide the basis for numerous combinations and variations, individual or team work stations on casters so that they can be aggregated or separated by means of partitions, and containers to make the office better organised and more practical and convenient, i.e. comfortable. As Rolf Fehlbaum puts it, "Antonio has a very rational approach to his design work that is highlighted in his *Mobile Elements*. Good design is what resolves problems, and Citterio's furnishings resolve a lot of problems: of comfort, ecological sustainability and ergonomics. A designer has to be a problem solver with an aesthetic sensitivity, just like Antonio."[22]

Comfort for the City and Territory

Metalco: Sedis*; Vighizzolo bus stop shelter, Cantù; Piazza Cordusio bus stop/multifunctional kiosk with shelter, Milan; ATM Restyling MM1 underground line, Milan; Guardiano Sud pier, Ravenna Marina; Michele Alboreto new piazza, Rozzano*

Beyond the domestic or working environments, comfort can also be interpreted on the urban scale in terms of services, amenities and infrastructure improvements. In this context, Citterio's work (exemplary among his urban design projects are the pier in Ravenna, the piazza in Rozzano and the restyling of Milan's MM1 underground line) is strongly permeated by his search for innovative solutions that combine ease and practicality of use with harmonious environmental integration. The practicality of use (well represented by the Vighizzolo bus stop in the township of Cantù, or the bench designed for Metalco) is principally associated with urban fixtures and is applied both on the human and the territorial level. The concept of "environmental comfort" has to do with the way the object relates to its surrounding landscape. A bench has to be comfortable for those who choose to sit on it, but also has to be a nice addition to the urban landscape. "The bench is a public asset, it fulfils an important social role," states Citterio. "It is an urban design object that allows one to perceive the culture of a city and the quality of life of its inhabitants."[23] And so Citterio took part in the design contest of the Urban Land Institute Italia, "Have a seat with ULI, a bench for Milan", proposing a bench with seat and back in wooden slats supported on a solid and durable cast iron frame. Although it did not win first prize, the bench went into production and was installed in Piazza Michele Alboreto in Rozzano, which was inaugurated in December 2006. The bench is available in two versions: simple and contoured. It is an experimental product suitable for industrial production with a cleverly contoured back that affords a variety of seating positions. Citterio's usual attention to detail is seen in the flush-mounted metal plate for the sponsor's logo. "This project was inspired by the intention to design a bench that could, thanks to its form and the quality of its materials, dialogue with the city of Milan, a city with a contemporary vocation."[24]

The same vocation characterises other urban fixtures designed by Citterio, such as the bus stop/kiosk in Piazza Cordusio in Milan, whose lightness and austerity well represent the spirit of the Lombard capital. In analogous fashion, as a result of the design contest held by the Milan Urban Transit Authority (ATM), Citterio worked on the restyling of the Milan MM1 underground line, originally designed by Albini. The programme of the contest involved redesigning the mezzanine levels of the stations with the objective of improving the service and shopping areas. Patricia Viel's comments on the contest theme are particularly indicative: "The very concept of mezzanine as an intermediate access level between the city and the platforms located the project theme more in the cultural world of the commercial space, of the mall, than in the realm of technical infrastructural connective tissue." While maintaining the charac-

[22] Rolf Fehlbaum, conversation with the author, February 2006.

[23] Conversation with the author, May 2005.

[24] Ibid.

[25] Andrea Branzi, *L'architettura cronache e storia*, April, no. 234, 1975.

[26] Luigi Prestinenza Puglisi, *Antonio Citterio*. Rome: Edilstampa, 2004, p. 159.

teristics of Albini's original decor, Citterio worked on the illumination, the colours, the maintenance programme and the signage. The reference points for his project were safety, accessibility, quality of the subsurface environments and the profitability of the commercial areas, components which are not typically architectural, but that have a high value in terms of the quality of use.

As Andrea Branzi believes, architectural quality is still implicit in any urban form; however, it is completely extraneous to the scientific criteria on which territorial planning may be based. "It is one thing to use an urban service, a house, a school, a hospital; it is another to pick up the cultural message that the architectural form of that service continues, in spite of everything, to transmit to the user."[25] This cultural message, even if expressed via poor or virtually uncontrolled cultural and linguistic qualities, in reality constitutes a serious impediment to the "scientific" organisation and function of the urban territory.

The Guardiano Sud pier of the Ravenna Marina, designed in collaboration with the architect Anna Giorgi and the lighting technicians of Metis Lighting, was the winning project of the 2004 contest on the theme of environmental quality. The linearity of the surrounding landscape was captured by and transferred into the project, which employed "soft" technological means to transform a disused part of the city into a gathering place with a clear urban identity. The project has two elements that characterise it: a sand dune where one can stop and take the sun, meet friends, read or play, and a white fibreglass seashell, the last strip of land before open sea, that stands as an ornament visually marking the end of the pier. The lighting design is particularly evocative with underwater and perimeter lighting marking out the limits of the pier, which is thus transformed into "a sort of stage for sporting events or happenings, a moored boat, emphasised by counter-lighting effects."[26] So here we have comfort being interpreted as a service to people through architecture that gives new qualities to urban spaces and their social functions.

This is also what happens in Citterio's piazza for Rozzano, just south of Milan, designed in 2005 and inaugurated in 2006. The new piazza is a space occupying 8,000 square metres, originally used for the local street market, in the centre of the residential neighbourhood in the former Romagnoli area. It is surrounded by porticoes and residential buildings with commercial establishments at street level. The ease of use as part of the design is clearly explained by Patricia Viel: "For this reason, the choice was made to create the roadway in *serizzo*, a very durable grey stone, so that people could go to the stores in their cars and park them nearby for a limited period of time." The internal part of the piazza, tiled in red terracotta, is divided into two different areas: in one section, acacias and lindens are planted to provide shade for mothers, the elderly or anyone else on hot days; and there is an open area with a cylindrical steel and glass information booth, providing an important service to the people. Yet again, Citterio has executed his work with surgical precision, recapturing the tradition of the Italian piazza in a contemporary key, marked by discretion, familiarity and, above all, comfort.

COMFORT

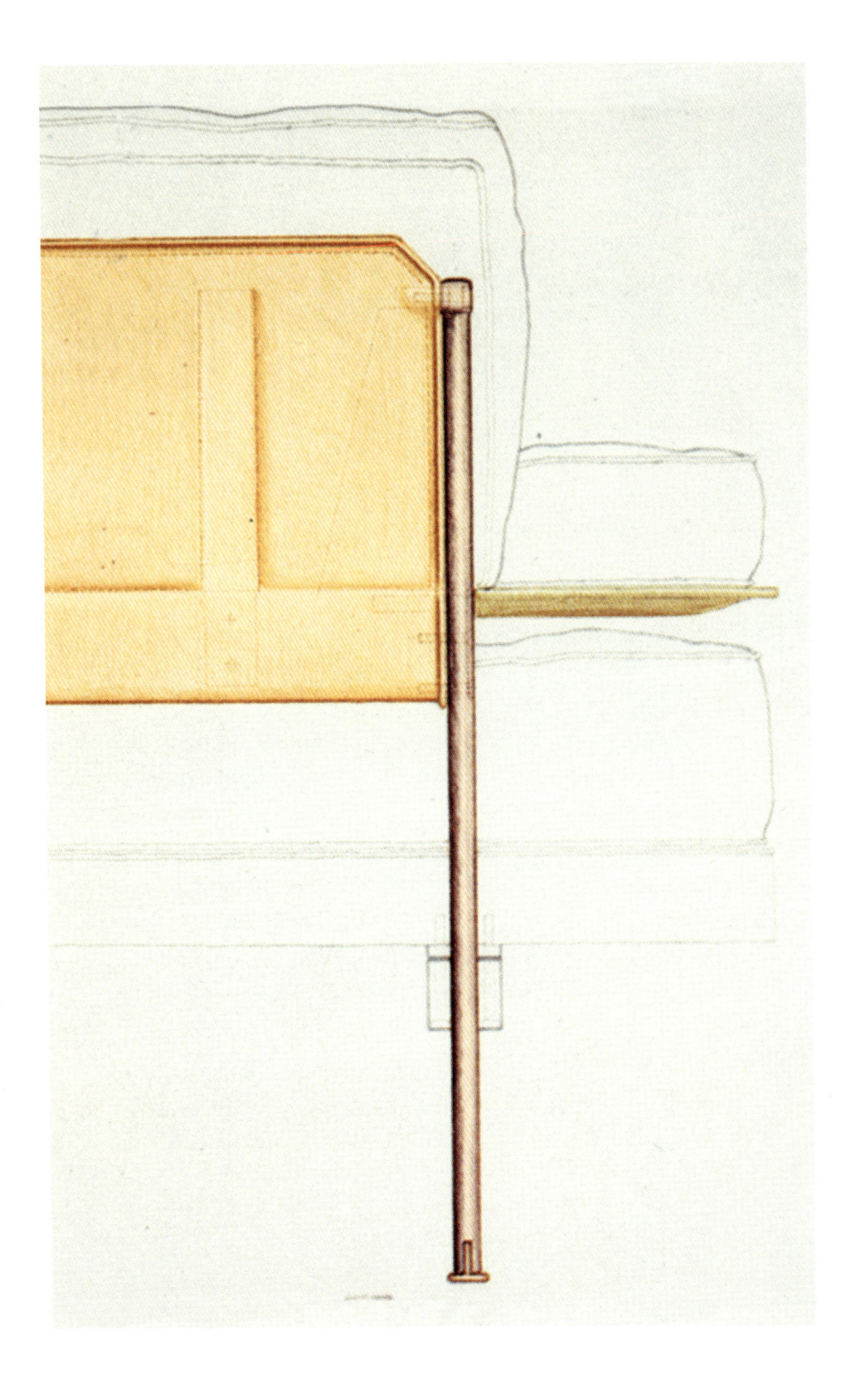

"For me, comfort is like technology. In the design phase, I try to ignore them, but there's no way around it. They always crop up. I can't manage to forget that an object has to function and also be comfortable at the same time."
Antonio Citterio

1979 Diesis, B&B Italia

Antonio Citterio and Paolo Nava

"Among the projects that Antonio has done for B&B, the *Arne* and especially the *Diesis* are the ones I like best because they required the greatest pains. The *Diesis* was so tremendously essential for the years in which it was produced that it was still selling twenty years later. But time has vindicated Antonio. He was the first to understand that people's habits had changed, and that the living room was no longer the showcase of the bourgeois household, but had become a place for people to relax or entertain their friends. Antonio does not consider himself an innovator, but he's wrong. His works are silent, but inexhaustible innovations. And there is no turning back."
Giorgio Busnelli

COMFORT

A comfortable sofa is a broad, soft, cosy and informal "island" that invites you to lie down more than sit and that gently responds to your desire to relax without giving up its distinct identity within the domestic space.

COMFORT

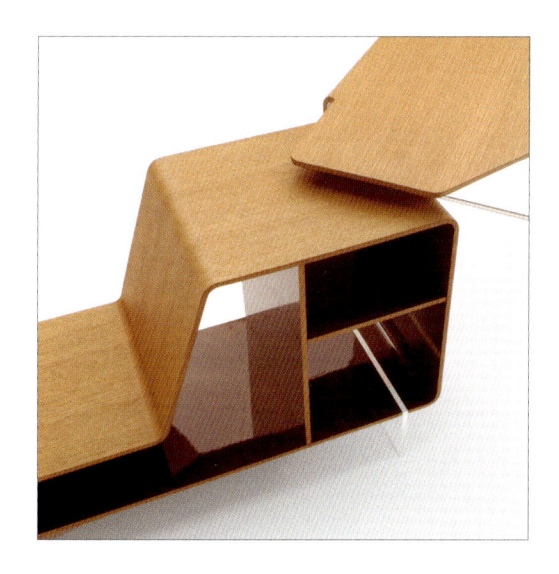

< 1999 Freetime, B&B Italia
< 1995 Harry, B&B Italia
< 1997 Charles, B&B Italia

> 2005 Arne, B&B Italia

"My sofas seem very simple,
but they're not."
Antonio Citterio
In Citterio's statement, simplicity
takes on the characteristic features
of a constructive makeup rather
than a formal choice.

COMFORT

COMFORT

< 2003 Mart, B&B Italia
> 2005 J.J., B&B Italia

COMFORT

< 2005 Air, Flexform

> 2004 Timeless, Flexform
> 1998 ABC, Flexform

On a par with the masterpieces of the masters of Italian Design, Antonio Citterio's seats interpret innovative technologies and materials in the familiar forms of tradition. *ABC* in particular represents an icon of contemporary design not merely for the grace of its form, but also for the comfort of its seat, which reclines and stretches out to follow the anatomy of the body's movements.

COMFORT

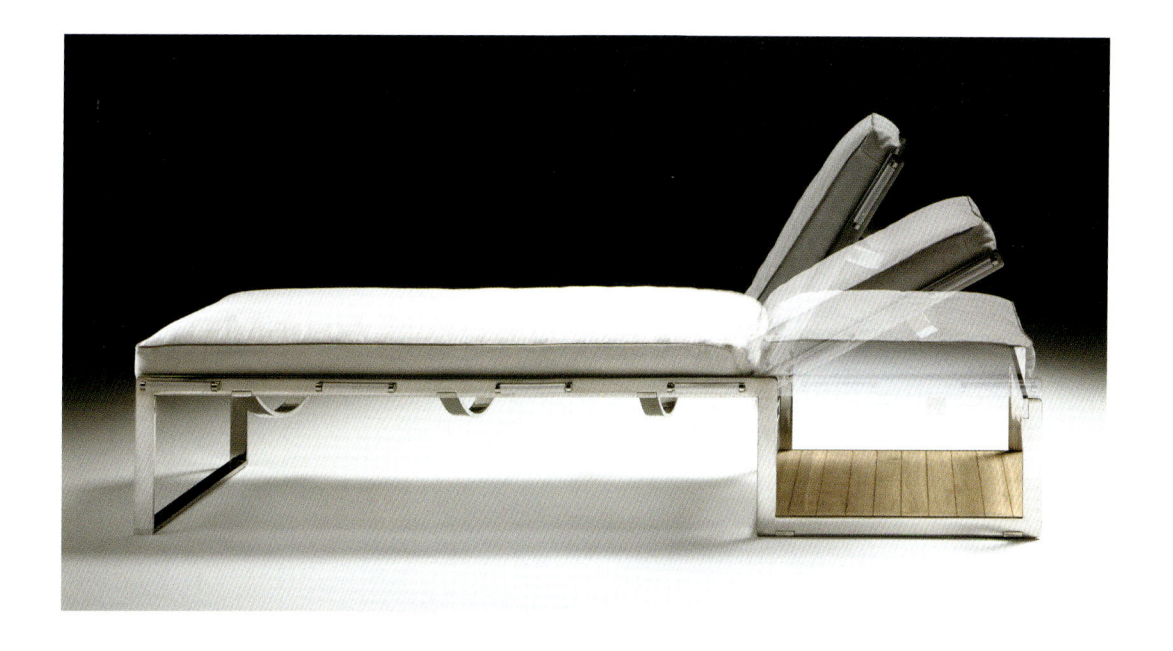

COMFORT

2005 Decanter, Iittala
with Toan Nguyen

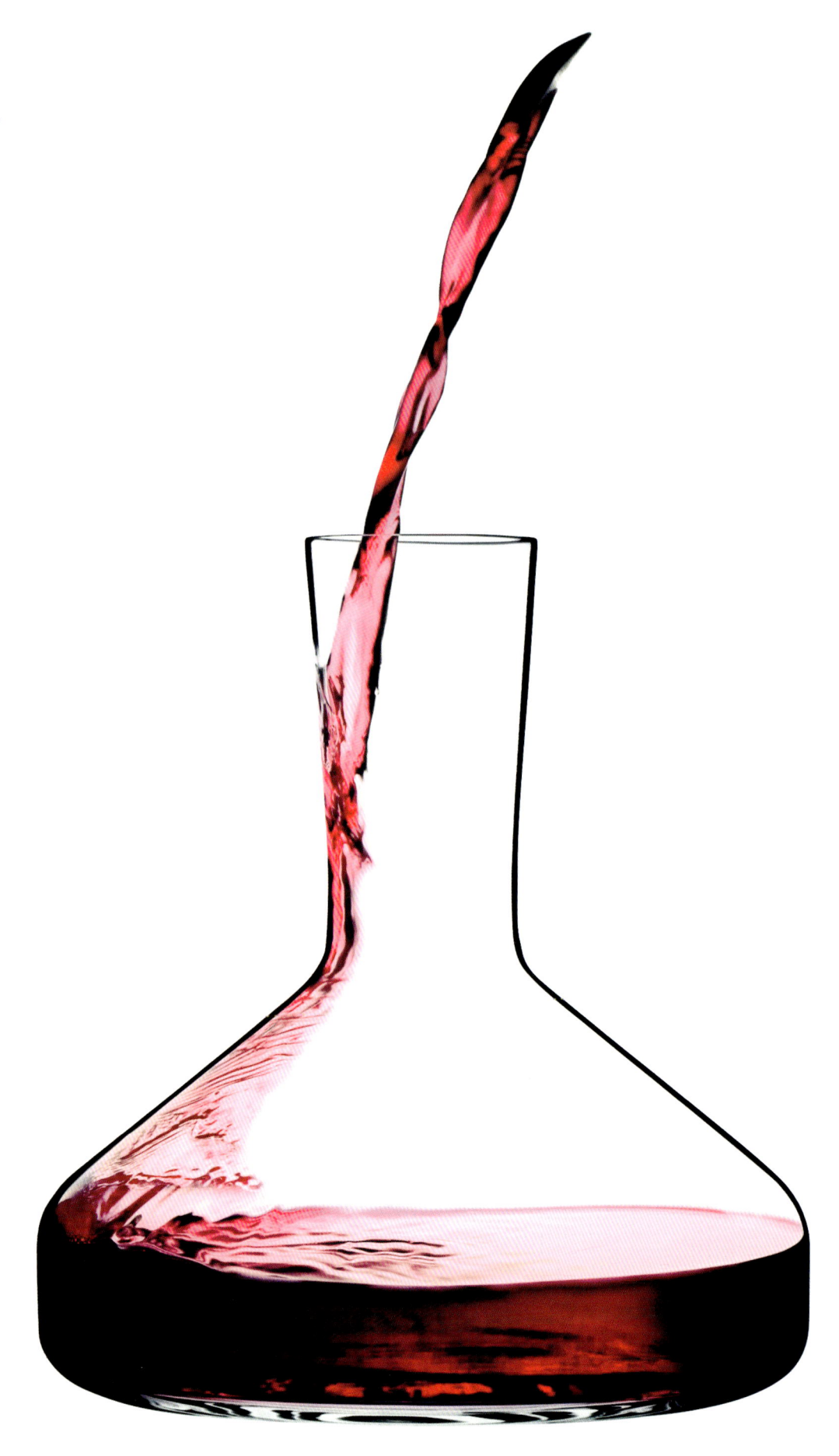

2000 Collective Tools, Iittala

with Glen Oliver Löw

COMFORT

COMFORT

2004 Shaker, Skantherm

with Toan Nguyen

COMFORT

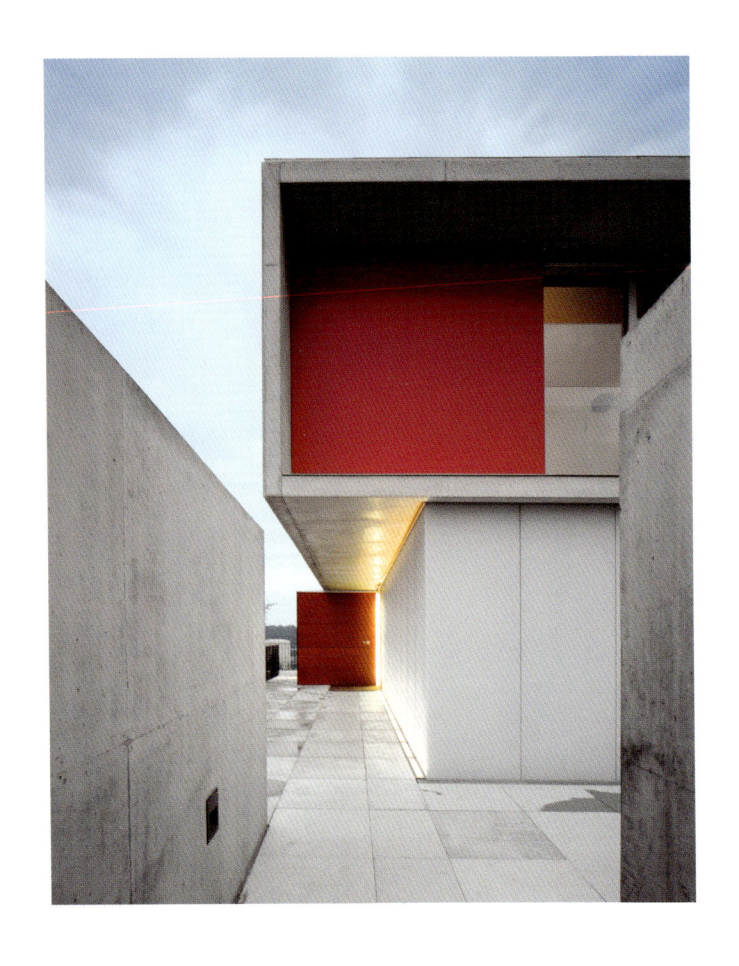

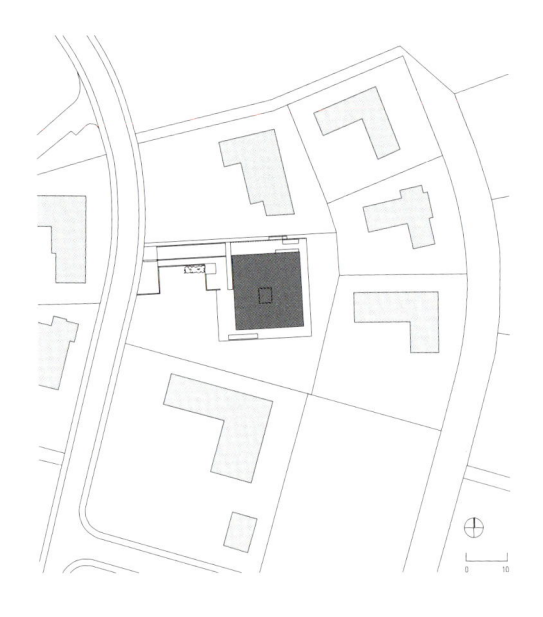

COMFORT

2003–2005 Switzerland

with Jan Hinrichs
Private residence
850 sq. m

"Comfort is not found in the Italian-style house only as a response to necessity, to needs, to our life's ease and to the organisation of services. This comfort is in something higher: it is in providing us with a measure for our thoughts through architecture, in giving us with its simplicity a salute to our lifestyles, in giving us with its open receptivity the feeling of a confident and abundant life and lastly, it is found in the invitation that the Italian-style house offers to our spirit to recreate itself in relaxing visions of peace, in sunny nature. This, in the full sense of the Italian word *conforto*, is what it means."
Gio Ponti

COMFORT

COMFORT

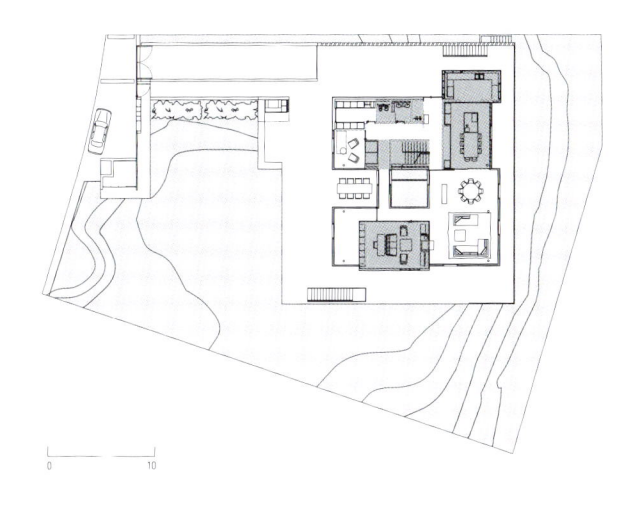

"We are all descendants of John Stuart Mill. After all, what is the architecture of a building if not the comfort of those living in it?"
Philip Johnson

COMFORT

2005 Comparto Te Brunetti, Mantua

Design competition
76,000 sq. m

COMFORT

COMFORT

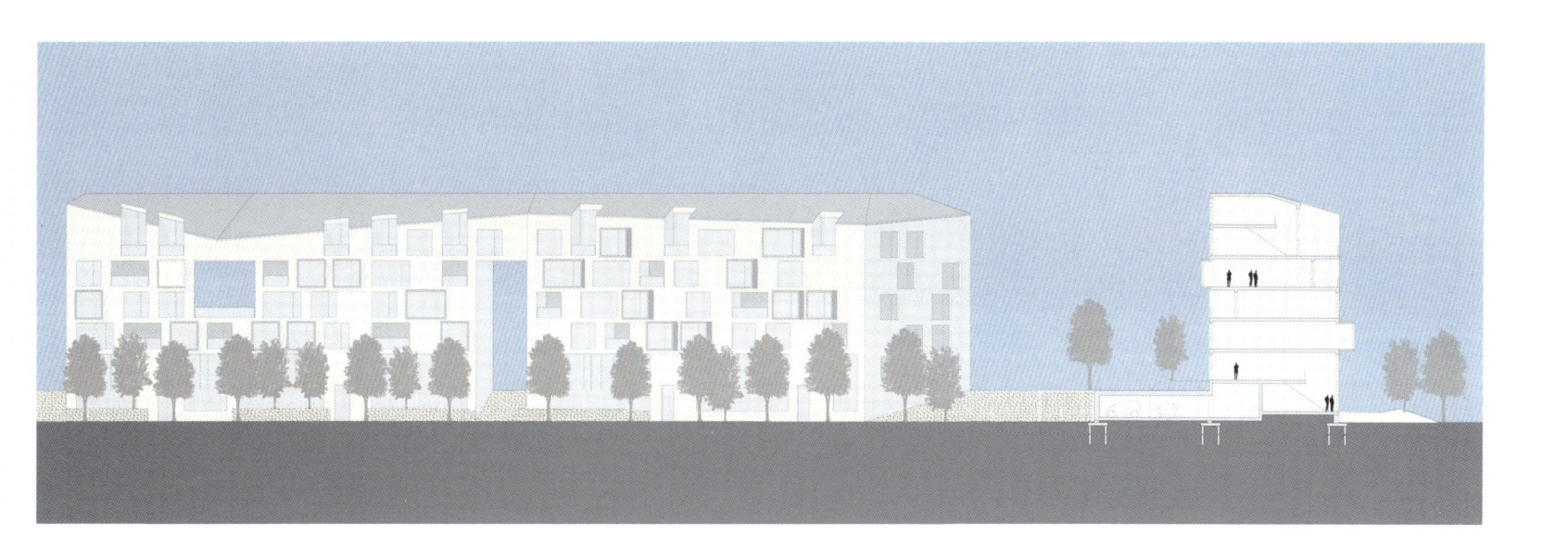

COMFORT

COMFORT

2003–2006 Eden, Bormio

Residence under construction
1,100 sq. m

Prospetto nord 1:300

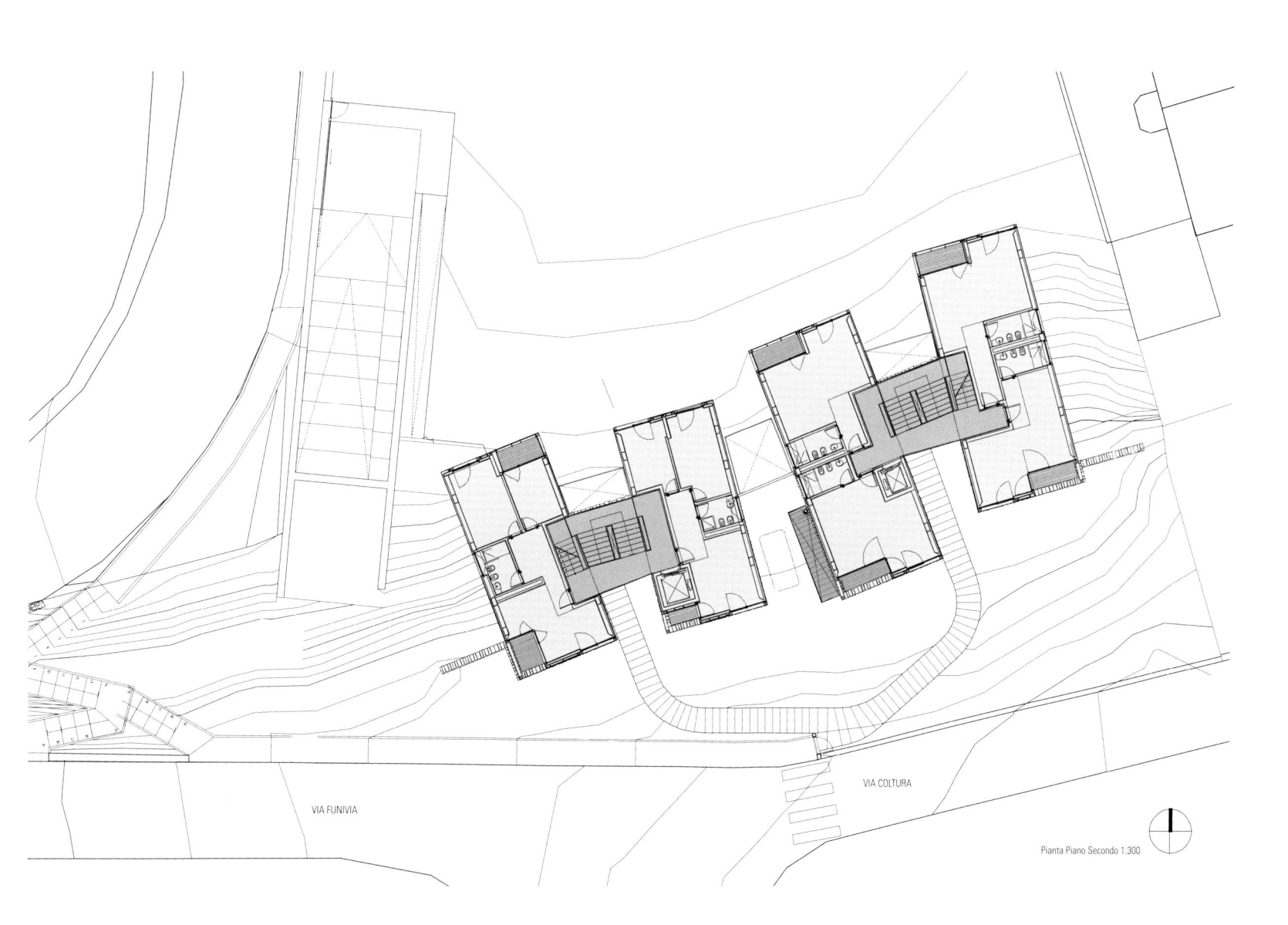

Pianta Piano Secondo 1:300

VIA FUNIVIA

VIA COLTURA

COMFORT

1984–1988 Esprit, Milan

*Headquarter offices and showroom
3,000 sq. m*

Citterio restores the industrial spirit of
the building, a former torrefaction works,
through the use of materials such as
hot-dip galvanised steel for the stairs,
coated cement floors and visible ductwork.

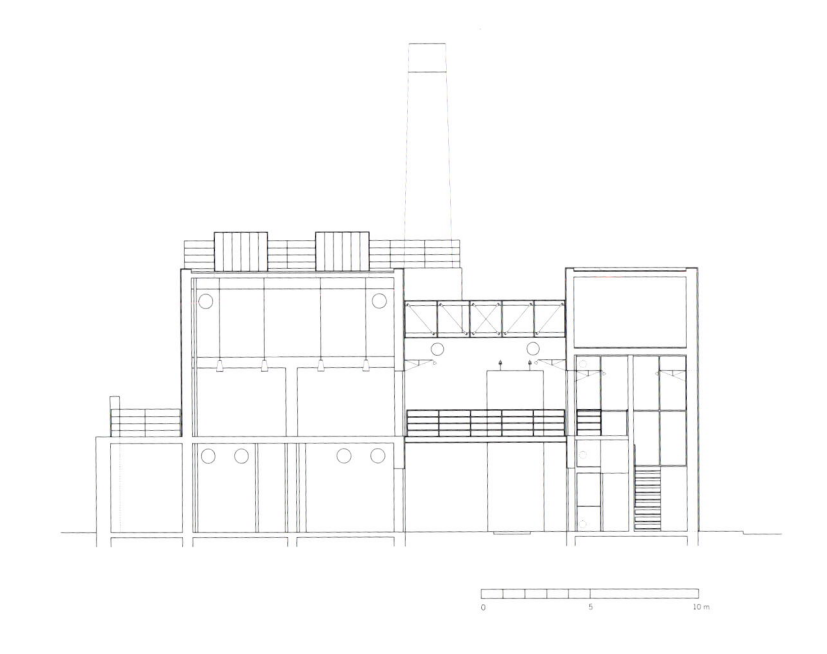

COMFORT

ESPRIT
ITALIA

COMFORT

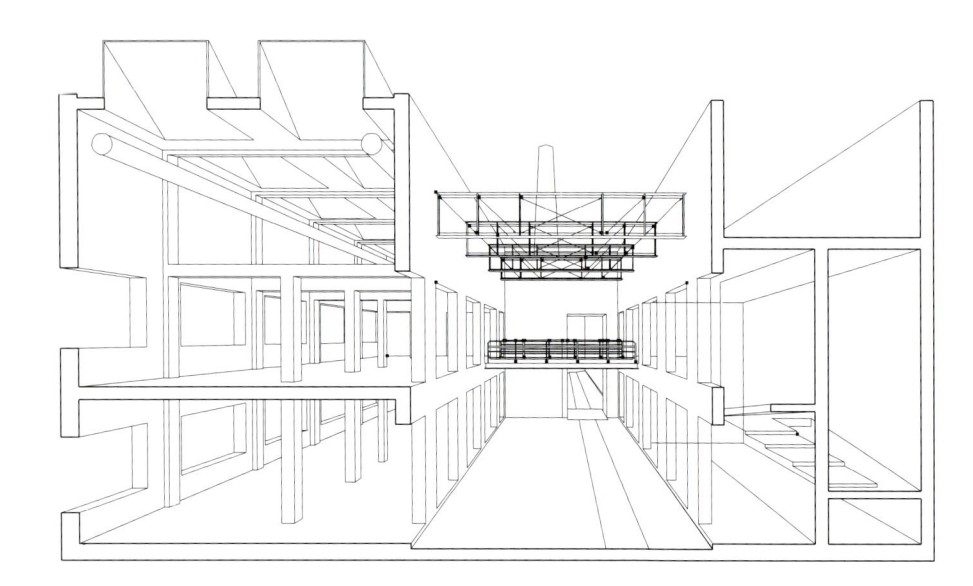

COMFORT

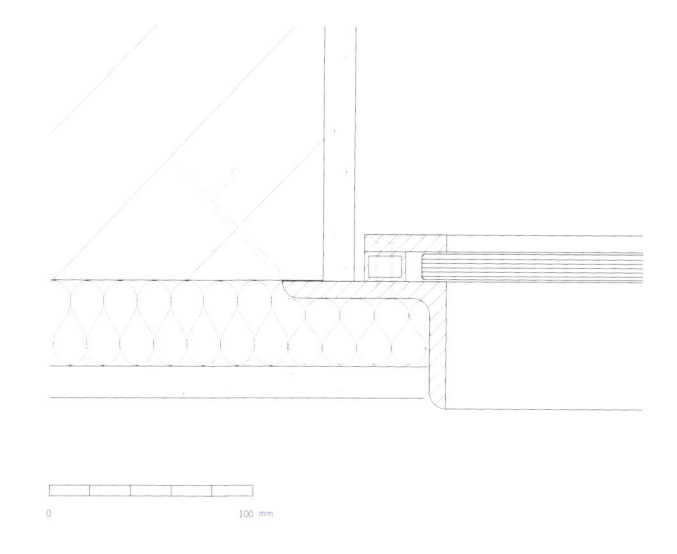

0   100 mm

COMFORT

2002 Mobile Elements, Vitra
with Toan Nguyen

"The quality of a project depends on the degree, however small, of cultural change that it sparks."
Enzo Mari

COMFORT

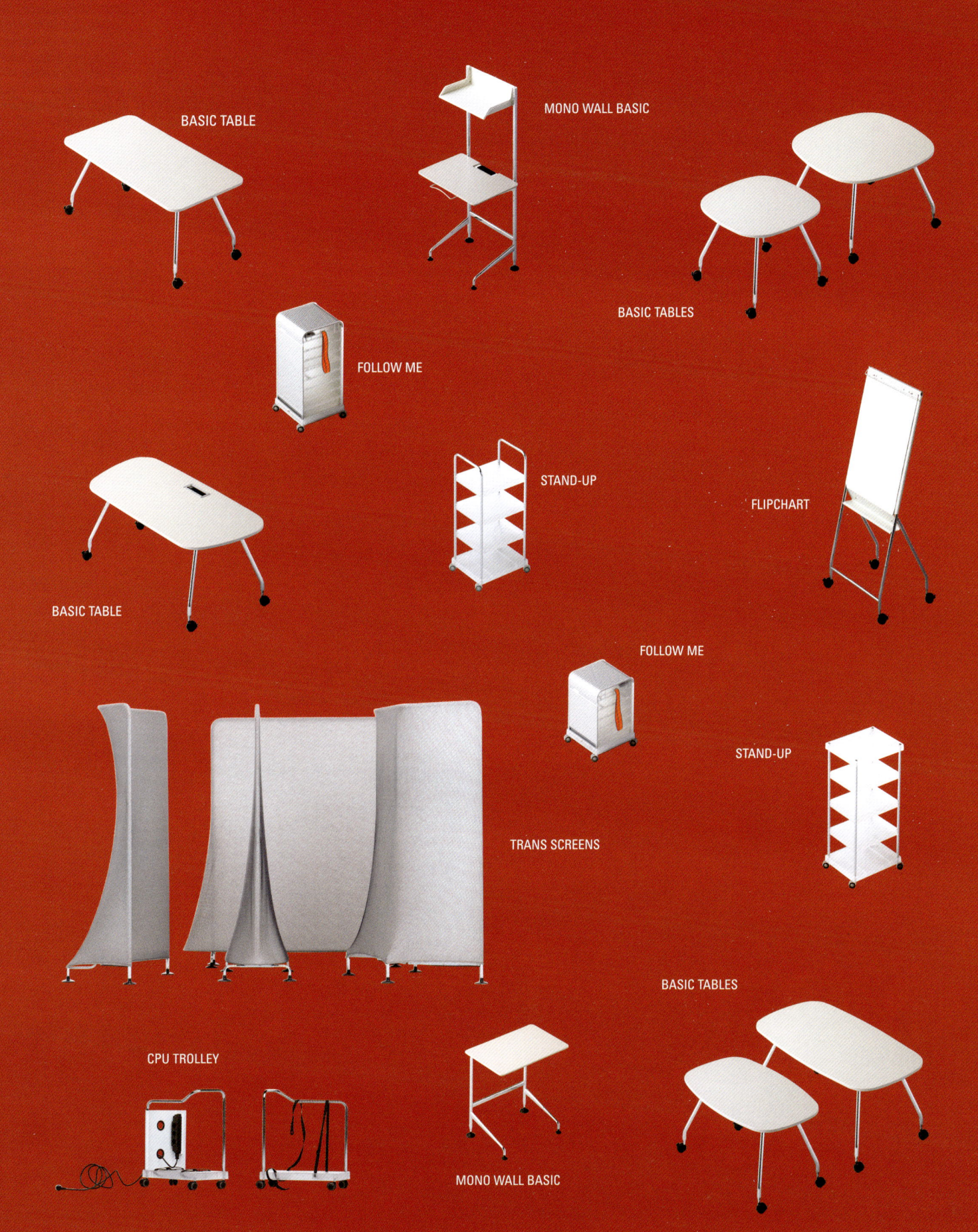

BASIC TABLE

MONO WALL BASIC

BASIC TABLES

FOLLOW ME

STAND-UP

FLIPCHART

BASIC TABLE

FOLLOW ME

STAND-UP

TRANS SCREENS

BASIC TABLES

CPU TROLLEY

MONO WALL BASIC

COMFORT

1998 VISASOFT	2002 OSON S	1992 VISAVIS
1994 T-CHAIR	1996 QUATTRO	1990 AC2
1992 AXION	1990 AREA	

COMFORT

2002 OSON C

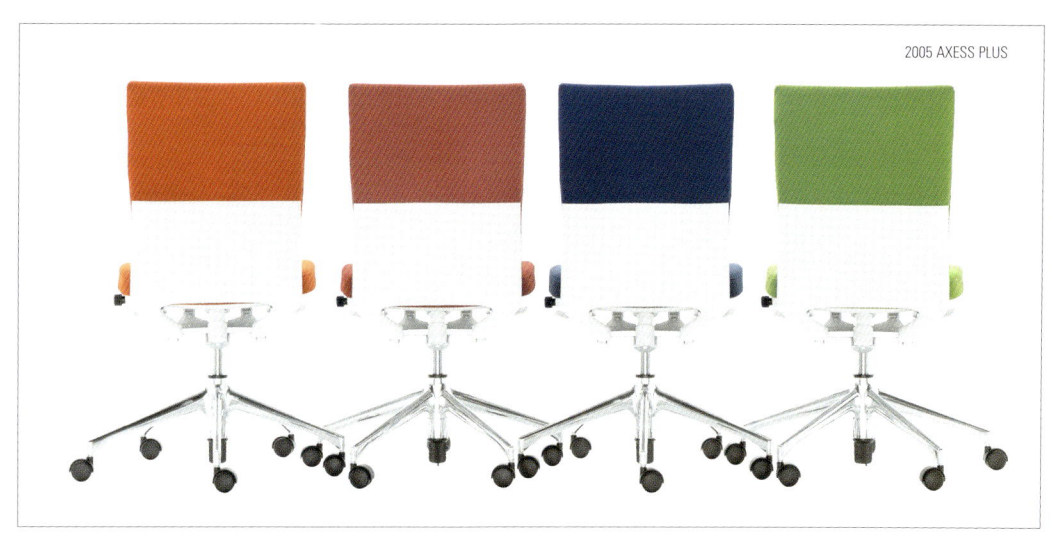

2005 AXESS PLUS

2004 VISASTRIPES

2004 VISAVIS 2

1990 AC1

2002 VISALOUNGE

1996 AXESS

2002 TONIX

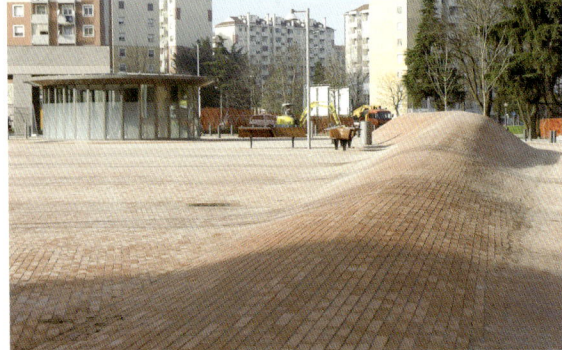

2005–2006 Rozzano, Milan

"Michele Alboreto" Square
8,000 sq. m

Citterio has executed his work with surgical precision, recapturing the tradition of the Italian piazza in a contemporary key, marked by discretion, familiarity and, above all, comfort.

COMFORT

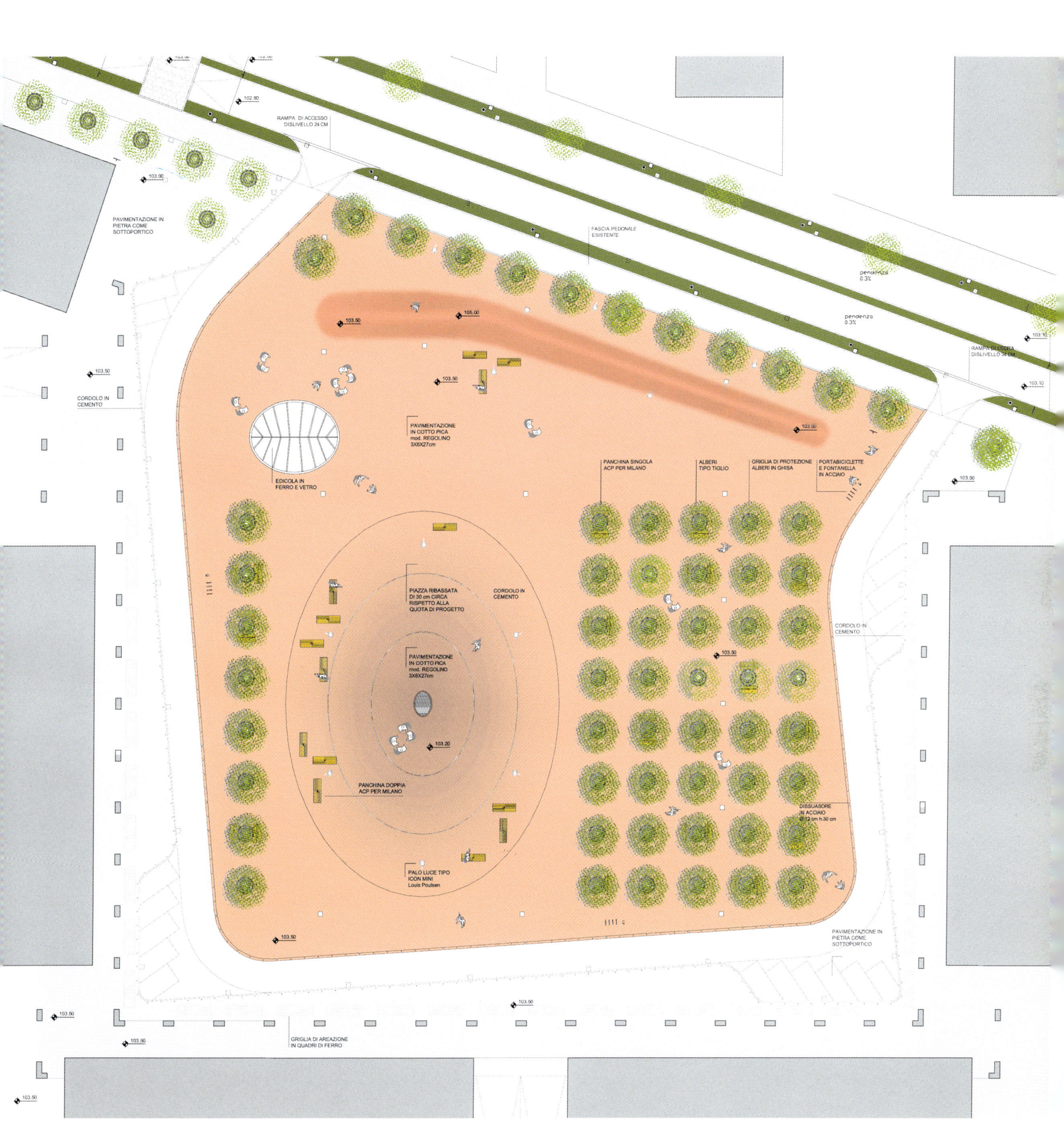

COMFORT

2006 Vighizzolo, Cantù

Bus stop shelter

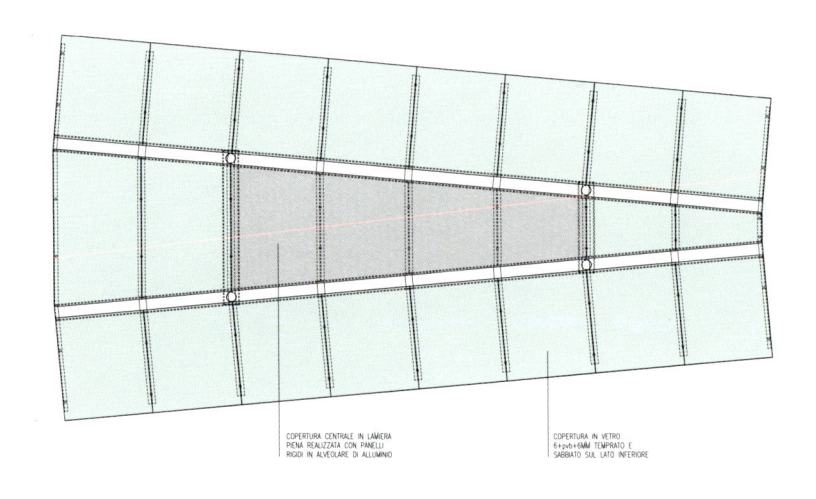

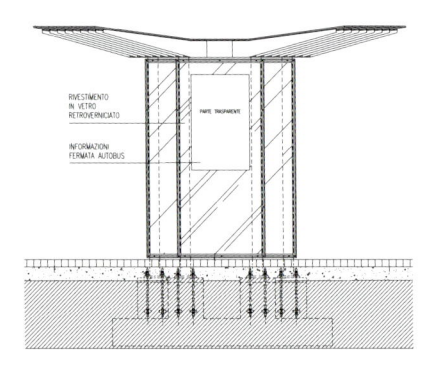

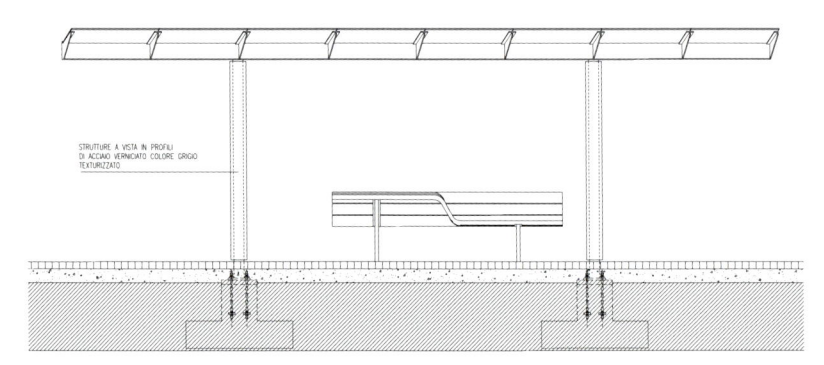

COMFORT

2005 Sedis, Metalco

with Toan Nguyen

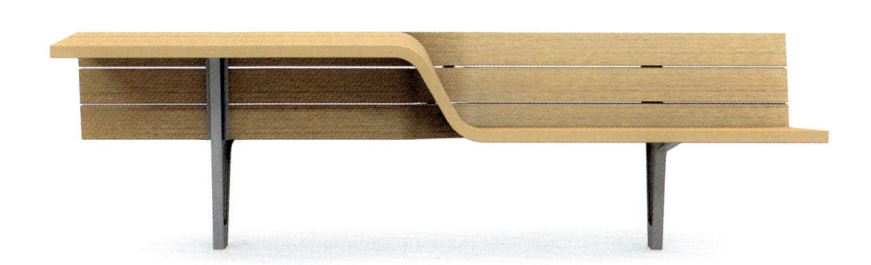

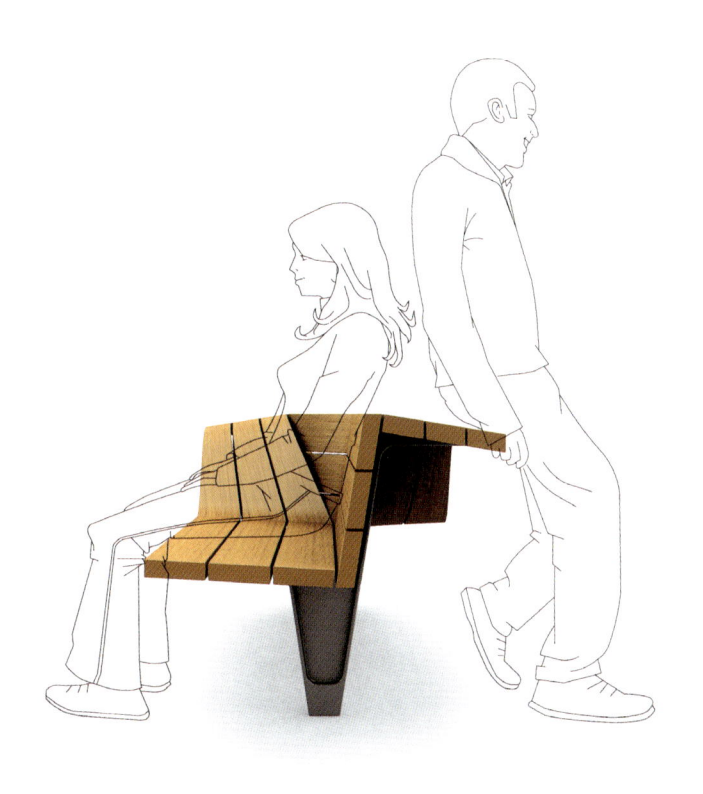

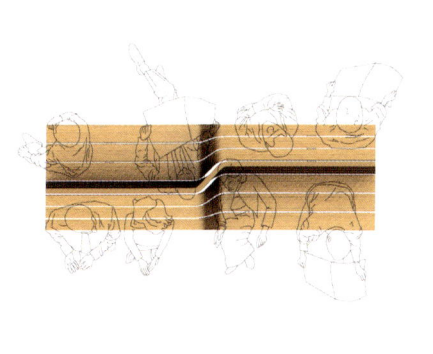

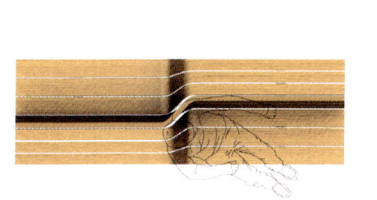

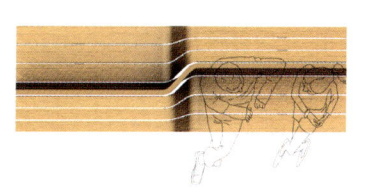

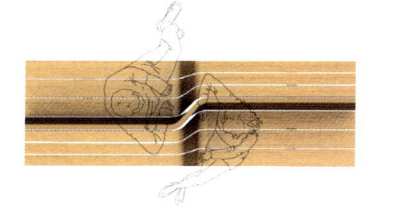

COMFORT

1998–1999 Piazza Cordusio, Milan

ATM multifunctional kiosk with shelter

COMFORT

COMFORT

2004–2005 Underground, Milan

Restyling Duomo-MM1 Line stop

"The very concept of mezzanine as an intermediate access level between the city and the platforms located the project theme more in the cultural world of the commercial space, of the mall, than in the realm of technical infrastructural connective tissue." Patricia Viel

COMFORT

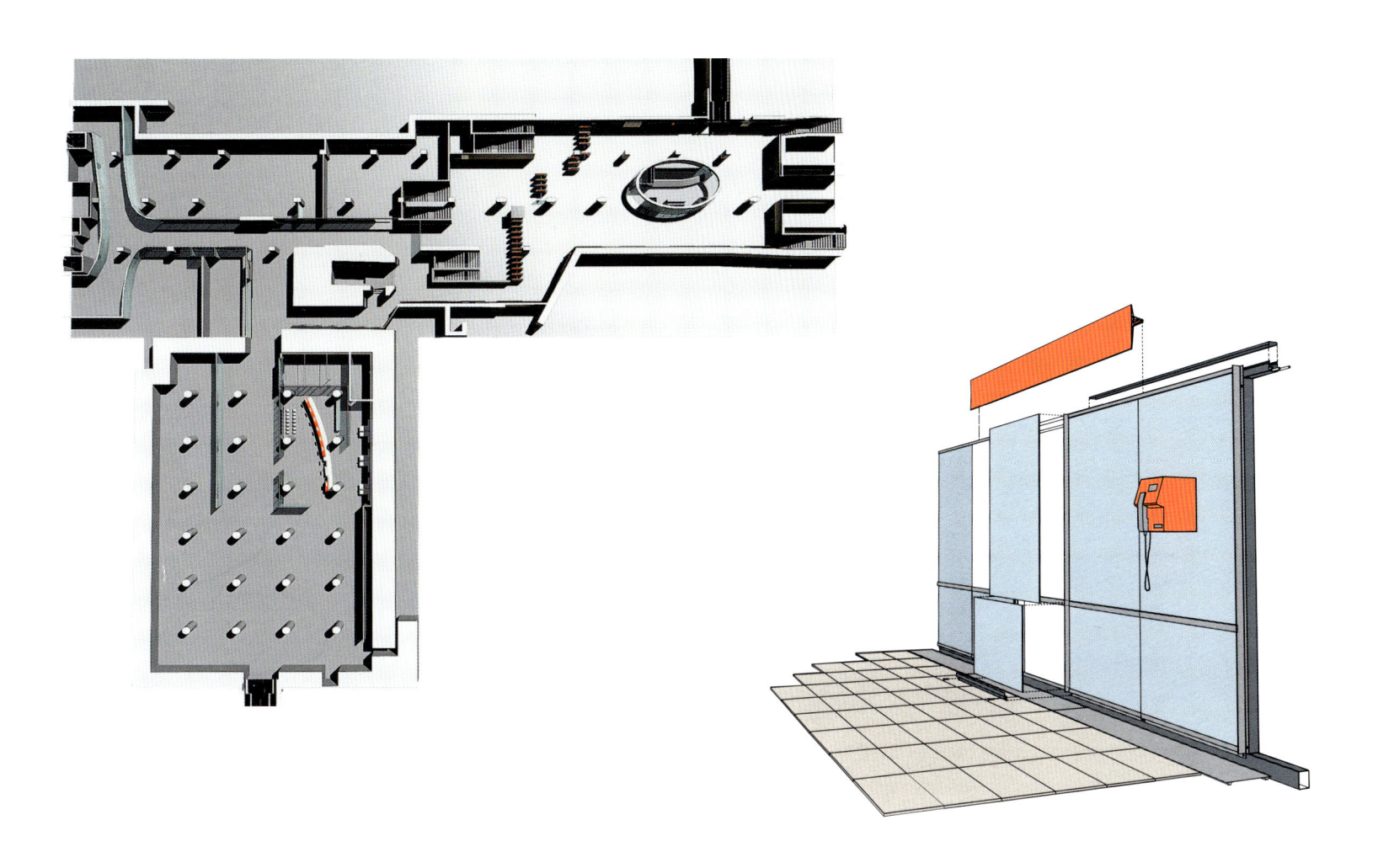

COMFORT

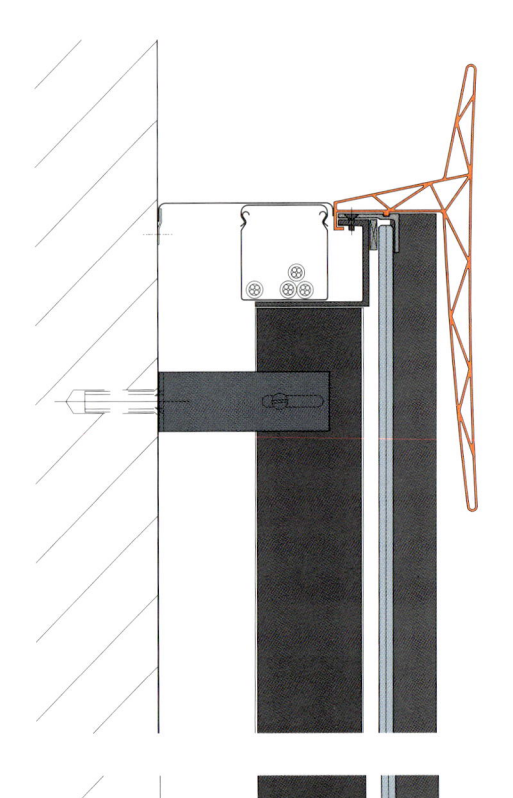

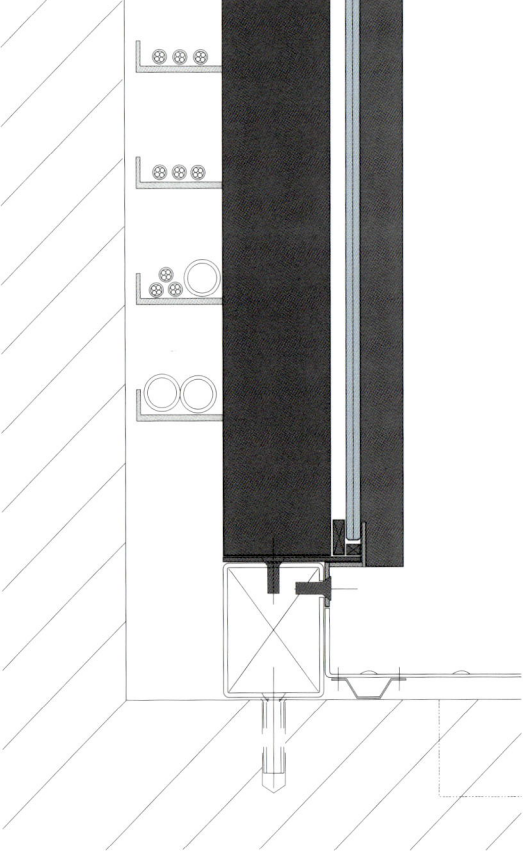

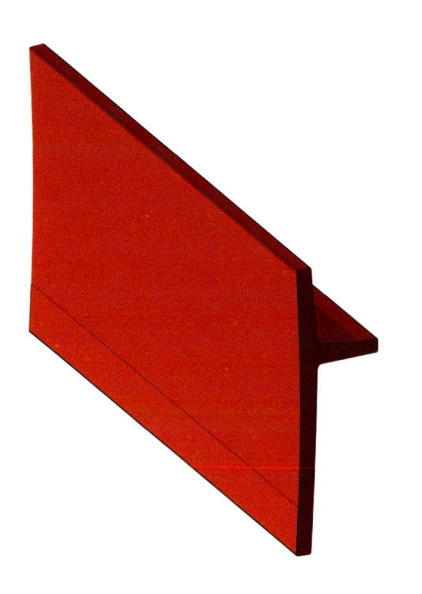

106

COMFORT

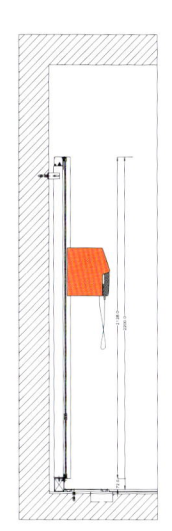

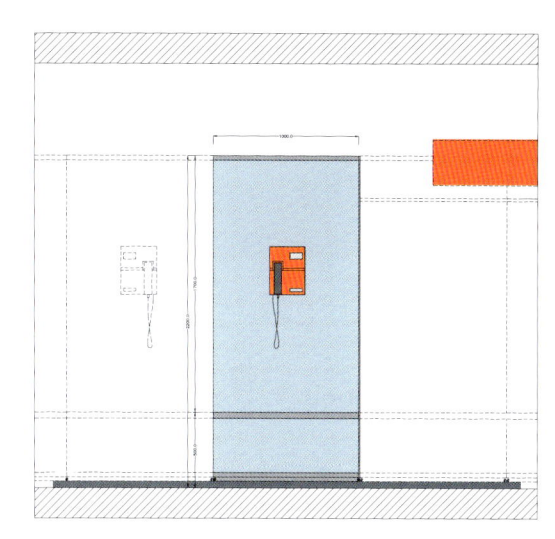

COMFORT

2004–2007 Ravenna Marina

Winning competition entry for the functioning, furnishings and safety of the Guardiano Sud pier. Project partners: Anna Giorgi, Metis Lighting

COMFORT

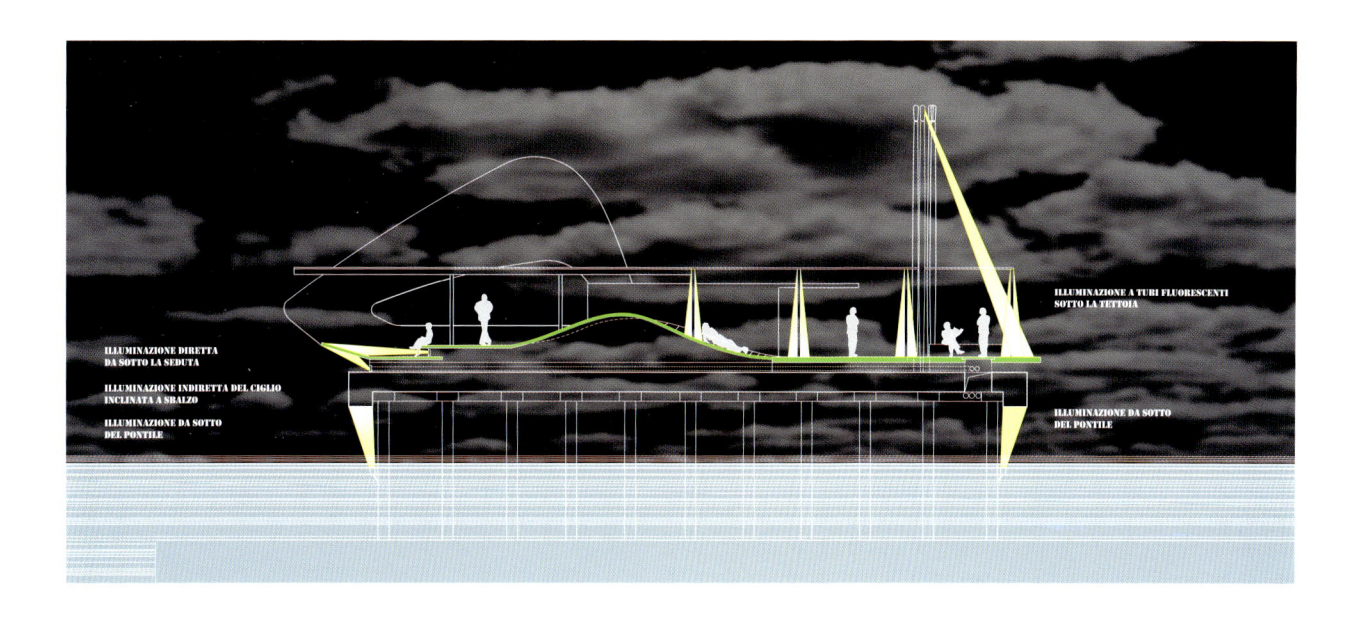

ILLUMINAZIONE DIRETTA
DA SOTTO LA SEDUTA

ILLUMINAZIONE INDIRETTA DEL CIGLIO
INCLINATA A SBALZO

ILLUMINAZIONE DA SOTTO
DEL PONTILE

ILLUMINAZIONE A TUBI FLUORESCENTI
SOTTO LA TETTOIA

ILLUMINAZIONE DA SOTTO
DEL PONTILE

UTILITY.3

In 1796, Goethe wrote to Mayer that it would be better to tie a millstone around the necks of artists and drown them instead of letting them slowly wither away in a quest for the useful.[1] Philip Johnson was even more to the point when he wrote about the crutch of utility saying that people believe a building is beautiful if it works, pointing out that that is a rather silly statement because all buildings work. The Parthenon probably worked excellently for the ceremonies for which it was designed. The fact that a building works is not enough – we expect it to work. We expect hot water to come out of a hot water faucet. We expect the architect to put the kitchen in the best spot. If making the house work takes priority over a feeling for design, then what is created is not architecture, but simply an assemblage of different parts.[2]

The fact that we live in a materialistic age, in a world of businesses and school boards that demand useful buildings,[3] does not mean that the crutch of utility is all that props up architecture. There is no question that the practice of architecture arose in response to a need. Architecture is clearly a utilitarian art, and this utility has always lain in the creation of delimited spaces, within which people are free to move as they will.[4] If for no other reason than this particular genesis, functionality has remained one of the basic requisites of quality building in every age, but it must not be confused with Johnson's assemblage of different parts. The primitive hut built by early Homo sapiens with extreme logical simplicity was described by Vitruvius in the second book of *De Architectura* to indicate the archetypical design that gave origin to the long and complex development of architectural forms.[5] His principle of *utilitas* has endured through numberless metamorphoses, marking both the limits and the allure of architectural design. Paraphrasing Louis Kahn, the difference between the total creative freedom of the artist and the use-bound creativity of the architect lies in the simple fact that a painter can paint a square wheel – an architect cannot, because it won't roll. Nevertheless, if it is true that *utilitas* is a timeless postulate, it is equally true that architecture – if it is to be valid – must also possess beauty, or *venustas*, the third and decisive quality in Vitruvius's triad. The essence of architecture cannot be reduced to mere utilitarianism, to the pure and simple resolution of practical needs. It also responds to a deeper need: to construct the quality of our living spaces.

In spite of its periodic resurfacing in Western culture, the equation *useful = beautiful* cannot stand up to the simplest test; there has never been a strict correspondence between functionality and beauty. As Johnson so acutely observed, even an ugly object can perfectly fulfil its purpose.

Johnson is right in considering functionality a condition that does not determine the real qualities of architecture, but rather one which can have a paralysing effect on the culture of architectural design, even though architects and designers currently seem to prefer the narcissistic matrix over the functional one. Contemporary magazines exalt the spectacular architecture of the "archistars", while deliberately eclipsing modern "ethical" themes (from the question of habitations to the poetics of rationality) because the clients demand a *Wunder-architektur* based on inspiring the "awe" inherited from the shock treatment approach of avant-garde art or from clever advertising vehicles, in adherence to the

[1] Konrad Fiedler, "Aphorismen", in Herman Konnerth, *Konrad Fiedlers Schriften über Kunst*, Munich: 1914.

[2] Adapted from Philip Johnson, "The Seven Crutches of Modern Architecture", *Perspecta 3*, 1955, pp. 40–44.

[3] Philip Johnson, adapted from a speech at the eleventh Annual Northeast Regional Conference of the American Institute of Architects, Oceanlake, Oregon, 12 October 1962.

[4] Alois Riegl, *Die Spätrömische Kunst-industrie*. Vienna: W. Braumüller, 1901. Adapted from the Italian translation *Tardoromana*, edited by Licia Collobi Ragghianti. Florence: Sansoni, 1981.

[5] It was in the eighteenth century that Vitruvius's *utilitas* gave way to illuminist functionalism. The contribution of the Jesuit Marc Antoine Laugier on the primitive hut as the functional origin of architecture as a response to baroque ornamentalism is fundamental. He states in his *Essay on Architecture* that of all utilitarian arts, architecture is the one that demands the greatest effort and the broadest knowledge. The small primitive hut is the model on the basis of which all architectural magnificence is conceived. Our buildings must be solid, functional and decorous. Buildings are made to be lived in, and to fulfil this purpose they have to be functional. Adapted from Marc Antoine Laugier, *Essai sur l'Architecture*. Paris: 1753.

[6] Paul Valéry, *Eupalinos ou l'Architecte*, 1921; public domain.

[7] Antonio Citterio in an interview with the author, May 2005.

[8] Le Corbusier, *Verso un'architettura*, in Pierluigi Cerri and Pierluigi Nicolin, ed. Milan: Longanesi Editori, 1984, p. 6.

[9] On the development of space distribution in houses, see Riccardo Montenegro, *Abitare nei secoli, Storia dell'arredamento dal Rinascimento a oggi.* Milan: Mondadori, 1996.

economic principles of city marketing.

Nevertheless, as in any other era, our desire for wonders is overshadowed by the demand for "distributed quality". An increasingly strong need is felt for planners and designers who are capable of conceiving objects and structures that are logical, minimal and free of emphasis. This calls to mind a famous piece from Paul Valery's *Eupalinos ou l'Architecte*. In the imaginary dialogue, Socrates asks his architect friend: "Tell me (you who are so sensitive to the effects of architecture), have you not observed, walking around the city, that among the buildings populating it, some are mute, others speak and yet others – the rarest of all – sing?"[6]

This is a typical trait in Antonio Citterio's work. He prefers the quality of primary social functions – dwelling and working – to the exhibition of form. Nevertheless, Citterio is well aware of architecture's ethical value, its social impact and its ability to relate to – and thus modify – the urban context. The outcomes are not always positive, as contemporary cities show us. "I consciously renounce sensationalism, I stubbornly remove all that is vainly ostentatious or self-referential. I do not like grand gestures; I do not think they help the project. We are living in a period of consolidation and I do not think innovation can rightly be represented by making things spectacular the way they do in Hollywood."[7]

Utility for the Home
Citterio-Dwan private residence, Milan; Private residence in Sagaponack, project; Arclinea: Convivium*; Hansgrohe:* Axor *mixer; Guzzini:* My Table*; Fusital:* AC3*; Tre Più:* Planus

People live in old homes and do not worry about building houses in line with their needs.[8] With this *j'accuse*, Le Corbusier captures the lack of correspondence between the house and its intended functions. The disciplinary separation between architecture and interior design has gradually led to a schism between container and contents, and to the arrangement of interior spaces as the simple result of a constructional grid. From the Middle Ages to the twentieth century, the spaces in the house have been rigidly hierarchised on the basis of their assigned functions, and only the ones used for receiving guests were deemed worthy of efforts at design.[9] In the process of redefining built forms and reorganising interior space that has been underway over the past fifty years in the "bourgeois" house, two approaches prevail. On the one hand we have the opening up of space with the open-space plan, where the circulation patterns are not determined by the arrangement of the furnishings, but by the functions that are carried out within the space. On the other hand we have a rigorous and traditional organisation of interior spaces, pathways and functions that rigidly impose the way the house is to be used.

Citterio counters the idea of a house subdivided on the basis of function with a unitary conception in which the correspondence between the architecture, the interiors and the furnishings is the result of a quest applied to the poetics of dwelling. We can see this in the Citterio-Dwan house in Milan (1998), where the arrangement of the furnishings represents one of the constituent elements of the interior design. The wall cuts, the different levels and the interaction of planar surfaces and materials that characterise the architectural design are echoed in counterpoint in the furnishings, where the materials and colours of the upholstery along with the lamps, tables and cabinetry, contribute to enhancing the equilibrium of the interior space. The distribution of space is flexible, and can be modified over time to adapt to changing needs.

Here we see the lesson of the Milanese school, but there is also the clear influence of Pierre Chareau's exploration of transparency in the house for Jean Dalsace, or the interplay of volumes in Charles Eames's house in Santa Monica, where the furnishings represent a happy synthesis of integration with the architectural design.

The fluidity of the space and the comfort of the furnishings respond to the evolution of domestic habits, to the change in dwelling types induced by the real estate market and to new family use and consumption patterns. For this reason they represent an example of habitational utility. And this utility is interpreted according to the paradigm of the culture of excellence, which, as opposed to traditional luxury, seeks to increase personal pleasure and wellbeing and not, as per a well-established practice, to show off one's wealth or social status.

As Citterio puts it, "utility is associated with time and with day-to-day life. It is closely tied to the use of objects, to the relationships we establish with them. For this reason the nature of the utility changes as the house changes. My idea of habitational utility is indissolubly linked to lifestyle, to changing family habits. For example, in the 1980s, the sofa was not very deep, since it was mainly a support for conversation; now it is a place to relax. Before, the television had to be hidden. The contemporary awareness is that of inhabiting the house as a retreat where you can let yourself relax, eat and sleep without restrictions. Analogously, in 2000, the kitchen represents the centre of the house, an intimate gathering place and the place where the rite of preparing meals is performed. Receiving your friends in the kitchen has become a metaphor for affection, interchange and warmth."[10] It was thus inevitable that the kitchen space would have to be modified and transformed from an inhospitable and sequestered utility area into the pulsating centre of the house.

A representation of this design sensibility is the house in Sagaponack, where the distributive fulcrum and incipit of the home is the kitchen, designed as the centre of mass of its planimetric composition and the meeting place for the family. Incorporating a suggestion from the client, Citterio designed the house from the inside out, simplifying the indoor-outdoor relationship through large plate glass windows and creating a terraced garden to ensure privacy. Inside, a wood and glass court distributes light and connects the swimming pool to the kitchen and living room areas. The kitchen is the domestic traffic hub and an application of the study of kitchen system design that sees Citterio leading the way in developing the island format. This type of kitchen represents an innovation in design most notably elaborated further in the different collections created for Arclinea. Starting with the *Italia* kitchen in 1988 and especially with the *Convivium* kitchen in 2002, these collections redefined the components of the kitchen space in the contemporary house and popularised the island-style kitchen.

In dwelling spaces that tend to get smaller and smaller, the kitchen has expanded to

[10] Conversation with the author, 26 May 2005.

[11] Henry Focillon, *The Life of Forms in Art*, adapted from the Italian translation *La Vita delle forme, seguito dall'elogio della mano.* Turin: Einaudi Piccola Biblioteca, 2002.

[12] Federico Butera, *Il castello e la rete. Impresa, organizzazioni e professioni nell'Europa degli anni '90.* Milan: Franco Angeli, 2005, p. 21. Design is a foundational contributing element also to *Total Quality Management*. Giovanni Mattana observes, "*Total Quality Management* is a spreading phenomenon. It is understood as management focussing on quality, based on the participation of all workers, oriented towards long-term profitability resulting from customer satisfaction and including benefits for the greater society", in his "Un quadro di riferimento per la qualità totale", *Esperienze originali di Qualità Totale*, 'L'Impresa', 2, 1991, p. 9 and in *Qualità, affidabilità, certificazione. Strategie, tecniche e opportunità per il miglioramento dei prodotti, dei servizi, delle organizzazioni.* Milan: Franco Angeli, 2002.

become a living room/dining room as well. Citterio also dedicated his attention to details that improve the performance and use of the kitchen cabinets and cupboards and the division of elements by function: cabinets for storing food and utensils, countertops for preparing food. Citterio's design offers a rational response to the various needs associated with the main steps in cooking. From washing and preparing to cooking and eating, the cabinets and areas around the island are designed around user movements and facilitate all operations. The convivial urge represented by the kitchen space is associated with the desire for objects offering semi-professional performance, such as the hood over the stove for Arclinea and the Hansgrohe *Axor*-series mixer faucet, semi-professional objects that testify to and exalt the day-to-day passion for cooking.

The curiosity of the designers applies the same sensibility to the creation of the tableware and kitchen utensils designed for Guzzini, Hansgrohe, Sawaya & Moroni and Hackman-Iittala. The forms were conceived on the basis of their intended functions and to respond to the anatomy of the hand that will grasp them. It is not a question of ergonomics, but of utility, the possibility to enhance the forms of objects by picturing the movements that will be associated with them. Hence the *My Table* tableware for Guzzini narrows elegantly at the base of the grip to emphasise the pressure of the fingers and then broadens at the end to amply accommodate food.

Citterio's praise of the hand by designing objects that give it the role of protagonist reminds us of Focillon's memorable praise in *The Life of Forms in Art* when he says that through their hands people make contact with the hard substance of thought; they succeed in unlocking it. The hands are what impose form, outline.[11] We see this again in Citterio's door handles for Fusital. They crystallise his vigilant quest for detail and his ability to rethink commonplace objects. In the *AC3* handle from 2003, in particular, the enwrapping line encloses the movement of the hand while responding to specific production demands. "The production of the handles by robots," states Citterio, "involves a specific necessity of form in relation to the means of producing it, whether we are processing a metal tube or a cast piece."

Antonio Citterio's extraordinary ability to design in a systemic way is clearly evidenced in his doors for Tre Più. They are objects that respond to the same logic and were produced via the same design method. While his study of door handles was guided by his thinking about archetypical forms, his exploration of the door motif derived from a personal experience. Not having found doors on the market that had the characteristics of flexibility and engineering he sought, Citterio had an artisan make the doors for his house and for his studio. This led to the conception of the flush-mount hinged *Planus* door system that can easily be incorporated into any wall, and the sliding *Pavilion* door system that liberates space from the constriction of the wall and subdivides it with flexible and lightweight furnishing elements.

Utility for the Workplace

Pharmaceutical company offices, Verona; Research & Development Centre B&B Italia, Novedrate; Vitra: Ad Wall, Ad One

In the contemporary period, as observes Federico Butera,[12] the idea began to crumble that work can be programmed like a huge machine whose sole purpose is to produce more and more at a lower cost for markets in continual expansion. "The economy of flexibility substantially changes company management criteria. The first criterion that changes is that of economic efficacy, which in this [new] model regards the appropriateness of a response to the market. Lowering unit production costs is not the only important thing; it is also important to produce products and services appropriate to the timeframes, locations and ways that they are demanded by the market . . . The second criterion that changes regards efficiency, which indicates the amount of time that passes from the emergence of market demand to the physical delivery of the product or service into the hands of the customer."

It follows that the contemporary office has to address specific demands and produce solutions that are in line with complex requirements regarding work, coordination and communication. With his signature determination and lucidity, Citterio has moved in response to this, working both on the contents and on the container, starting from the principle that the architectural space determines the quality of work every bit as much as the chair on which one sits.

The offices created for a multinational pharmaceutical company in Verona are quite significant in this regard. Citterio redesigned an existing building according to the parameters of dynamic and flexible organisation of work. Echoing the exploration of translucency whose main interpreters are Herzog & De Meuron, this building is distinguished by the lightness and transparency of its spaces, which incorporate different functions without sacrificing spatial unity.

The glassed volumes are the main spatial elements. With their different fittings, depending on whether they are exterior or interior, they create scenographic spaces such as the entrance foyer, with its steel staircase encased in a stratified and coloured glass volume leading up to the President's offices. The U-glass (a moulded industrial glass) emergency stairway unit is another example with its full height partitions in serigraphed glass that creates a screen between one space and another without sacrificing the feeling of lightness.

"We addressed the redesign work," explains Patricia Viel, "by identifying a series of sensitive areas – the entries, the presidential offices, the executive offices – and also shaping the project guidelines to address the other work areas."[13]

The planimetric pivot is the central patio that breaks up the rectangular floor plan and separates the utility areas from the office areas. It is flanked by the boardroom, which opens onto the open space for the secretarial staff, the eleven 6 x 4-metre office modules and the two free offices for receiving guests from abroad. The "smart" distribution of space is accompanied by the aesthetic and functional integration of the interiors with the furnishings to create sober environments far removed from the mechanisms of so many other "office systems". The final effect reminds one of the care and warmth of the home environment rather than the alienating effect of the work environment. The choice was made to emphasise "an alternative work dimension," continues Viel, "in which the priority given to values linked to quality of life and fluidity of interrelations is complemented by the calm and contemplation of a cultural cli-

[13] Cited in A. Boisi, "Spazi fluidi", *Interni*, May 2006, pp. 32–33.

[14] Ibid., pp. 35–36.

[15] Conversation with the author, March 2006.

mate such as might typically be found on a university campus, conceived to favour and stimulate thought as well as to facilitate order and achievement."[14] The use of light, which Citterio wields not only as a source of illumination, but also as a construction material, is a determining factor in achieving that end. The lighting design exalts the fluidity of the space, highlighting the glass volumes and marking out the circulation pathways.

Citterio also had to deal with preexisting material in his work for the B&B Research & Development Centre. In this case, it was prized material: the building designed by Tobia Scarpa in the 1970s, with Renzo Piano subsequently enlarging the façade overlooking the Novedratese road. And it was a mixed-use building, neither industrial nor commercial. The challenge represented by this research centre project was an unusual architectural theme: the reorganisation of the complex required the relocation and grouping of some management facilities and the creation of an architectural element on the perimeter to accommodate the research lab and design centre. All the functions of the R&D Centre are accommodated within the 10,000 square metres of Citterio's project, including product planning and technical design, advertising, exhibition, sales and sales staff training.

Citterio unified the preexisting components in a unitary project and placed the accent on a vocation for research not belonging precisely to the Italian industrial culture. The R&D Centre has introduced a new methodology into the Italian furniture industry: research as a support for design and production.

"The conception of the office has changed," states Citterio. "The rigidity of the mega-systems of the 1980s has been supplanted by a demand for flexibility in work spaces, corresponding to the increasing mobility of the labour market. The computer, for example, has radically modified the way we conceive office furniture."[15]

The void left by the lack of an ideal office design has now been filled in by the custom-made solution, created ad hoc to suit the specific needs of the client. It follows that office furnishings as well have to meet needs that are no longer standard, but more personal. And also for furnishings in the office environment, the challenge is represented by the need to allow the space to be organised in a flexible manner.

The office systems created for Vitra are characterised by the flexibility of the combinations, which can be personalised on the basis of the dimensions of the given space and the type of office required. They are designed both as individual objects and as components of a greater system.

Citterio created the autonomous walls of *Ad Wall* (2000), where the module has elements that can be varied in height, dimensions and form, and combined to become an integral part of the overall office design, and *Ad Hoc* and *New Ad Hoc* (2005), which are autonomous workstations that separate and organise the office workspace in line with specific needs. The personalisation is not limited exclusively to a reiteration of all the variations on the theme of the finite partition-desk-chair module, but also extends to compact, freestanding workstations such as the *Vademecum* work station, or to individual elements – oval or trapezoidal tables, reticulated partitions, itinerant bookcases, integrated or individual illumination – that allow effective ad hoc customisation and improve user ease and comfort. This marks a significant change in the realm of the office, one that increases the utility of office space management, the utility of employee efforts and the utility of single components in terms of enhanced performance.

A company's networked office system is now diversified on the basis of the work performed, using different configurations to suit its primary purpose. So you may have a front office with the leadership role of the overall office system and thus the responsibility for outlining strategic orientations and objectives, a back office providing support to the front office in the process of determining objectives and a virtual office, a finely branched network of telematic offices providing dense coverage, but lacking the physical form that conditions the needs of the other two types.[16]

Utility for the City and Territory

Technogym Village, Cesena; Antonio Citterio and Partners studio, Milan; Neuer Wall, Hamburg

The Wellness Valley is slowly taking form in the area near Cesena. It is a unique example of enhancement and promotion of the productive resources of an area. Citterio has given form to Nerio Alessandri's enlightened vision to contribute to what he calls an "improvement in the quality of life through education, regular physical activity, proper diet and a positive attitude." The ambitious objective is translated into a series of community services that highlight the utility of the project for the surrounding territorial context.

Without relying on government contributions, but by applying the approach of industrial districts, the Technogym Village takes the form of a hub for Italian wellness and offers a variety of services to the neighbouring communities: sports facilities, a park and an efficient, nonpolluting production facility. Citterio's project unites the office buildings overlooking the park and adds the labs of the Research & Development Centre and the Wellness Centre, a building with an oval floor plan of some 2,700 square metres immersed in the park with its gymnasium and swimming pool. Here the architecture establishes a holistic relationship with its contents: glass walls create a fluid relationship between indoors and outdoors, and high performance natural materials (laminated wood and glass) emphasise the organic nature of the project.

Technogym Village has a well-defined identity that is evident right from the motorway exit, where motorists will immediately see the long flank of the production facility. Like the Brembo Centre in Bergamo by Jean Nouvel, the dimension of the façade along the motorway enhances the visual impact and orients the spatial approach. While Nouvel bases his impact on the chromatic vibrations of red to capture and surprise the motorist's eye with the unexpected, Citterio favours the lighter and more rarefied dimension of a very long glassed-in stoa where the volutes of the roof echo the soft contours of the Romagna landscape.

An equal delicacy is found in the urban projects where Citterio's approach is the antithesis of that of the "archistars". Citterio intervenes with a surgeon's skill to incorporate his buildings into the urban fabric without making "noise", without indulging in any individualistic ostentation. He counters the narcissism of the personal mark with the dignity of mimesis that translates into urban quality, in harmony with a well-established trait of Milanese culture.

The Antonio Citterio and Partners studio in Milan's Via Cerva is a clear demon-

[16] See Alessandra Vasile, *New Offices in Italy*. Milan: L'Archivolto, 2003; Fabio Fabrizzi, *Uffici*. Milan: Federico Motta Editore, 2002; Michele Furnari, *Gli Uffici*. Rome–Bari: Editori Laterza, 1995.

stration of this. On a long, narrow plot on a residential street, Citterio eliminated all decoration and ornament to lay bare the entire façade of the structure: large windows framed by Ceppo stone facing that reveal externally the active operations in the building while allowing the metropolitan humours to penetrate inside. It is a very discreet façade that respects its surroundings, does not obscure its neighbouring buildings and is highlighted only at night by the lights on the five open office floors. Inside, in fact, the building is empty of all walls and partitions so that every floor is an open-space area. Antonio Citterio's office is on the top floor, conceived as "a house when I am not at home": a terrace with a wooden *brise soleil* structure that modulates the light and complies with the offset stipulated in building regulations.

We see Citterio's signature attention to the urban context in the Neuer Wall office building in Hamburg, where the façade dialogues with the canal running through the heart of the city. With its position right in the centre of town, Citterio's Neuer Wall incorporates an elegant curtain of grey stone, where the glass of the parapets and the wooden slats of the sun shades create a texture of stunning visual impact, emphasised on close view by the refinement of the horizontal bevelling of the walls. The apparent randomness of the door and window placement also creates interesting variations in the succession of filled and empty spaces.

Right from his earliest buildings – the Esprit Milan or the Antonio Fusco facility in Corsico – Citterio has demonstrated the unusual quality of being able to look at normal things with uncommon eyes. Lord Snowdon used to exhort us to look at usual things with unusual eyes. Citterio's merit in this work is precisely that of being able to elevate normalcy to the ranks of exceptionality; it is a project about details, materials, finishings, functional organisation, technological integration and performance. This is what determines the utility of use of a building, but also the utility of context, in the sense that it improves the urban setting without overwhelming it. In this attitude, we see the cultural watermark of a city – Milan – that has always reconciled project and production, design and manufacturing, and that historically has preferred discreet quality over pretentious exhibition.

1997–1998 Citterio-Dwan House, Milan

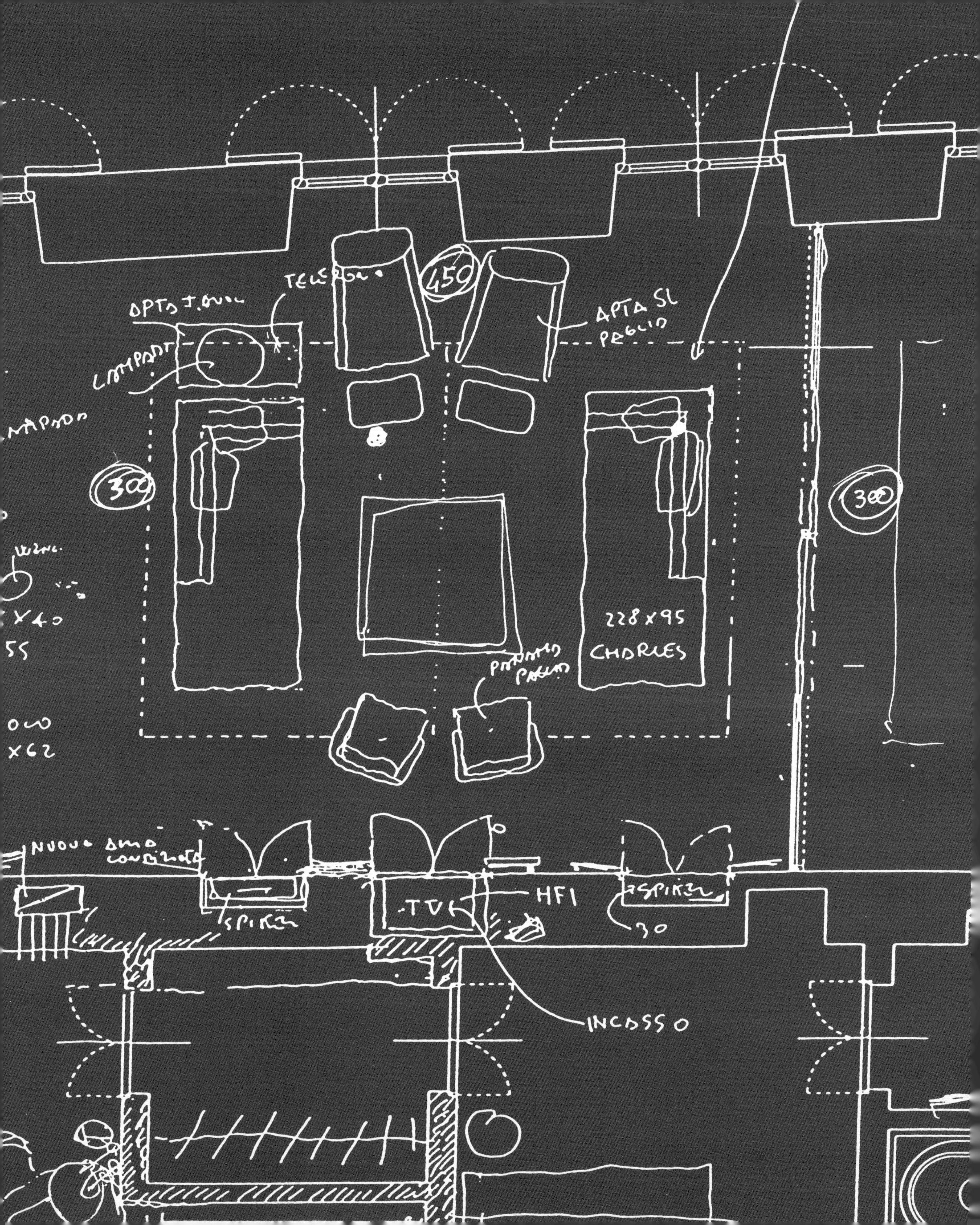
450
300
300
228 x 95
HFI
INCASSO

UTILITY

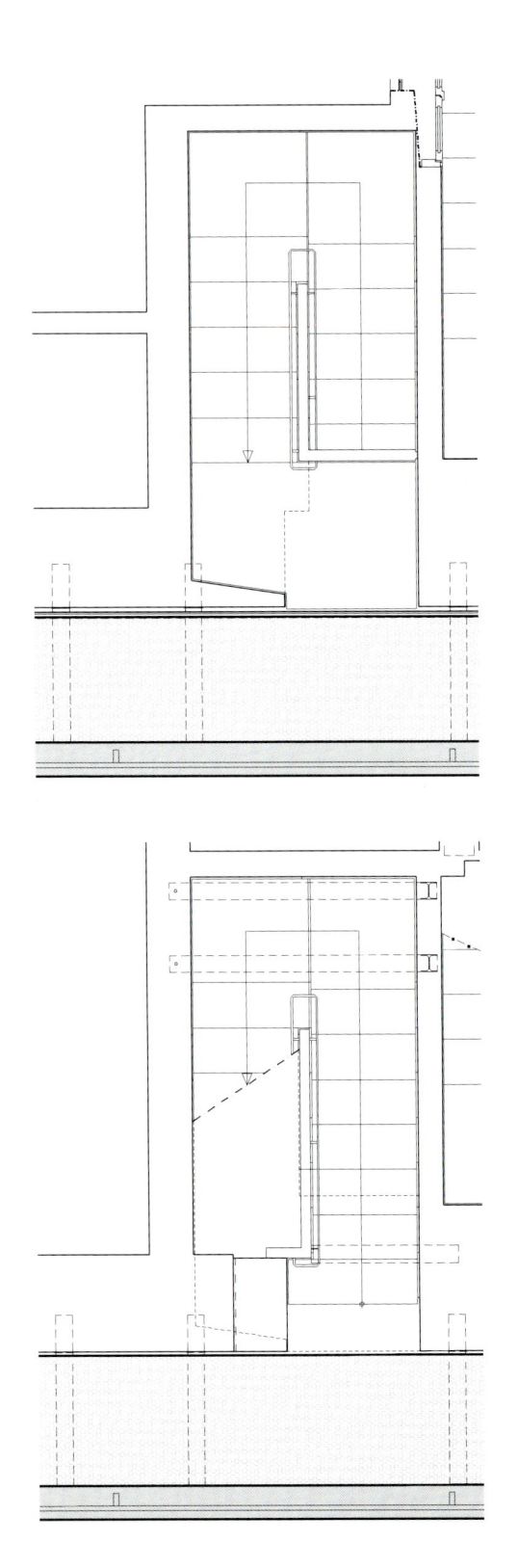

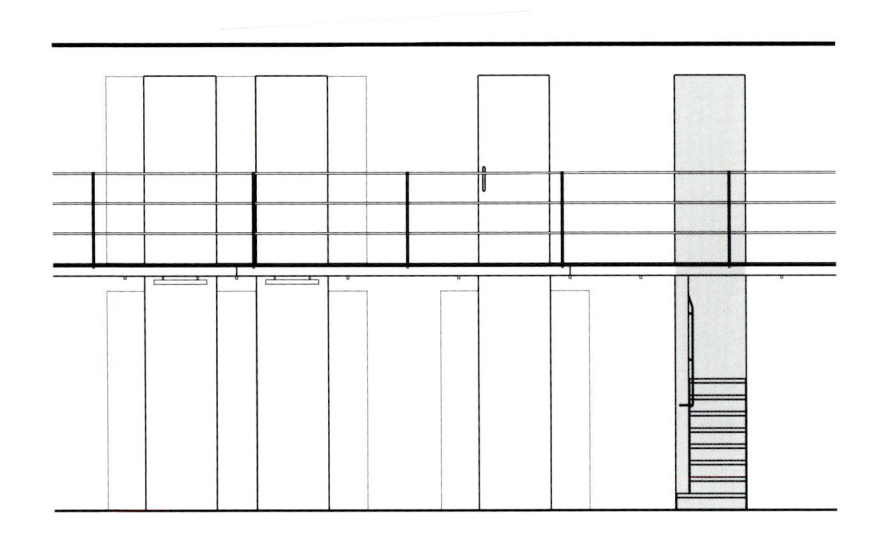

122

UTILITY

1997–1998 Citterio-Dwan House, Milan

Private residence
450 sq. m

The wall cuts, the different levels and the interaction of planar surfaces and materials that characterise the architectural design are echoed in counterpoint in the furnishings, where the materials and colours of the upholstery along with the lamps, tables and cabinetry, contribute to enhancing the equilibrium of the interior space.

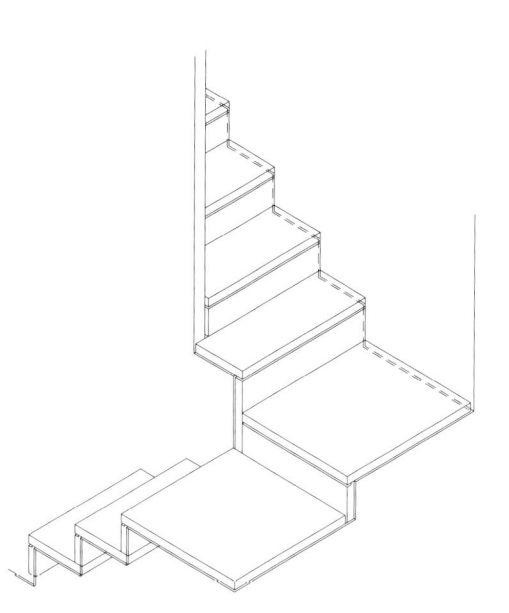

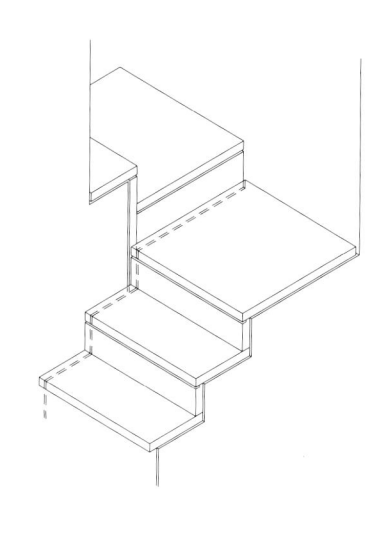

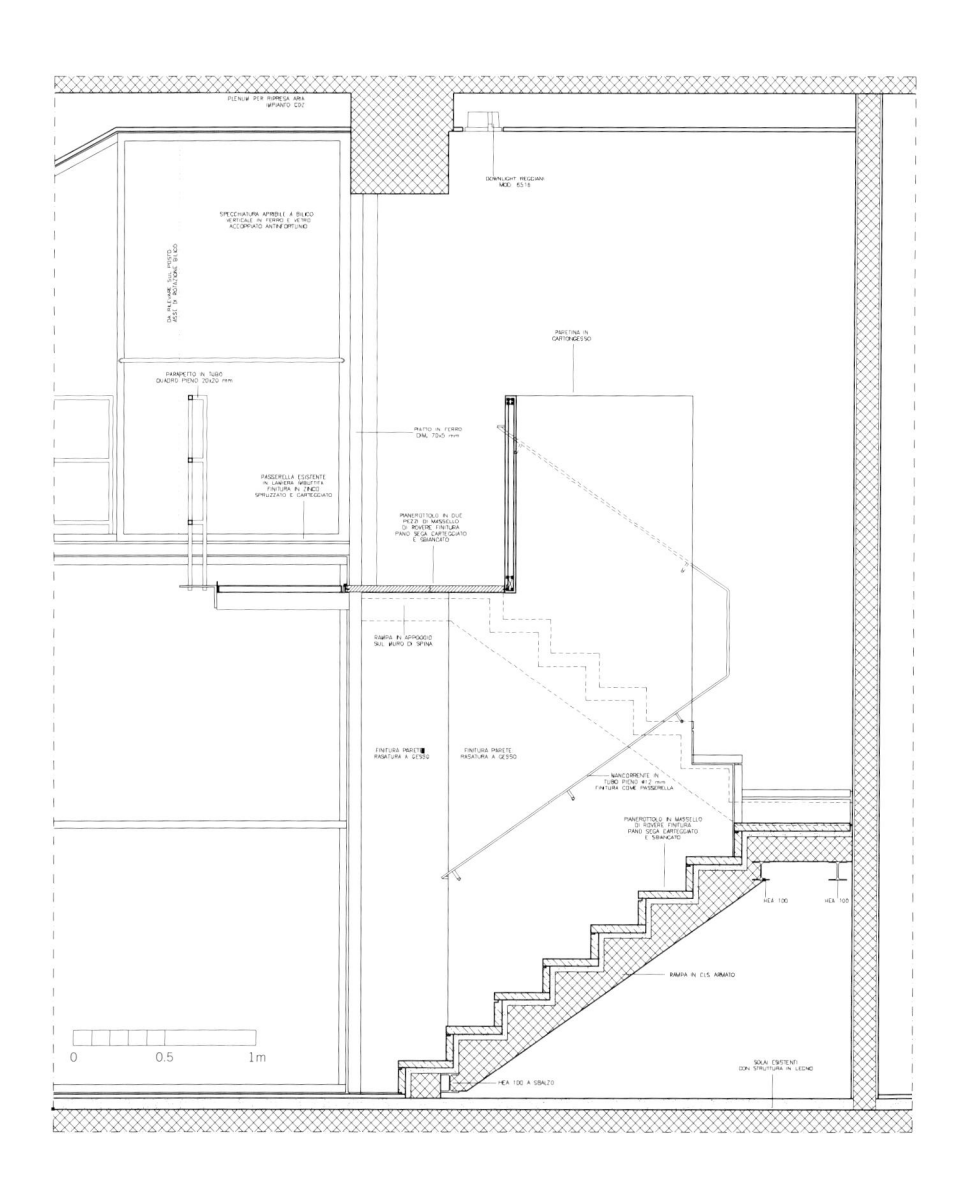

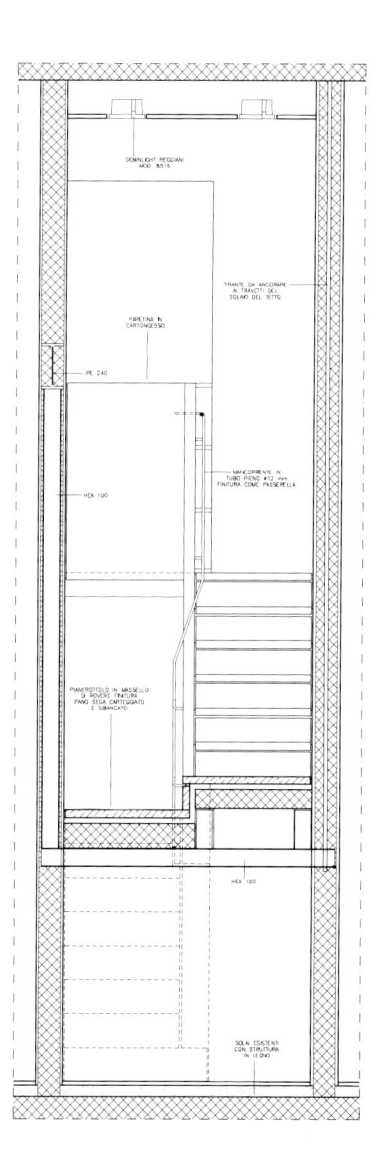

UTILITY

"Utility is associated with time and with day-to-day life. It is closely tied to the use of objects, to the relationships we establish with them. For this reason the nature of the utility changes as the house changes. My idea of habitational utility is indissolubly linked to lifestyle, to changing family habits."
Antonio Citterio

UTILITY

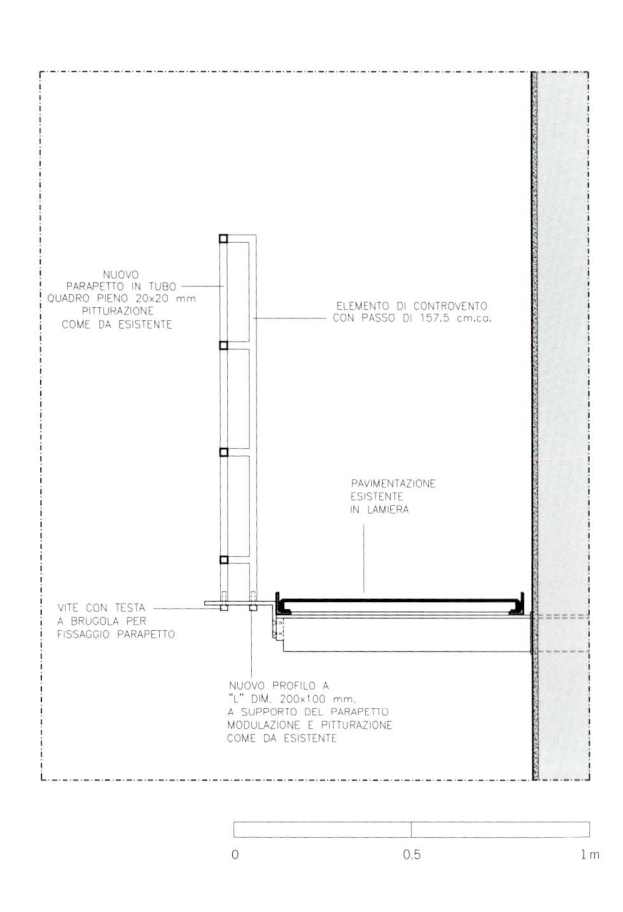

UTILITY

NUOVO
PARAPETTO IN TUBO
QUADRO PIENO 20x20 mm
PITTURAZIONE
COME DA ESISTENTE

ELEMENTO DI CONTROVENTO
CON PASSO DI 157,5 cm.ca.

PAVIMENTAZIONE
ESISTENTE
IN LAMIERA

VITE CON TESTA
A BRUGOLA PER
FISSAGGIO PARAPETTO

NUOVO PROFILO A
"L" DIM. 200x100 mm.
A SUPPORTO DEL PARAPETTO
MODULAZIONE E PITTURAZIONE
COME DA ESISTENTE

0   0,5   1 m

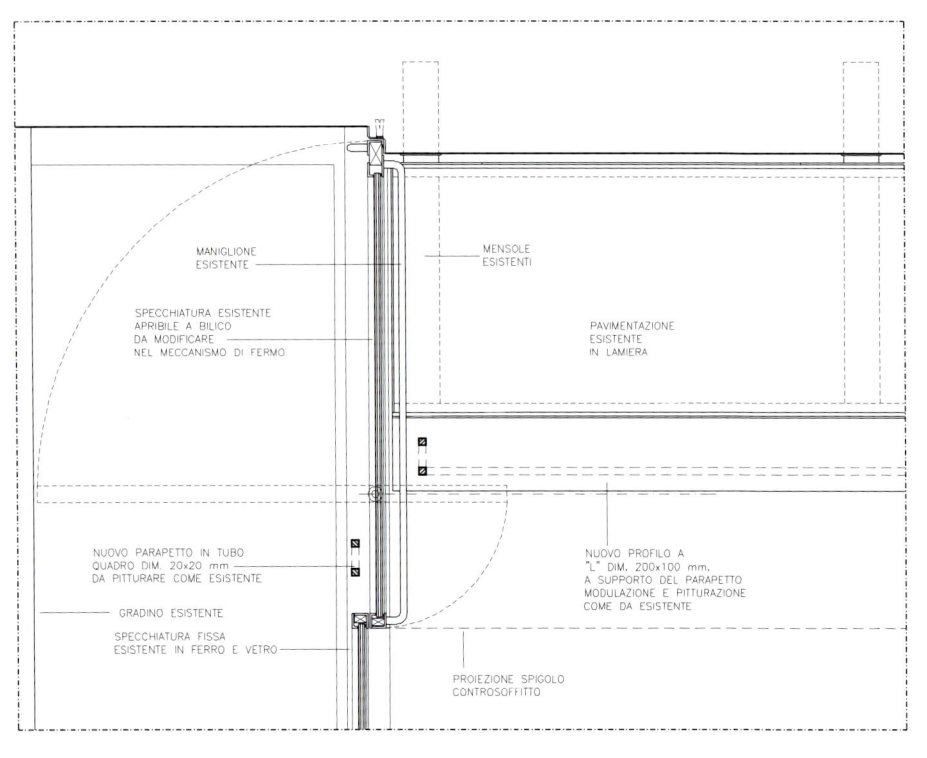

MANIGLIONE
ESISTENTE

MENSOLE
ESISTENTI

SPECCHIATURA ESISTENTE
APRIBILE A BILICO
DA MODIFICARE
NEL MECCANISMO DI FERMO

PAVIMENTAZIONE
ESISTENTE
IN LAMIERA

NUOVO PARAPETTO IN TUBO
QUADRO DIM. 20x20 mm
DA PITTURARE COME ESISTENTE

GRADINO ESISTENTE

SPECCHIATURA FISSA
ESISTENTE IN FERRO E VETRO

NUOVO PROFILO A
"L" DIM. 200x100 mm.
A SUPPORTO DEL PARAPETTO
MODULAZIONE E PITTURAZIONE
COME DA ESISTENTE

PROIEZIONE SPIGOLO
CONTROSOFFITTO

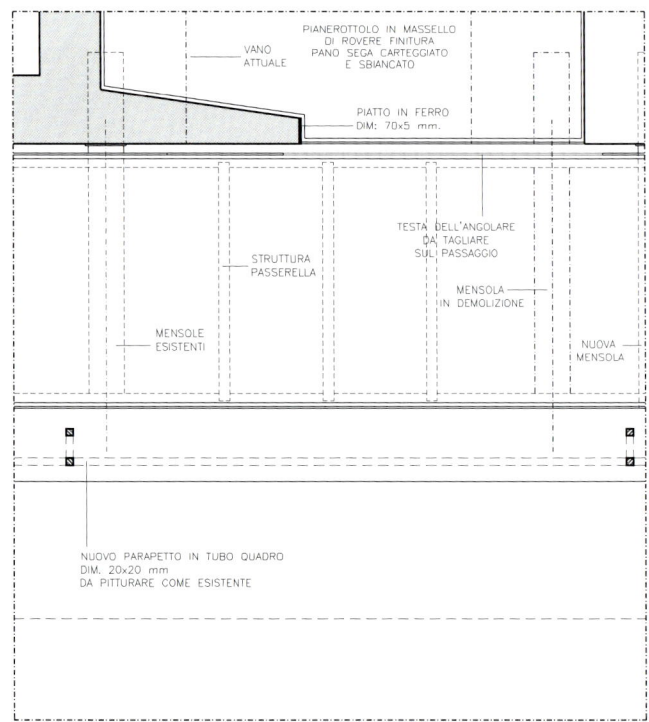

VANO
ATTUALE

PIANEROTTOLO IN MASSELLO
DI ROVERE FINITURA
PIANO SEGA CARTEGGIATO
E SBIANCATO

PIATTO IN FERRO
DIM: 70x5 mm.

STRUTTURA
PASSERELLA

TESTA DELL'ANGOLARE
DA TAGLIARE
SUL PASSAGGIO

MENSOLA
IN DEMOLIZIONE

MENSOLE
ESISTENTI

NUOVA
MENSOLA

NUOVO PARAPETTO IN TUBO QUADRO
DIM. 20x20 mm.
DA PITTURARE COME ESISTENTE

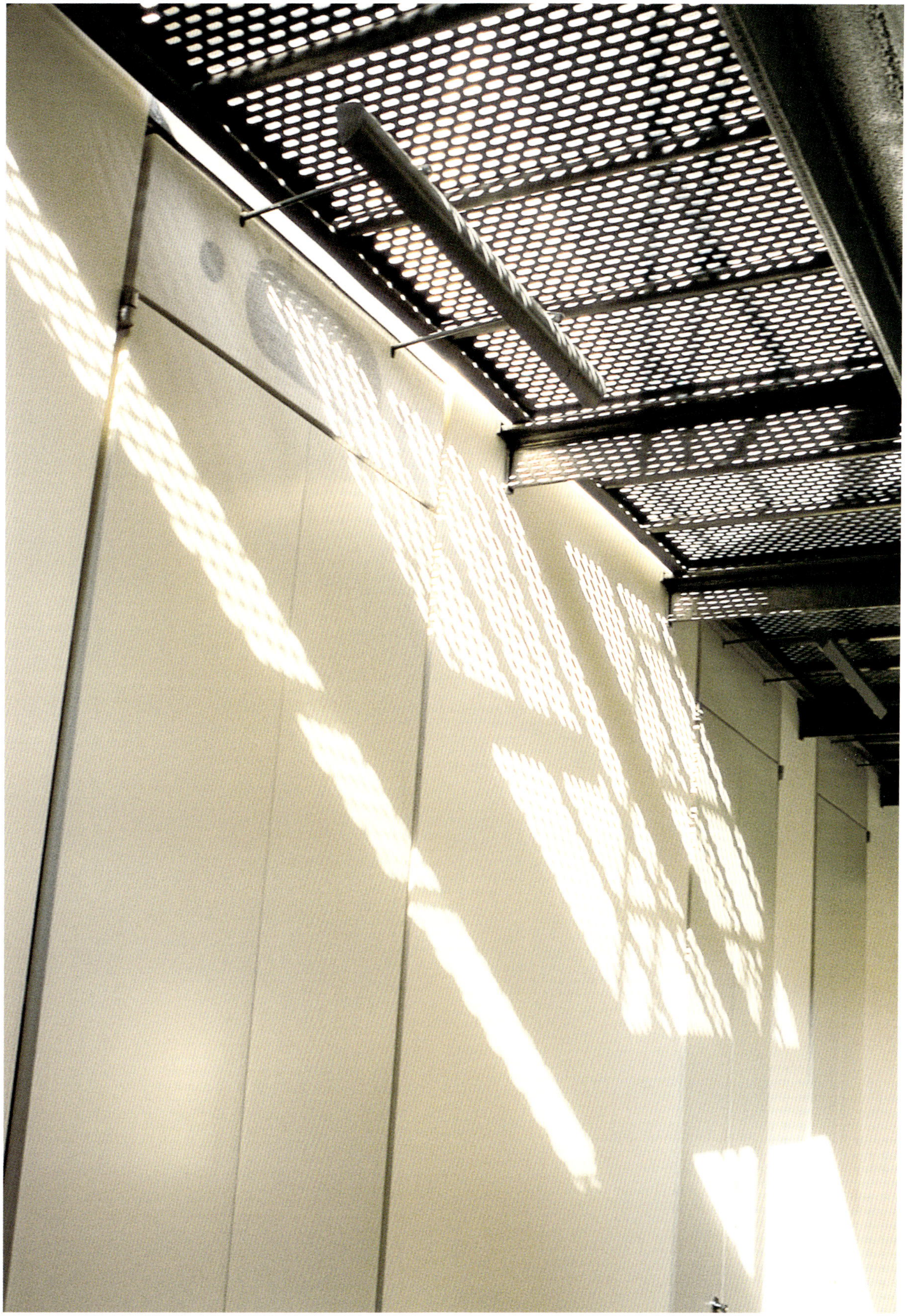

1999 Planus, Tre Più

UTILITY

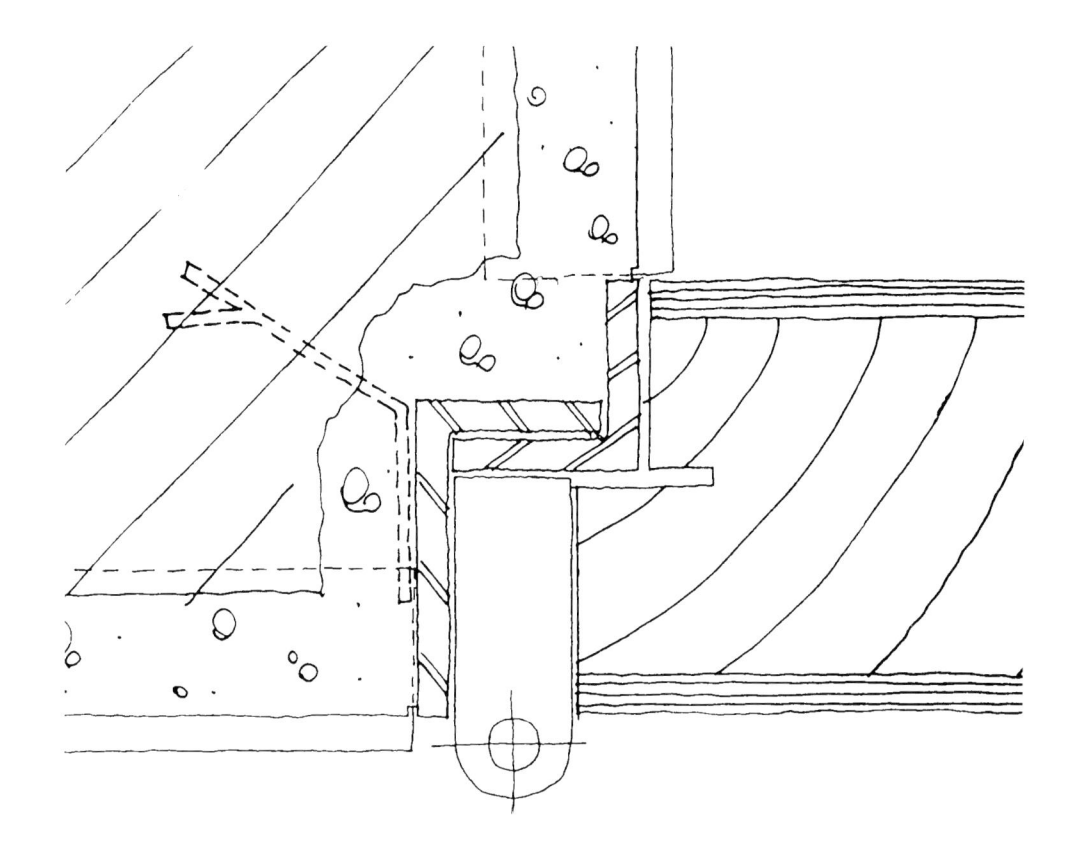

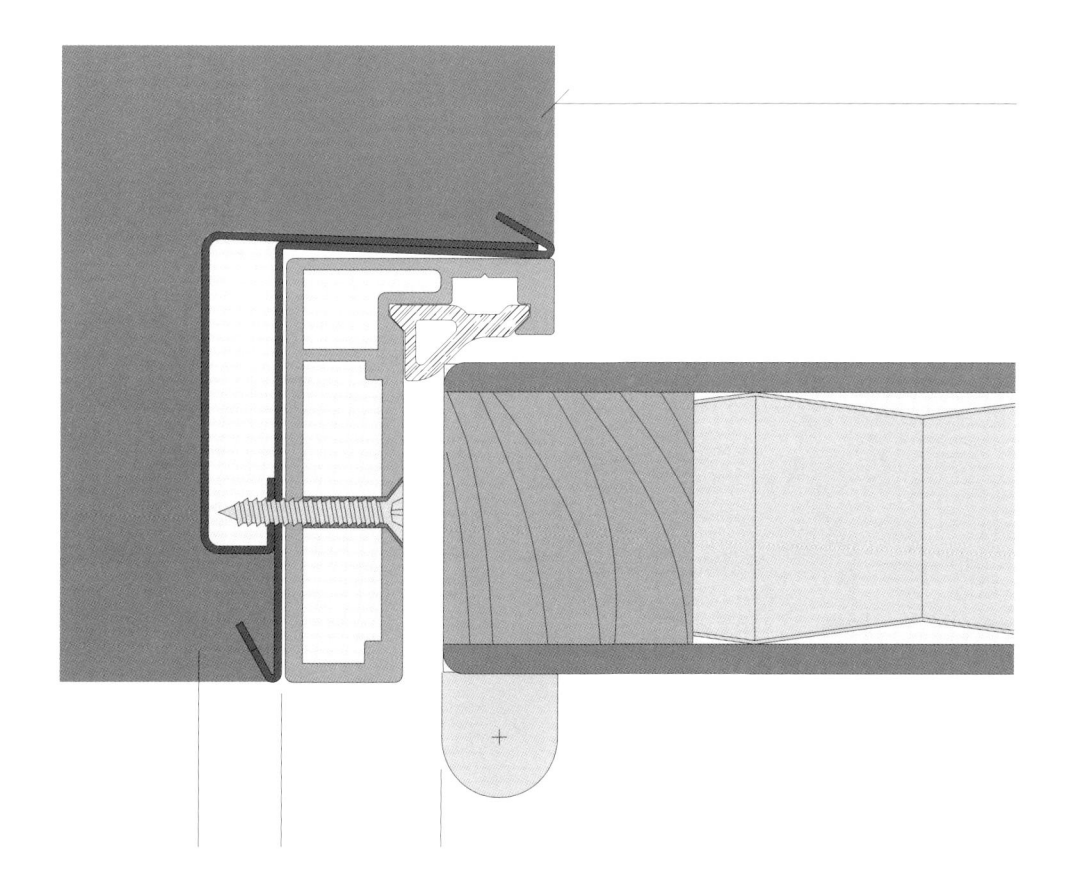

UTILITY

2002 House in Sagaponack

Private residence
340 sq. m

The project is part of the "Houses at Sagaponack" programme promoted by The Brown Companies, Inc., in association with Richard Meier. The masterplan includes the construction, in Southampton, Long Island, of a residential community, for a total surface area of 800,000 sq. m. Thirty-four internationally renowned architects were invited to design a residence.

UTILITY

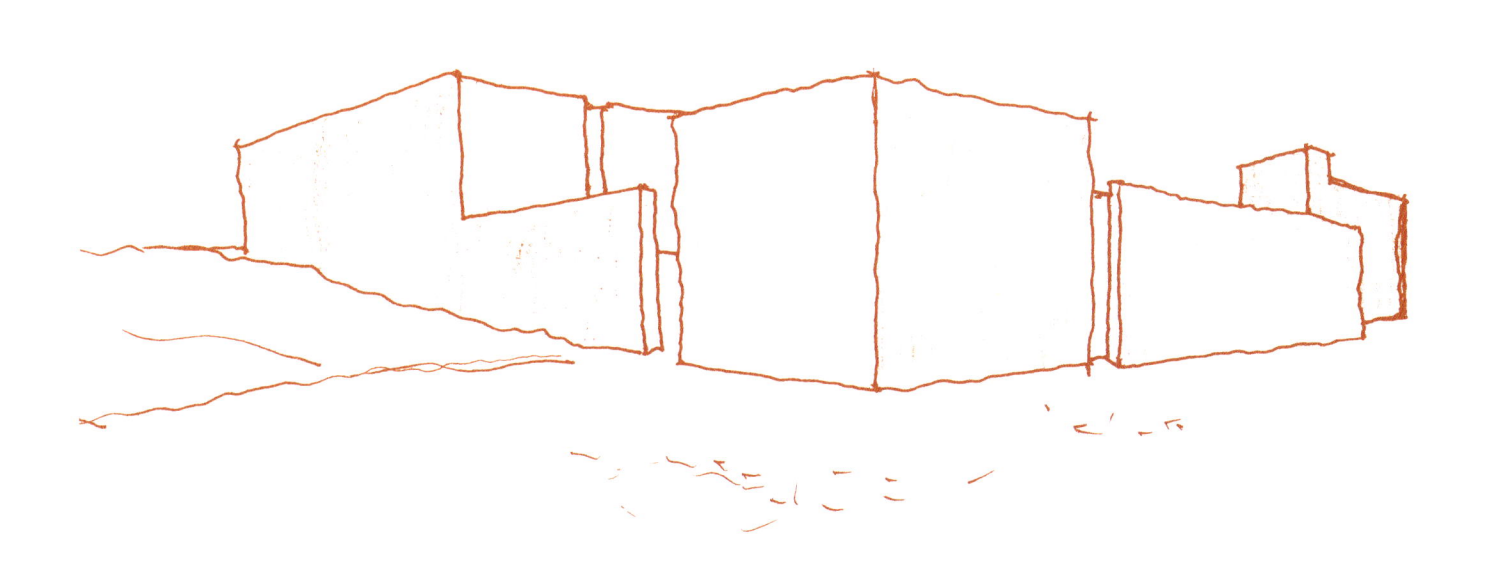

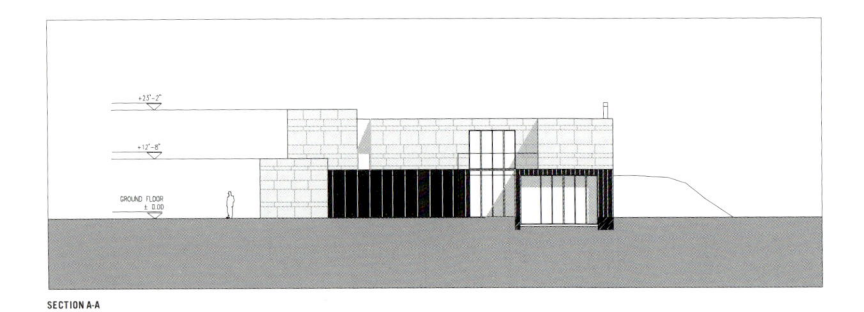

Incorporating a suggestion from the client, Citterio designed the house from the inside out, simplifying the indoor-outdoor relationship through large plate glass windows and creating a terraced garden to ensure privacy. Inside, a wood and glass court distributes light and connects the swimming pool to the kitchen and living room areas.

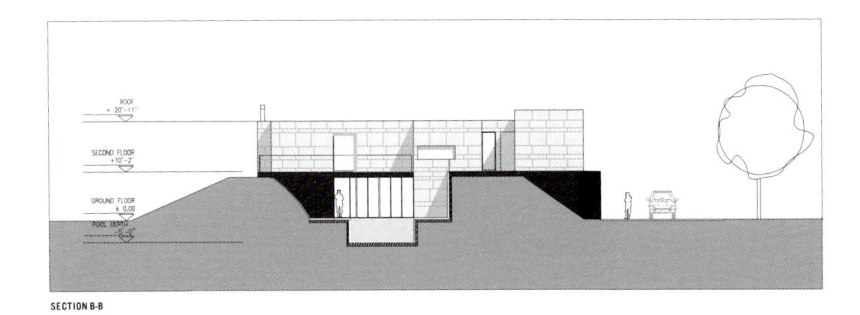

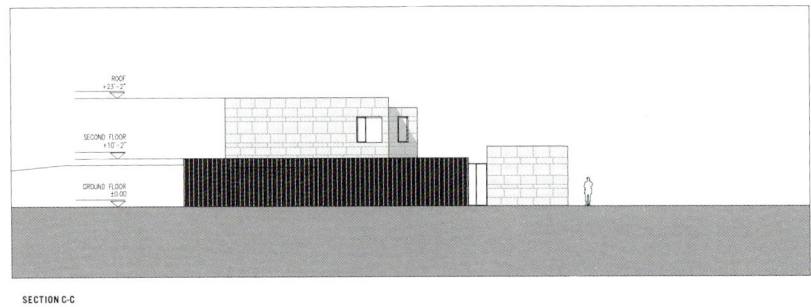

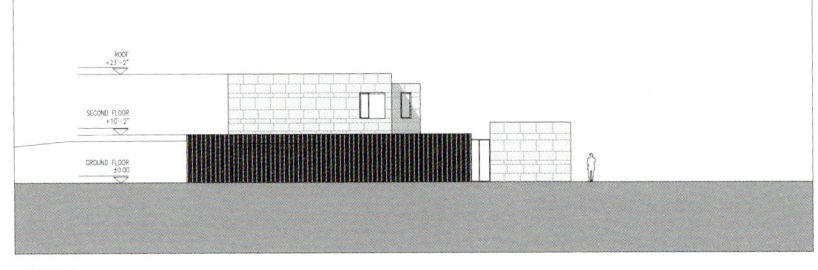

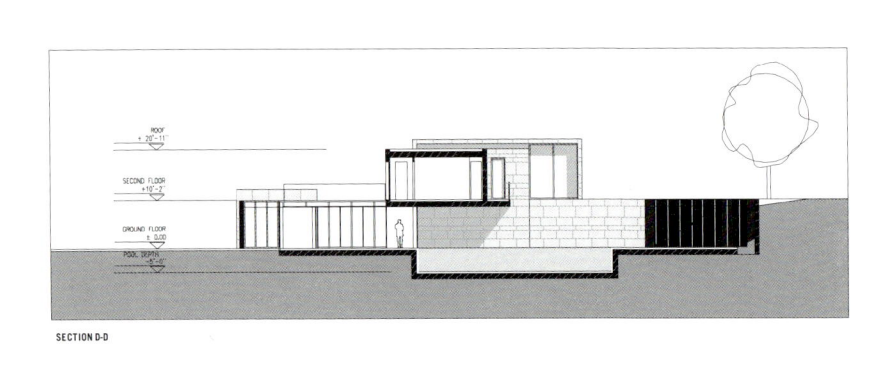

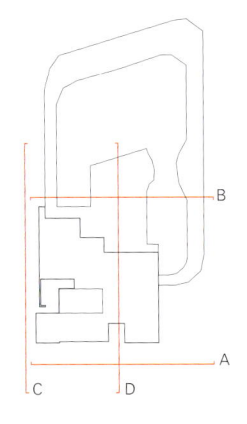

SECTION A-A

SECTION B-B

SECTION C-C

SECTION D-D

0 5 10 m

UTILITY

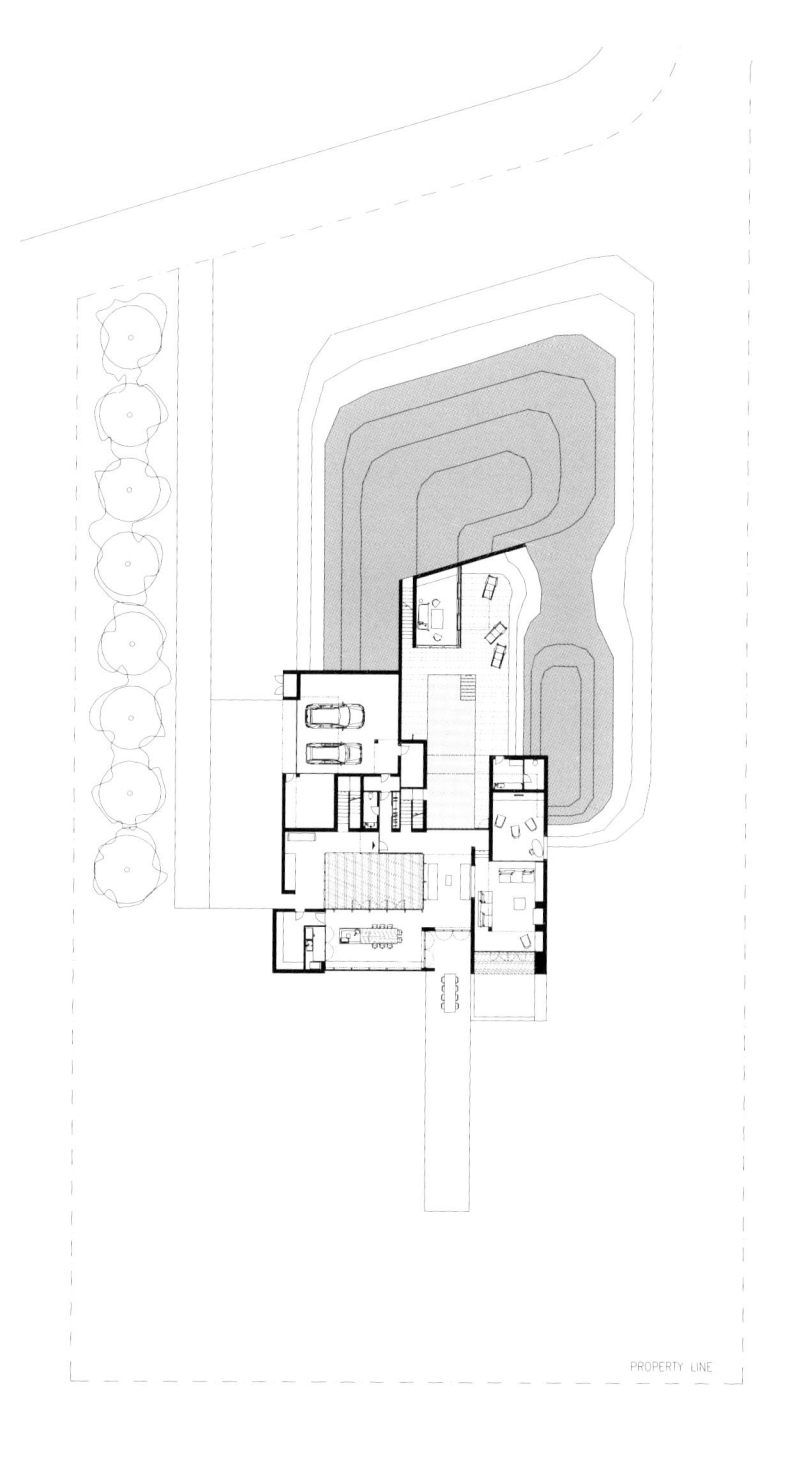

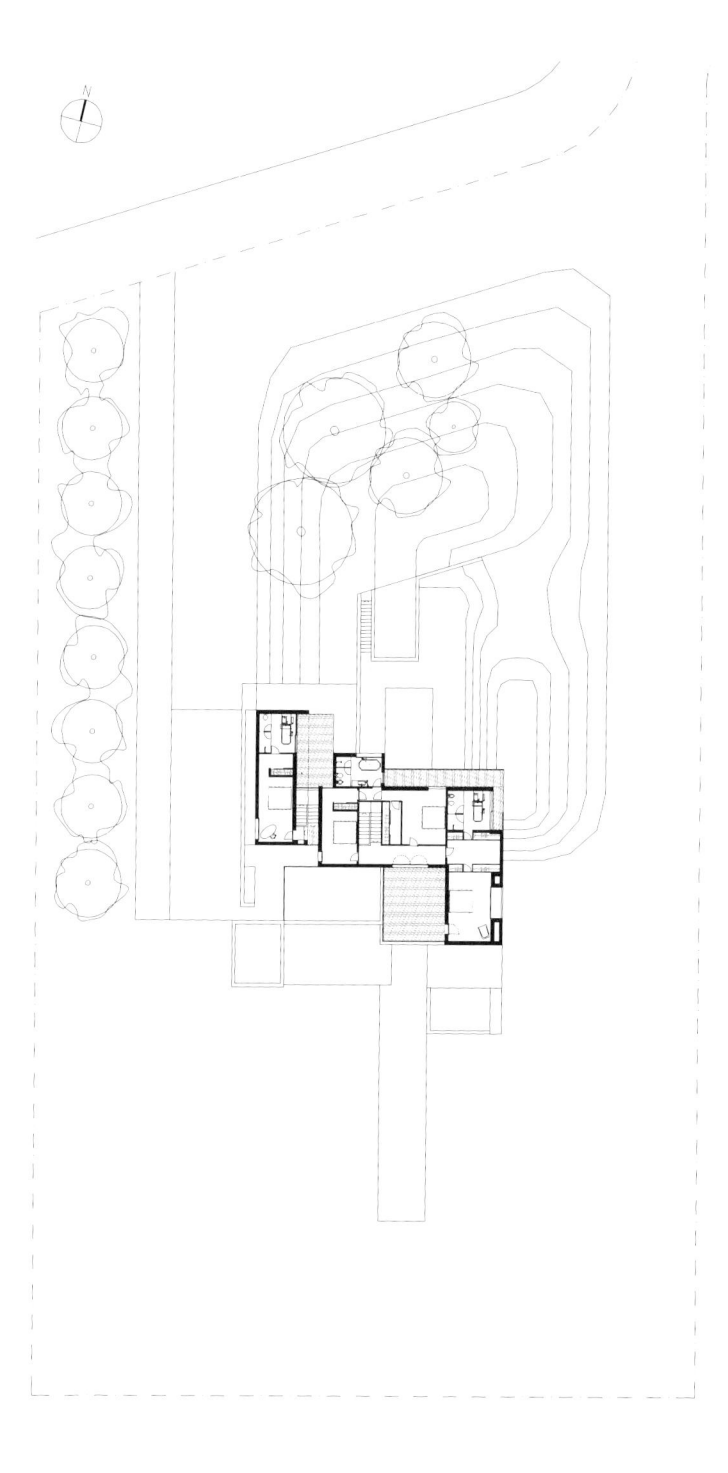

PROPERTY LINE

UTILITY

134

UTILITY

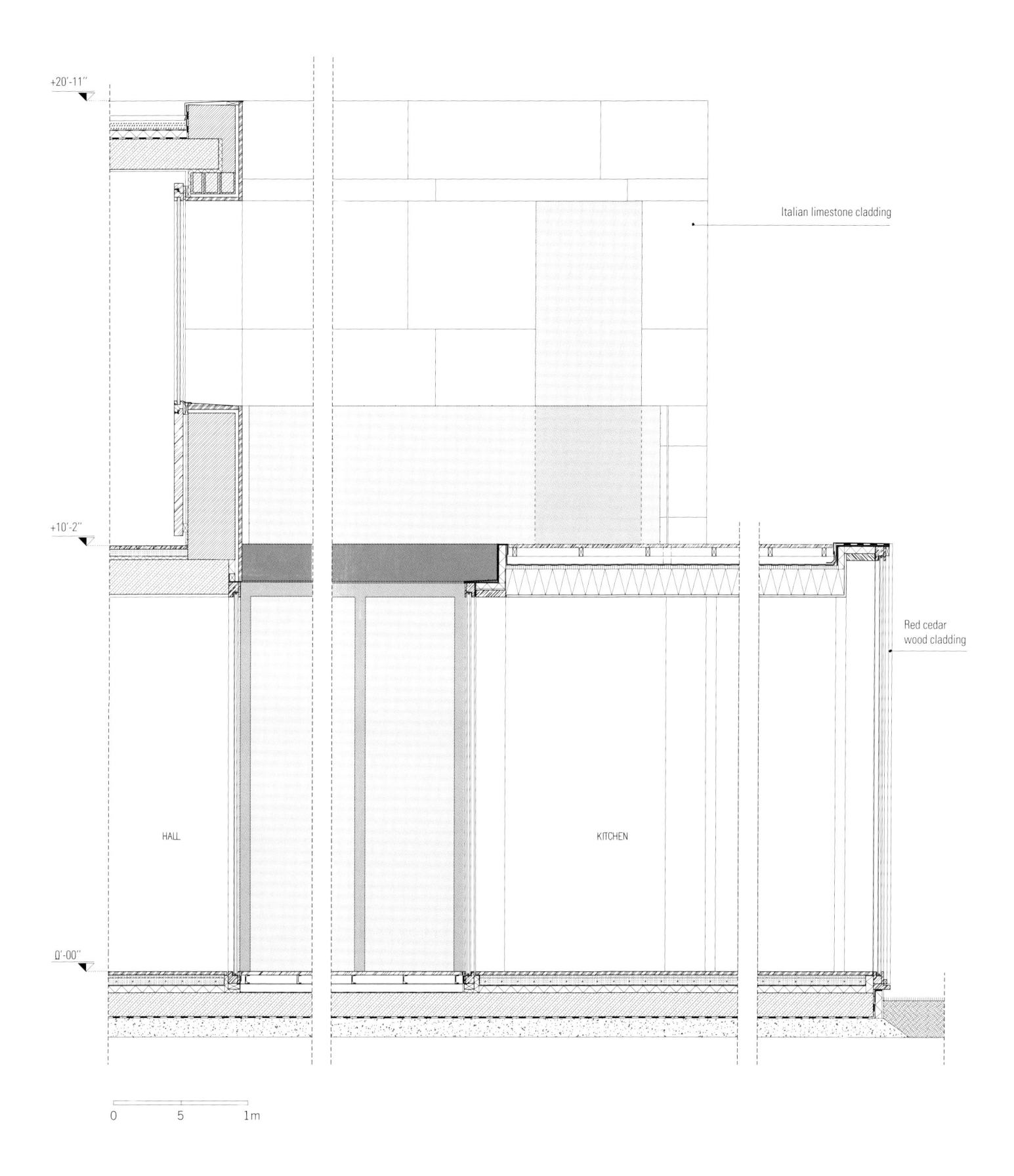

+20'-11"

+10'-2"

0'-00"

HALL

KITCHEN

Italian limestone cladding

Red cedar wood cladding

0   5   1m

135

UTILITY

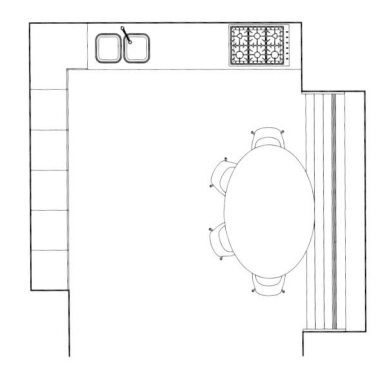

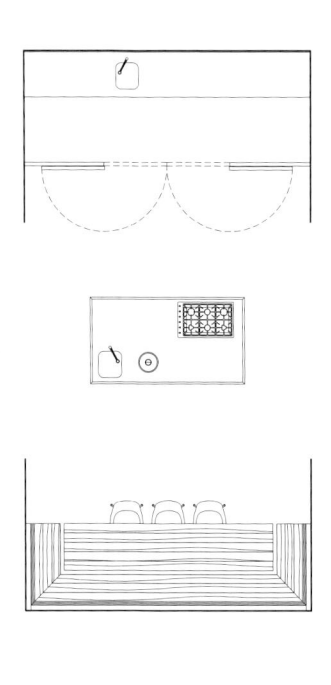

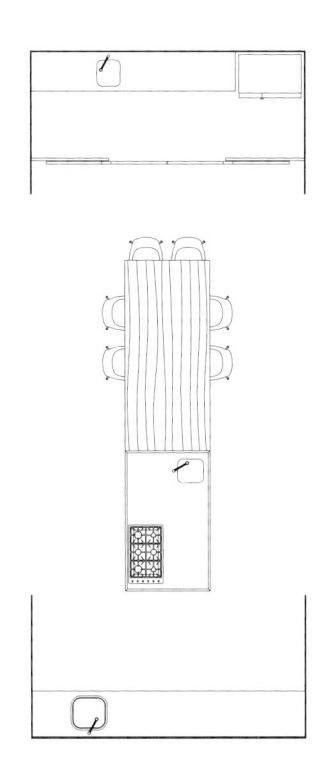

"The kitchen represents the centre of the house, an intimate gathering place and the place where the rite of preparing meals is performed. Receiving your friends in the kitchen has become a metaphor for affection, interchange and warmth."
Antonio Citterio

2002 Convivium, Arclinea

Citterio's design offers a rational response to the various needs associated with the main steps in cooking. From washing and preparing to cooking and eating, the cabinets and areas around the island are designed around user movements and facilitate all operations.

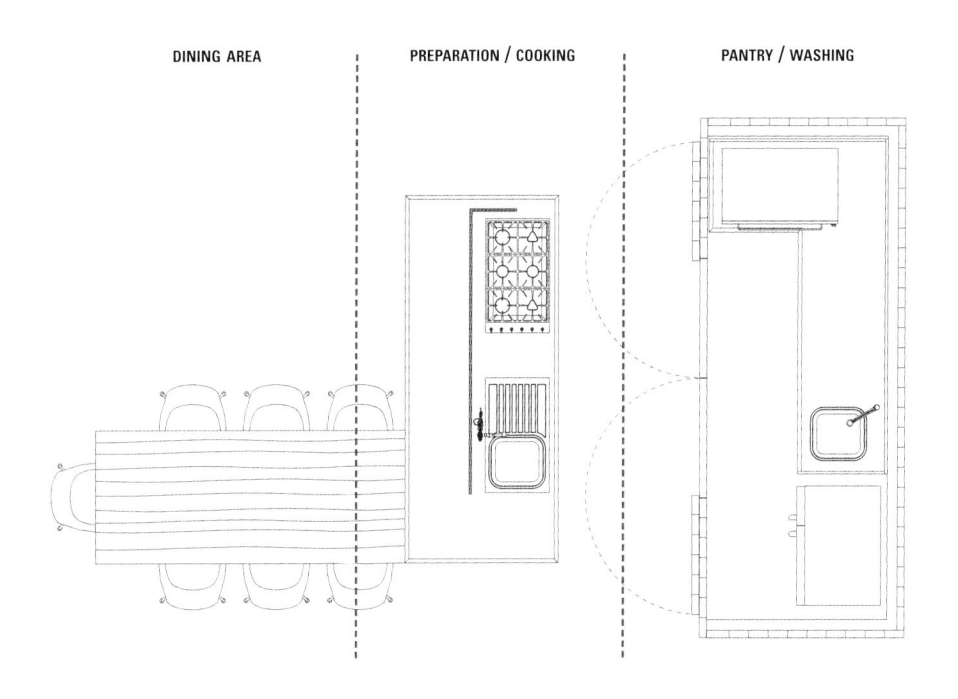

DINING AREA | PREPARATION / COOKING | PANTRY / WASHING

UTILITY

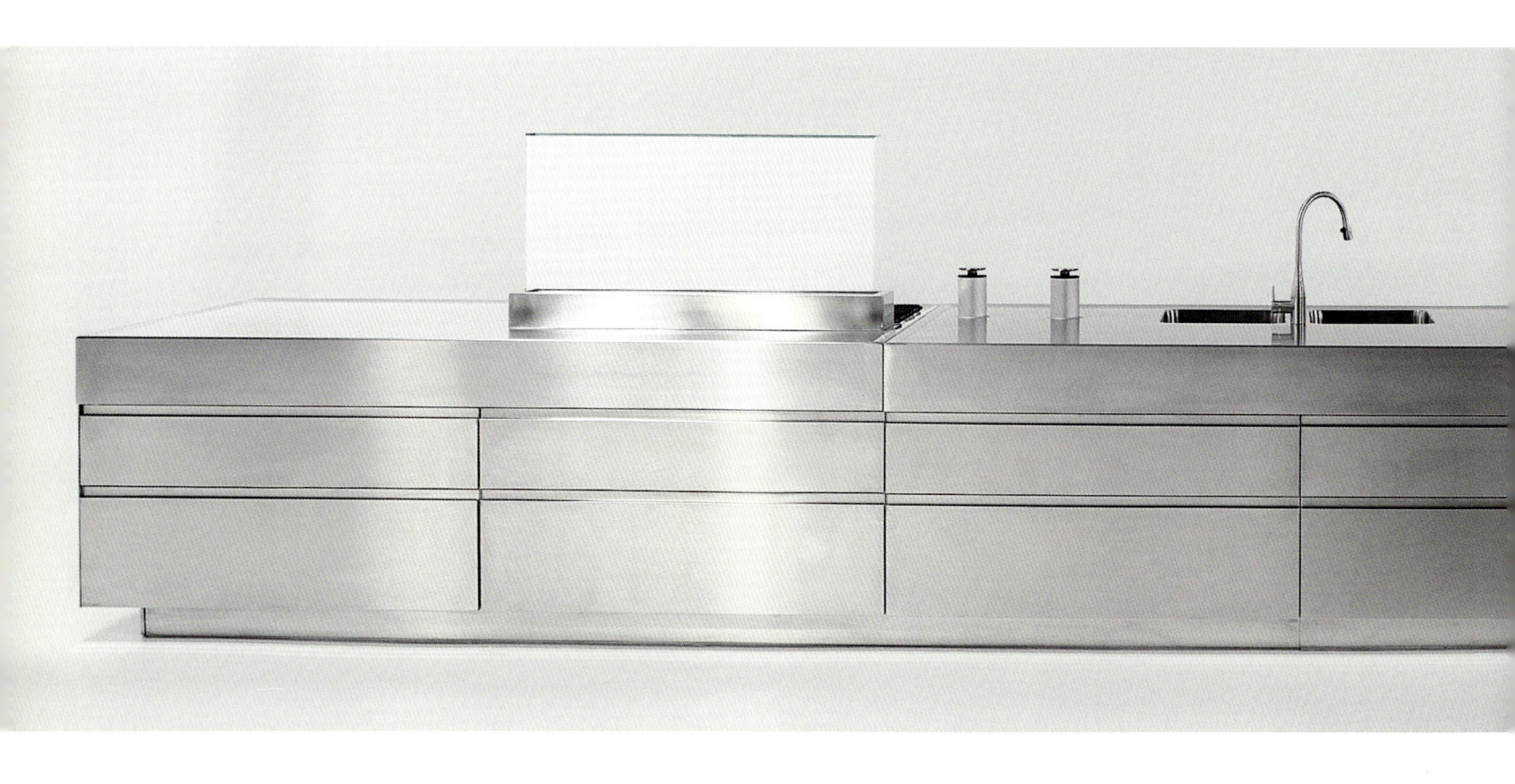

UTILITY

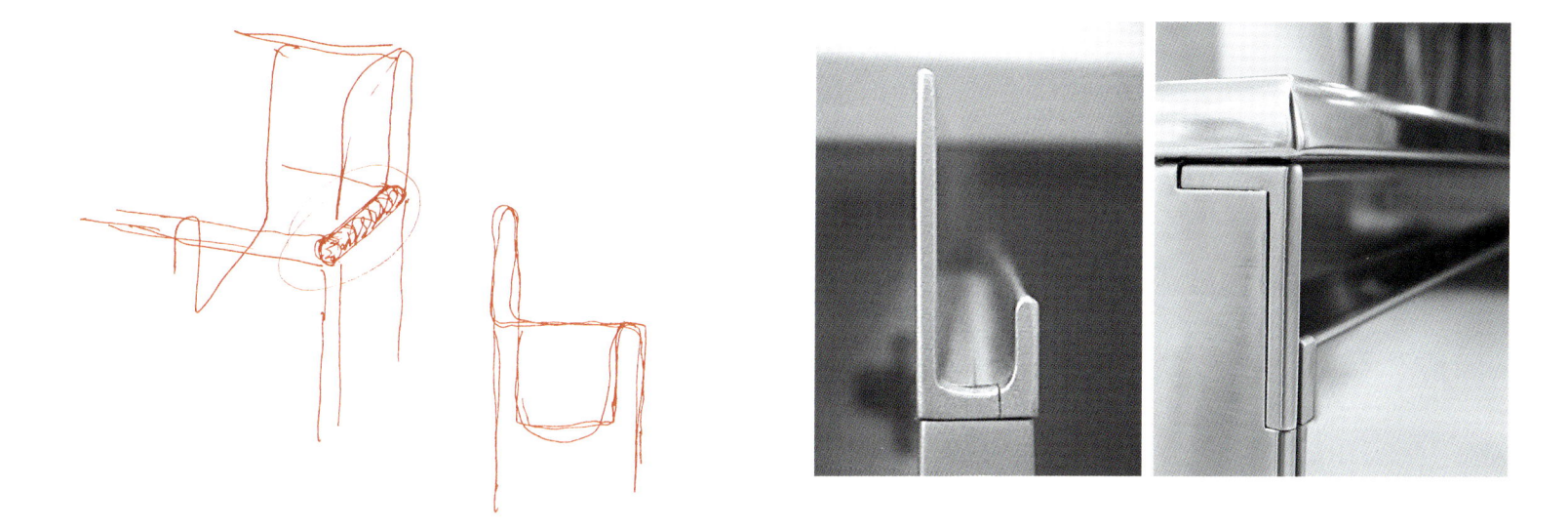

2006 Convivium, Arclinea

Hood with vanishing glass panel and surface suction

UTILITY

2006 Axor Citterio Kitchen, Hansgrohe

with Toan Nguyen

"Through their hands people make contact with the hard substance of thought; they succeed in unlocking it. The hands are what impose form, outline."
Henry Focillon

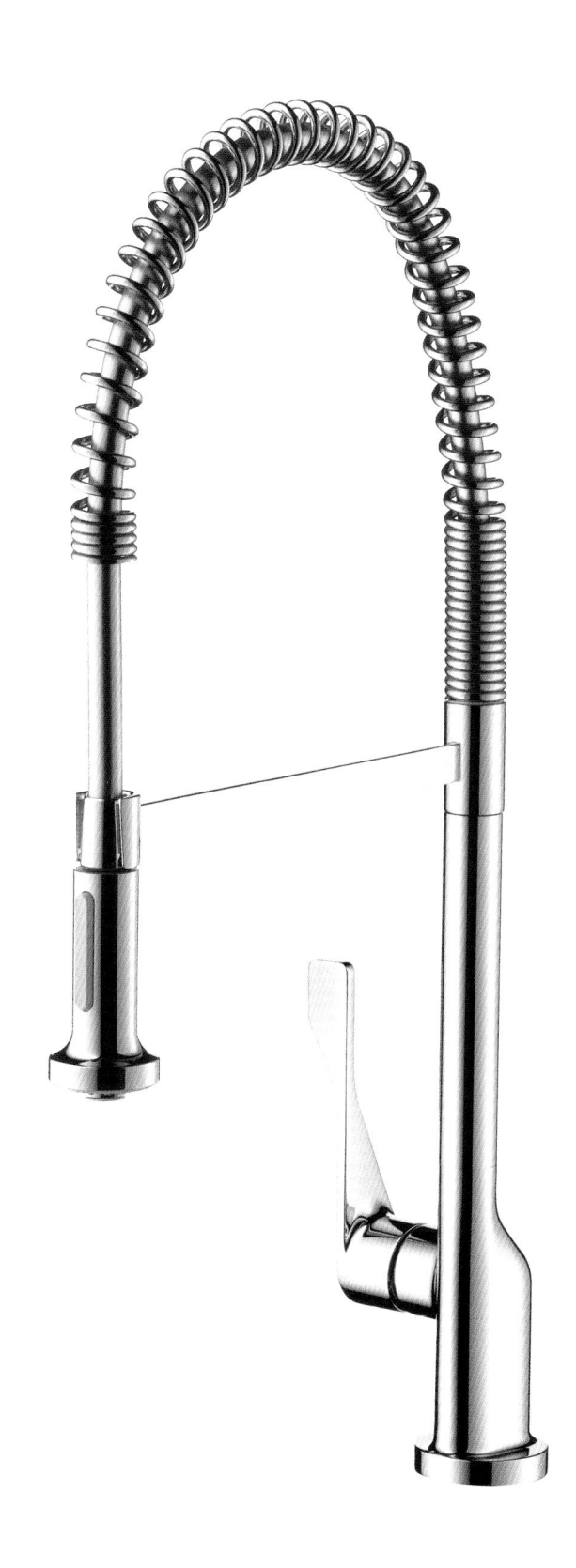

UTILITY

UTILITY

2005 My Table, Guzzini

with Toan Nguyen

The forms were conceived on the basis of their intended functions and to respond to the anatomy of the hand that will grasp them. It is not a question of ergonomics, but of utility, the possibility to enhance the forms of objects by picturing the movements that will be associated with them.

UTILITY

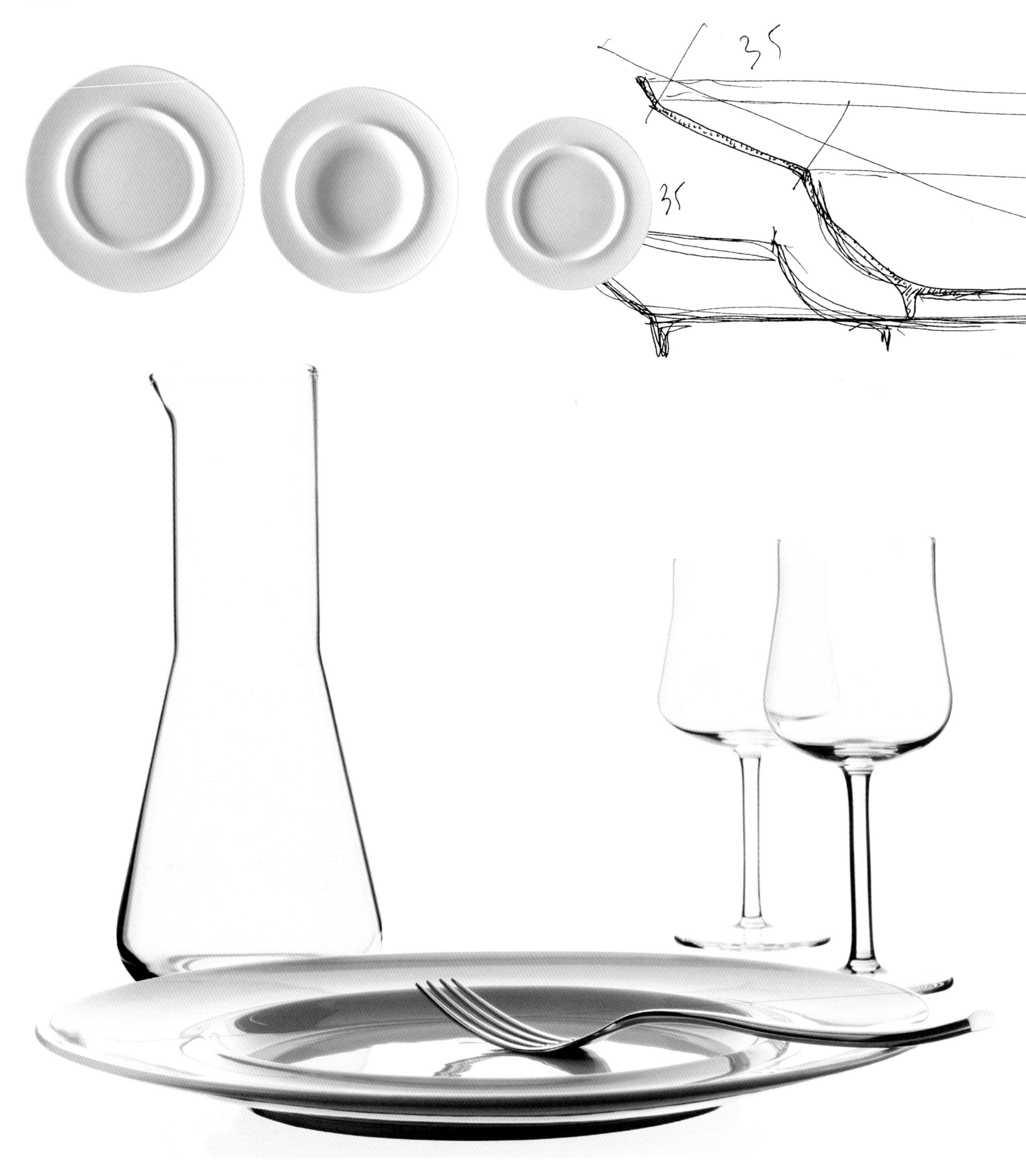

144

UTILITY

< 2005 **My Table**, Guzzini
> 2005 **Square**, Guzzini
with Toan Nguyen

UTILITY

> 2000 K2, Fusital

< 2004 AC3, Fusital

with Toan Nguyen

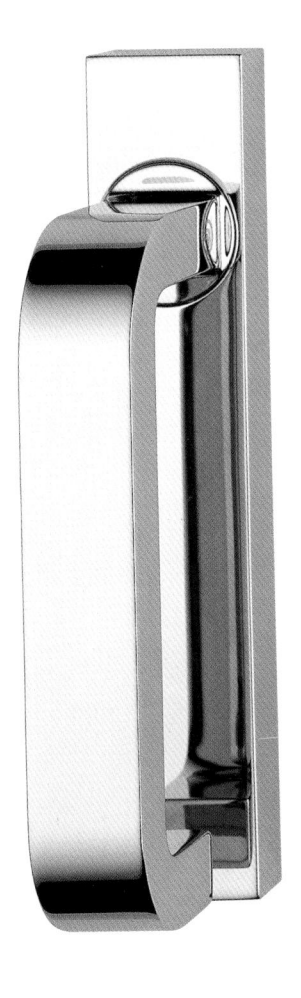

UTILITY

UTILITY

2004 Lecce

Private residence
600 sq. m

Project for residence within a palazzo in the historic centre of Lecce. The inside courtyard was created with typical stone blocks from Lecce upon which olive trees rest so as to evoke the architecture and vegetation of the Salento area.
The ground floor is characterised by vault ceilings, in stone, and intended for guests; instead, the first floor is for the family.

UTILITY

UTILITY

2003–2005 Multinational Pharmaceutical Company, Verona

President's offices
2,400 sq. m

The glassed volumes are the main spatial elements. With their different fittings, depending on whether they are exterior or interior, they create scenographic spaces such as the entrance foyer, with its steel staircase encased in a stratified and coloured glass volume leading up to the President's offices.

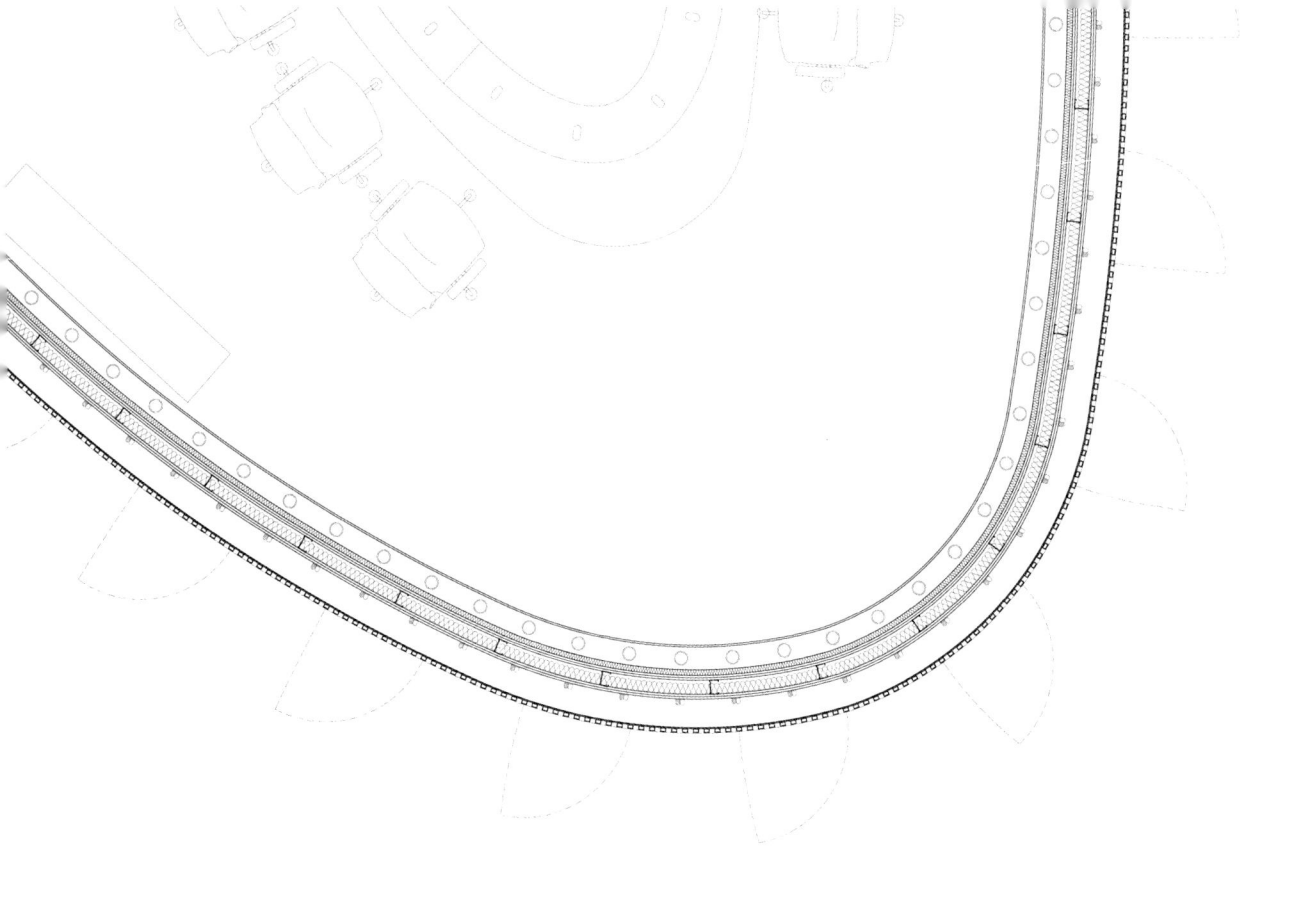

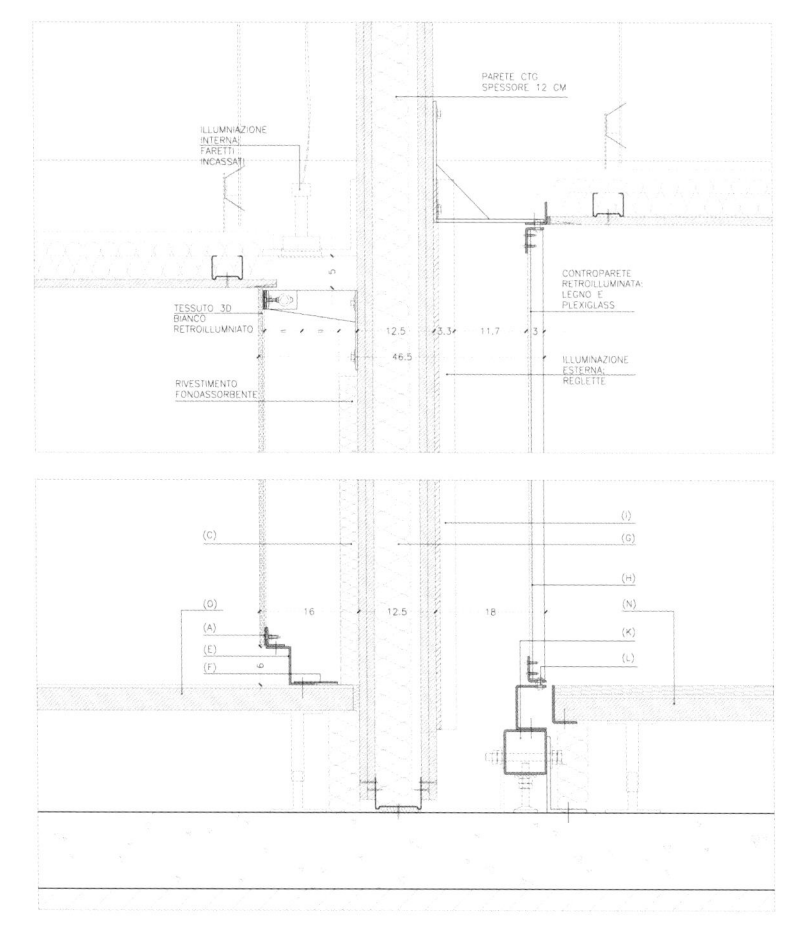

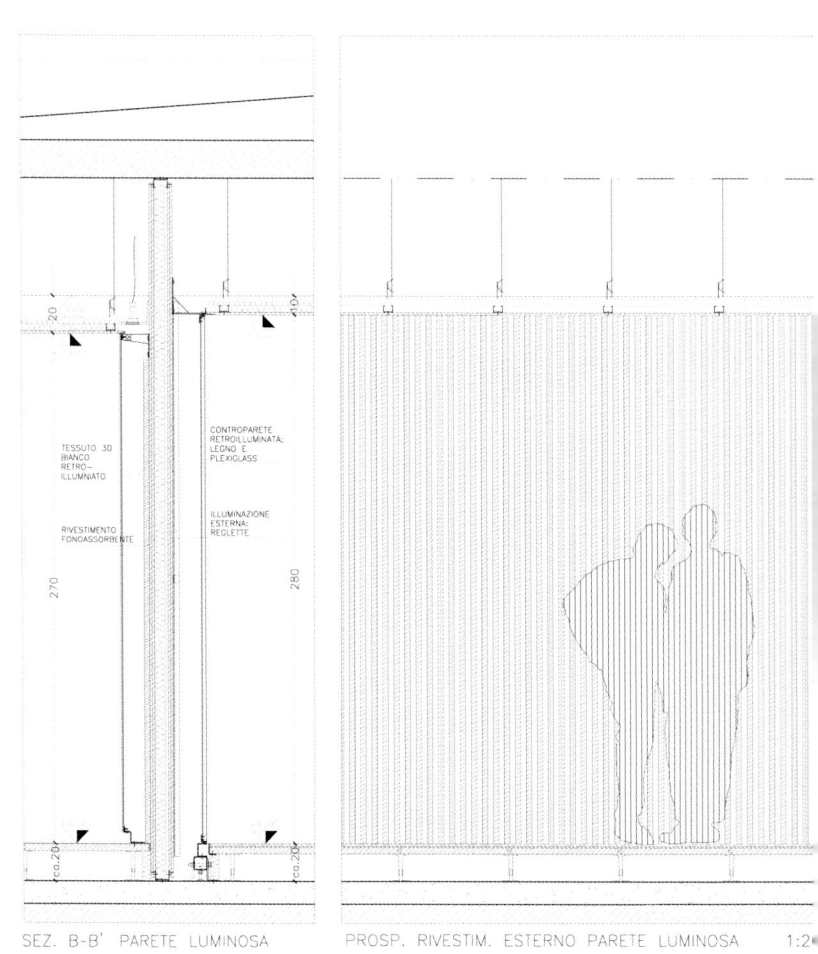

SEZ. B-B' PARETE LUMINOSA   PROSP. RIVESTIM. ESTERNO PARETE LUMINOSA   1:2

UTILITY

UTILITY

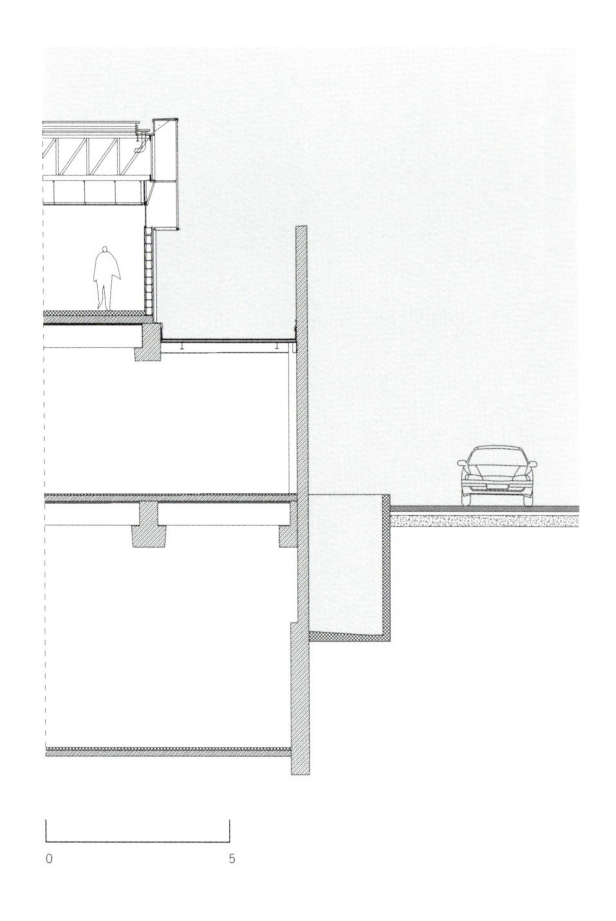

2000–2002 B&B Italia, Novedrate

*R&D Centre, offices and showroom
8,000 sq. m*

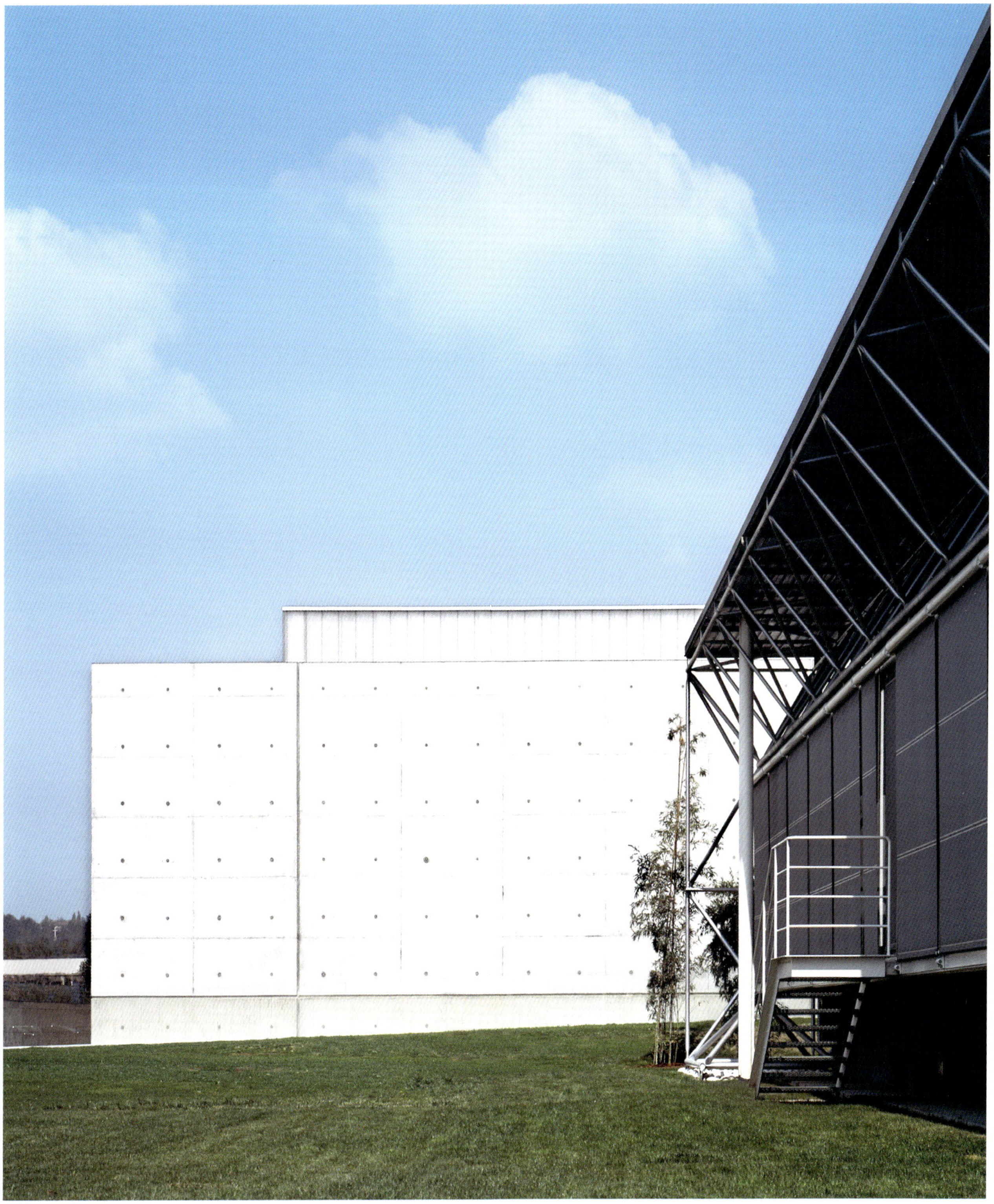

UTILITY

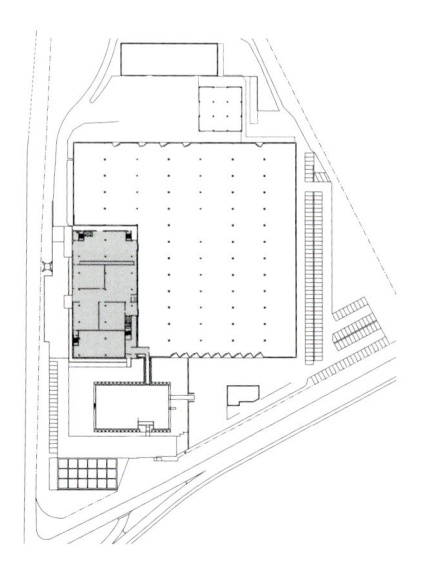

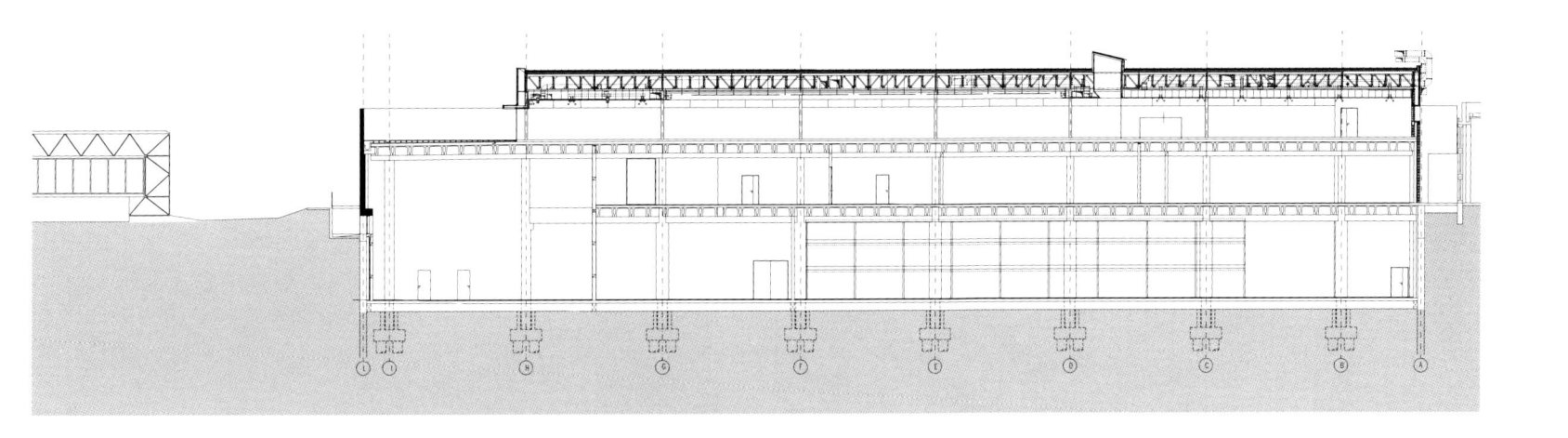

The R&D Centre has introduced
a new methodology into the Italian
furniture industry: research as a support
for design and production.

UTILITY

> **2002 Ad One, Vitra**

with Toan Nguyen

The office systems created for Vitra are characterised by the flexibility of the combinations, which can be personalised on the basis of the dimensions of the given space and the type of office required. But above all they manifest Citterio's capacity for approaching design in a systematic way, where the single furnishings – tables, chairs, cabinets, storage units – are designed both as individual objects and as components of a greater system.

< **1994–2004 Ad Hoc, Vitra**

Ad Office

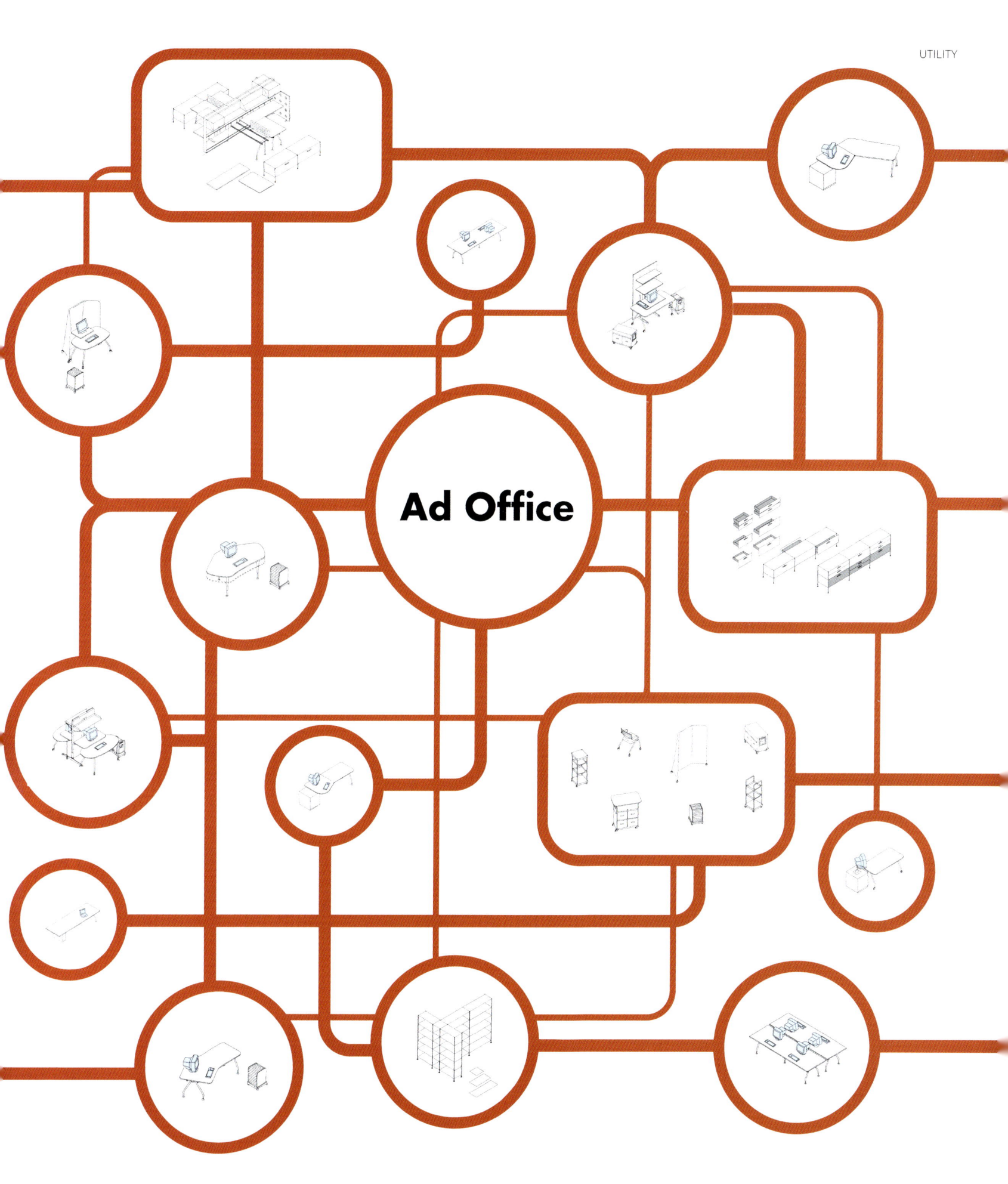

UTILITY

UTILITY

2000 Ad Wall, Vitra

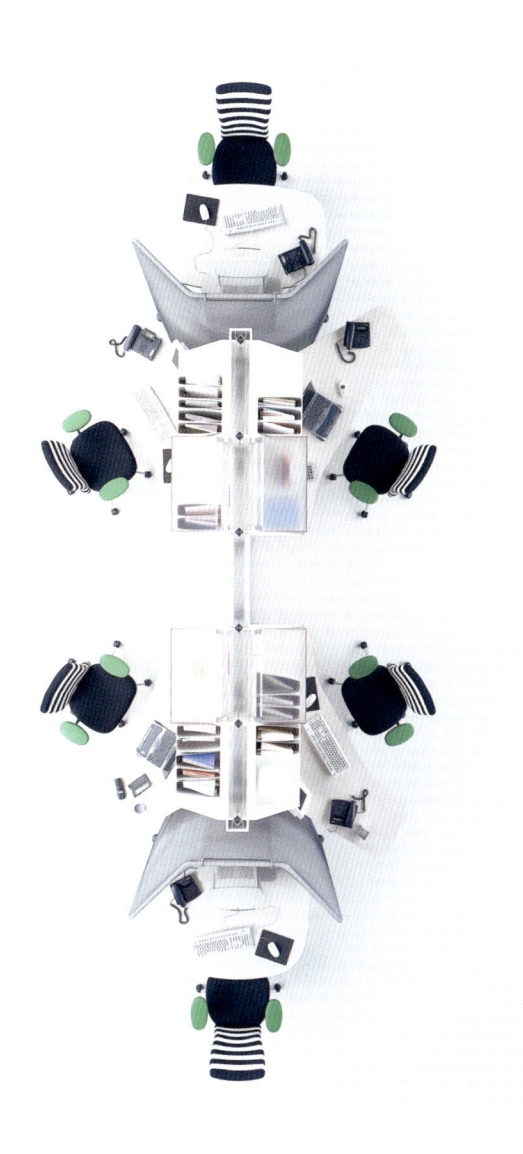

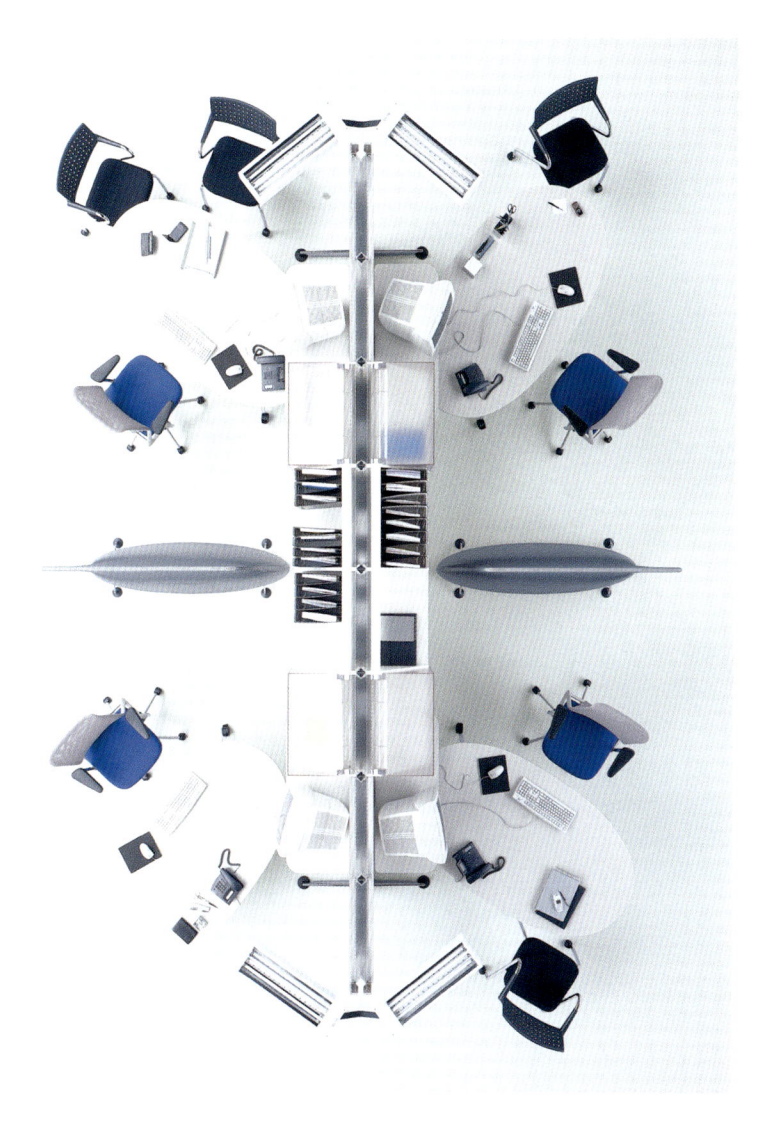

UTILITY

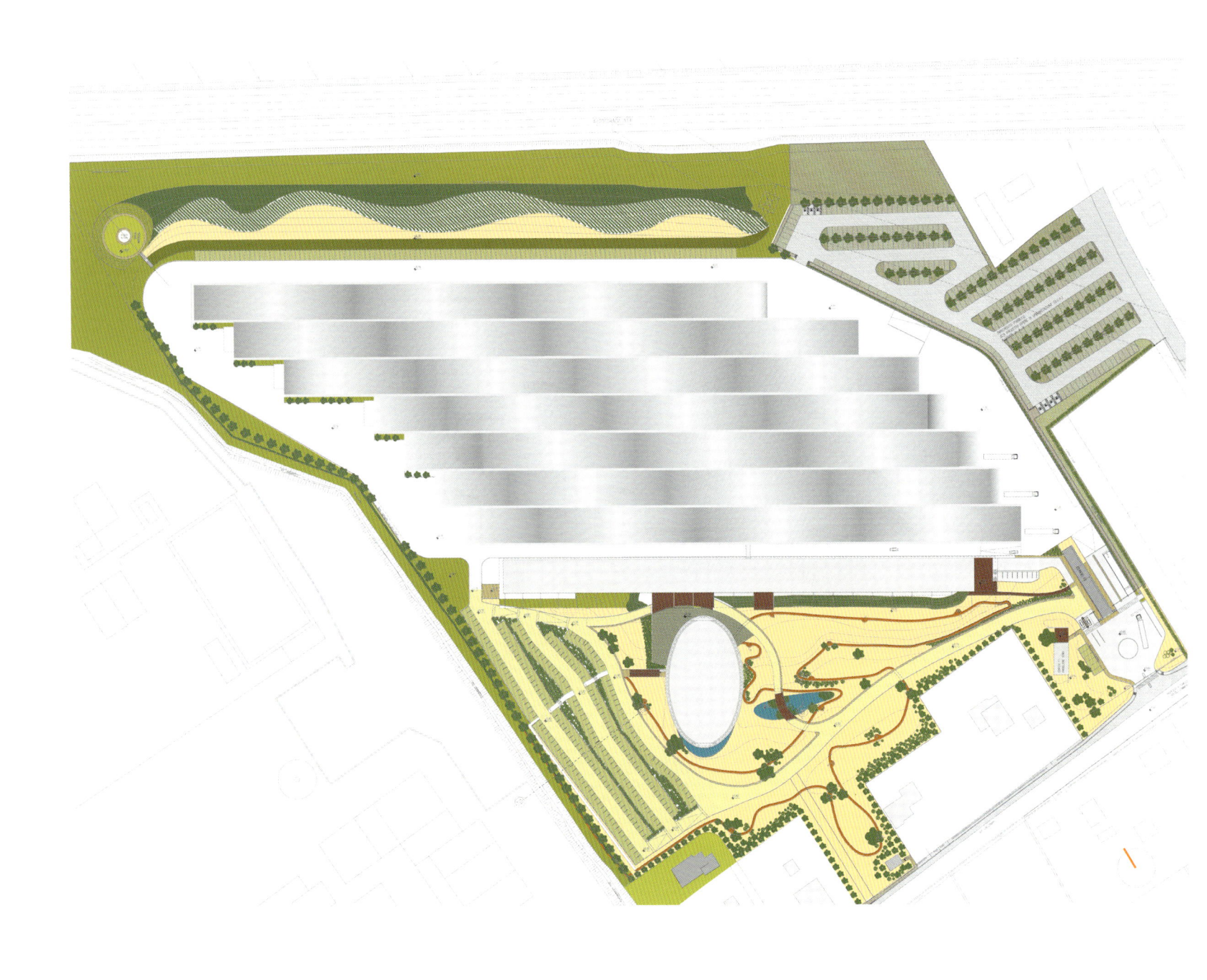

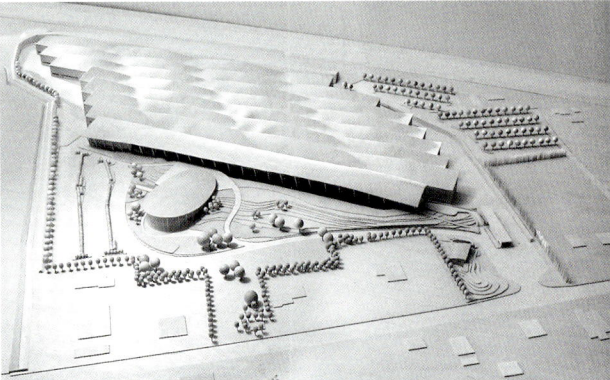

162

FIRST PHASE

2002–2007 Technogym, Cesena

*Direction offices, production facility,
R&D Centre, Wellness Centre
54,000 sq. m*

SECOND PHASE

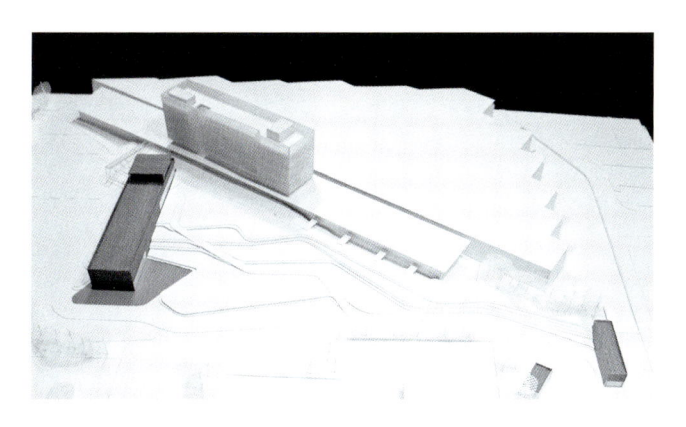

THIRD PHASE

FOURTH PHASE

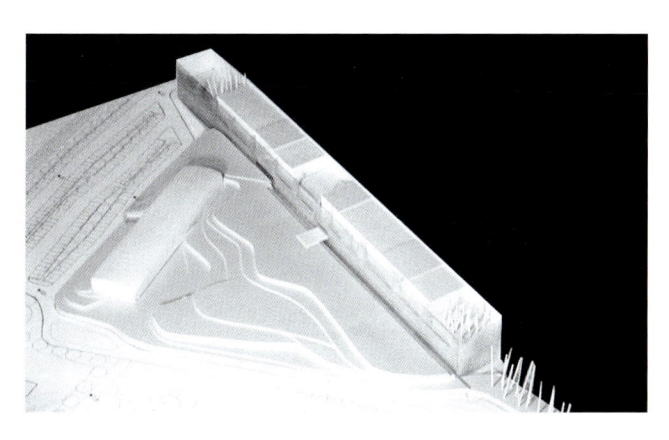

FIFTH PHASE

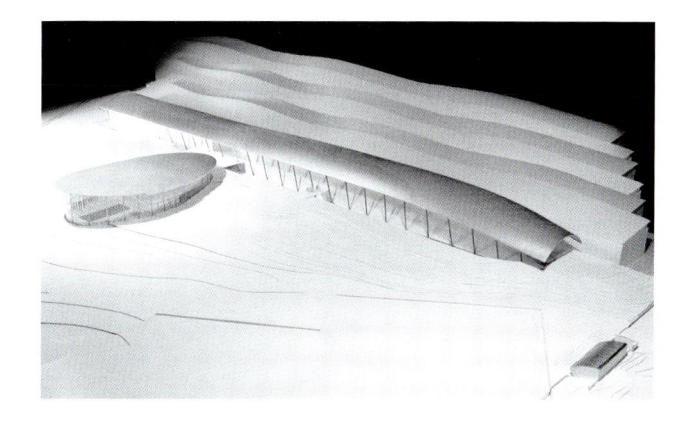

UTILITY

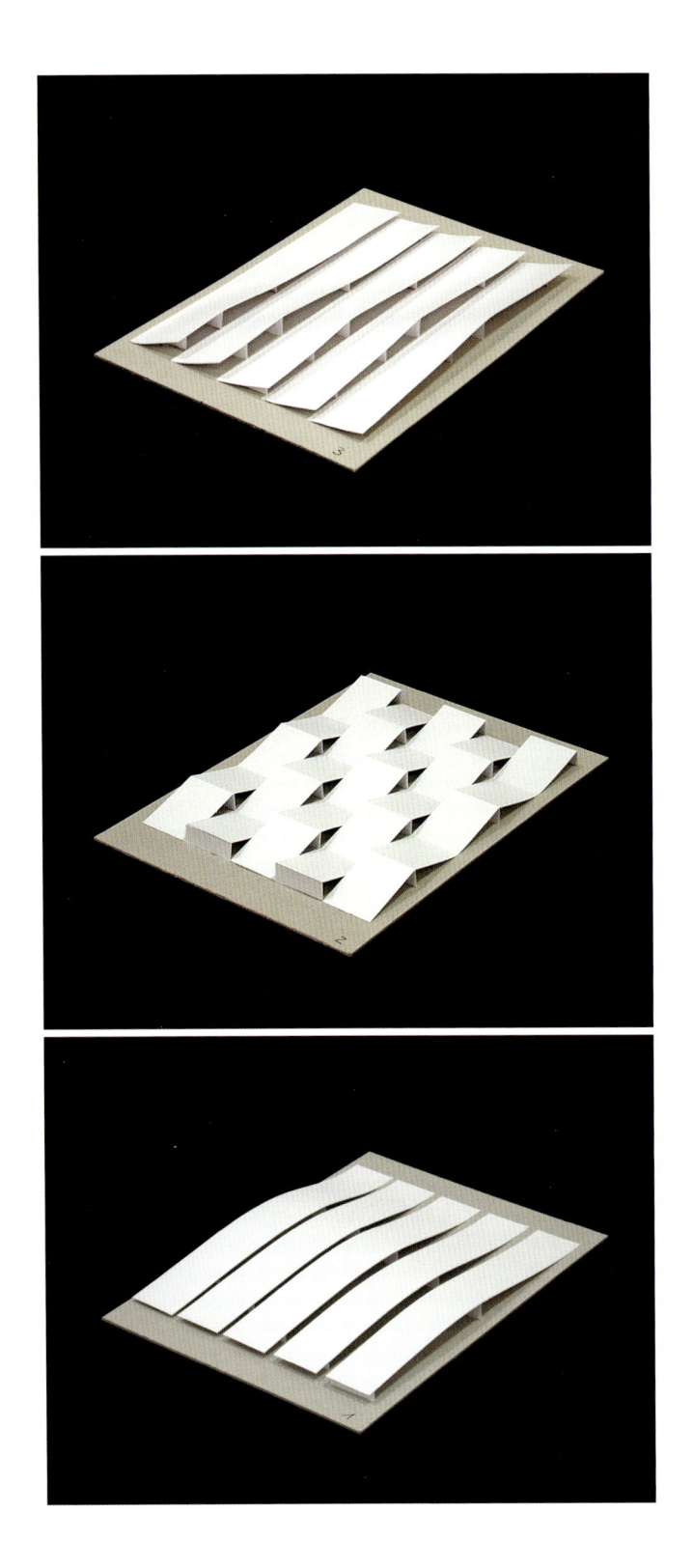

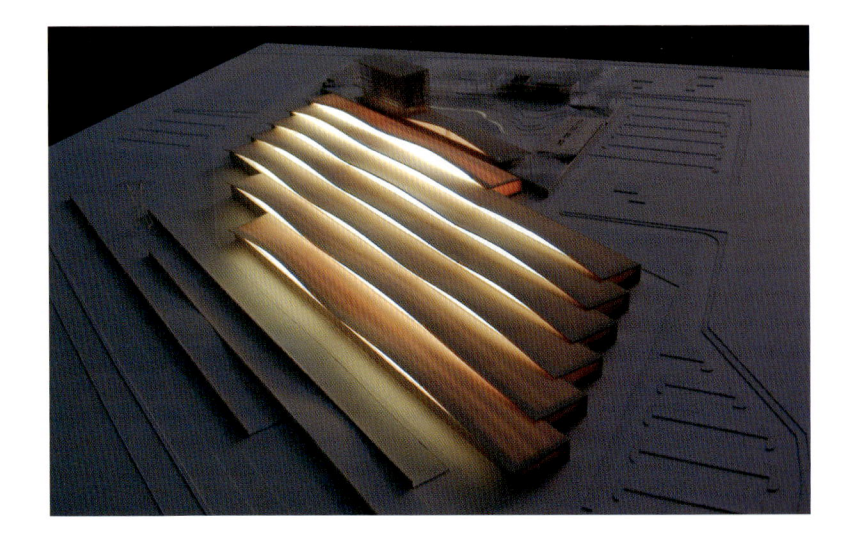

164

UTILITY

UTILITY

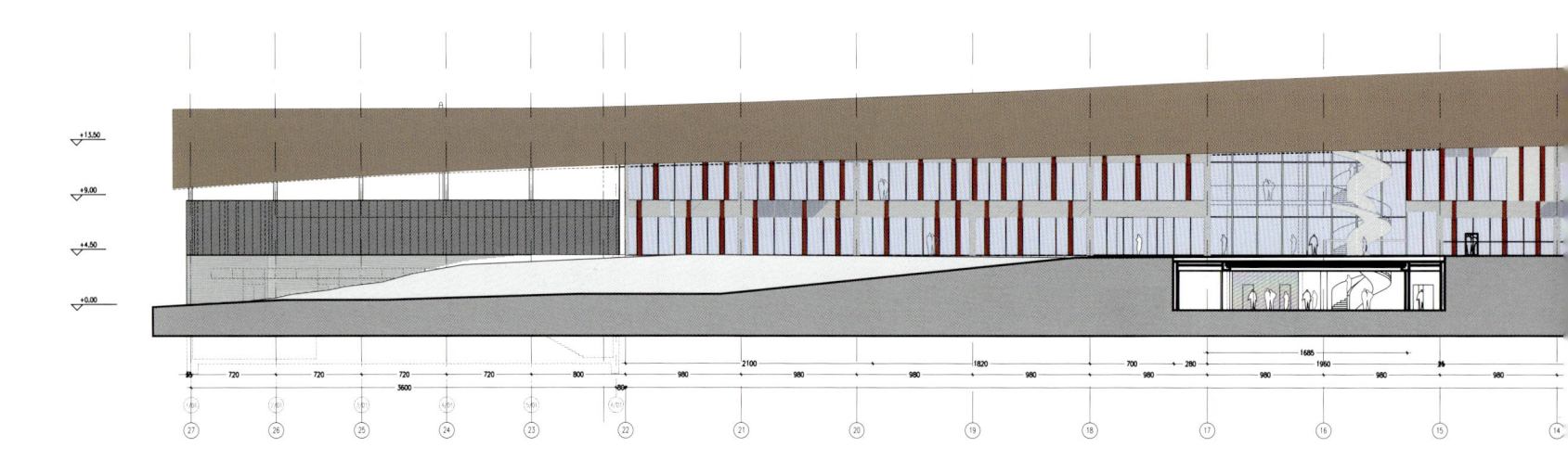

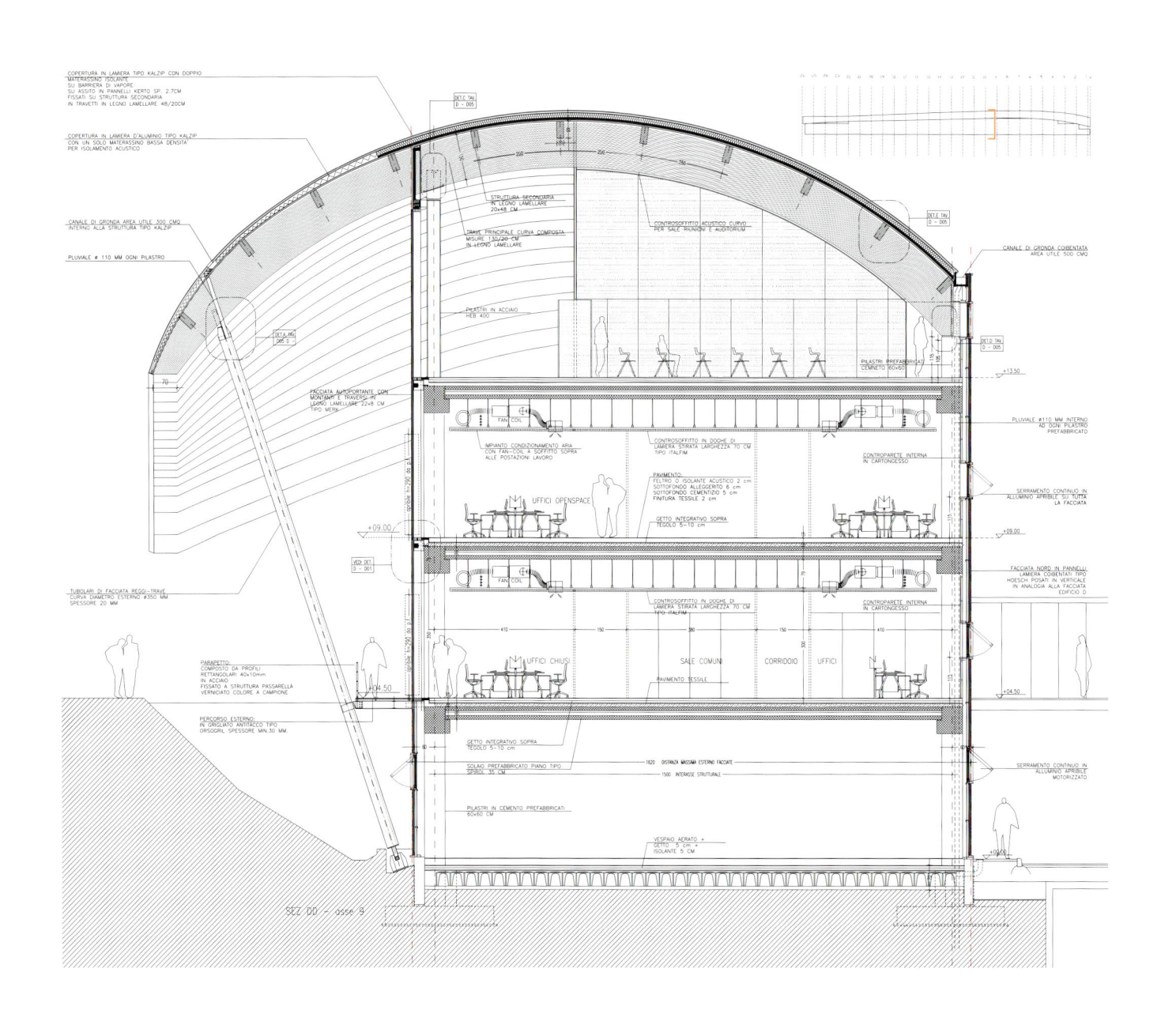

SEZ DD - asse 9

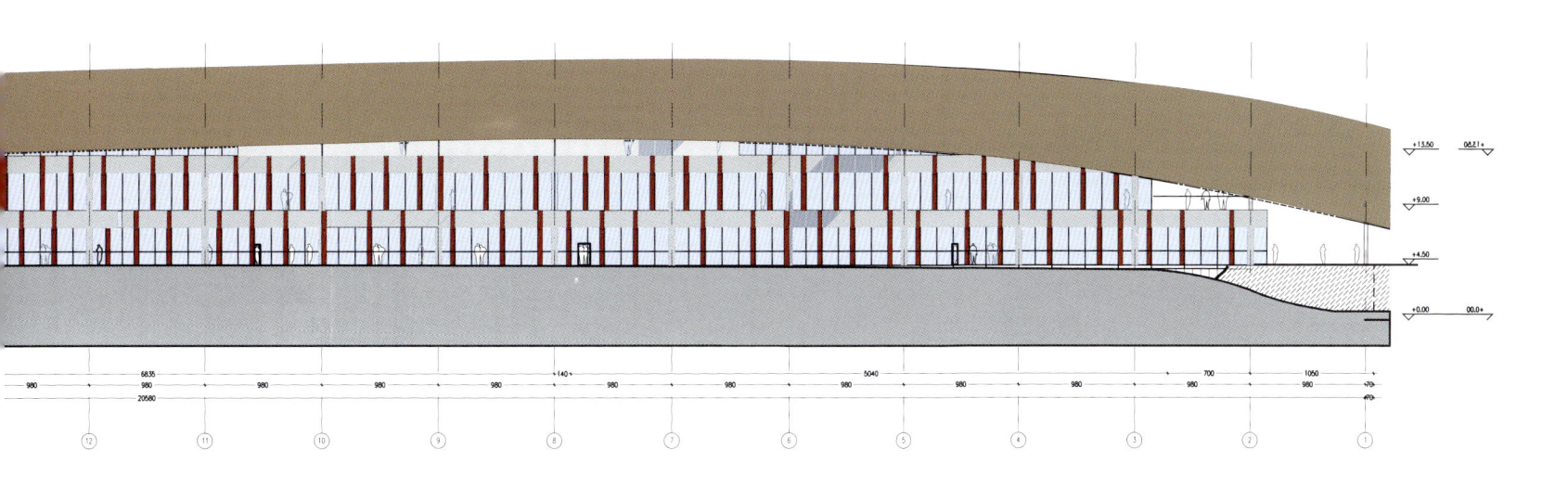

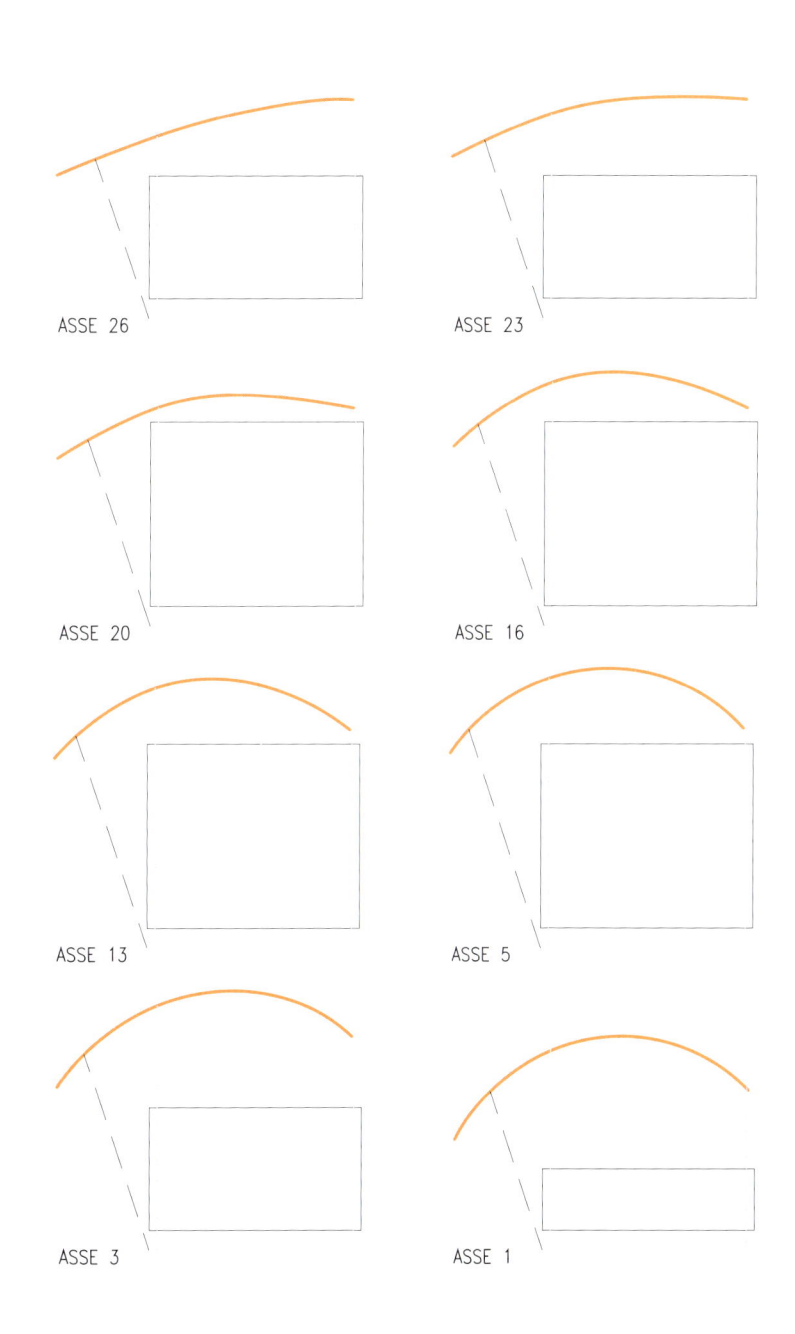

UTILITY

ASSE 26

ASSE 23

ASSE 20

ASSE 16

ASSE 13

ASSE 5

ASSE 3

ASSE 1

UTILITY

Here the architecture establishes a holistic relationship with its contents: glass walls create a fluid relationship between indoors and outdoors, and high performance natural materials (laminated wood and glass) emphasise the organic nature of the project.

1998–2000 Antonio Citterio and Partners, Milan

1,700 sq. m

Citterio intervenes with a surgeon's skill to incorporate his buildings into the urban fabric without making "noise", without indulging in any ostentation. He counters the narcissism of the personal mark with the dignity of mimesis that translates into urban quality, in harmony with a well-established trait of Milanese architecture culture.

UTILITY

UTILITY

UTILITY

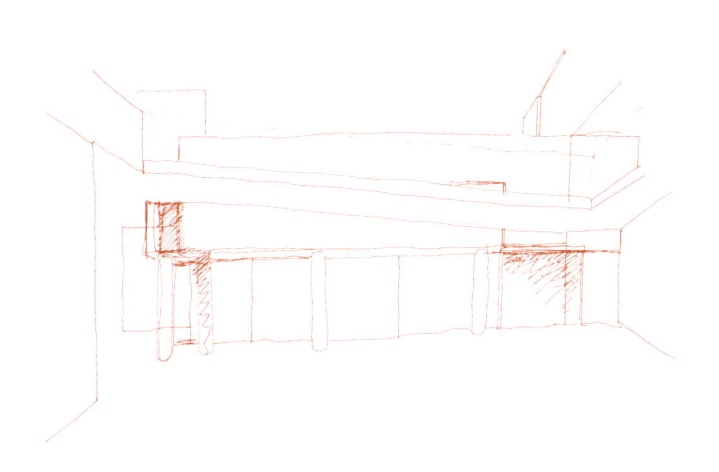

173

UTILITY

2000–2002 Neuer Wall, Hamburg

Commercial-use building and offices
3,500 sq. m

With its position right in the centre
of town, Citterio's Neuer Wall incorporates
an elegant curtain of grey stone, where
the glass of the parapets and the wooden
slats of the sun shades create a texture
of stunning visual impact, emphasised
on close view by the refinement
of the horizontal bevelling of the walls.

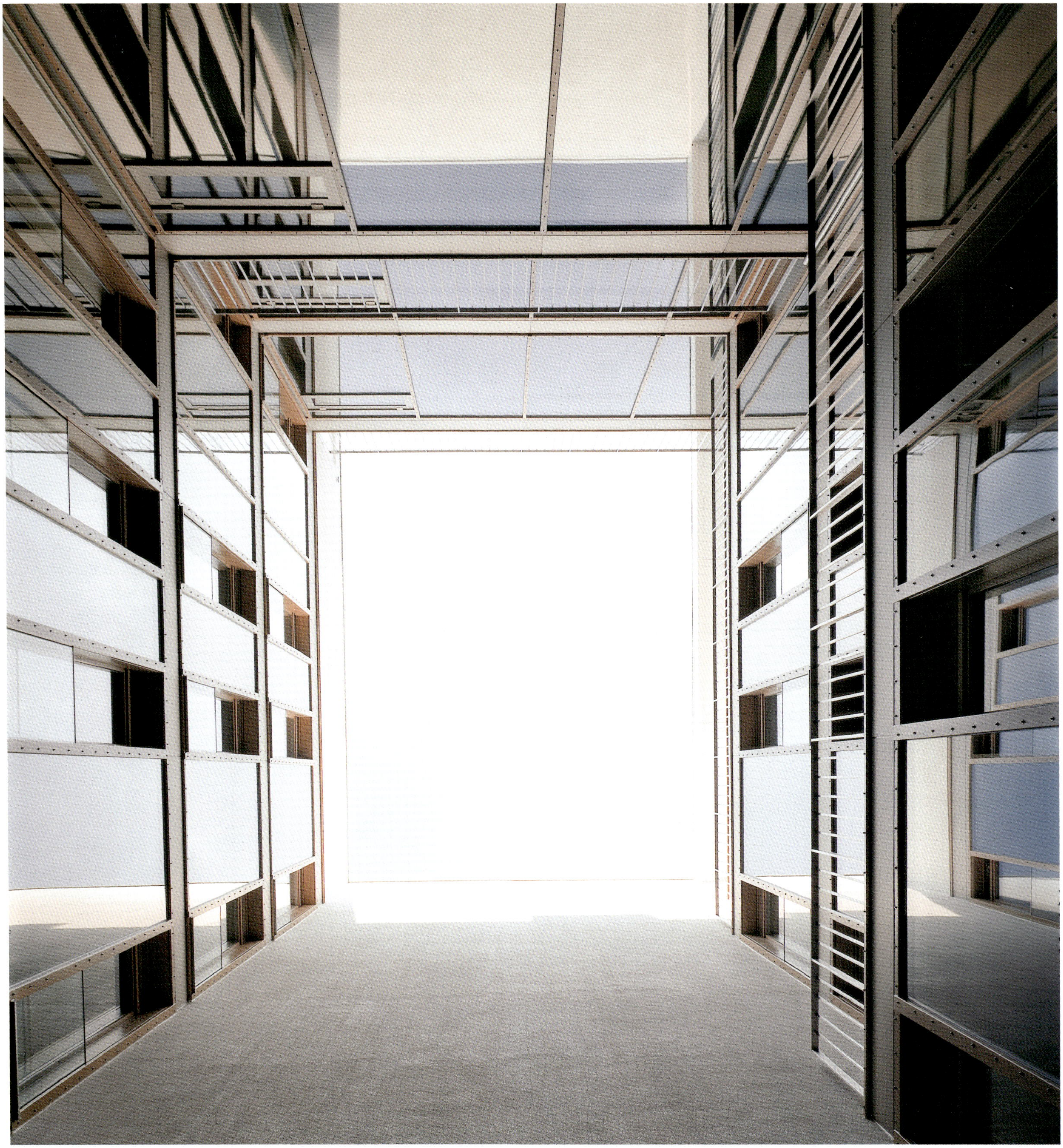

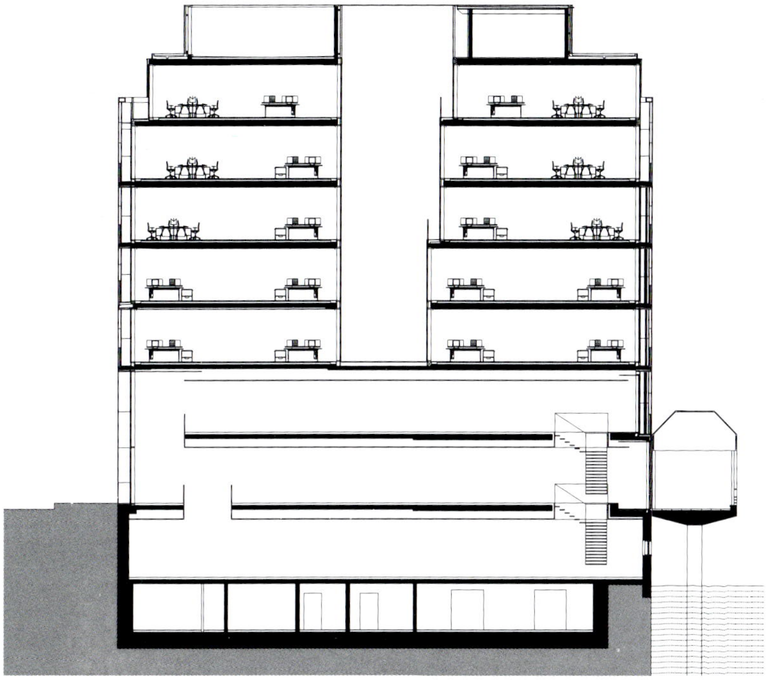

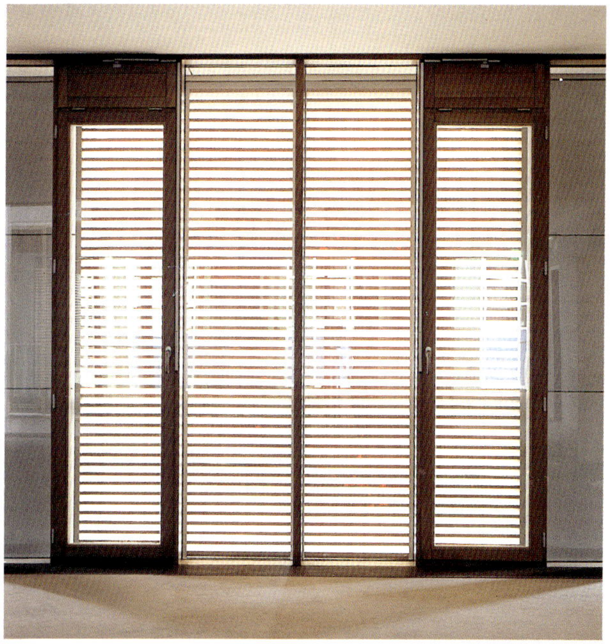

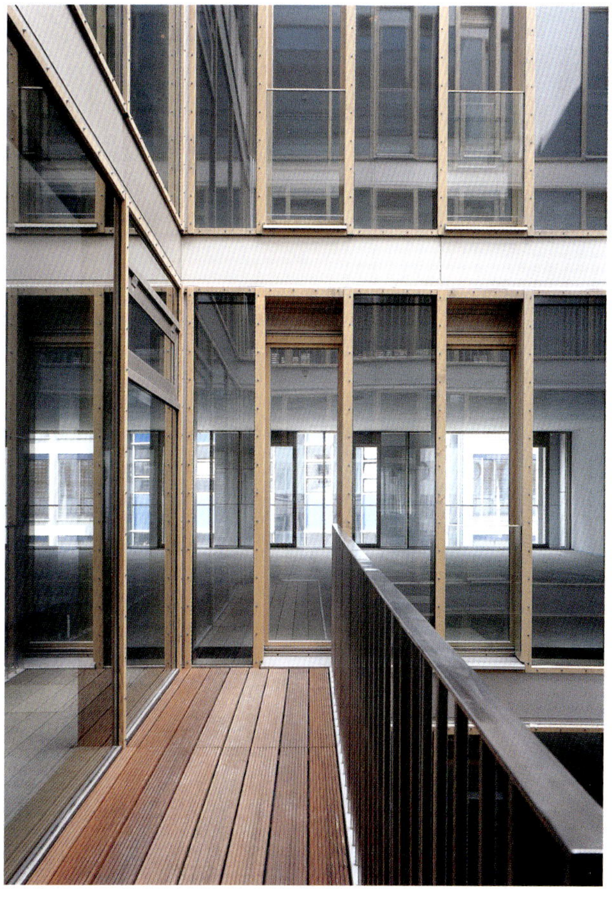

STRUCTURE.4

Philip Johnson said that structure was a dangerous element to focus on. He cautioned against equating *clearly expressed structure* with architecture and thinking that *nothing more was needed*. He admitted that at one time he had found himself in the same trap; it was a very easy way to look at things, since it is very unlikely that an architect's project will lack clarity when all its bays and windows are identical.[1]

Another point of view was held by the famous structurist Mario Salvadori, who left no room for doubt on the matter: "In architecture, structures are and always have been an essential component. Whether a man was building a simple shelter for himself and his family or erecting spacious halls where hundreds of people could worship, trade, discuss politics or enjoy shows, he had to use certain materials in specific quantities and form them so that his structures could withstand the force of gravity and other dangerous loads. They had to stand up to wind, lightning, earthquakes and fires . . . and since from time immemorial man has had an innate sense of beauty, all his structures were conceived in accordance with certain aesthetic criteria, which often impose demands on the crafting of structures that are much more rigorous than those of soundness and economy."[2]

Salvadori intimates that the structural component has always been a determining factor in the architectural project. However, while his affirmation well represents the buildings of the past it does not hold true in contemporary times, where architects have called structure into question in favour of a mechanistic conception of technology, giving rise to a separation between structural types and building types that continues to characterise our scientific culture. This separation has also led to a schism between the world of architecture and the realm of technics, almost as if these two aspects cannot share space in the same building. The language of architecture has grown increasingly refined, fluid, distilled, captivating and oriented toward formal rigour, while technics has become increasingly schematic, classifying, numerical and oriented toward technical rigour.

Perhaps the postmodern movement of the 1980s with its Chippendale tympana and its curtain wall cathedrals sought to display the ineluctability of this rupture as a form of provocation. Structure and building type are no longer apodictically indivisible. After more than four thousand years we have finally freed ourselves of the slavery of "structural honesty". Architecture is, only in appearance, as free as the layout of reinforced concrete structures. The act of separating structure from form, of stripping columns of their function as supports, is not a capricious mannerism, but an attempt to assume a new attitude toward the column "form". "Structural invention, that which permits the most efficient resolution of new problems arising day after day in the relentless development of construction in all its aspects," stated Pier Luigi Nervi, "can only be the fruit of a harmonious fusion of personal inventive intuition and impersonal, objective, realistic and inviolable static science."[3]

While planners such as Frank Gehry, Ron Arad, Zaha Hadid, Richard Rogers or the latest Pritzker honouree Paulo Mendes da Rocha focus on the plastic weight of the structures, others like Herzog & de Meuron, Renzo Piano, John Pawson, Jean Nouvel or Kazuyo Sejima, to name just a few, tend toward maximum lightness as the outcome of a methodology based on reduction. Antonio Citterio belongs to this last group. He is not interested in employing minimal or reductive solutions for resolving structural problems, but rather seeks to develop his language in the "skin" of the building.

---

[1] Philip Johnson, "The Seven Crutches of Modern Architecture", *Perspecta 3*, 1955, pp. 40–44, passage here based on the Italian translation, "I sette puntelli dell'architettura moderna", in Philip Johnson, *Verso il Postmoderno. Genesi di una deregulation creativa*. Genoa: Costa&Nolan, 1985, p. 103.

[2] Mario Salvadori, "Lo sviluppo storico", in Mario Salvadori and Robert Heller, *Le strutture in architettura*. Milan: Etas Libri, 1983, p. 1.

[3] Pier Luigi Nervi, "Presentazione", in Mario Salvadori and Robert Heller, Ibid., p. IX.

[4] Antonio Citterio, conversation with the author, May 2006.

[5] Gio Ponti, *Amate l'architettura*. Genoa: Editrice Vitali e Ghianda, 1957, p. 46. Published in English as *In Praise of Architecture*.

[6] Ibid., p. 106.

His work may be interpreted by examining the development of the wall. Primogenital structural element of construction, the boundary line between inside and out, the wall recounts the tale of Citterio's intense quest, his conquests, hesitations and reconsiderations.

From the emptied walls of the first Busnelli or Seregno houses to the lightness of his buildings in Hamburg or the Zegna building in Milan, and also from his *Diesis* sofa to his lamps *Lastra* and *Kelvin*, and his *Eileen* tables, Citterio manifests the mutations of the skin, its stretching. He exalts its transparency and texture in his architecture as well as in his industrial design. "The wall is the zero element of my language," he states. "When I design, the wall defines the volume. I designed a villa near Como based on the theme of the wall that gave me the opportunity to work with a double layer. When you design something you have to confront complex steps that cannot be resolved until they have been identified. In spite of the fact that technology changes and evolves with time, being familiar with the production process is the key to dominating structure. And today's approach to structure is different from that in the past. You work with a skin and reproduce this skin on the façade, using, for example, polymeric materials that separate the internal part of the work from the external part, and the relation between surface and structure becomes the main element in the project."[4]

It appears that Gio Ponti's prophecy has come true: "Structure is not a mineral. Architecture began with stones, the stones evolved into cement; stones will disappear from architecture."[5]

Structure for the Home

Private residence, Villasimius; Private residence and studio, Sondrio; Flexform: Lightpiece, Infinity; *Hansgrohe:* Axor Citterio bathroom; *Inda:* H2O; *Sanitec Group/Pozzi Ginori:* Q3, Easy, Quinta, 500, Join

Gio Ponti wrote in his 1957 work *Amate l'architettura* that "the Italian house is not an insulated and provisioned refuge against the harshness of the climate, as are the houses across the Alps where life seeks a haven from inclement nature for many long months. The Italian house is the place we choose to enjoy, during our lives, with happy possession, all the beauty that our land and our sky give to us during long seasons . . . The perfect house is one that makes us pause on the open threshold, awed by its human secret and its architectural beauty."[6]

Citterio took this lesson to heart, as evidenced by his houses in Villasimius and in Sondrio.

Villasimius is an agricultural enterprise on forty hectares in Sardinia planted in vineyards and olive groves. The only structure on the property is the farmhouse built in the 1960s, which Citterio redesigned in the name of ascetic reduction – although he left nothing lacking. Here the structure is a filter between indoors and outdoors. The strength of the wall offers protection from the heat while its openings welcome in the surrounding landscape. The main theme in Citterio's project is the redesign of the landscape, and the relationship between nature and the built elements is interpreted mimetically in accordance with the Milanese architect's guiding stars: discretion and lightness. The estate represents an elegant episode of "domestic" nature where the house, set at four metres above sea level in the lowest part of the property, is just one piece in the mosaic. Around it the property climbs the hill and extends southwards in vineyards, citrus orchards and olive groves. The large porticoes with their flexible alternation of inside and outside provide a spatial link and luminous filter, enhancing the usability of the house in the different seasons while softly tracing out the changes in elevation.

"The hardest part of this project," states Patricia Viel, "was to create a natural volume within the landscape. And so the choice was made to face the structure in irregular, coarse lime stucco that brings shadows to life, to create long patios woven into the surrounding greenery, for teak framing, and the cuts in the wall that open onto the sea and the sky." The original building had an irregular outline that was complicated by a conspicuous system of pergolas that exaggerated the impact of its volume. Citterio chose to reduce the volume, replacing the peaked roof with a flat one in order to better fit the architecture into its setting near the sea. Here, Citterio's Cartesian minimalism encountered the materiality of stone and succeeded in creating an ideal material and chromatic continuity with the landscape. The ground floor is faced in granite as are the outer walls, which follow the ground contours and result in an enlargement of the building footprint and the creation of outdoor areas, *horti conclusi*, walled olive gardens, that integrate well with the internal layout of the house. The upper floor is a white prism whose thick perimeter walls obviate the need for curtains. The walls are approximately forty-five centimetres thick, creating shady windows, while the splayed jambs afford an ample view of the surrounding landscape.

The house and studio Citterio built in Sondrio are also characterised by a lower section in stone and a similar expressive intensity. The house stands upon its stone-faced base, elevated upon a sort of ersatz acropolis, and the articulated perimeter of its upper floor opens generously onto its surroundings. The primordial power of stone, emphasised by the plastic mass of the volumes and by the broad sloping roof, marks out the lower perimeter while releasing above it the transparency and lightness of glass. Much of the volume of the house is underground. Indeed, in section, it cuts across an entire part of the hillside from the garage at the lower road level to the north entrance with access from the upper road next to the vineyard. The structure of the house is sunk into the mountain, anchored to it along one side, while the southern wall is completely transparent, as is the entire volume of the living room and kitchen area of the house. "The structure of the retaining walls plays an important geotechnical role," explains Patricia Viel. "The walls are made of reinforced concrete and are insulated and designed to allow groundwater to drain away. Above ground they are faced in stone. This results in walls that are some sixty centimetres thick and a house that appears completely different when viewed from the south and from the north."[7]

Seen from the north, the house appears low-slung with vertical windows echoing the pattern of the roof. Openings provide glimpses of the stone face-work, copper details of the rain gutters and the stone-shingled roof. The view from the south is characterised by the sequence of large openings and glass walls. The largest opening to the south, a dual sliding glass door that opens to almost six metres, opens onto the swimming pool. The architrave above the door is faced in black granite, as are all the arches on the façade, and supported by a cruciform one-piece stainless steel pillar.

The house is articulated in a sequence of stone-faced retaining walls, where the massiveness of the structure is juxtaposed with the lightness of the glassed openings, and the weight of stone with the transparency of glass. The interior space and the furnishings mediate this antonymy with Citterio's signature mimetic aptitude.

[7] Patricia Viel, conversation with the author, July 2006.

[8] Jean Baudrillard, *The System of Objects*. London–New York: Verso, 1996, p. 50. English translation by James Benedict.

In the studio, designed for the same client in Sondrio, the gravity of the rough-hewn stone face-work is balanced by the levity of the *Visavis* chairs and the choice of lamps, such as the *Lastra*, whose regular profiles lighten the structure.

Citterio creates overt and hidden structures where the materials follow their own nature, and form opens to accommodate new gestures. As Baudrillard put it, "[w]e know from practical experience how very far the mediation of gestures between man and things has been stretched."[8] Citterio reduces structure to its essence. We see this, among other cases, in his container-furniture *Lightpiece* and *Infinity* for Flexform, where the plain module represents the synthesis of its flexibility, its numerous variations on the theme. It comprises a metal frame that can be composed in different ways with shelves, drawers and doors. These well-defined and fully formed objects can be intermixed on the basis of the changing needs of space and function in this triumphant expression of changeable lifestyles.

Citterio forces us to interact with the objects, to compose furniture and, something even more important, to give body back to the objects by synthesising their movements. His rarefied mark is not a stylistic orientation, but rather a crystallisation of gestures and functions. His reflection on the kitchen, one of the household environments most deeply explored by Citterio, also extends to the bathroom system, he transforms from a random assemblage of sanitary fixtures into a temple of wellbeing, a place to regenerate oneself and bring time to a halt. His bathroom becomes a meditation chamber complete with chaise lounges and bookcases arranged around sculptural tubs. It communicates with the adjacent rooms via container-cabinets and glass walls, as we see in his projects for Sanitec/Pozzi Ginori, Hansgrohe and Inda. In *Axor Citterio* for Hansgrohe, for example, the partition wall has disappeared, replaced by the close rhythm of glass alternating with the materiality of wood in the cabinets to create a novel spatial continuity. Citterio's combinatory art is also applied in small spaces, favouring the succession of functions over the dimensions of the space. He enriches the arrangement and functional distribution by reworking the forms of the traditional components of the bathroom: sanitary fixtures and faucetry.

He creates faucets and sinks with sculptural forms (who ever said that a faucet necessarily had to have a cylindrical section?) that characterise the space with the purity of their volumes. The *H2O Frame* sink by Inda marked a historic turning point in the monotonous and traditionalist sink market. The sink is a field of exploration especially for Pozzi Ginori, where the *Q3*, *Easy*, *Quinta*, *500* and *Join* series offer compact volumes marked by inviting geometries and represent an evolutionary leap in the column-type sink and in suspended sanitary fixtures.

Freed of the supporting cabinet, the sink acquired an expressive identity and functional autonomy. Citterio's intuition has been celebrated in countless attempts at imitation, proving that the ability to vary the scale of a project confers new qualities on spaces and generates innovation.

Structure for the Workplace
Edel Music Headquarters, Hamburg

"Originally there was an architecture of walls, with the sense of fullness, weight and material," affirms Citterio. "Then something changed and the wall became almost insubstantial. Technology, systems engineering and construction techniques all contributed to an 'emptying out' of the wall. Today you no longer design the wall, but rather the skin, the covering of a structure."[9]

In the Edel offices in Hamburg, completed in 2002, the structure is raised on pilotis and suspended somewhere between the Elba River and the sky, ethereal in the ample windows of its five floors and mutable in the reflections in its façade. The skin creates an osmotic indoor-outdoor relationship, and the ample cornice, dimensioned to suit the scale of the building, defines its perimeter. It is one of the projects that better represents Citterio's ability to integrate the different scales of a project: structure, interiors, furnishings.

The elegant building is distinguished for its lightness and the anonymity of its contiguous volumes, which are harmonised by a predefined master plan. Arranged around a courtyard that is open to the river, the two lower levels of the structure contain shared services – restaurant, foyer, bar, showroom and auditorium – while the upper three floors contain the offices. The first two of these three floors project outwards for about eight metres towards the water, which gives the offices an extraordinary view of the river. "To obtain this section," states Patricia Viel, "the supporting floor is nearly one metre thick, it has an incredible density of reinforcement rods and was made prestressed in order to reduce strain. The structural grid leaves the prefabricated circular pillars in plain view. They were made using a centrifugal process that gives them excellent performance characteristics and a flawless surface. The intention was to create a building in cement and wood. Since we had to adhere to regulations which have become pretty much international regarding building insulation, the edges of the floors were finished with prefabricated elements whose outline reduces the structural section while preserving the coarse aspect of the material. Between one floor and the next we built a façade entirely in red oak with windows that can be opened, produced according to designs and finished with a special protective coat that can stand up to the Elba atmosphere, which is often briny."[10]

The sophistication of the structural design does not give in to exhibitionist temptations; on the contrary, it conserves the stately calm required of workspaces. The details were handled with Citterio's usual care, and the architectural shell effectively transmits the company values. This building also clearly represents the model for subsequent efforts to lighten the design of the façade and empty the walls in the quest for a transparent, vibrant skin. The geometry marked out by the windows and the regularity of their placement herald the arrangement of the façades of later buildings, such as the Barvikha Resort or the Bulgari Hotel in Milan, where the lesson of the modern masters finds mature expression.

Structure for the City and Territory
Convention Centre and Hotel in Palma de Mallorca, competition project

In 1957, Luigi Moretti wrote: "The world of forms is revealed to us by way of the differences that are triggered between one form and another. Differences are the inescapable, ineluctable flashes of reality and of forms; they are the forms . . . A non-elementary form is constituted by a group of differences that are bound together by relations that express and force their order and their consequentiality. The complex of these relations is the structure of form, which may thus be expressed in the ab-

[9] Michele Reboli and Matteo Vercelloni, "Antonio Citterio and Partners", *Interni*, December 2001, no. 517, p. 99.

[10] Patricia Viel, conversation with the author, June 2006.

[11] Luigi Moretti, *Spazio*, June–July 1957.

[12] Cesare Brandi, *Struttura e architettura*. Turin: Einaudi, 1967.

stract as a system of pure relations . . . In works of architecture, more than in those of the other arts, the realm of relations is comprehensible, that is, the structure that binds and regulates the various forms that compose it . . . the structure of chiaroscuro, the structure of static relationships, the structure of the spaces, the structure of the plastic relationships and the structure of the surfaces."[11]

A project submitted to a design contest in 2005, the new Convention Centre and Hotel in Palma de Mallorca outlines the complex interpretation that Citterio attributes to structure, precisely, as Moretti suggests, in its plastic, superficial and chiaroscuro interpretation. Here structure becomes light, the light that filters through the densely sequenced portico, a recurring element in architecture of the same period (for example David Chipperfield's Museum of Modern Literature in Marbach am Neckar, Stuttgart), and unites tradition and innovation in the irregular simplicity of the profiles and materials.

The Convention Centre and Hotel were designed to play a connective role between the urban fabric of the historical centre and the more fragmentary fabric of the post-WWII urban expansion. In an urban continuum interrupted only by the pedestrian paths leading down to the seaside, a large roof at a height of eleven metres covers the sequence of built volumes containing the main convention hall, the cafeteria, the meeting rooms and the exhibition space. The paths to the seaside offer occasions for passing through, creating a sort of stoa that gives the complex its clear public character. This character is also recognisable in the design of the atrium outside the main convention hall, which is the only public space under the large roof, embellished with a garden that is strategically raised with respect to the roadway.

The cafeteria garden offers a second permeation point for the public, while a third point of passage is located not far off to the east, near the separate entrance to the exhibition space and the meeting rooms, which can also be reached via the hotel. The hotel complex is laid out between a small street that divides the lot and the new building that is part of the master plan. This building overlooks the tourist harbour across a public area shaded by the roof and beautified with a small garden. Between the guestroom towers, located at the easternmost edge of the project area, and the adjacent building, there is a last point of passage across the block.

Citterio forcefully opposes fragmentation, separation and noncontinuity assumed as a method more than as a principle, as a contemporary way of planning. Against the effects that have led to the thought that the contemporary city and territory have to be understood as a sort of grand museum, a sort of archaeological area covering the entire country, where architecture and art are confined to a few historical or modern works, Citterio opposes an urban vision built with painstaking patience starting from each single element of the composition. Cesare Brandi interpreted the general sense of this feeling by stating that "when architecture is not art, it is mere tectonics, the practical fulfilment of a need."[12]

STRUCTURE

Primogenital structural element of construction, the boundary line between inside and out, the wall recounts the tale of Citterio's intense quest, his conquests, hesitations and reconsiderations.

"The wall is the zero element of my language."
Antonio Citterio

186

2003–2004 Villasimius, Sardinia

Private residence
750 sq. m

The estate represents an elegant episode of "domestic" nature where the house, set at four metres above sea level in the lowest part of the property, is just one piece in the mosaic. Around it the property climbs the hill and extends southwards in vineyards, citrus orchards and olive groves.

STRUCTURE

The main theme in Citterio's project here is the redesign of the landscape, and the relationship between nature and the built elements is interpreted mimetically in accordance with the Milanese architect's guiding stars: discretion and lightness.

"The hardest part of this project was to create a natural volume within the landscape."
Patricia Viel

STRUCTURE

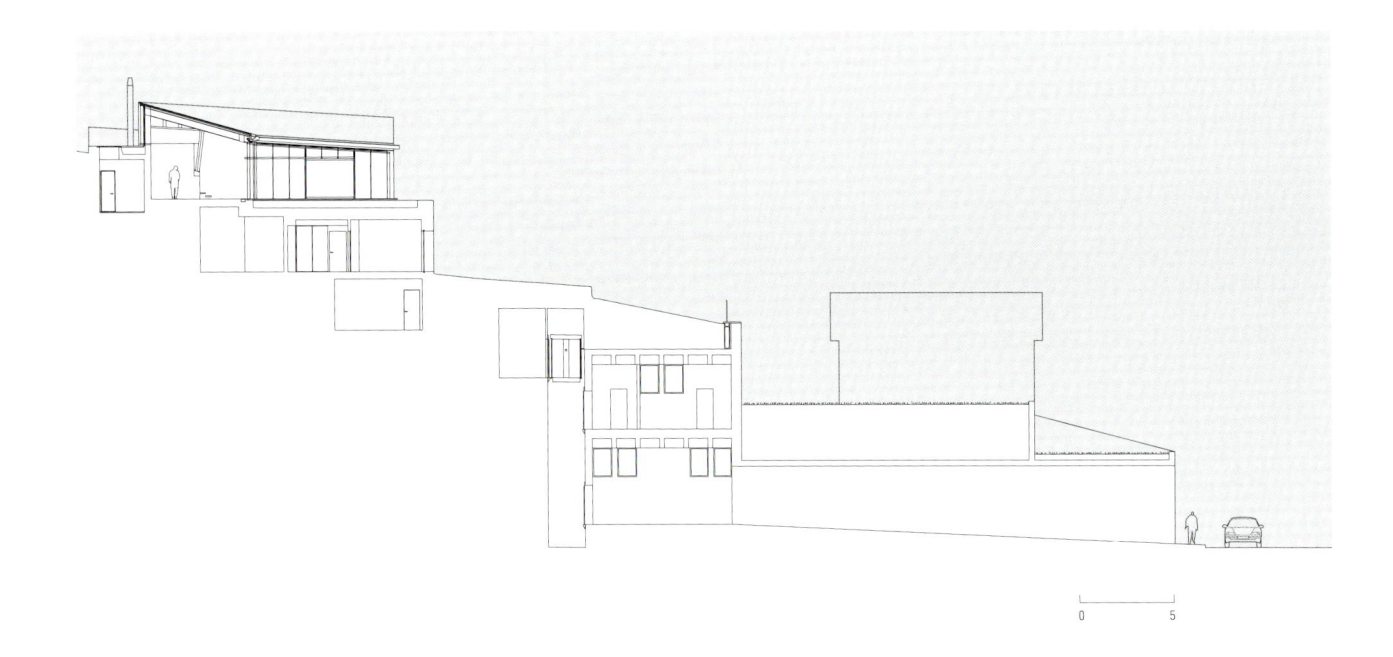

STRUCTURE

0 5

2003–2007 Colda, Sondrio

Private residence
850 sq. m

The house stands upon its stone-faced base, elevated upon a sort of ersatz acropolis, and the articulated perimeter of its upper floor opens generously onto its surroundings. The primordial power of stone, emphasised by the plastic mass of the volumes and by the broad sloping roof, marks the lower border while releasing above it the transparency and lightness of glass.

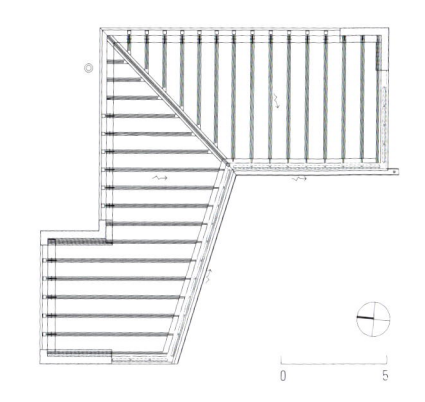

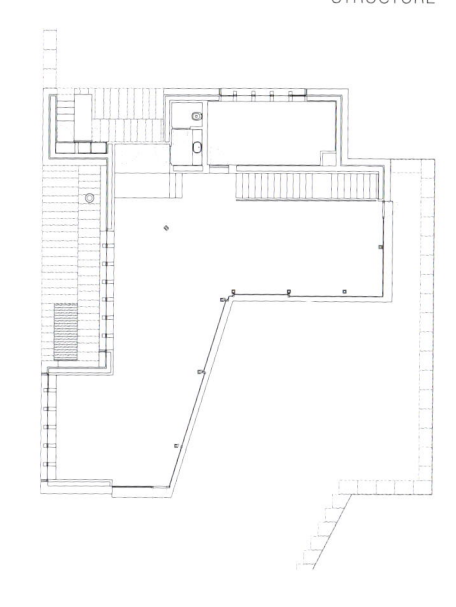

STRUCTURE

"Structure is not a mineral. Architecture began with stones, the stones evolved into cement; stones will disappear from architecture."
Gio Ponti

2002–2004 Sondrio

Notary's studio
450 sq. m

STRUCTURE

STRUCTURE

STRUCTURE

2002 Lightpiece, Flexform
2005 Vic, Flexform

Citterio reduces structure to its essence. We see this, among other cases, in his container-furniture *Lightpiece* and *Infinity* for Flexform, where the plain module represents the synthesis of its flexibility, its numerous variations on the theme.

2004 Infinity, Flexform

It comprises a metal frame that can be composed in different ways with shelves, drawers and doors. These well-defined and fully formed objects can be intermixed on the basis of the changing needs of space and function in this triumphant expression of changeable lifestyles.

STRUCTURE

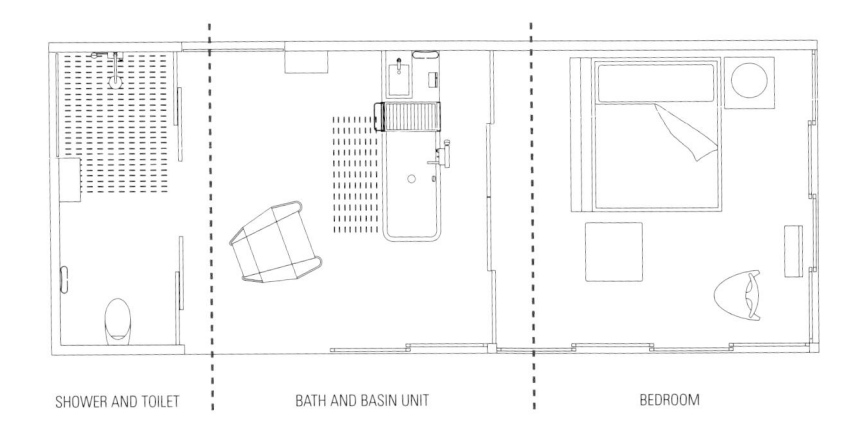

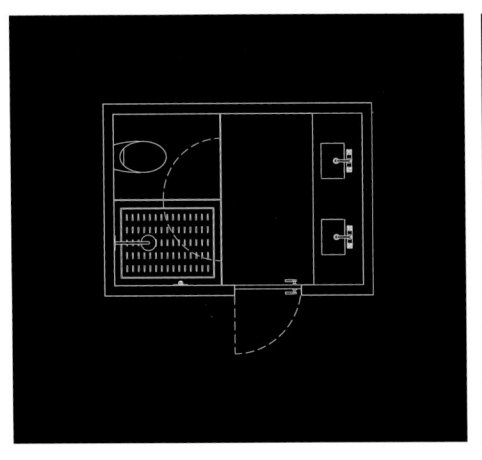

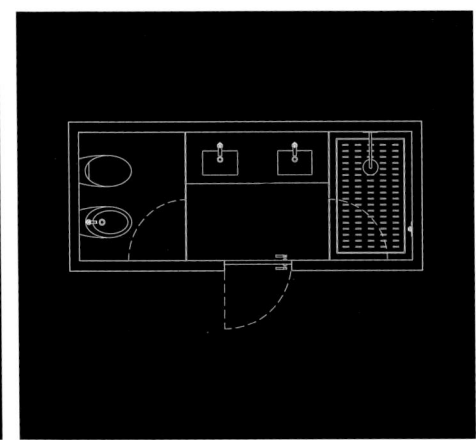

SHOWER AND TOILET | BATH AND BASIN UNIT | BEDROOM

6 SQ. M

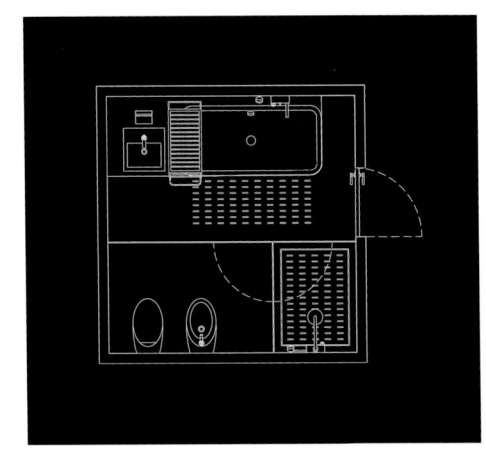

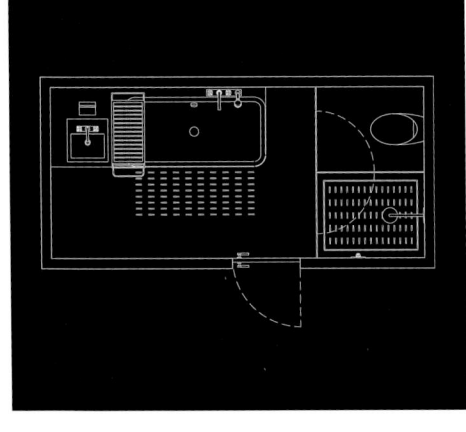

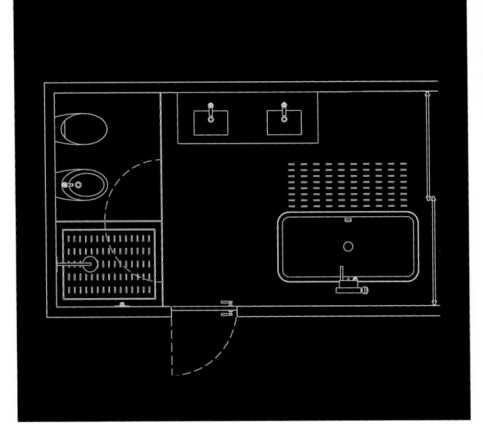

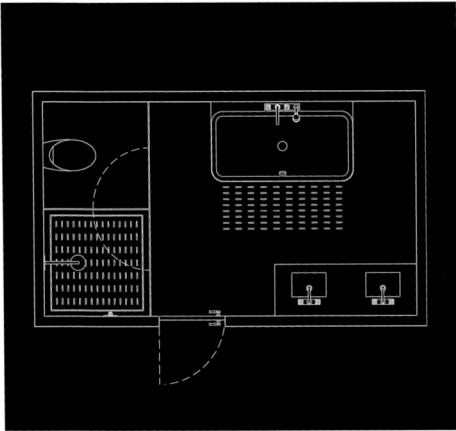

9 SQ. M

12 SQ. M

STRUCTURE

2001–2003 Axor Citterio, Hansgrohe

with Toan Nguyen

Citterio transforms the bathroom from a random assemblage of sanitary fixtures into a temple of wellbeing, a place to regenerate oneself and bring time to a halt.

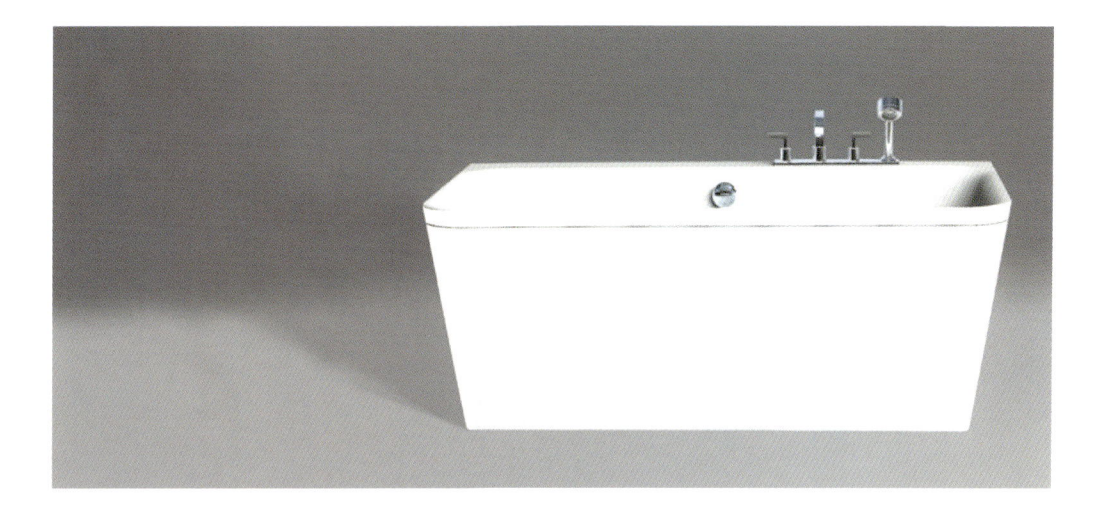

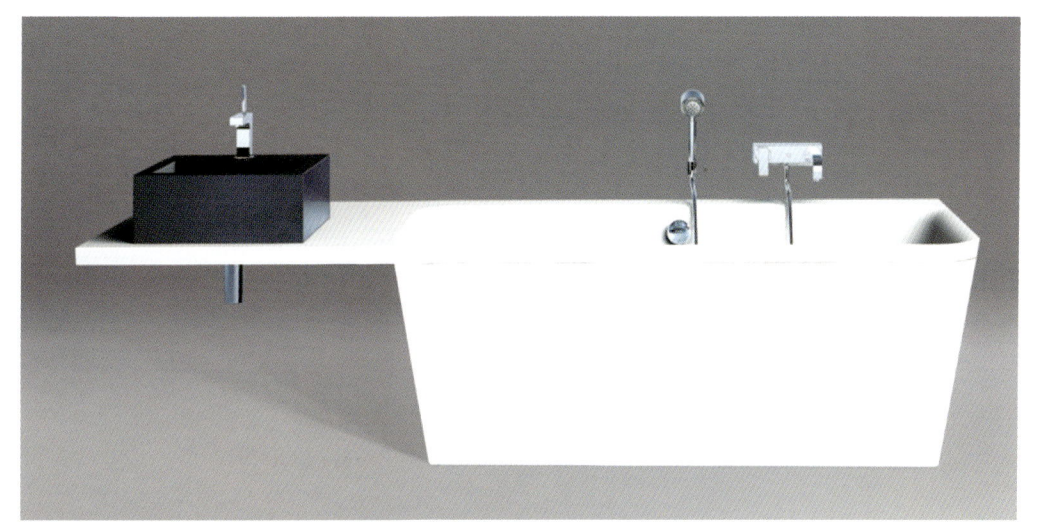

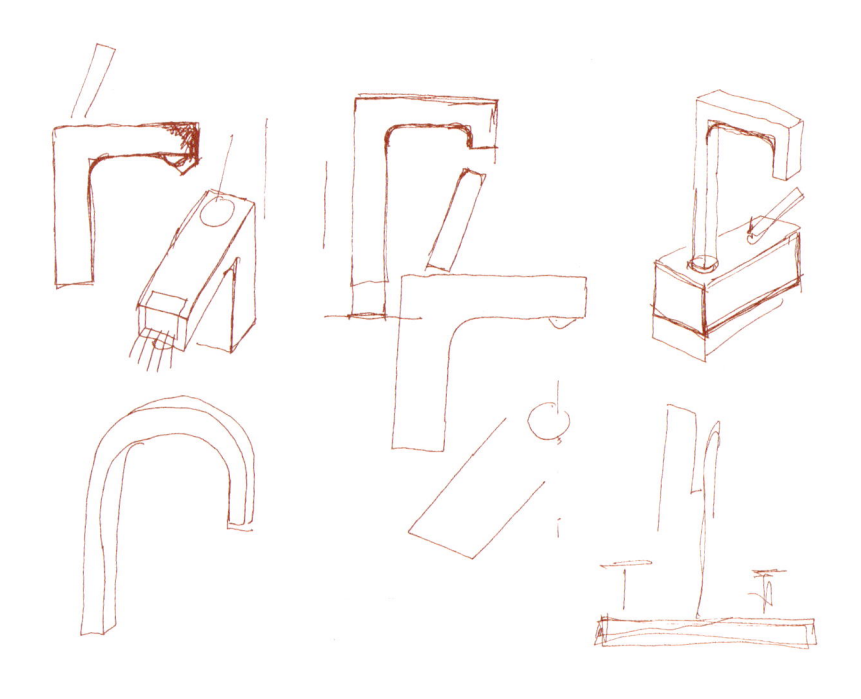

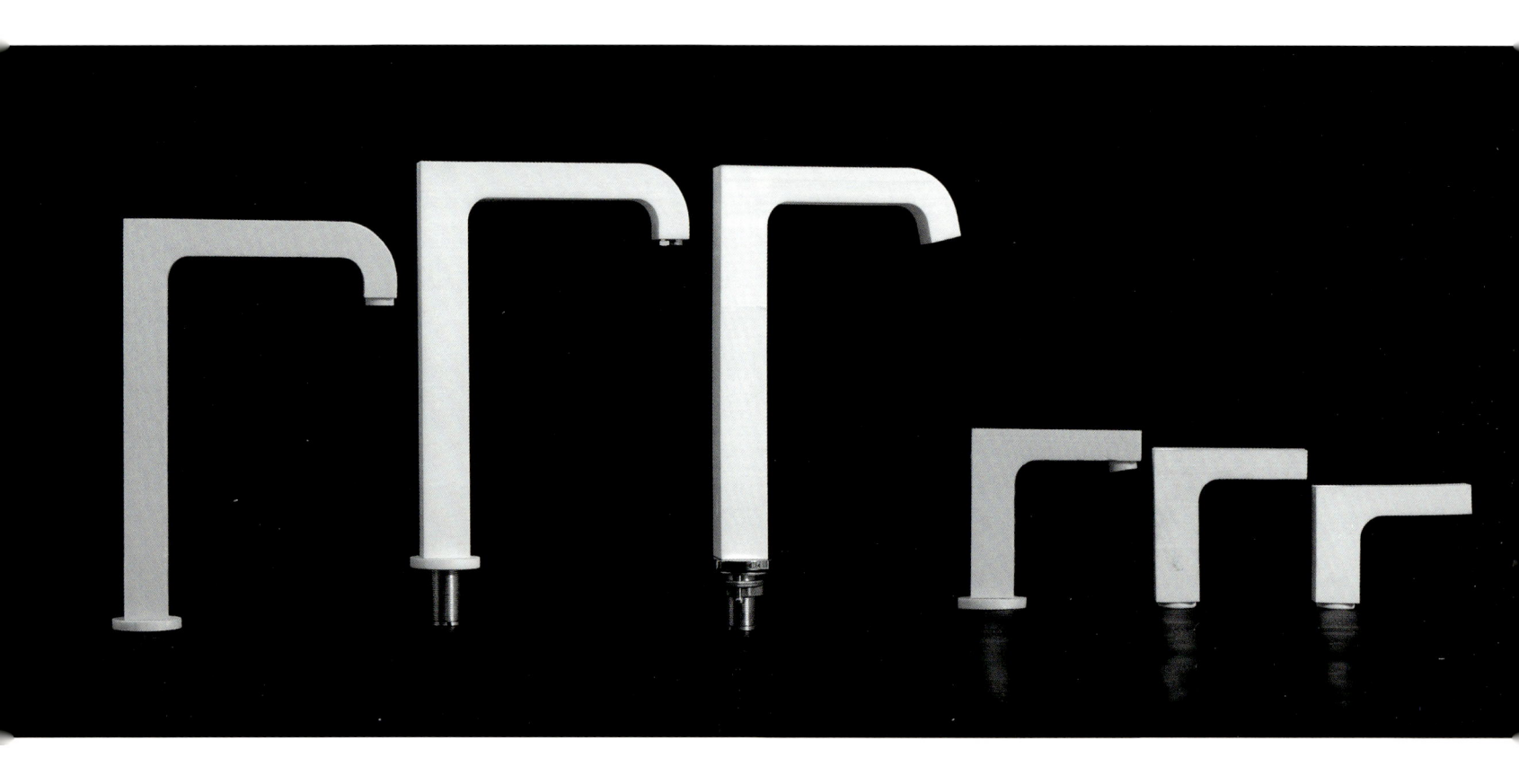

STRUCTURE

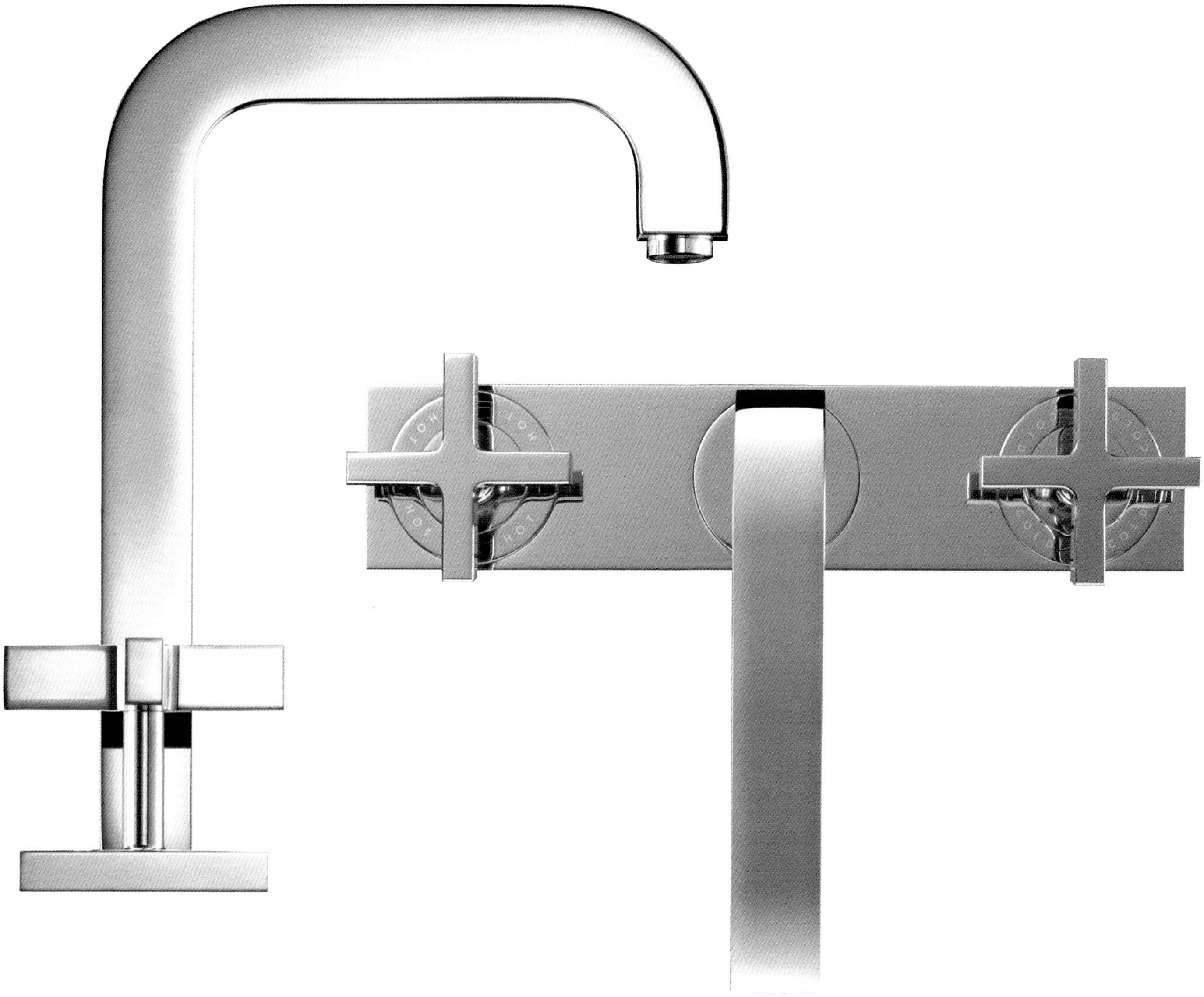

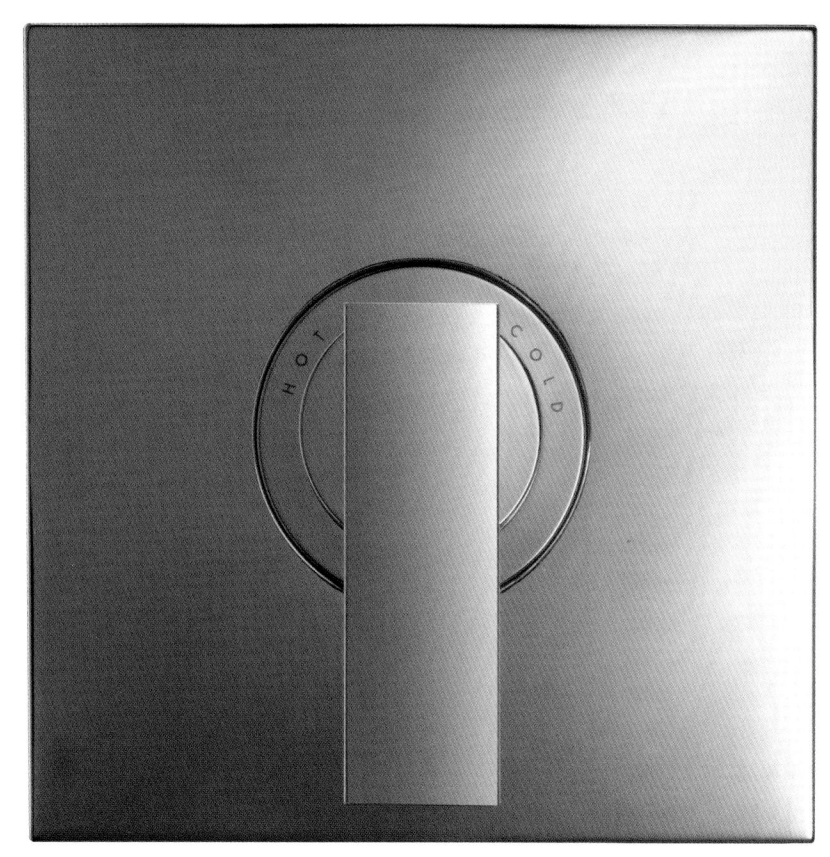

STRUCTURE

STRUCTURE

STRUCTURE

2001 H2O, Inda

with Sergio Brioschi

The *H2O Frame* sink by Inda marked a historic turning point in the monotonous and traditionalist sink market.

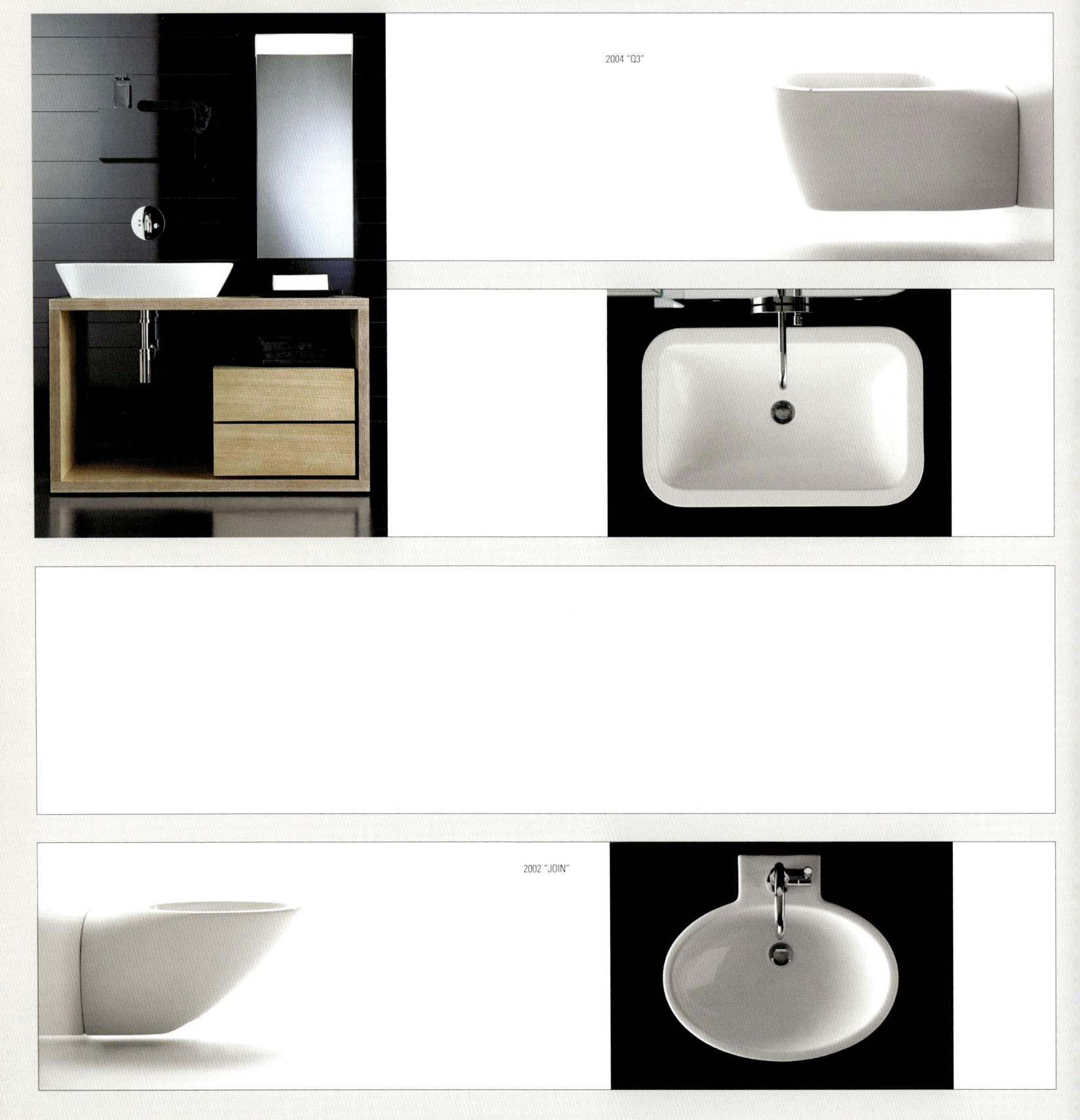

STRUCTURE

2004 "Q3"

2002 "JOIN"

STRUCTURE

2004 "QUINTA"

Pozzi Ginori, Bathroom Collections

with Sergio Brioschi

2000 "500"

207

STRUCTURE

STRUCTURE

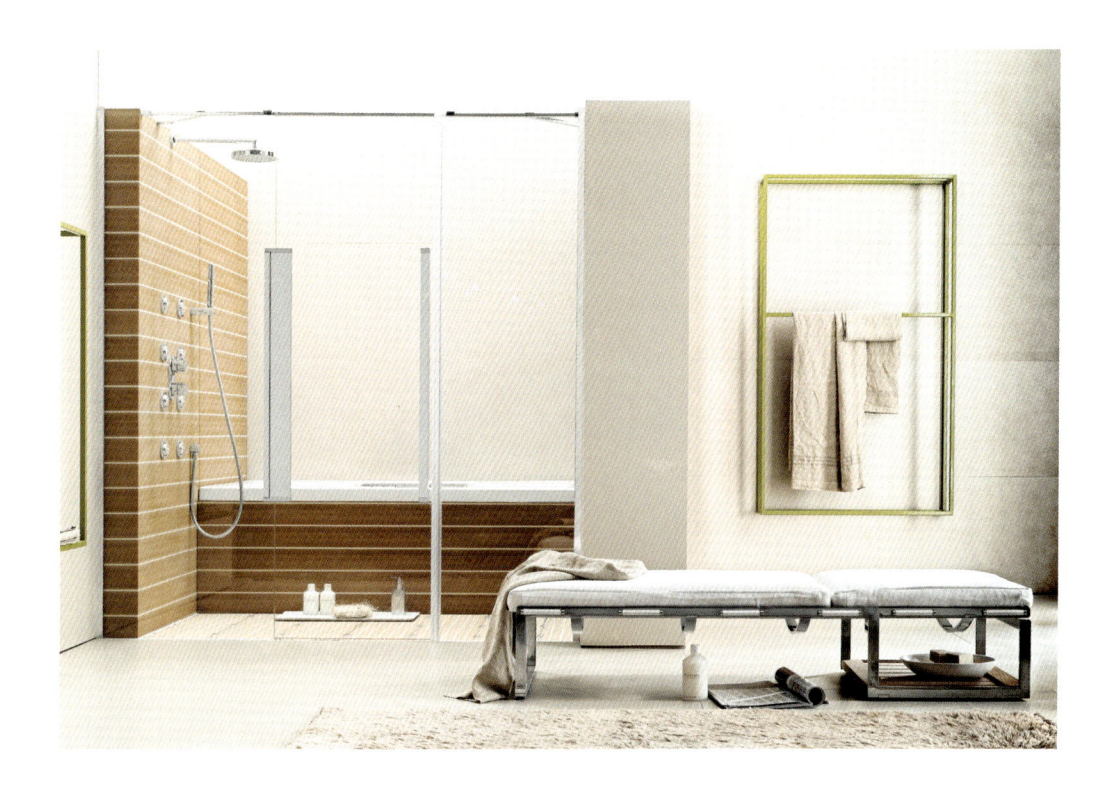

2005 Cube, Albatros

with Sergio Brioschi

209

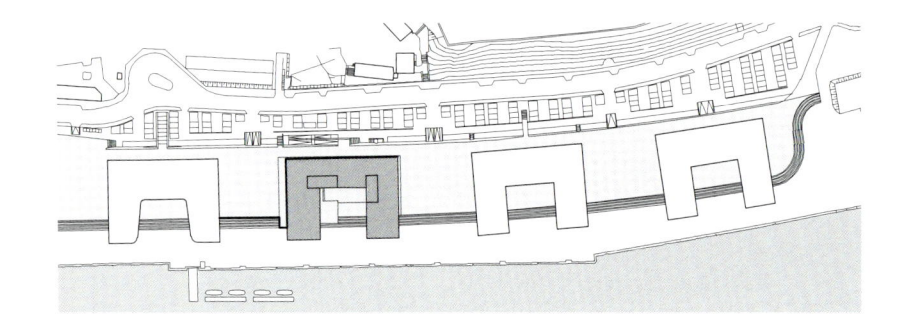

STRUCTURE

STRUCTURE

1998–2002 Edel Music, Hamburg

Headquarters with direction offices, recreational and commercial spaces, restaurant
6,000 sq. m

In the Edel offices in Hamburg, completed in 2002, the structure is raised on pilotis and suspended somewhere between the Elba River and the sky, ethereal in the ample windows of its five floors and mutable in the reflections in its façade.

STRUCTURE

STRUCTURE

"The structural grid leaves
the prefabricated circular pillars in plain
view. They were made using a centrifugal
process that gives them excellent
performance characteristics and
a flawless surface."
Patricia Viel

The sophistication of the structural design
does not give in to exhibitionist
temptations; on the contrary, it conserves
the stately calm required of workspaces.

"In architecture, structures are
and always have been an essential
component."
Mario Salvadori

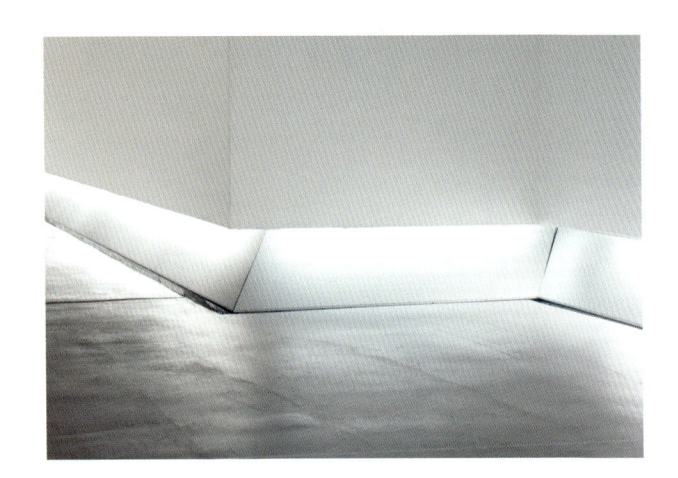

STRUCTURE

2006 Aspesi, Milan

Boutique on Via Montenapoleone
750 sq. m

"We feel de-schooled, free to uncover the history of old places, to reveal their structure, to exalt their materials and create a sense of a huge industrial workshop." Patricia Viel

STRUCTURE

2005 Convention Centre, Palma de Mallorca

Design competition
Convention Centre 16,500 sq. m
Hotel 10,575 sq. m
Parking area 11,100 sq. m

The Convention Centre and Hotel were designed to play a connective role between the urban fabric of the historical centre and the more fragmentary fabric of the post-WWII urban expansion.

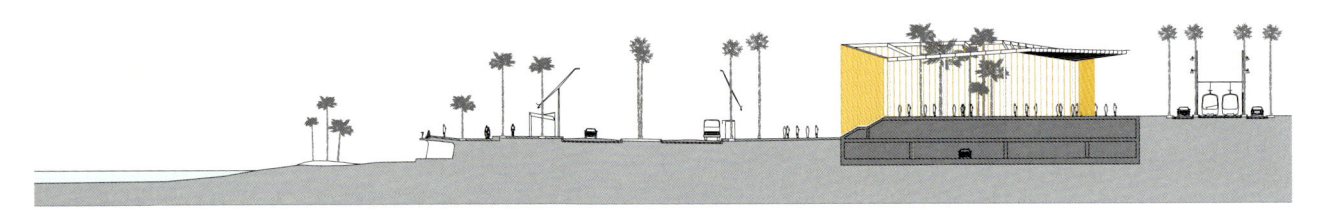

Sezione AA - Area ingresso principale

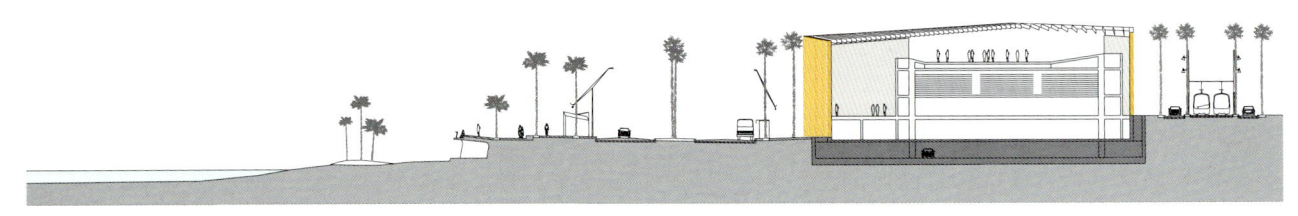

Sezione BB - Auditorium / Sala congressi e belvedere

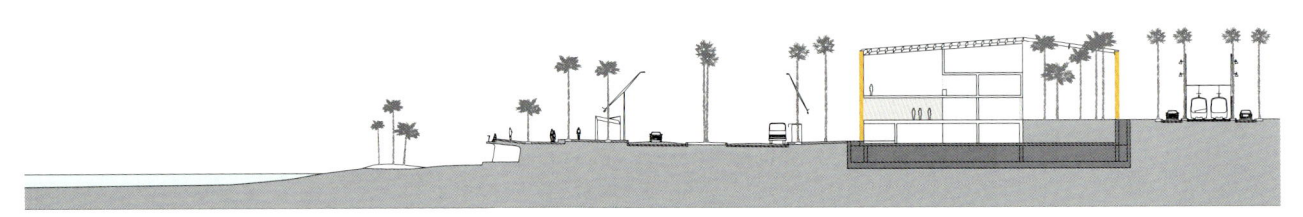

Sezione CC - Ristorante e giardino interno

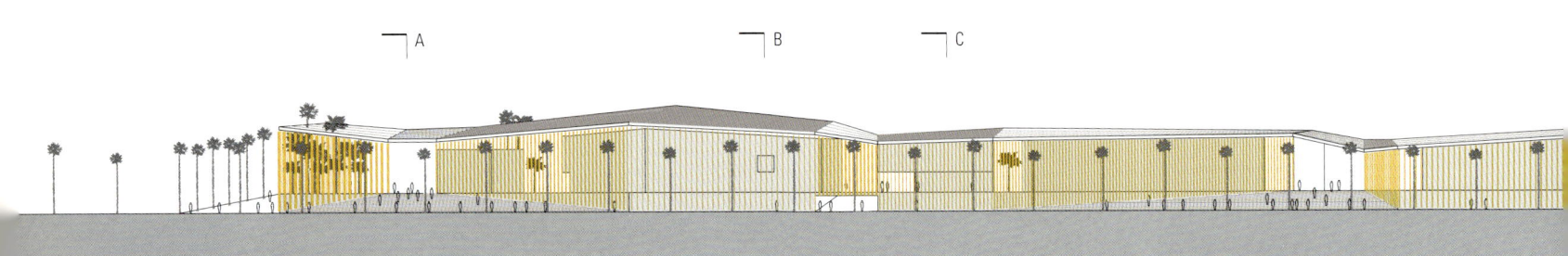

0   20 m

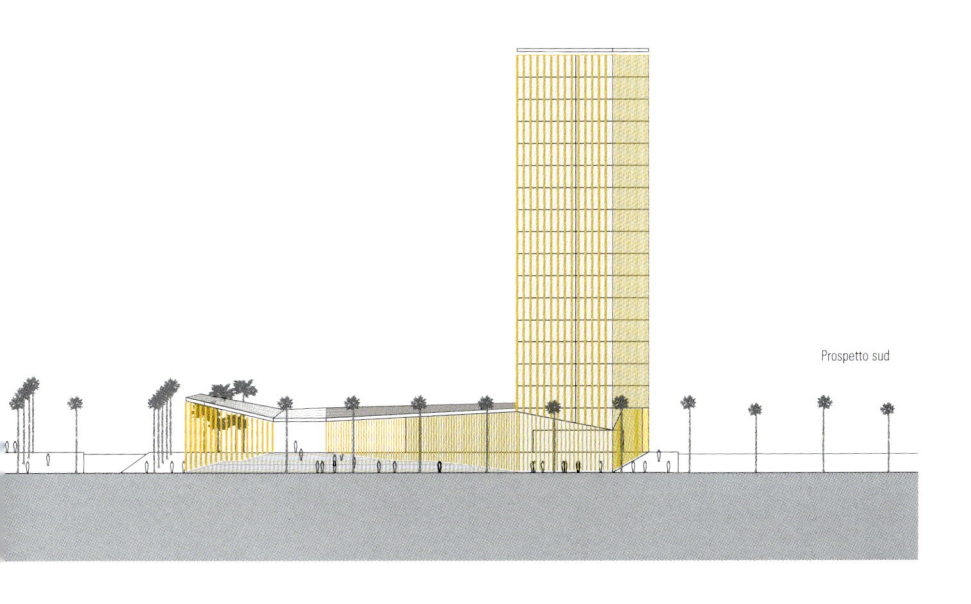

STRUCTURE

0 25 50

Prospetto sud

217

STRUCTURE

STRUCTURE

"Structural invention, that which permits
the most efficient resolution of new problems
arising day after day in the relentless
development of construction in all its aspects,
can only be the fruit of a harmonious
fusion of personal inventive intuition
and impersonal, objective, realistic
and inviolable static science."
Pier Luigi Nervi

TECHNOLOGY.5

In a 1962 talk about the crutch of technology, Philip Johnson acknowledged that a roof shaped like a hyperbolic paraboloid was a new technology, but questioned whether it could ever be considered art.[1] His challenge echoes the more famous polemic of J.J.P. Oud, who declared in 1925, "I bow the knee before the miracle of technology, but I do not believe that an ocean liner is comparable with the Parthenon". Oud's comment was part of the dispute between technics and art that permeated twentieth-century architectural culture[2] and then reemerged in the contemporary era with the introduction of digital technology in architecture.

"Technics" corresponds to the Latin *Ars*, since the Greek *teknè* refers more to skill or know-how in specific areas, and is not concerned with causes or the thing that is done.[3] Vittorio Gregotti's thoughts on the matter are very incisive: "Since there can be no art without technics, the reciprocal position of these two aspects is of critical importance in creating and judging things in architecture and in the arts in general . . . Good brushes do not make good painters, but the tradition of European art is filled with extraordinarily compelling discourses on painting technique."[4] Even though arts cannot be separated from their techniques, in the current era, as Jean-Luc Nancy has observed, "the division often separates the product, *poiesis*, from the means of production, *teknè*."[5] In the current day, "technics" is a synonym for "technology"[6] and represents the set of tools and procedures by which people pursue their goals and build their world. In this sense, Andy Warhol's famous 1963 quip, "The reason I'm painting this way is that I want to be a machine and I feel that whatever I do and do machine-like is what I want to do", expresses the need, albeit with strong critical ambiguity, to bring art closer to the science-technics-production system.

Etymologically, "technology" refers to a critical and systematic discourse (*logos*) on technics. In our specific case, the role of technology in architecture would include the critical and systematic discourse on technics for architecture. The history of the term "technology", however, has much deeper roots than those of "technics". "Technologos" initially signified not so much he who spoke and thought about *teknè* as much as he who spoke artfully, thus in an elaborate, rhetorically and dialectically refined fashion, if not indeed with perfidy and untruth. In this sense, a church father could call heretics *technologoi*. The term "technology"[7] appeared, perhaps for the first time, in the sixteenth century in a little known work by Alcal-Barral, *Encyclopédie technologique*,[8] in which the concept of "technology" is associated with the art and the study of the methods of constructing artefacts.

The term entered the Italian language much later. In nineteenth-century Italian bureaucratic and academic parlance, the term *tecnica* was used exclusively. *Tecnologia* was adopted from the English, where "technology" had developed in parallel with the Italian *tecnica*. The Oxford English Dictionary gives as the first definition of "technology": "A discourse or treatise on an art or arts; the scientific study of the practical or scientific arts", after the meaning of the Greek composite term.

One of the major works on the subject of technology applied to architecture is the *Handbook of Architectural Technology*, by the famous Henry J. Cowan. It assembles all the necessary knowledge for critically developing the constructional choices in an architecture project: mathematics, material science, structural theory; structures made of wood, steel, reinforced concrete, bearing walls; foundations, acoustics, safe-

---

[1] Philip Johnson discussed this in a speech given at the Eleventh Annual Northeast Regional Conference of the American Institute of Architects, Oceanlake, Oregon, on 12 October 1962.

[2] See Lewis Mumford, *Art and Technics*, where he upholds the primacy of the symbolic character of art, i.e. man's tendency to translate his experiences into symbols so that by employing technics he can once again become master of his own destiny.

[3] On the relationship between art and technics, see Tomas Maldonado, ed., *Tecnica e cultura. Il dibattito tedesco tra Bismarck e Weimar*. Milan: Feltrinelli, 1979.

[4] Vittorio Gregotti, *Architettura, tecnica, finalità*. Rome: Editori Laterza, 2002, p. 3.

[5] Jean-Luc Nancy, *Le Muse*. Reggio Emilia: Diabasis, 2006.

[6] "The words 'technics' and 'technology' are often used interchangeably in current usage, although the latter term has a somewhat more modern flavour." Vittorio Gregotti, *Op. cit.*, p. 12.

[7] For a compendium on the history of technology, see Donald S.L. Cardwell, *Technology, Science and History*. London: Heinemann, 1972; or A. Sposito, *Elogio della tecnologia: prolegomeni alla storia di artefatti*. Palermo: Alloro, 1993.

[8] Alcal-Barral, *Encyclopédie technologique. Dictionnaire des arts et manufactures, de l'agricolture, de miner, . . .* Paris: 1583–1584.

[9] Gottfried Semper, *Der stil in den technischen und tektonischen Künsten oder Praktische aesthetik*, Vol I: Dietextile Kunst, Kunst und wissenschaft, Frankfurt, 1860-1863; 2nd ed. Friedrich Bruckmann, Munich, 1878-1879; Vol. II: Keramik, Tektonik, Stereotomie, Metallotecnik, Friedrich Bruckmann, München, 1863; based on the Italian translation, *Lo stile nelle arti tecniche e tettoniche, o estetica pratica: manuale per tecnici, artisti ed amatori*, by A.R. Burelli, C. Cresti, B. Gravagnuolo, and F. Tentori, preface by Vittorio Gregotti. Rome: Editori Laterza, 1992, p. 109.

[10] Homer, *Odyssey*, E, 455, 529.

[11] Vittorio Gregotti, *Op. cit.*, p. 23.

ty, durability, systems and so forth. In the nineteenth century, an important contribution to the art-technics debate came from Gottfried Semper, who believed that materials and technics had to be taken into consideration in any artistic practice. He stated that "technics" had become the word of the day. In speaking, it had been roughly equivalent to "art", but had then become the more often used word. The simple folk, the laity, still used the word "art", while the word "technics" sounded better in the mouths of clerics and specialists.[9]

From this it derives that the proper construction technique is a necessary, but not sufficient, condition for distinguishing architecture from construction. For this reason, the *Corso di tecnologia dell'architettura* (Course in architectural technology) emerged from Bairati and Muzio's teaching of "constructional elements" in the 1950s. They taught the details of construction organised in accordance with the classic scheme: retaining structures and foundations, bearing structures, roofing, partition walls, doors and windows, fixtures, facings, coatings, flooring. In 1964, with the arrival in Turin of Professor Ciribini, the course was radically changed and technology began to be taught as a *strumento per il progetto* (designing tool). Ciribini used this title as a blanket category to teach almost everything. His lessons substantially regarded "method", philosophy of planning, philosophy of standards, philosophy of design, philosophy of conception and management. Ciribini, too, held to the etymological definition of the term "technology" when he affirmed that "technology is the treatment and rule of execution of astute art",[10] in brief, "knowing why" (intention) and "knowing how", of which technics would be the "knowing what" (the way of being).

Ciribini's interpretation of technology as a discipline in support of planning and design is shared today by numerous architects. For Citterio as well, architecture is indissolubly bound to technological innovation, without it being, because of this, a crutch or an end, according to what Philip Johnson suggested. Citterio fully represents the figure of the "designer as a technician",[11] or better, the technician as a specialist, who shifts the skills of the trade, the manual dexterity of artistic practice, toward the capacity to think about and to know the rational processes of fabrication separately. It is no coincidence that Citterio is one of the few Italian designers recognised by industry for his capacity as a knowledge broker who can interpret the project in accordance to the principles of production organisation. Auguste Perret said, "il n'y a pas de détails dans la construction" (there are no details in construction). The same attachment to detail as an essential element in the definition – and hence in the quality – of an architectural work or an object is also found in Citterio. He excels in the art of the technique of detail – that is, of difference, discretion – and its morphological necessity in respect to the whole, to reveal the nature of a joint, or the rhythm and material of a surface. Technology is the means that allows Citterio to enter into the poetics of the detail, creating a perfect correspondence between form and function. A tireless attendee of tradeshows, Citterio is an omnivorous connoisseur of the most advanced production technologies and often is someone who offers suggestions for new technologies, touching a variety of industrial sectors with his broad ranging experience.

While in the 1960s technology as a science was grounded on knowledge of the use of materials in relation to structural loads, today evolution in structures is indissolubly linked to virtual design and planning. Technology has become a synonym for the application of informatics and telecommunication to the various human activities. Craftily invasive, and yet indispensable, technology, in its myriad possible forms, is everywhere. It unleashes the creativity of designers, or perhaps it kills it. The use of computer and digital technologies has allowed for the construction of astounding works. Think of the Centre Georges Pompidou, built in Paris in the 1970s by Renzo Piano and Richard Rogers. In addition to having been the manifesto of high-tech architecture, it was also one of the first projects to be designed entirely on a computer. Today, a rather outstanding example of the application of technology to architecture is the Guggenheim Museum in Bilbao designed by Frank Gehry, whose complex construction was made possible by the use of programs such as CATIA (Computer Aided Three-dimensional Interactive Application), which transformed studio models of the work into mathematical formulas. But there is another instrument offered by digital technology for virtual construction that is now used by architects, too: Virtual Reality Modelling Language (VRML). The Dutch group NOX designed the Water Pavilion, an example of "fluid architecture", in Rotterdam using VRML.

Antonio Citterio considers architecture and design, precisely for their connections with production techniques to be above all "the completion of a job, the noble aspect of human endeavour, endowed with a collective purpose as well as a subjective one precisely in that they are a product of art."[12] His is a highly specialised job with high ethical content to be developed for those enterprises like B&B Italia, Vitra, Flos and Technogym, to name just a few, who have invested in new materials and innovative technologies. But Citterio also creates works for advanced technology companies such as his PCs for Max Data (1997), his televisions for Brionvega (1999), interiors for Alfa Romeo (2000) and hospital structures for Malvestio (1992), where he proves that he knows how to optimise his resources – technological or productive – while keeping clearly in mind Adolf Loos's motto that there is no point in inventing something if it does not represent an improvement.

Technology for the Home

Technogym: Kinesis Personal; *B&B Italia:* Otto Chair; *Kartell:* Dolly, Mobil, Battista, Spoon

Citterio uses the effects of technological innovation to improve the conditions of use of objects, creating unusual crossbreeds, for example between furniture and fitness equipment. We see this in his *Kinesis Personal*, a home workout machine produced by Technogym. Introduced at the 2006 Salone del Mobile, *Kinesis* was the first example of a multipurpose fitness machine conceived to be part of the furniture. Technogym states that the *Kinesis* project embodies the idea of bringing the person back to the centre and leaving technology in the background, so that it will no longer be the person who has to adapt to technology, but technology that adapts to the person.[13] The patented "full gravity technology" is capable of providing movement in three dimensions while maintaining resistance at a fixed level, thus allowing the user to move freely. The machine is a platform for the free movement of the body, but also an object that integrates well into the homescape. With his usual elegance, Citterio has designed a piece of fitness equipment that is every bit as refined as a furnishing complement, where the horizontal pattern of the slats of the back is amplified by the mirrored surfaces, and the chrome-plated rigour of the stays creates effects on a par with sculpture. It is a machine that becomes part of the interior design, integrating gracefully

[12] Ibid., p. 110.

[13] Based on a Technogym press release in the *Financial Times*.

[14] Claudio Luti, cited in Alberto Bassi, *Antonio Citterio. Industrial Design.* Milan: Electa, 2004, p. 108.

[15] Ibid.

into the domestic space. *Kinesis* thus represents a successful synthesis of technology and design, uniting performance characteristics with aesthetics. It allows the user to do over two hundred different exercises in less than a square metre of floor space, and marks the beginning of a new conception of the home environment dedicated to psycho-physical wellbeing, as well as a new conception of a piece of fitness equipment as a furnishing element.

And similarly to the way design is associated with and exalts a complex technology such as "full gravity" in Technogym's *Kinesis*, in his *Otto Chair*, Citterio creates a lightweight and easily handled chair using dual component moulded plastics. Produced by B&B in 2006, *Otto Chair* is a collection of chairs characterised by its backrest composed of a matte "skeleton" with transparent coloured fields that enhance flexibility and highlight the structural tension. Here we find cutting-edge technology and user-friendly design in a chair whose appeal is based on its contrasts: chromatic, tactile, ergonomic. The chair is available in a chrome-plated version with a central rod stand, or in aluminium with four legs, with or without armrests or casters. This seating system offers additional proof of Citterio's capacity to think of design as a system.

Citterio's quest for integration between advanced technology and design finds one of its maximum expressions in his products for Kartell. "Unlike with other companies," claims Claudio Luti, company owner, "Citterio works to design a single piece or a series of pieces. The trolleys, which were the first objects we did together, required a long search for solutions."[14] And so we have the trolleys/tea tables *Battista*, *Leopoldo* and *Gastone*, the *Dolly* chair and the *Spoon* stool, which unite the formal elegance of the design with a sophisticated and solid structural system. In the *Dolly* chair (1996), for example, the characteristic element is the use of a new plastic, batch-dyed polypropylene modified by the addition of minerals, that can be made in different thicknesses without shrinkage problems. The versatile *Dolly* is offered in two versions: with the seat in whitened red oak, or in the same plastic as the rest of the structure. *Dolly* fits well in the home, in the office or in collective settings, and is characterised by being a stackable chair with armrests, where comfort is united with practicality of use. The same principles underlie Citterio's exploration of possibilities for trolleys, an object neglected by designers until the advent of *Battista* in 1991. "When I got married, in 1989, I was looking for a trolley, but couldn't find anything interesting on the market. So I designed one."[15] The ability to picture the user in the setting where he or she will use the product is now considered an extraordinarily valuable input in innovating new products: the greater the quality of the input, the greater the possibility for proposing radical innovations. And so here we have a moment of personal need leading to a process of thoughtful design of a traditional household object that is radically modified without, however, sacrificing its familiar flavour. *Battista*, *Leopoldo* and *Gastone* are a family of trolleys in steel, aluminium and plastic, which innovate the trolley, usually made of wood. In the heterogeneity of their forms, Citterio offers a contemporary image of the trolley, where the bending of the spring is the only concession to decoration in the structure, which is otherwise Euclidean in the shape of the top and the delicacy of the legs. The elements are reduced to a minimum and assembled in such a way as to reveal their structure.

The rigour of the structural skeleton finds consummate expression in *Mobil*, a drawer unit designed in 1994 that is still one of Kartell's best selling products and one that has given new impetus to plastic, modifying its perception as a cheap material. *Mobil* is a system of lightweight, portable, functional, strong and durable containers that adapt well to any space in the home or office, fulfilling a variety of purposes. Tops, shelves and drawers are available in three finishes: semitransparent, opaque and glossy in the version made of transparent Polymethylmetacrylate (PMMA). The drawers, alternating with the shelves and the tops, are the basic element in the system. *Mobil* is a versatile system with a range of possible configurations on casters or feet allowing it to be used in a variety of settings: bedrooms, living rooms, bathrooms, as a stand for the stereo, or in the office or studio as a drawer unit for the desk. "In this project," continues Luti, "the reduction of the elements to a minimum was of fundamental importance. It was a sort of deconstruction of the object. And then there was the union of plastic with the lightweight metal frame. *Mobil* is both one of our best-selling pieces and one that provides great visibility and recognisability."[16]

"When I designed *Mobil*," comments Citterio, "sand-finished transparent plastic did not exist. What happened afterwards – which products and how many of them were created starting from *Mobil* – is there for everyone to see. While looking at a coloured, sand-finished glass ashtray, I got the idea to obtain the same effect with plastic, which meant changing the moulding process of the raw material."[17]

A unifying thread running through Citterio's background is his dedication to innovation – product innovation, service innovation, process innovation – combining the most advanced technologies with traditional forms. In a world saturated with chairs and lamps, he succeeded in designing objects which, as Le Corbusier put it, "sing". Among these, the lamps *Kelvin* (2003) and *Lastra* (1998) for Flos represent an innovation in performance based on Citterio's observations of how lamps are *used*. *Lastra* grew out of Citterio's observation of the scenic representation of light in the United States, where it was associated with the rites of the new luxury before the same thing happened in Europe. It is a hanging lamp designed to dialogue with the table below it. It is a plate (*lastra*) of transparent tempered glass with six or eight (depending on the model) pressed glass diffusers painted white. The inspiring motif was the rear window defrosters on American cars, which also dictated the electrical transmission system. *Lastra* is a high-tech object whose formal minimalism is tempered by its dialectic with the table below. "*Lastra* is a technological household object," states Citterio, "that grew out of my attention to seeking solutions to a problem – that of direct light on the table – rather than out of a quest for form."[18] Hence, if the table becomes the stage for household rituals, then the lighting has to dramatically illuminate the scene. The concept that Citterio proposed to Flos was "a scenographic connotation of light."[19] *Lastra* is a surface hovering in the air, in a specular relationship with the table below it, whose surface it doubles. Its orientable spotlights reproduce on the domestic scale the drama of stage lighting found in American interiors.

Technology for the Workplace

Flos: Lastra, Kelvin; *Ansorg:* lighting systems; *Esprit, Amsterdam and Antwerp; Ermenegildo Zegna, Milan*

"Why do young people believe in technics?" wondered Gio Ponti, and immediately responded, "Because of technical morality."[20] In the sudden and flighty rushes of con-

[16] Ibid., p. 109.

[17] Matteo Porrino, interview with Antonio Citterio, Parma Architecture Festival, 21 April 2005.

[18] Alberto Bassi, *Op. cit.*, p. 142.

[19] Francesco Zurlo, "L'osservazione inconsapevole", in F. Zurlo, R. Cagliano, G. Simonelli, R. Verganti, *Innovare con il design, il caso del settore dell'illuminazione in Italia*. Milan: Il Sole 24 ore, 2002, p. 216.

[20] Gio Ponti, *Amate l'architettura*. Genoa: Editrice Vitali e Ghianda, 1957, p. 250.

[21] Ibid.

[22] Conversation with the author, June 2006.

temporary life, speaking of morals and ethics of work may appear to be decidedly *démodé*. And yet Citterio shows us that a contemporary designer may prefer the "morality of technics" over the narcissism of the personal mark. If, as Ponti affirms, "the purposefulness (*Zwecklichkeit*) of a product requires, a priori, the use of materials that best lend themselves to its creation and the use of specific technical procedures . . . then formal and aesthetic questions automatically lead to the issue of materials."[21]

The use of new materials does indeed derive from technological research, but their application in different types of products and their correspondence to the form and function of an object fall within the purview of the designer. While in Citterio's *Lastra*, light represents a precise point of reference, and not just a question of function, within the dwelling space, in a similar manner *Kelvin*, created for Flos in 2004, is a reflection on the orientable clamp-on lamp, the reworking of a classic model using advanced technology. The dual-layer diffuser has an inner reflector in aluminium and an outer polycarbonate shell that allows the user to handle it without getting burned. "In *Kelvin*, the diffuser functions like a thermos," says Citterio. "You can touch it and it isn't hot; you can use it to regulate the light. It provides different responses to different needs. This lamp took four years of work, because it had to compete with classics on the market such as *Tolomeo* and *Tizio*, which are benchmarks in table lamps."[22] Citterio explores the spring system and, as in *Lastra*, constructional details. Springs and clamps are deliberately left visible according to the principle of structural honesty that represents a characteristic trait in Citterio's work: revealing the structure and its component elements to communicate both technological allure and ease of use.

While with *Kelvin* the innovative aspect derives from observation of the new situations and contexts of use, in the Ansorg lighting system, formal discretion has become the main quality making it suitable for application in exhibition settings. Ansorg is a company in the Vitra group and the *Elettra* (1993), *Quadra* (1994), *Camera* (1996), *Alumina* (1998) and *Brick* (2002) lighting systems represent the response to the demand for flexibility and neutrality in exhibition spaces. The lamps are constructed of two materials that respond to well distinguished needs: the natural anodised aluminium of the inner reflector acts as a heat dissipater, while the outer plastic shell allows the user to grasp and orient the light without getting burned. The spot lamps, such as *Cargo* (1990) and *Kado* (1999), are designed for use in exhibition spaces such as the Vitra shop.

The conceptions that have marked office and exhibition space design in the past are plotted on a new coordinate system associated with communications technology and a new vision of production and relational dynamics. Company offices, service and Internet companies, studios of fashion designers and professional studios are emblematic of a way of interpreting the workspace that is no longer standard, but the result of a design process that has to satisfy needs of corporate image, functionality and human resource organisation. They are containers that bring together exquisitely architectural contents, as we see, among other examples, in the Esprit buildings in Amsterdam and Antwerp. Together with the building in Milan, these represented Citterio's first opportunity to experiment with the global project, where the company identity (and that of its designer) could find a clear response in the architectural project as well as in the internal architecture and decor.

The Esprit buildings in Amsterdam and Antwerp are historical buildings that have been refurbished and reworked. The Antwerp building was completely demolished, preserving only the external walls by means of a system of mechanical buttresses that made it possible to excavate two underground floors before rebuilding the entire interior of the building. Both buildings represent regional group headquarters with offices and showrooms on the upper floors and a megastore on the ground floor. In both the Amsterdam and Antwerp buildings, which were begun shortly after the Milan worksite opened, the project guidelines called for the reuse of existing industrial buildings and the preservation of a factory spirit in their organisation. Following on the Milan experience, galvanised steel and stairway design became the dominant characteristics in these two projects.

The hot galvanising process both finishes and protects steel for structures, frames and especially for exterior uses. "In the projects for Esprit, the theme of natural materials, without skins, led us to use this process for all metal elements: stairways, railings, door and window frames and doors," comments Patricia Viel. "The stairways, which are open, visible, vertical spaces used to express the complex section of these projects, were a project in their own right."[23] The Esprit stairways are structures with galvanised steel frames. The design of the treads and risers in bent and perforated sheeting made it possible to achieve continuity in stair detail. The perforation of the sheeting, which is indispensable for allowing the natural lighting from the skylights to filter through, was done with a specially designed oval punch in a diagonally staggered pattern. The punch design meets all safety regulations. The tubular railings, the vertical partition mesh and the large doors and windows represent a vocabulary of recurring elements in the project, clearly derived from the industrial landscape.

It is the same landscape that characterises the Milanese offices of Ermenegildo Zegna, built in 2004–2007 in collaboration with the Beretta studio. Located in the former Riva Calzoni plant in an industrial area converted over to fashion, the new Zegna group building conserves little of the pre-existing building. It contains offices, showrooms and a theatre-auditorium for the different divisions of the group. The preexisting industrial building was razed to make way for a new structure that borrows only a few morphological elements from the industrial aesthetic, such as the shed roof. The organisation and distribution of spaces creates a succession of inner courts that look outwards through a long glassed-in concourse connecting to the entrance on Via Stendhal. The homogeneous exterior texture of the structure is fragmented in the rapid horizontal succession of exhibition spaces (a showroom for each of the group's collections) that are laid out around a glassed-in patio, which serves as a spatial circulation node and visual centre of mass of the various activities going on within the complex. The structural clarity counterbalances the complexity of layout in the luminous reflections in the large windows, which become the spatial centre for the entire complex.

Technology for the City and Territory
Company day-care centre, Verona

The company day-care centre, created in 2006 for GlaxoSmithKline in Verona, offers a service to the surrounding territory as well as to the employees of the multinational pharmaceutical company. Some one thousand five hundred people work on the GSK

[23] Patricia Viel, conversation with the author, November 2006.

[24] Conversation with the author, September 2006.

[25] Ibid.

[26] Patricia Viel, conversation with the author, September 2006.

[27] Ibid.

"campus" in administrative, commercial, production and research capacities. The campus is thus a densely inhabited organism, a metaphor for the organisation and dynamics of a city. The organisational culture is Anglo-Saxon, characterised by strong interaction between the individual, the team and company objectives. Antonio Citterio was first asked to design the President's office and then the day-care centre.

The entire project is part of the company objectives to improve people's quality of life, allowing them to do more, feel better and live longer. Alongside facilities for work, it dedicated approximately 680 square metres to a day-care centre. The entire building is realised using technology to minimise energy consumption for heating and air conditioning. It is characterised by eco-compatible architecture having low environmental impact and using, in spite of the tight budget, natural materials such as wood which "we had already applied widely in the project for the President's office," explains Citterio, "with the intention of creating a very homey setting in an otherwise very technical environment. Light-coloured wood and the colour orange are the basic motifs of the various campus redesign project modules."[24]

The day-care centre is situated in a long, irregularly shaped court with a continuous perimeter and a peaked roof. The conditions of the layout imposed "an introverted floor plan that carved out a safe space protected by the corner of the property line."[25] An internal garden links the surrounding structures, whose irregular pattern breaks up the monotony of the rectangular geometry and echoes the interplay of roof slopes, in line with a correspondence between indoors and outdoors that characterises Citterio's most recent works. "The architectural design orbits around the large wooden roof," states Patricia Viel, "with its different slopes and heights, mainly supported on a perimeter wall made of prefabricated wooden panels. The doors and windows in the façade overlooking the garden are made of wood and aluminium and allow connection between indoor activities and the outdoor play area."[26] The interior is characterised by the closed cells of the service areas and the children's rest area in the more intimate and protected zone. The classrooms are served by a distribution pathway that leads through the closed cells, but is not a simple closed corridor.

In spite of the introverted nature of its use, this building plays a very strong aggregative role in adherence to company philosophy and its sensitivity to its employees. "Rendering a simple geometry complex," explains Citterio, "is an operation that almost always brings good results because it enriches the visual perception of the architecture. Making it buildable, however, is not always feasible. The structure and the shell are completely built of wood and thus move the building closer to the world of objects than to that of architecture. The building was produced and preassembled in the factory, and final assembly took place on site."[27]

The innovation represented by this building is more a question of process than product. The visual grace and equilibrium of the day-care centre are united with a low environmental impact and a design-for-assembly process aimed at reducing the number of constructional components because, as Marshall McLuhan might have put it, technology is an extension of our bodies and our senses.

TECHNOLOGY

TECHNOLOGY

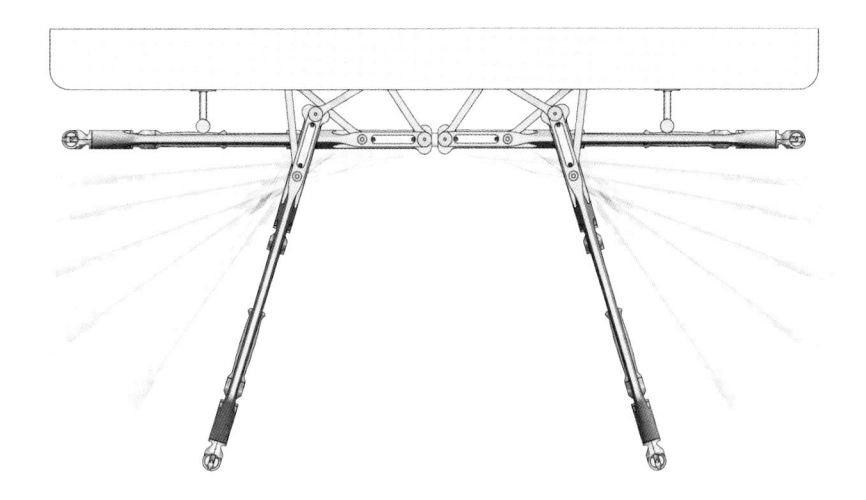

2006 Kinesis Personal, Technogym

with Toan Nguyen

Citterio uses the effects of technological innovation to improve the conditions of use of objects, creating unusual crossbreeds, for example between furniture and fitness equipment. We see this in his *Kinesis Personal*, a home workout machine produced by Technogym.

TECHNOLOGY

TECHNOLOGY

TECHNOLOGY

Citterio fully represents the figure of the "designer as a technician", or better, the "technician as a specialist", who shifts the skills of the trade, the manual dexterity of artistic practice, toward the capacity to think about and to know the rational processes of fabrication separately.

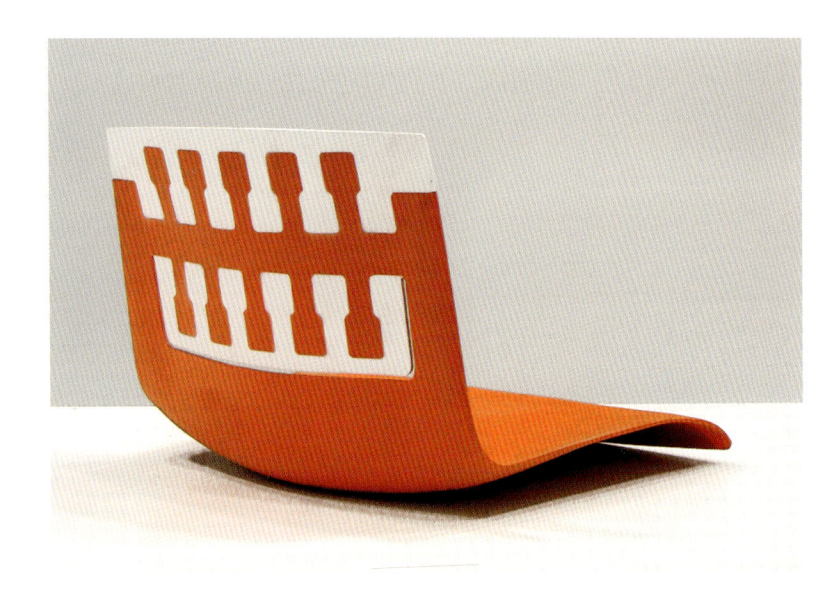

2006 Otto Chair, B&B Italia

with Toan Nguyen

And similarly to the way design is associated with and exalts a complex technology such as "full gravity" in Technogym's *Kinesis*, in his *Otto Chair*, Citterio creates a lightweight and easily handled chair using dual component moulded plastics.

TECHNOLOGY

1991 Battista, Kartell

with Glen Oliver Löw

Battista, Leopoldo and *Gastone* are a family of trolleys in steel, aluminium and plastic, where trolleys have traditionally been made of wood. In the heterogeneity of their forms, they offer a contemporary image of the trolley, where the bending of the spring is the only concession to decoration in the structure, which is otherwise Euclidean in the shape of the top and the delicacy of the legs.

"When I got married, in 1989, I was looking for a trolley, but couldn't find anything interesting on the market. So I designed one."
Antonio Citterio

TECHNOLOGY

> **1994 Mobil, Kartell**

with Glen Oliver Löw
Compasso d'Oro 1995
On permanent display at MoMA, New York, and the Centre Pompidou, Paris

The rigour of the structural skeleton finds consummate expression in *Mobil*, a drawer unit designed in 1994 that is still one of Kartell's best selling products and one that has given new impetus to plastic, modifying its perception as a cheap material.

< **1996 Dolly, Kartell**

with Glen Oliver Löw
On permanent display at the Centre Pompidou, Paris

In the *Dolly* chair, the characteristic element is the use of a new plastic, batch-dyed polypropylene modified by the addition of minerals, that can be made in different thicknesses without shrinkage problems.

237

TECHNOLOGY

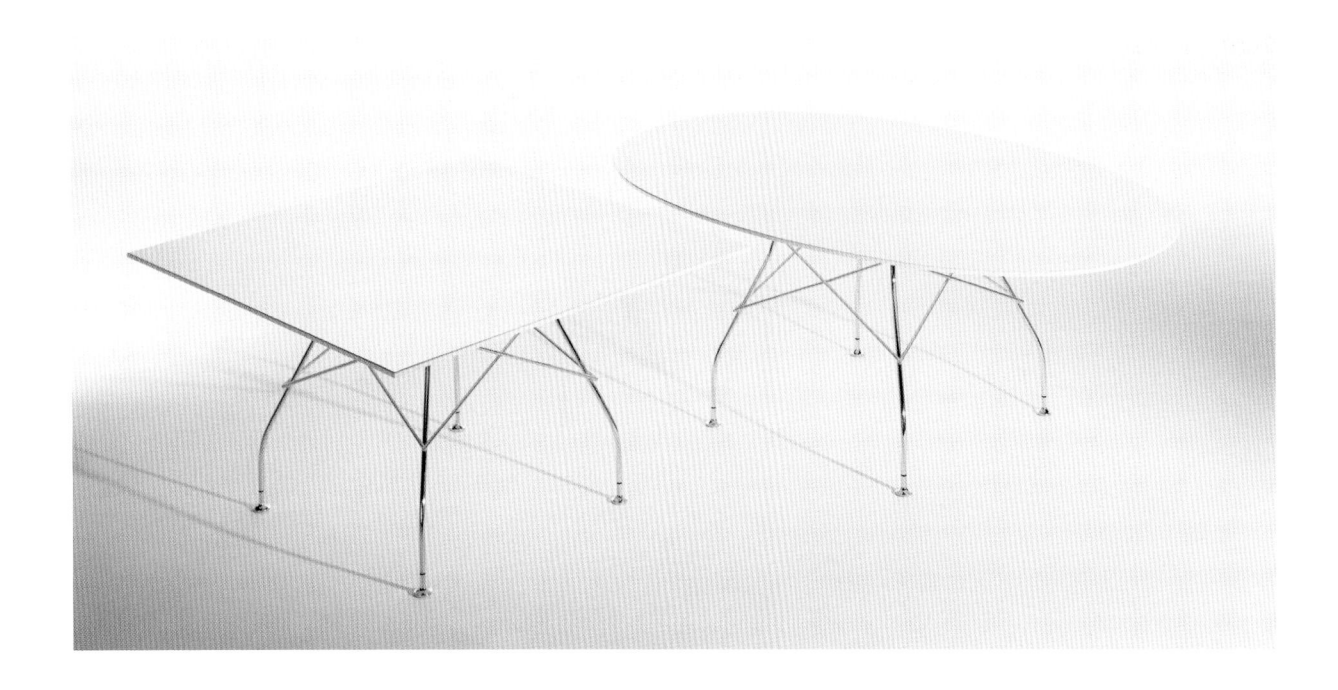

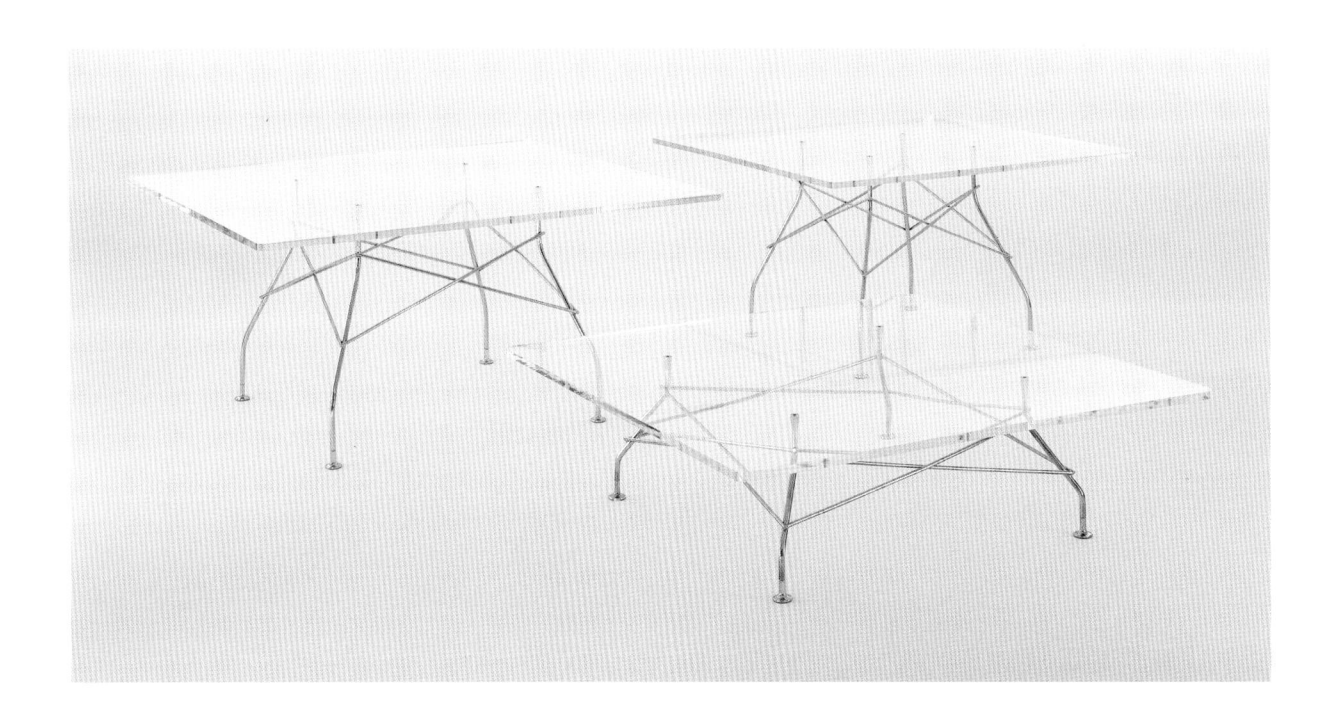

< **2000 Glossy, Kartell**
with Glen Oliver Löw

> **2006 Flip, Kartell**
with Toan Nguyen

TECHNOLOGY

> 2005 Spoon Chair, Kartell
< 2002 Spoon, Kartell

with Toan Nguyen

TECHNOLOGY

241

TECHNOLOGY

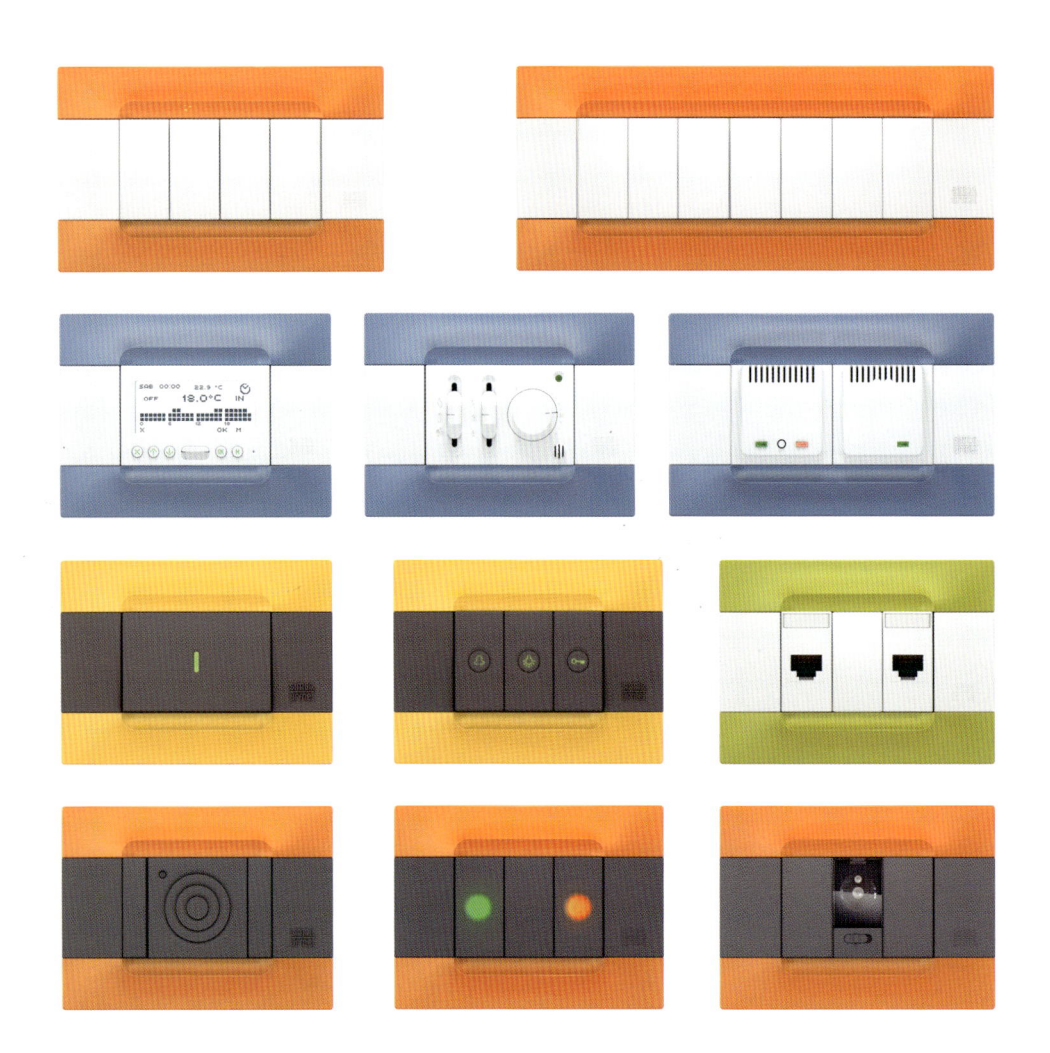

242

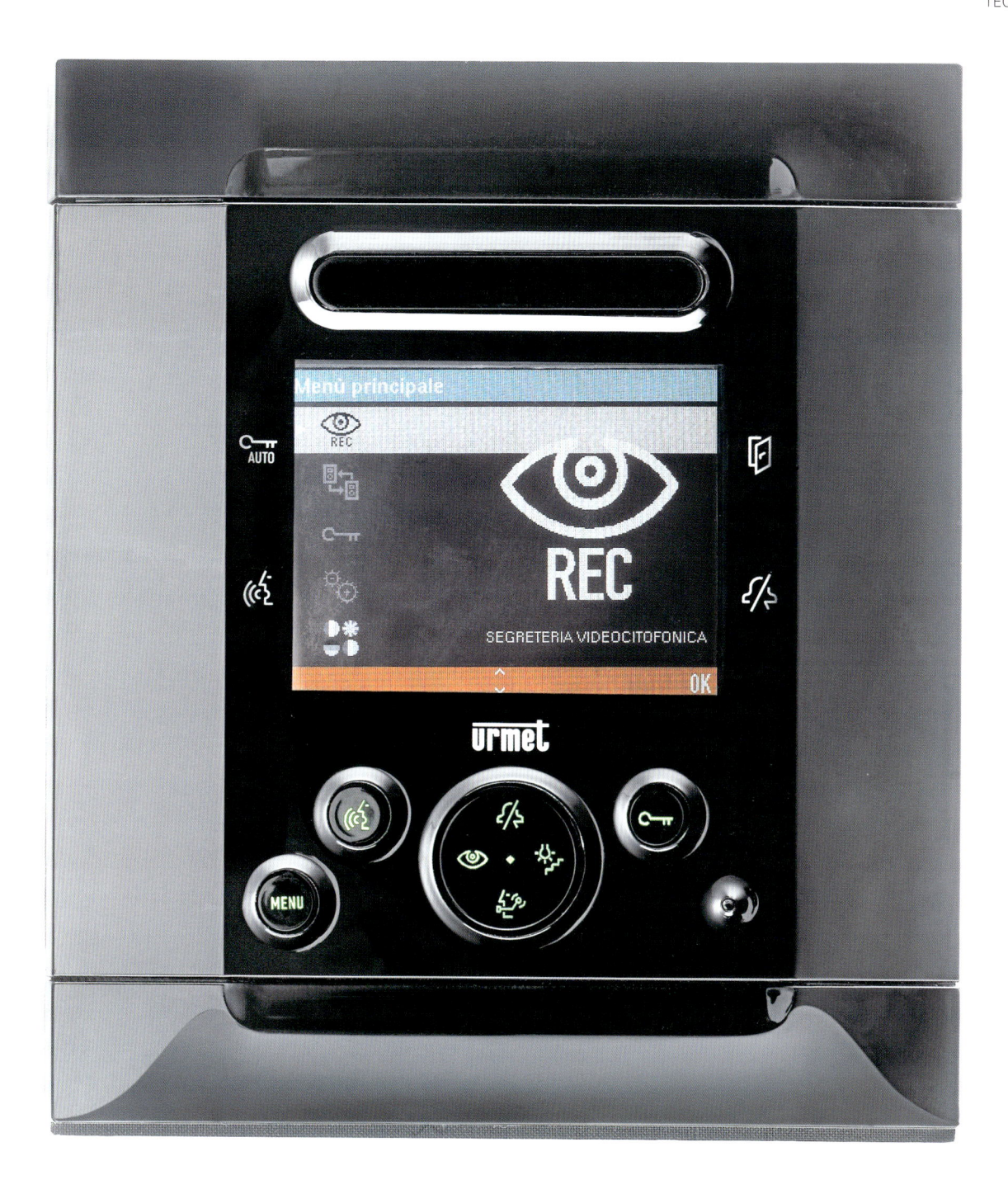

TECHNOLOGY

< 2007 Nea, Simon Urmet
> 2007 Folio, Simon Urmet

with Toan Nguyen

TECHNOLOGY

1998 Lastra, Flos

with Glen Oliver Löw

Lastra grew out of Citterio's observation of the scenic representation of light in the United States, where it was associated with the rites of the new luxury before the same thing happened in Europe. It is a hanging lamp designed to dialogue with the table below it. It is a plate (*lastra*) of transparent tempered glass with six or eight (depending on the model) pressed glass diffusers painted white. The inspiring motif was the rear window defrosters on American cars, which also dictated the electrical transmission system.

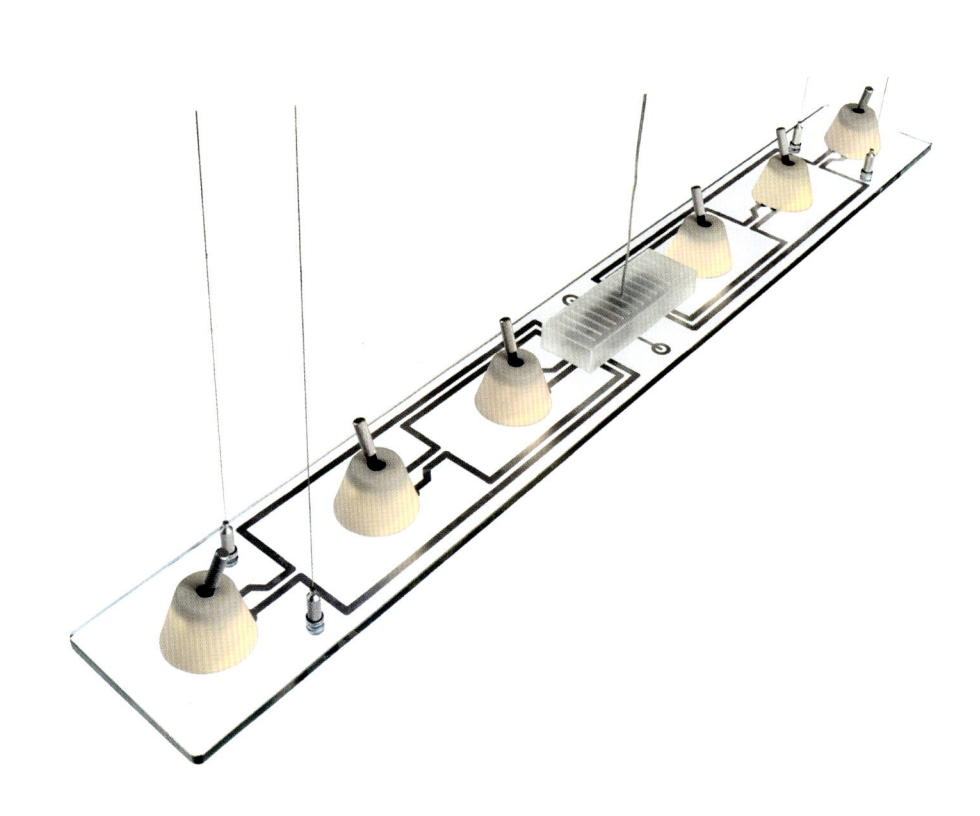

2003 Kelvin, Flos

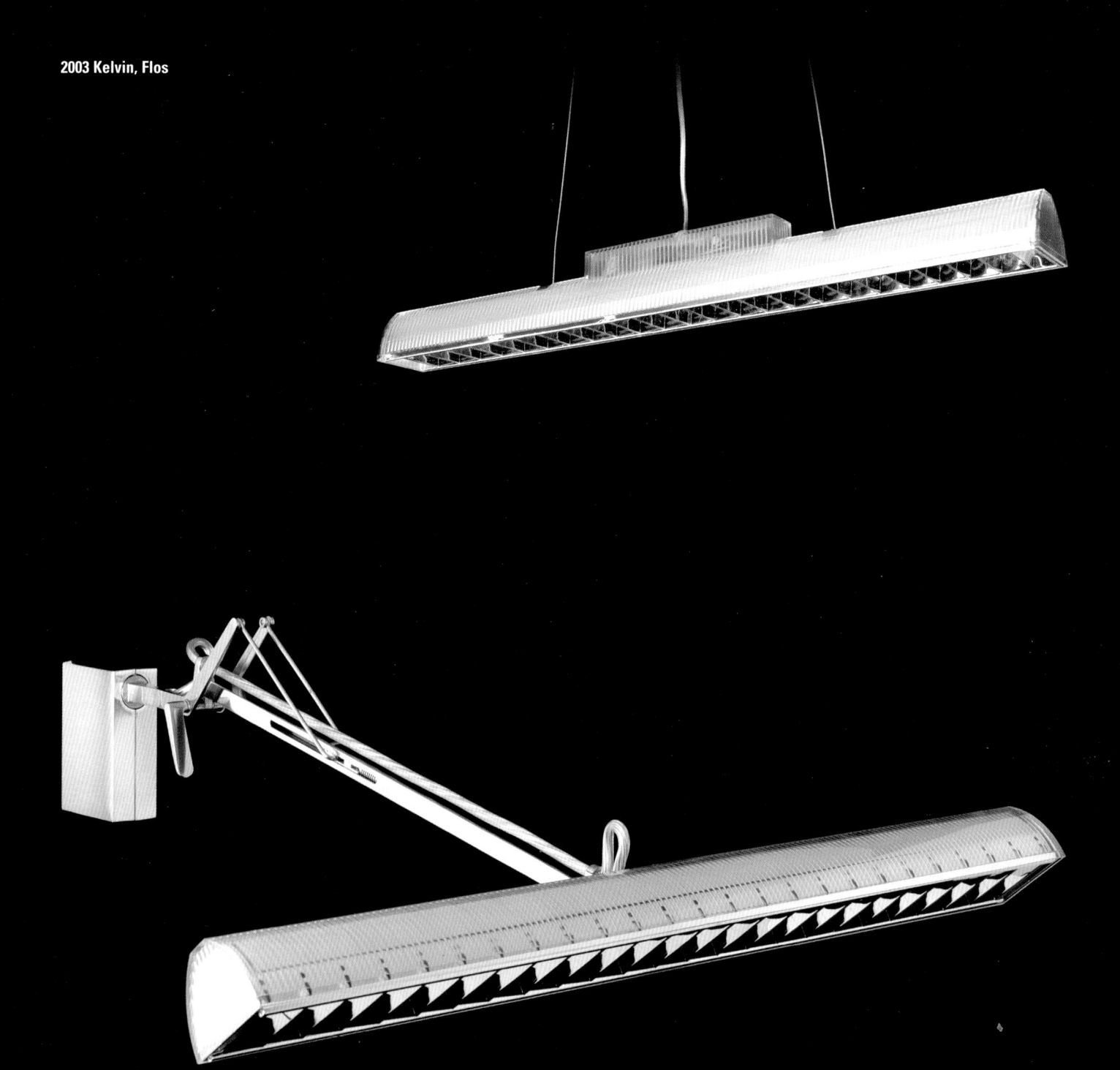

TECHNOLOGY

2003 Kelvin, Flos

with Toan Nguyen
Red Dot Design Award 2004

Kelvin is a reflection on the orientable clamp-on lamp, the reworking of a classic model using advanced technology. The dual-layer diffuser has an inner reflector in aluminium and an outer polycarbonate shell that allows the user to handle it without getting burned.

"There is no point in inventing something if it does not represent an improvement."
Adolf Loos

TECHNOLOGY

1993 Elettra, Ansorg

with Glen Oliver Löw

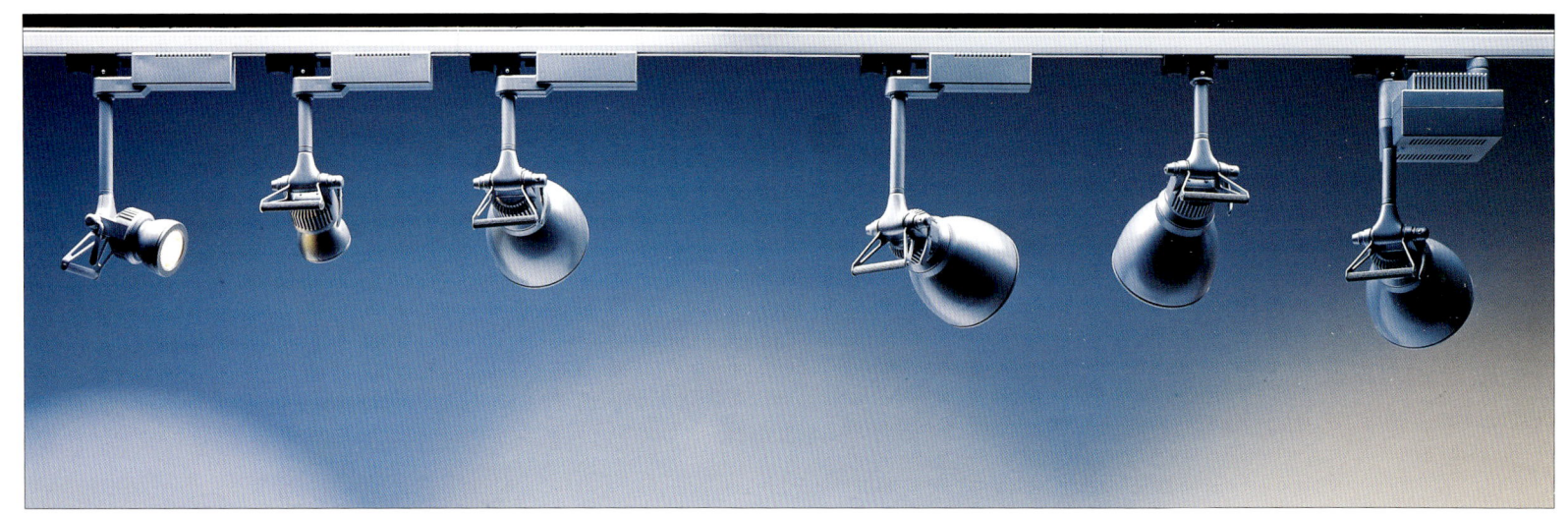

TECHNOLOGY

2002 Brick, Ansorg

1996 Camera, Ansorg

with Glen Oliver Löw

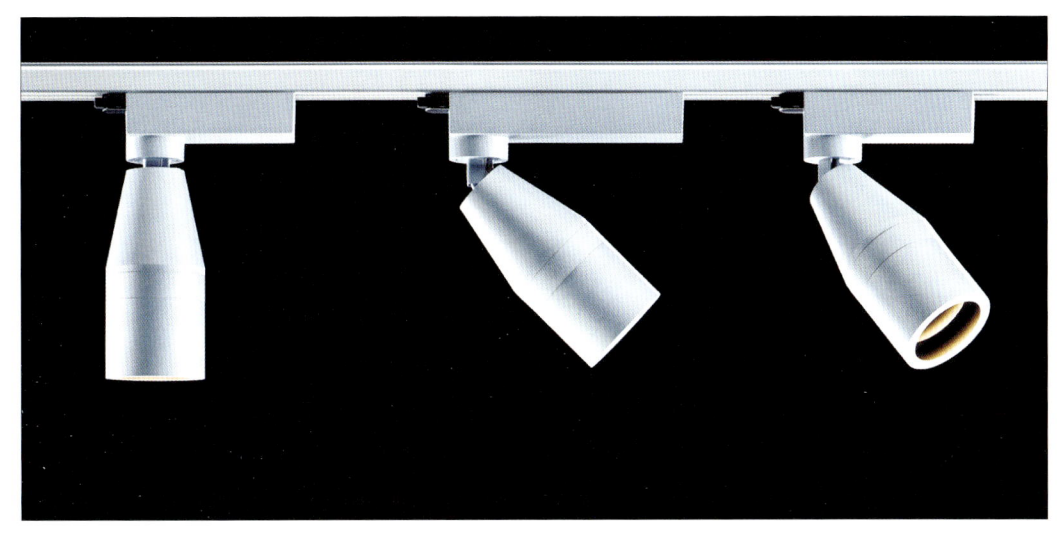

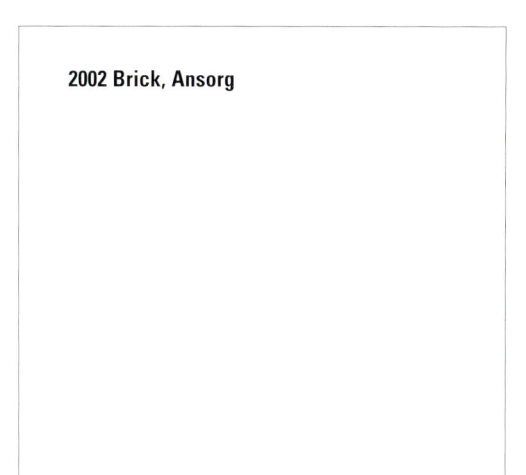

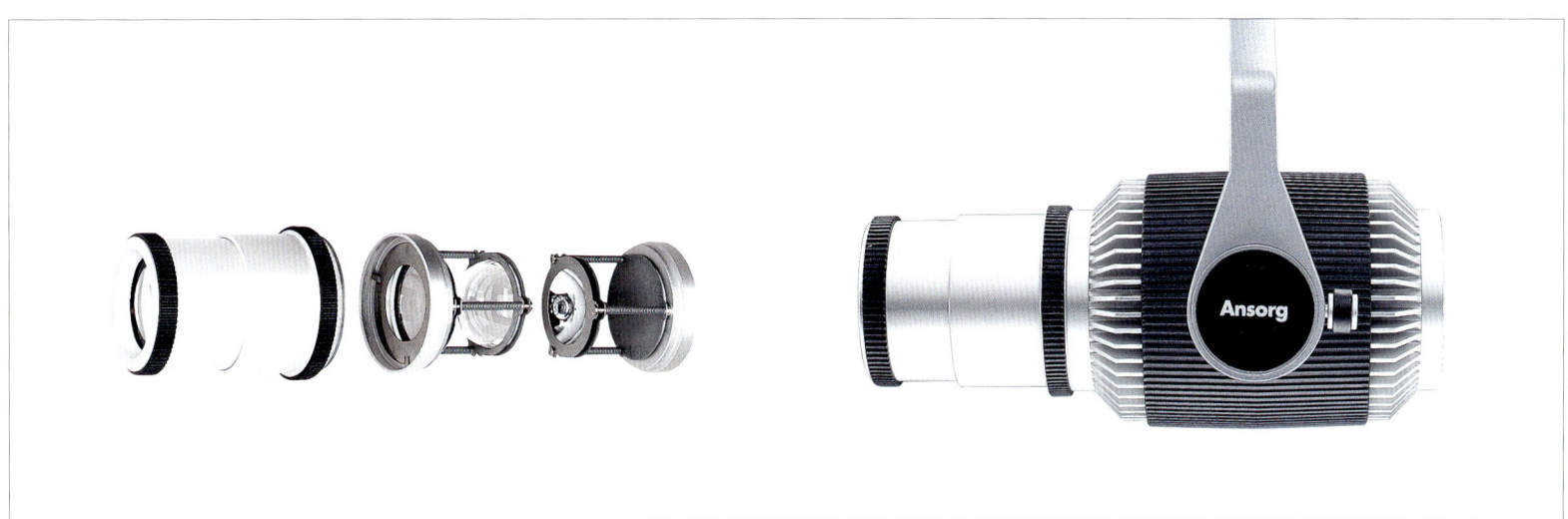

TECHNOLOGY

1985–1987 Esprit, Amsterdam

Showroom, café, offices
4,000 sq. m

"In the projects for Esprit, the theme of natural materials, without skins, led us to use this process for all metal elements: stairways, railings, door and window frames and doors. The stairways, which are open, visible, vertical spaces used to express the complex section of these projects, were a project in their own right."
Patricia Viel

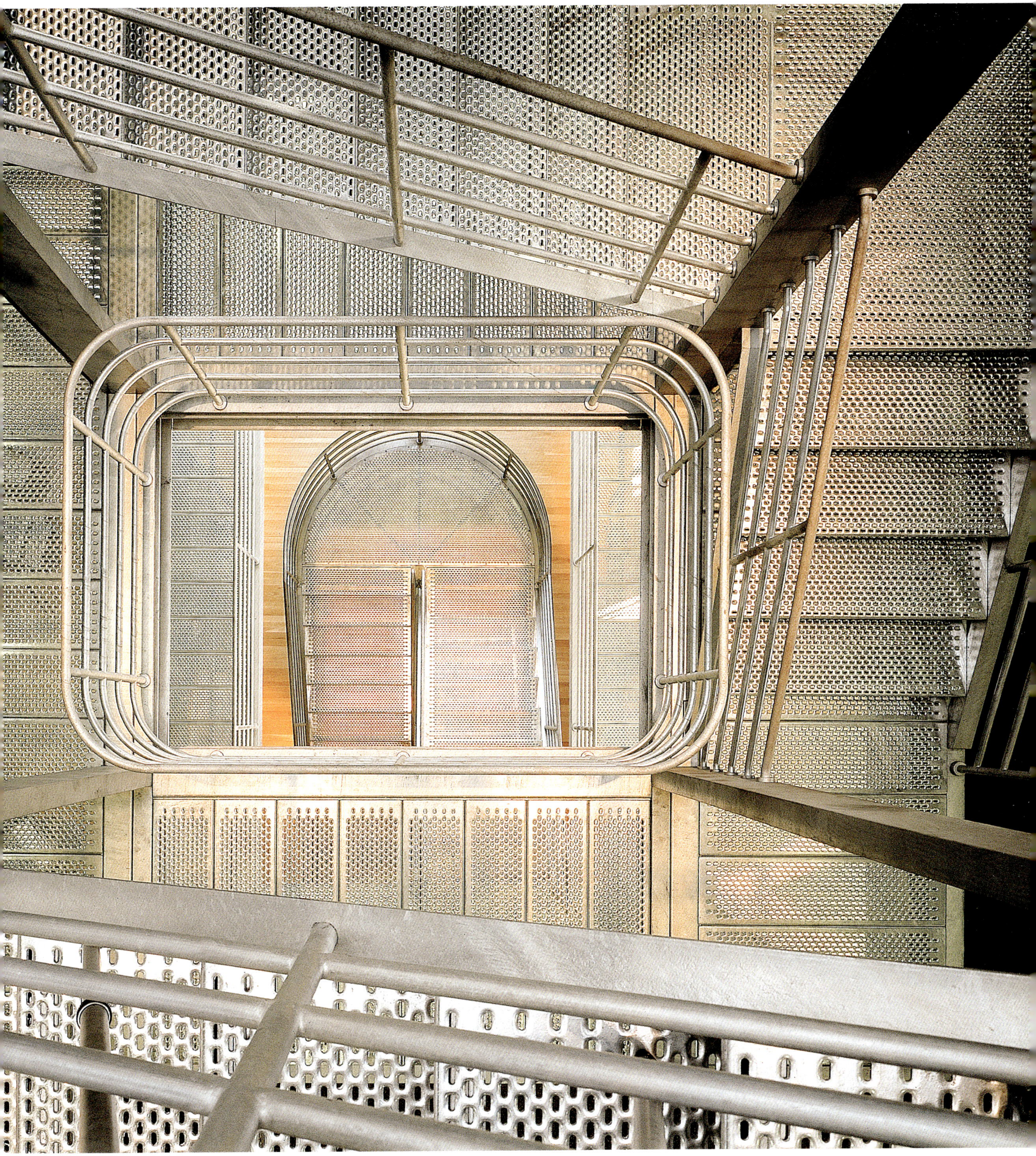

TECHNOLOGY

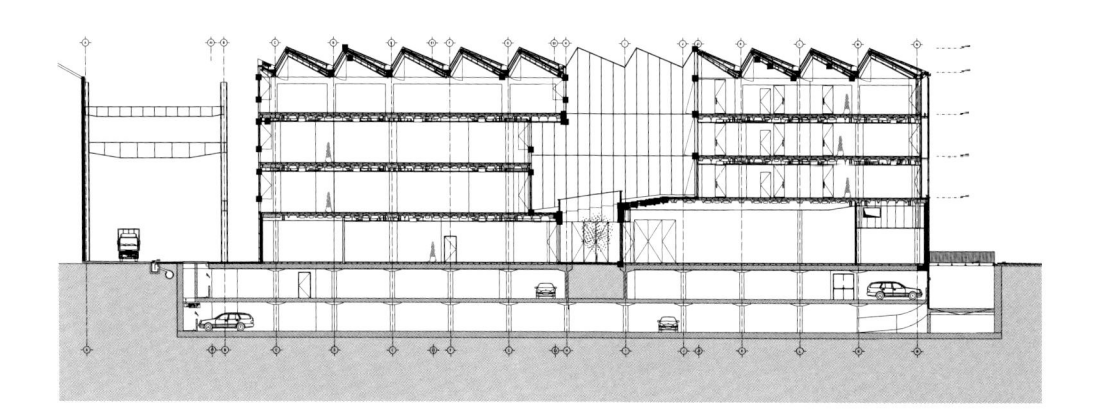

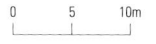

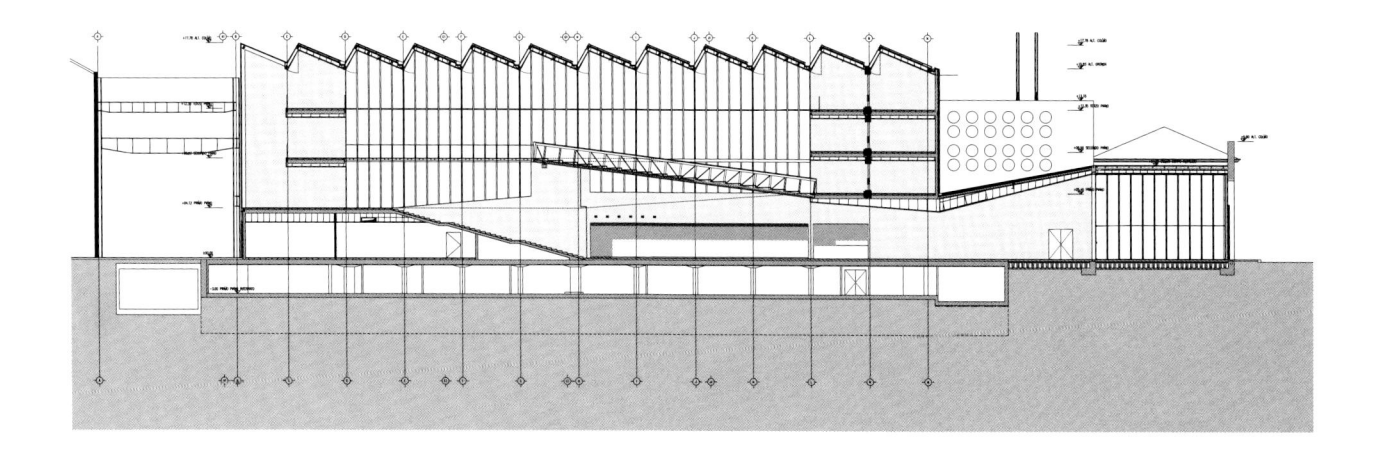

2004–2007 Ermenegildo Zegna, Milan

*New corporate headquarters of the Ermenegildo Zegna Group
Project partner: Studio Architettura Beretta Associati*

The structural clarity counterbalances the complexity of layout in the luminous reflections in the large windows, which become the spatial centre for the entire complex.

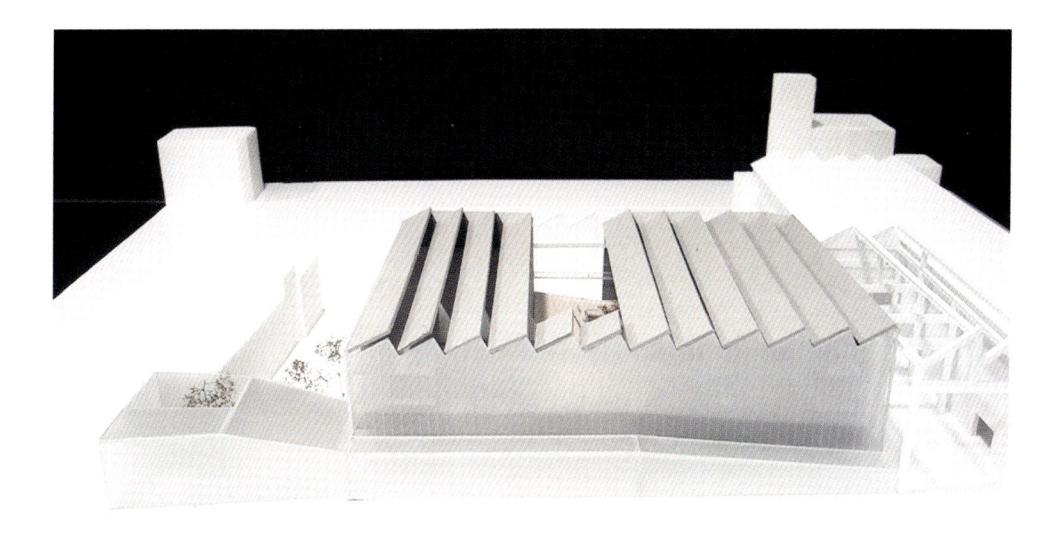

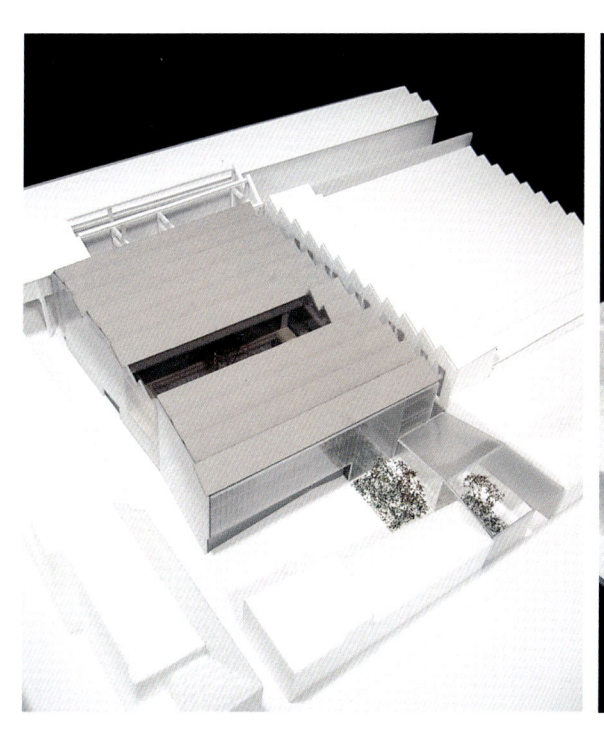

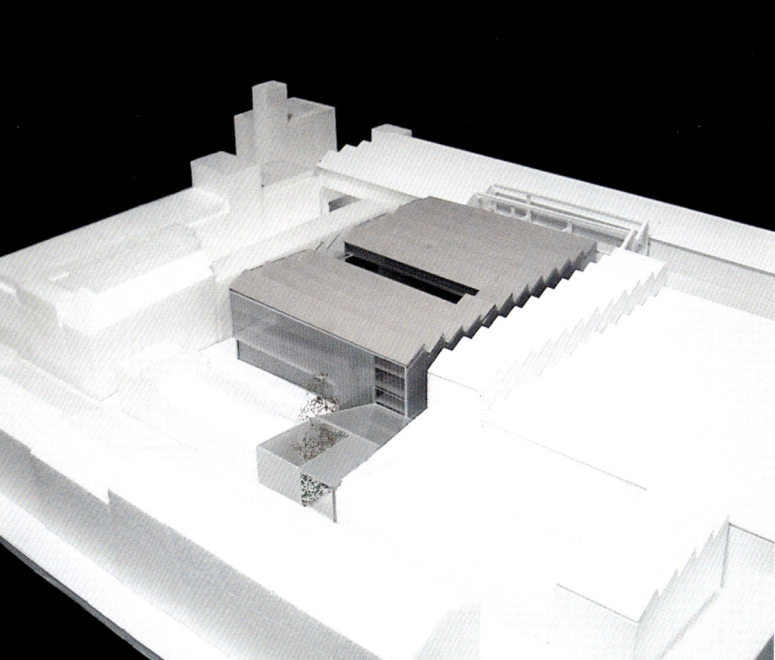

TECHNOLOGY

"Antonio Citterio considers architecture and design, precisely for their connections with production techniques to be above all the completion of a job, the noble aspect of human endeavour, endowed with a collective purpose as well as a subjective one precisely in that they are a product of art."
Vittorio Gregotti

TECHNOLOGY

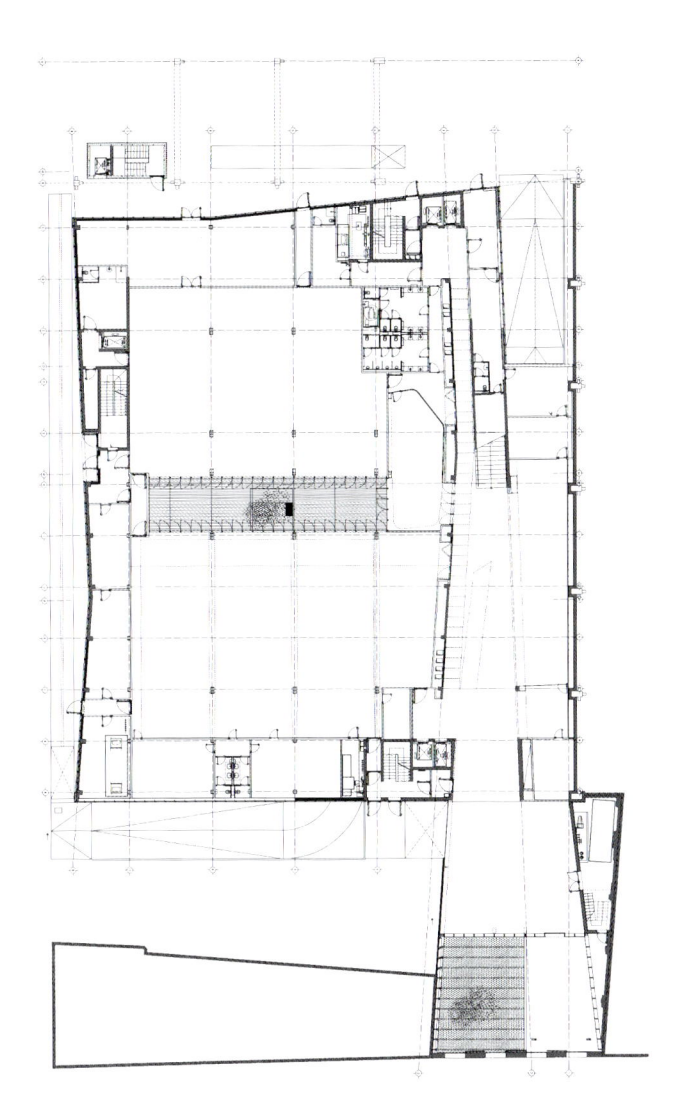

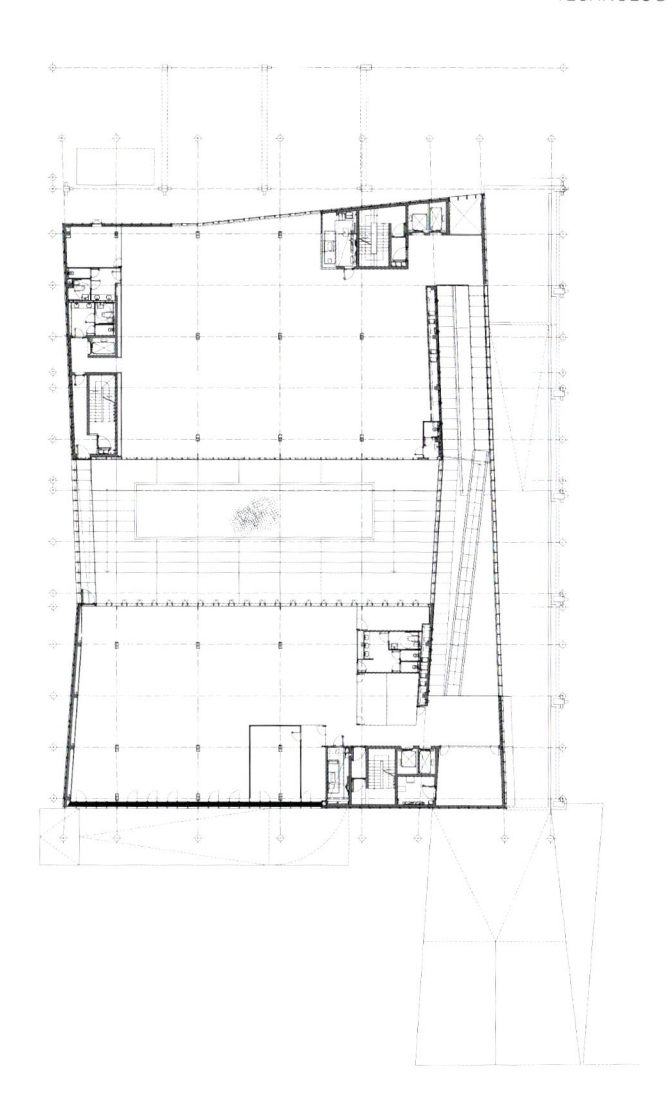

255

TECHNOLOGY

2004–2005 Company Day-care Centre, Verona
420 sq. m, 560 sq. m of garden

"The architectural design orbits around the large wooden roof with its different slopes and heights, mainly supported on a perimeter wall made of prefabricated wooden panels. The doors and windows in the façade overlooking the garden are made of wood and aluminium and allow connection between indoor activities and the outdoor play area."
Patricia Viel

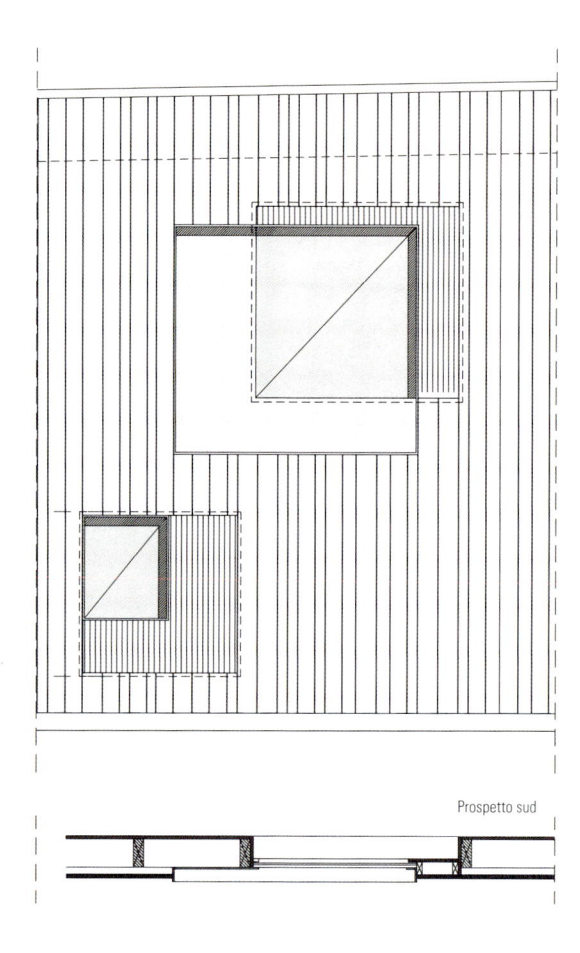

Prospetto sud

TECHNOLOGY

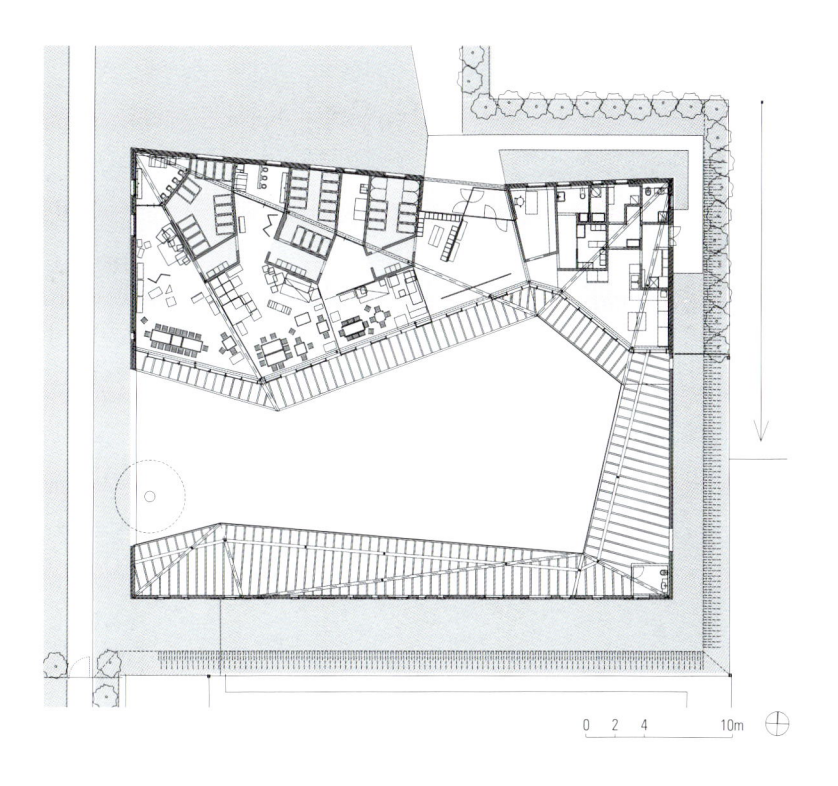

TECHNOLOGY

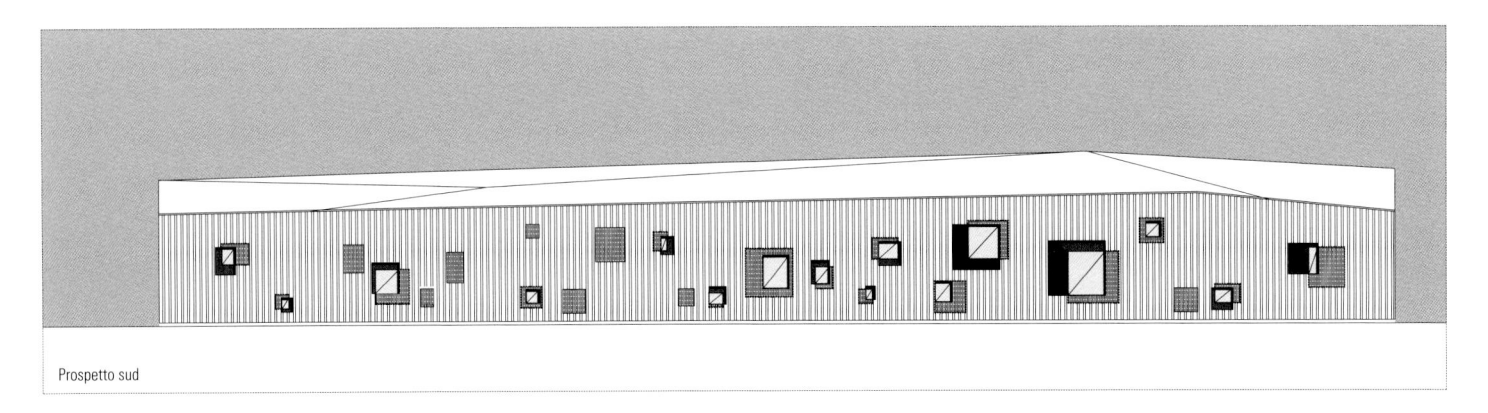

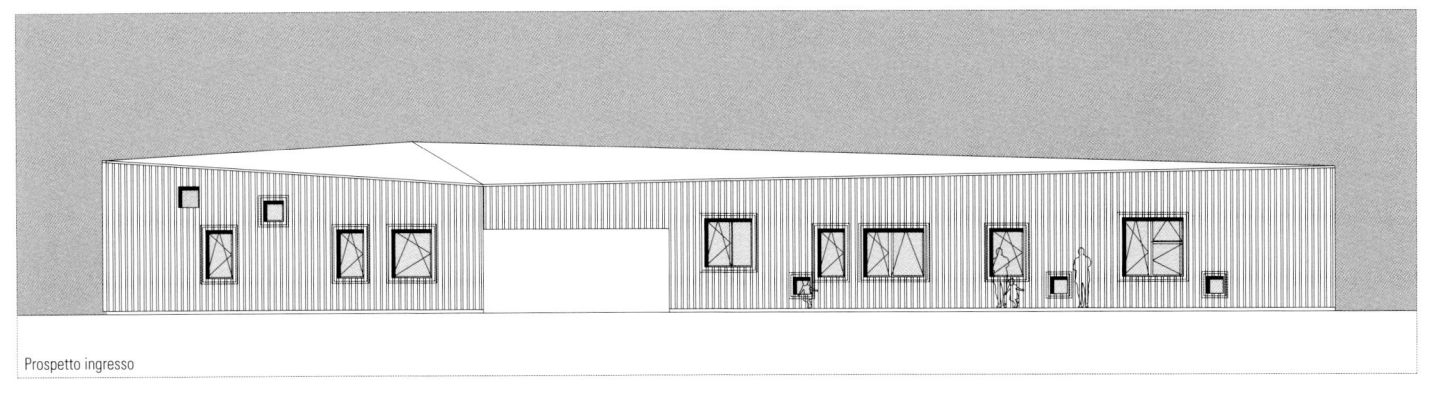

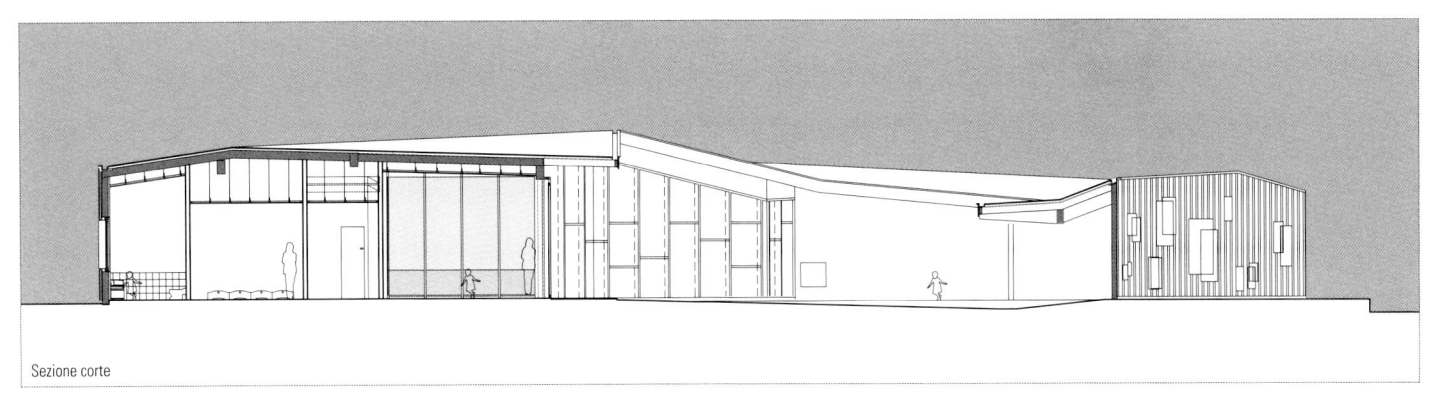

Prospetto sud

Prospetto interno corte

Prospetto ingresso

Sezione corte

0 2 4 10m

TECHNOLOGY

ECONOMY.6

Philip Johnson was of the opinion that being able to build on a tight budget was certainly a virtue, but questioned whether the result could be called art. Were not all the world's most famous structures costly? He once tried to work out how much it would have cost to build another Parthenon. He figured that it would have taken most of the labour and brainpower exerted in America over the previous thirty years and would have cost around twenty billion dollars. Of course that is not so much when we think that a trip to the moon costs forty billion. But with all that marble and all that bronze, for the architectural profession it would have been heaven.[1]

These words set Johnson apart from the tradition of American architecture, where so much attention is paid to the tradeoffs between profit and creativity. On this topic, in an article written in 1900 titled "The Financial Importance of Rapid Building", Cass Gilbert described one of his extraordinary skyscrapers as "a machine that makes the land pay".[2] It would seem that Gilbert had been quite impressed in 1893 by an impassioned speech by Barr Ferree, editor of *Engineering Magazine*, at the annual conference of the American Institute of Architects. Ferree commented that American architecture has more to do with economy than with art. A building had to pay or no entrepreneur would ever invest in its construction. For Ferree, this was both the cross to bear and the delight of architecture.[3] Taking things further, his colleague, the real estate expert George Hill, writing in *The Architectural Record*,[4] reminded architects that the function of a commercial building was to produce profit, and that consequently, the architectural project is strongly conditioned by economic factors.

In more recent years, Carol Willis, author of *Form Follows Finance*,[5] pointed out that the commercial nature of architecture must not necessarily be considered an impediment to good quality – as Johnson seems to suggest. On the contrary, budget limitations often generate innovative solutions and groundbreaking experimentation. The history of twentieth-century architecture, especially in the chapters dedicated to the European avant-garde movements which were more sensitive to relations with mass mechanisation, contains numerous testimonials in this regard. This is the scenario for Antonio Citterio's work, for whom the relation to the budget is part of the logic of industrial production and something that cannot be ignored by the designer. "Architecture and industrial design must per force recognise," he says, "the relation between an object and its market. Industry often has to make large investments to make an object recognised on the market. Many architects and designers are not concerned with this aspect, erroneously believing that creativity must not be sullied by economic considerations. But it cannot be denied that in architecture and in industrial design there is an economy that constrains the budget and therefore the project. But there is also an urban economy in which the building will have to find its place, a national economy like the one that favoured the birth of Italian Design, and an economy of details, materials and forms."[6]

In this regard, Willis, director of the Skyscaper Museum of New York and discerning critic of American architecture, also believes that some of the icons of twentieth-century American architecture, such as the Empire State Building, are masterpieces not just because they were designed by great architects, but especially because they represent an intelligent synthesis of architecture and economics.

The relationship between profit and design is historically one of the essential components of commercial architecture, but it

[1] Philip Johnson, based on a speech at the Eleventh Annual Northeast Regional Conference of the American Institute of Architects, Oceanlake, Oregon, on 12 October 1962, in Philip Johnson, *Verso il Postmoderno. Genesi di una deregulation creativa*. Genoa: Costa&Nolan, 1985, p. 107.

[2] Cass Gilbert, "The Financial Importance of Rapid Building", *Engineering Record*, 30 June 1900, 41, p. 624. The article is cited in the excellent piece by Sharon Irish, "A Machine that Makes the Land Pay: The West Street Building in New York", *Technology and Culture*, April 1989, no. 30, pp. 376–397.

[3] Barr Ferree, "Economic Conditions of Architecture in America", in *Proceedings of the 20th-Century Annual Convention of the American Institute of Architects*. Chicago: Inland Architect, 1893, p. 231.

[4] George Hill, "Wasted Opportunities", *Architectural Record*, 1893, no. 3, p. 436.

[5] Carol Willis, *Form Follows Finance*. New York: Princeton Architectural Press, 1995.

[6] Antonio Citterio, conversation with the author, July 2006.

[7] Thomas Bender, *A Nation among Nations: America's Place in World History*. New York: Hill &Wang, 2006.

[8] Le Corbusier, *Quand les cathédrales étaient blanches*. Paris: Plon, 1937.

[9] See Le Corbusier and P. Jeanneret, *Œuvre complète 1910-1929*, edited by W. Boesiger and O. Storonov. Zurich: 1946.

is in the contemporary era that this relationship has shifted from the neutrality of anonymous architecture to the individualism of big name architecture. Starting in the postmodern period of the 1980s, real estate entrepreneurs – and Gerald Hines first among them – understood that what Johnson called "prima-donna architecture" had the added value not only of recharacterising the urban landscape, but also in terms of boosting sales of its spaces.

And so architects were asked not only to produce a rational project with well distributed spaces, but also a strong character for the façades which had remained deliberately anonymous up to that time. In the years marked by the rise of the brand and marketing, the ability of architecture to represent the values and power of the brand was encouraged. It had to be the image of power and a publicity vehicle. And it was thus, as observed by the historians Thomas Bender and William Taylor, that the "civic horizontalism" of the first urban developments were replaced by the "corporate verticality" of the contemporary metropolises.[7]

From the America of skyscrapers, the rationale of real estate market profits soon found a clear correspondence in the European capitals, London above all, and from there spread to the smaller cities, with targeted subdividing into lots, where architectural quality is guaranteed by designers of renown and the logic of profits is planned in detail.

It is perhaps partially for this reason that an examination of the state of the architectural discipline is so difficult.

The general lines of the crisis are undeniable and do not escape even the most incurable optimists. Architecture seems to have lost its *raison d'être* as a decisive witness to social transformations. The accusation is certainly not new. It echoes the prophecy that Victor Hugo, in 1830, put in the mouth of the archdeacon in *The Hunchback of Notre Dame*: "Alas, this will kill that. The book will kill the building."

Has printing killed architecture? There is no doubt reading these memorable pages in the light of more recent events. Architecture represented the technical and artistic development of human thought. Printing gradually took its place, and has now triumphed, because, as Hugo said, it is more economical.

Economic reality is what gives architecture its civic content, its role in contemporary society uniting utility and beauty, ethical values and aesthetic striving. In a travelogue from his trip to the United States in the 1930s, *Quand les cathédrales étaient blanches*, Le Corbusier expressed his admiration for the organisational methods applied in the Ford plants in Detroit. His admiration was focused on the success of planning in dealing with the issues of mass economy. He commented that when he went to a work site with ten one-thousand franc notes it was not even enough to build a room. In Detroit, for ten banknotes, Ford would sell you his well-known and prestigious automobile. In Le Corbusier's building site, the work went on with axes, picks and hammers. The workers sawed, planed and adjusted things to mere adequacy. On the one hand was barbarism, on the other, the modern times of Ford.[8]

Obviously this meditation on Ford cannot be dissociated from a comparison with the building sector in Europe, which Le Corbusier had been bent on radically changing ever since the 1920s, introducing buzzwords like "standardisation", "industrialisation" and "Taylorization".[9]

While the efforts by the master would only partially succeed in denting a building sector that virtually everywhere in Europe was still not ready to receive these stimuli, the situation was quite different in the United States where mass production and the example of the Ford assembly line burst forcefully into the construction sector.

By looking at the experiences, starting back in the 1910s, in the design of the kitchen space, the nerve centre of the modern "dwelling machine", we can get a fairly accurate picture of the roots of the relationship between economics, architecture and design.

The work done by the American scholar Christine Frederick to transpose industry's scientific methods of work organisation into the domestic economy, predated by a decade the numerous theories and works in many European countries on the specific issue of the kitchen as the motor of the home. From the kitchen to the city, the economic imperatives that govern industrial development defined the starting point for the new urban design pursuits of the modern avant-garde.

In the years between the two wars, the problem of the "economic house" and low cost residential developments was the object of much theorising and experimentation all over Europe, as was the search for new building types both on the scale of the single dwelling and on the greater urban scale. But the ideological mistake made by the architects of the modern avant-garde was that of selecting the "minimal house", whose minimalism was exclusively a question of its limited spatial extent, as the most perfect habitation from the distributive point of view. This way, the relation with economy became a search for the bare "minimum" necessary for dwelling, in terms of space and regarding construction solutions and use of materials.

Once the emergency of reconstruction and the anxiety of industrial conversion were behind it, the building sector could now identify a new current in which to assess its economic issues. It was no longer a question of seeking an economy of space, but rather a question of transforming the quantity of available space into an environment that can carry out functions with a clear economic benefit. On the other hand, while a reduction in space means nothing more than smaller dimensions for the dwelling space, a new arrangement and makeup of the technological elements can produce economic benefits that have a greater impact on the quality of life.

Similarly, the building process might become unexpectedly and significantly profitable if it moved away from a rationale of pure exploitation of the *quantity* of space to embrace a model of long-term urban development founded on the construction of an inhabited landscape with strongly innovative character.

Economy for the Home
Assago Milanofiori residential complex, competition project; Mercury Luxury Village Hotel in Barvikha, Moscow; Hotel facilities for the new Rho-Pero fairgrounds, competition project

In the plans for the Assago Milanofiori residential quarter submitted to the design contest called by the Gruppo Cabassi in 2005, Citterio employed a series of devices that optimised the ecological balance of the buildings, creating a well-defined image of metropolitan living in contact with nature. The gardens on the rooftops and in the open areas, the broad loggias and patios, the photovoltaic system, the wooden slat shading of the glassed façades, the use of door and window frames in wood and aluminium, high performance glass and the flexibility in lodging types give the entire complex a novel landscape character, associated both with its energy performance and with its constructional conception and spatial organisation.

His thinking about the new modes of dwelling and his ability to shape domestic spaces in accordance with economic principles make Citterio one of the most sought-after designers for hotels and other

[10] Luigi Prestinenza Puglisi, *Antonio Citterio*. Rome: Edilstampa, 2004, p. 116.

[11] Antonio Citterio, conversation with the author, March 2005.

hospitality facilities. The Bulgari Hotel has become an icon for contemporary hospitality because the quality of the architecture, the interior design and the decor transmits the quality of the brand to the guest. After this project, Citterio was asked to design a host of hotels that would become expressions of a domestic hospitality and a rational distribution of spaces and functions. Among these we have the Mercury Luxury Village in Russia, the interiors of Cooper Square in New York, the Brooktorkai Hafencity in Hamburg and the Shinsaibashi in Osaka. In particular, the Luxury Village Hotel in Barvikha, near Moscow, is configured as an urban fragment on the eastern outskirts of Moscow in an area of birch forests where prestigious residences have been built "surrounded by medium dimension lots with houses exhibiting an eclectic range of architectural tastes".[10] Mercury, a trading company specialised in the distribution of European luxury brands, is building a "golden mile" of luxury here, a road in the open countryside that will accommodate shopping malls and services. The American model of the mall as a connecting element between the suburbs and the city, and also extended to large shopping centres, finds application among the birches of Barvikha. The economics of the luxury mall, capable of generating profits in depressed or deserted areas by means of having big names in fashion set up shop there, is one of the most interesting phenomena in the relationship between architecture and economics. It is no coincidence that malls characterise the cities – for example, Dubai or Shanghai – that have received vital lifeblood from the new economy. And if the American and European metropolises succumb helplessly to financial upheaval and terrorist violence, "narcissistic cities" are blooming in great numbers in the desert or on the water, oblivious to the harshness of nature or to their own conformation. The unchallenged protagonists of the spectacle cities are the malls, where commercial rituals are celebrated according to the rationale of showy exhibitionism.

Commerce thus joins with architecture to amuse, astound and conquer new market segments and hence new consumers. The Muscovite complex juxtaposes the imperious vulgarity of the mall with the discretion of the high-end market with brands displayed in rarefied volumes of red cedar and glass. This luxury boulevard ends at a multipurpose exhibition space and Citterio's hotel. Here a wooden slat *brise soleil* elevated on pilotis echoes the delicate elegance of the nearby birches. The screen of slats modulates the light and gives character to the pattern of the façade. The geometry of the block is broken up by the inner courtyard, onto which the rooms open. Each room is large, some 65 square metres, and has its own private terrace delimited by the wooden partitions. The entrance to the building, marked by the green of the winter garden, opens onto a huge fireplace in set in counter-light, leaving the task of recounting the culture of the "Made in Italy" to the rigour of Citterio's refined furnishings.

Economy for the Workplace
Fausto Santini showrooms, Paris, Rome and Milan; De Beers, Los Angeles and London; Flos: U Beam, H Beam

"The store projects have been influenced by my experience with residential projects," states Citterio.[11] From his first stores for Santini in the 1980s to his recent creations for Aspesi and De Beers, his quest to conjugate the methods and processes of fashion with design is evident. Indeed, we hear with increasing regularity the binomial "fashion and design" as a symbol of Italianness in the world, characterising a universe of products that as a whole represent the "Made in Italy". Nevertheless, for those who are part of these worlds, it is difficult to think of them as part of a single productive apparatus, much less a unified cultural panorama. Citterio has proven that he knows how to dig back to three roots shared by fashion and design: the "culture of use", the "entrepreneurial culture" and the "productive culture". These common roots find a natural expression in an increasing closeness between the two realms. They increasingly conquer shared arenas of development as well as common areas of marketing and promotion. The traditional reciprocal indifference between the two is now dissolving – albeit with some resistance – in the face of the undeniable advantages of synergies between fashion and design regarding the image, but above all the productivity and development, of the overall national system. In the years when Italian fashion was gaining affirmation in prêt-à-porter and Italian brands were beginning to gain visibility and identity on the international scene, Citterio intuited that a heterogeneity of experience can represent a strategic advantage: for fashion, which is staked on the product-management dyad, in the development of a successful business model; and for design, in its shift from an artisanal production model to an industrial one. Citterio applied the characteristics of a "fashion system" to design and contributed to strengthening the identity of companies in the fashion industry by means of spaces that are strongly characterised, but also flexible and repeatable. "Antonio incarnates my ideal of the perfect designer," affirms Giorgio Busnelli. "He is not a sculptor like Zaha Hadid, Gaetano Pesce or Ron Arad, but he is among the very few who have a perfect understanding of the system. He knows how people live and buy. He told me that 'we have to do like they do in fashion. When a woman goes to Gucci, Cavalli or Valentino, she knows what to expect. We have to do the same thing with design.' And so we developed the B&B guidelines, as well as its identity and brand recognition, around this principle."[12]

Citterio designs numerous showrooms and collaborates actively with the big names in fashion: Esprit, Santini, Antonio Fusco, Aspesi and Enzo degli Angiuoni at the beginning and later Zegna, Valentino, Ungaro, Cerruti, Stefanel and De Beers, to name just a few of the companies for whom he has created offices and exhibition spaces. As Vanni Pasca and Pippo Ciorra observe, "it is always difficult for an architect to be identified with a fashion company through his projects for their production facilities, showrooms and commercial spaces. Here the presence of the customer tends to be more intense and the language of the architect risks being relegated to the role of a simple ornamental motif. That notwithstanding, a work of this type also represents an extraordinary opportunity to test and then develop design solutions."[13] Citterio's special knack lies in his ability to reconcile his identity with that of the company, often modelling the latter on his own. This is the case, for example, with the Santini stores. Santini is a major brand in shoes and leather goods, and Citterio has been designing their sales outlets since 1983. He creates an abstract and rarefied space, whose concept is based on the characteristics of the layout. In the Paris store, built in 1991, the irregular shape of the space on Rue du Cherche-Midi set the standards for subsequent projects. Citterio segmented the façade and connected two large spaces via a narrow corridor. The continuity of the space is enhanced by the hanging metal curtain that follows the entire length of the walls above the display units, evoking the rigour of Italian rationalism. The same elements are also found in the Rome store, built that same year, where the wood panelling on the walls and around the entrance, the symmetry of layout and the display niches create a peaceful and composed atmos-

[12] Giorgio Busnelli, conversation with the author, June 2005.

[13] Pippo Ciorra and Vanni Pasca, *Antonio Citterio/Terry Dwan*. Basel: Birkhauser Verlag, 1995, p. 166.

[14] Antonio Citterio, in Alberto Bassi, *Antonio Citterio. Industrial Design.* Milan: Electa, 2004, p. 160.

phere. The Milanese store, designed in 1993, is arranged around the ground floor area that has been transformed into a completely open sales floor with stairways in plain view. The display niches here are set apart from the main circulation areas, and the spatial organisation, centred visually around the stairway, creates a powerful effect. Citterio blurs the distinctions between retail, design and architecture by working side by side with the fashion designers, giving novel form to the architecture of fashion establishments. The new boutiques become the testing ground and the common ground for clearly distinct disciplines, which Citterio unites in the coherence and grace of his architectural language. Showing an unusual capacity for foresight, Citterio picks out visual metaphors for his clients that will transmit their image to the customer. The effectiveness of his projects is measured in terms of business and increased profits in an industry where spectacularisation has become an imperative, as also proven by Starck's Jean-Paul Gautier store in Paris, the Prada outlets by Herzog & De Meuron, Frank Gehry's Issey Miyake in New York and Ron Arad's Y's in Tokyo. Unlike many of his contemporaries, Citterio does not seek to dazzle people with special effects or futuristic technologies. Instead, his work is charac-

terised by his unfailing elegance and attention to detail, and by the harmony between interior design and the furnishing elements that welcome the customer into an environment where the space does not overwhelm the merchandise.

In his recent project for De Beers in Los Angeles, Citterio has interpreted the company philosophy with great elegance. Based on the display of jewellery, the characteristics of this project seek to emphasise the lighting effects of glass and the abstract nature of matter. Glass is used as a backdrop and as the enclosure for the display area and is juxtaposed and contrasted with heavy and opaque materials such as ebony and stone. The jewellery is arranged in a series of crystal boxes that appear to float in space. "We select our stones with care and experience," comments Andrew Coxon, President of De Beers. "But in the end, it is the diamond that chooses its owner." In order to let this happen, Citterio created a familiar and welcoming space, where the flashes of the diamonds are reflected in the transparency of the display cases, whose horizontal delicacy is balanced by the luminous vertical panels that partition the space and attract the eye. Colour and lighting design contribute to creating a balanced and harmonious space, where the light of

diamonds is interpreted architecturally in the creation of a magical and highly enchanting environment characterised by strong visual and tactile contrasts.

The control of lighting sources as an element of design is at the heart of Citterio's experimentation in lighting design. His *U Beam* and *H Beam* created for Flos in 2000 were developed with the precise objective of favouring the integration between different disciplinary realms. Light thus becomes the *fil rouge* uniting architecture, interior design and decor. "I felt it was necessary to design a family of large dimension devices that could measure up to the specific weight of architecture," declares Citterio, "that could be placed against it and become a permanent part of it."[14] Using a solution that was different from *Lastra*, the lamps gain their expressive power from technological innovation. They are suspended lamps that slice up the airspace like sharp blades. Their body is made of extruded aluminium painted opaque grey or white, and they are reflected in its neutrality. The production technology of aluminium allows for a noteworthy flexibility in the range of lamps, which is variable on the basis of the length of the lighting sources. In the economy of interior space, these lamps establish visual priorities and relations with the objects below. They regulate not only the emission of light, but also control its interaction with other light sources. In the versions with Smart Sensor Autodimming, a photocell adjusts the lighting intensity on the basis of other lighting sources to maintain a constant preset lighting level. This is a detail that makes a difference because, as Mies – not coincidentally a constant point of reference for Citterio – liked to say, "God is in the details."

Economy for the City and Territory
Former tobacco works in Verona, project; Wall: urban fixture; Aubrilam: urban fixture; Greenway exposition park, competition project for redevelopment of the historical Milan fairgrounds

In the field of urban redevelopment, Citterio has carried out a number of significant projects, focusing attention on a consolidated form such as the tower rising from a horizontal slab containing service establishments. However, in terms of recognisability, it takes on expressive qualities that are differentiated depending on use. Hence, in the new tourism and conference centre in Verona designed for the area between the fairgrounds and the railroad, the architect chose to work on two fronts, public and private, internal and external, developing an environment with a wealth of elements connecting it to the historical centre and elegant architectural figurations, such as the grand façade toward the city whose rhythmic pattern of glass panels evokes the internal courtyard of Le Corbusier's La Tourette convent.

Regarding service to the city, Citterio also designs urban fixtures such as the totems for the German company Wall, or the *Alba* collection for the French company Aubrilam, objects that improve the perception and usability of urban space. *Mon bijou*, the totem designed for Wall in 2003, is a covered bus stop that also acts as a publicity vehicle. "We are proud to have Antonio Citterio among our designers," states company President Hans Wall. "His language demonstrates an extraordinary correspondence with our products, where quality is aimed at satisfying the desires of the municipality and its people. The lightness of *Mon bijou* echoes the lifestyle of the contemporary city while offering at the same time complete protection for those waiting for the bus." The totem is a cylinder of galvanised steel with green trim and a glass and aluminium roof. Its compact profile represents a visual reference point and a refuge from the heat or cold for those waiting for the bus. The expressive power of *Mon bijou* is tempered in the delicacy of the *Alba* series for Aubrilam, a variegated system of urban fixtures. "I work with systems," states the designer. "In my projects, the work focuses on finding different expressions of the product in its different extensions. Every object has its own well-defined design identity while still being part of a broader collection."[15] And so we have streetlamps, barriers and benches made of wood slats and steel, characterised by the lightness of the visible structure and by the elegance of the coupling elements. *Alba* is a system of urban fixtures in homage to the work of Franco Albini. Citterio's support for his differently shaped outdoor lamps interprets Albini's characteristic pole initially designed for the Scipione exhibition at the Pinacoteca di Brera (1940) and then gradually gaining refinement until the designs for the Olivetti store in Paris (1960) with the beautiful version with the light bulb placed at the top. Citterio clearly renders the theme of the supporting elements interlocking with the functional structures (base and lamp) by means of a geometrical redesign of the wooden shaft. The bench employs the same characteristics as the pole, however, placing the emphasis on a more compact structure.

A revisitation of contemporary life is the theme of one of the more controversial

[15] Antonio Citterio, conversation with the author, April 2006.

[16] Vittorio Gregotti, "Ma il futuro di Milano non sarà nei grattacieli", *Corriere della Sera*, 6 July 2004.

projects of recent years, the project submitted to – but not winning – the design contest for the redevelopment of the historical Milan fairgrounds. Citterio, with Jean-Pierre Buffi, Michel Desvigne, Anna Giorgi, Pierluigi Nicolin, Ermanno Ranzani and Italo Rota proposed a meditation on habitation in the city centre in line with the new contemporary lifestyles. The dwelling spaces are based on improved environmental quality, something that is now impossible for structures in the historic centres of contemporary metropolises: contact with nature, energy savings, ecologically compatible materials and soft technologies aimed at favouring flexible dwelling conditions both in terms of the variety of social groups in the area and regarding the possibility of integrating home time with free time and professional time. Citterio designed a series of row houses and a few light and discrete tower houses that reflect the construction tradition and housing types typical of the Milanese school, integrating flexible and versatile services into the picture. He took special pains also regarding the environmental setting. The houses are immersed in greenery and have their own private gardens, while the tower houses front on a public park. While the Franco-Italian team of Rota and Citterio focused on recovering the Italian urban tradition and integrating the works into their setting, the winning projects by Zaha Hadid, Arata Isozaki and Daniel Libeskind opted for the titanism of the vertical scale as an element of rupture with the urban context.

Whether the new urban design will be represented by the Byzantine skyscrapers of Hadid, Libeskind and Arata is yet to be seen. What is true is that the contest was decided on the basis of the costliest proposal, and the victory of Citylife, in the Generali group, who offered 523 million euro with the skyscrapers of the three "archistars" has ignited numerous and often well grounded contestation. The economic factor prevailed over the environmental one, to the point that a trenchant Vittorio Gregotti termed it "one of the most sadly meaningful episodes of the low condition that the Milanese, the Italian and also to some extent the international architectural culture has sunk to. The contest was won by the financial-insurance group put together by Generali, SAI and RAS. Out of six participants, three were chosen. I am writing about the winner as a financial group, because the names and projects of the architects summoned by the various groups to participate hardly counted at all. What counted was the economic proposal and the financial trustworthiness that allowed the winner to overcome the competition."[16]

The Antonio Citterio studio was also invited by Sviluppo Sistema Fiera to participate in the design contest for the new hotel facilities at the new Rho-Pero fairgrounds. The iconic character of the architecture is well represented in the hotel, and the theme of the tall building, the focal point of the development, is here proposed in terms of an exaltation of the construction layout. But here it is softened by the fine texture of the façade planes, which mark out the two parallel vertical blades with different chromatic and luminous effects. What results is an image that echoes the classic tradition of modern architecture, a sort of interpretation of a Milan-style internationalism explored in the 1960s by Gio Ponti in the Pirelli skyscraper. Citterio's choice to follow the path of Cartesian serenity has the additional merit of entering into a dialectic with the twisting lines of Fuksas's Sail, composing a picture that clearly defines the dual soul, rationalist and organicist, of Italian architecture.

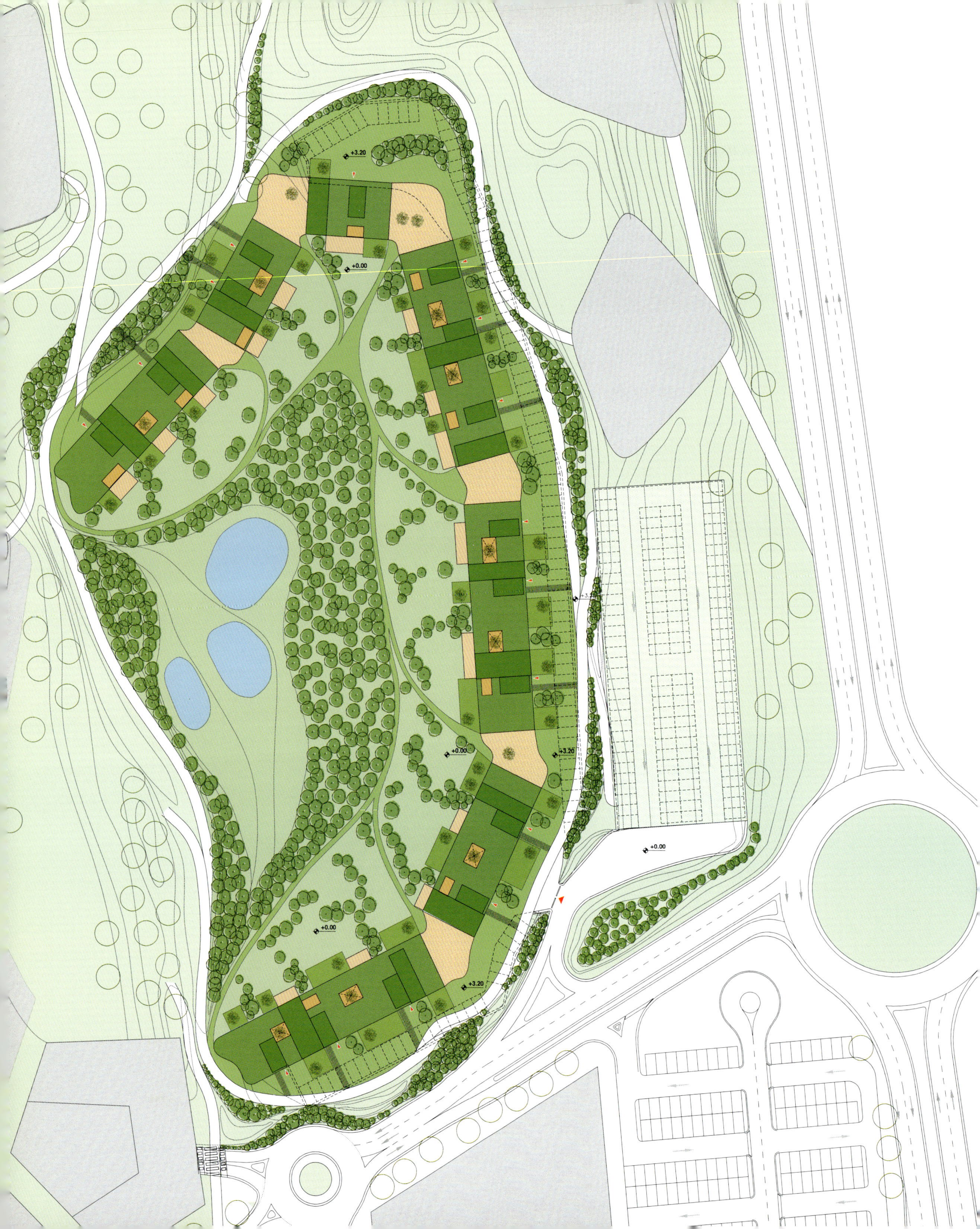
+3.20
+0.00
+0.00
+3.20
+0.00
+0.00
+3.20

ECONOMY

2005 Assago Milanofiori, Milan

*Design competition / Brioschi
Finanziaria – Gruppo Cabassi
Residential complex
7,345 sq. m*

In the plans for the Assago Milanofiori residential quarter, Citterio employed a series of devices that optimised the ecological balance of the buildings, creating a well-defined image of metropolitan living in contact with nature.

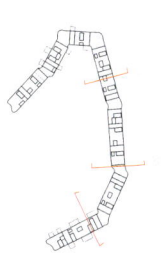

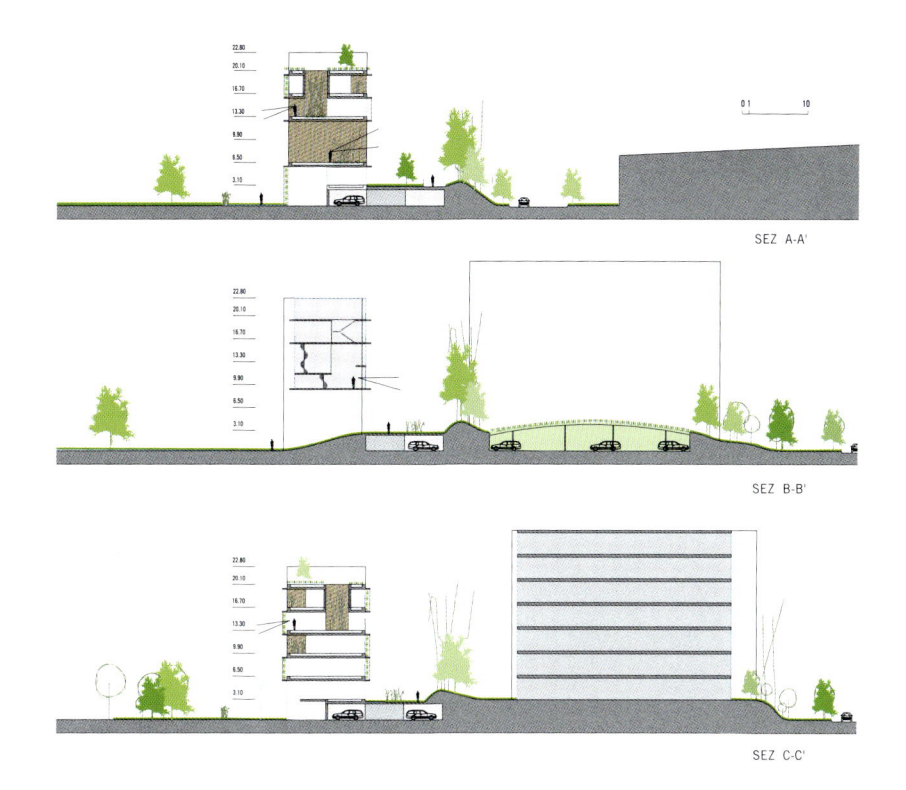

SEZ A-A'

SEZ B-B'

SEZ C-C'

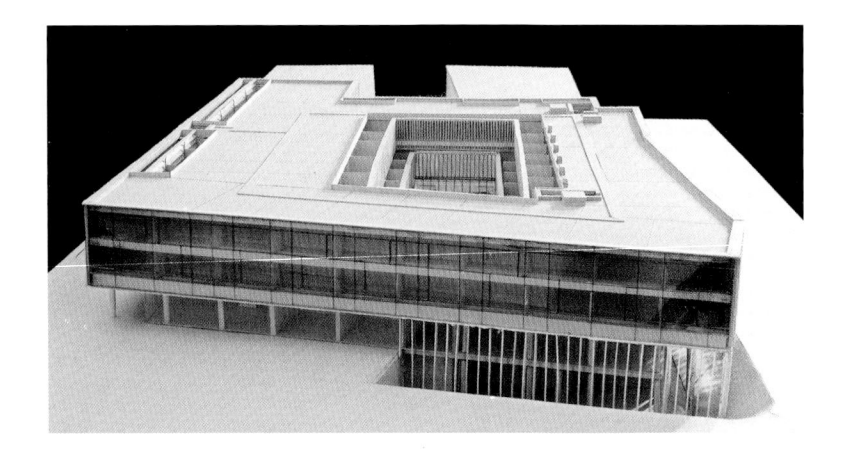

**2004–2007 Mercury Hotel
in Barvikha, Moscow**

15,000 sq. m

The thinking about the new modes of dwelling and the ability to shape domestic spaces in accordance with economic principles make Citterio one of the most sought-after designers for hotels and other hospitality facilities.

ECONOMY

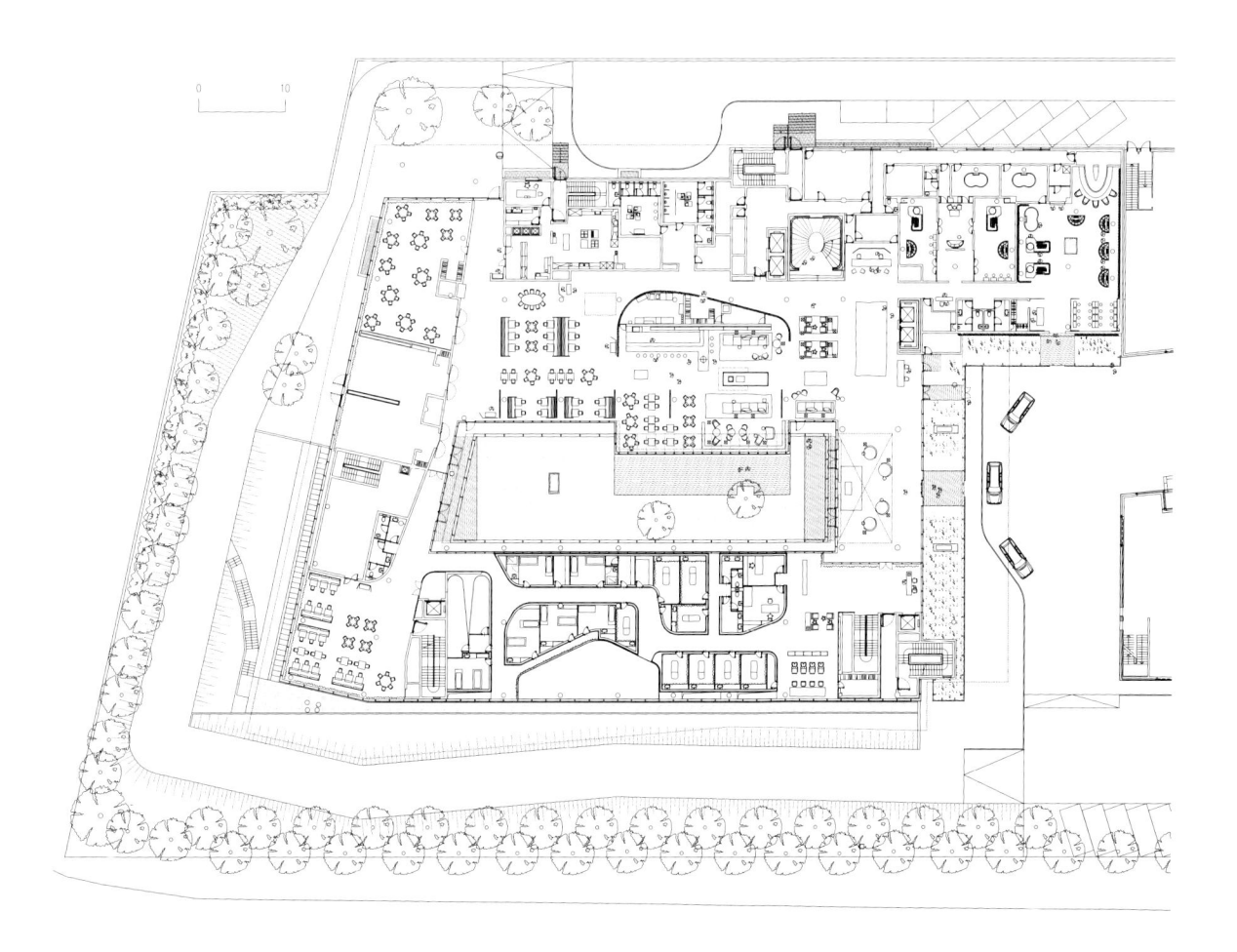

273

ECONOMY

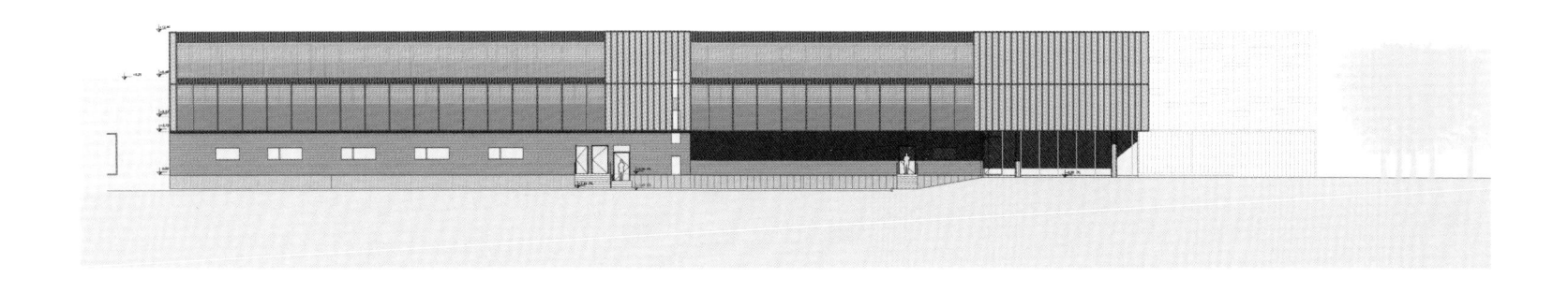

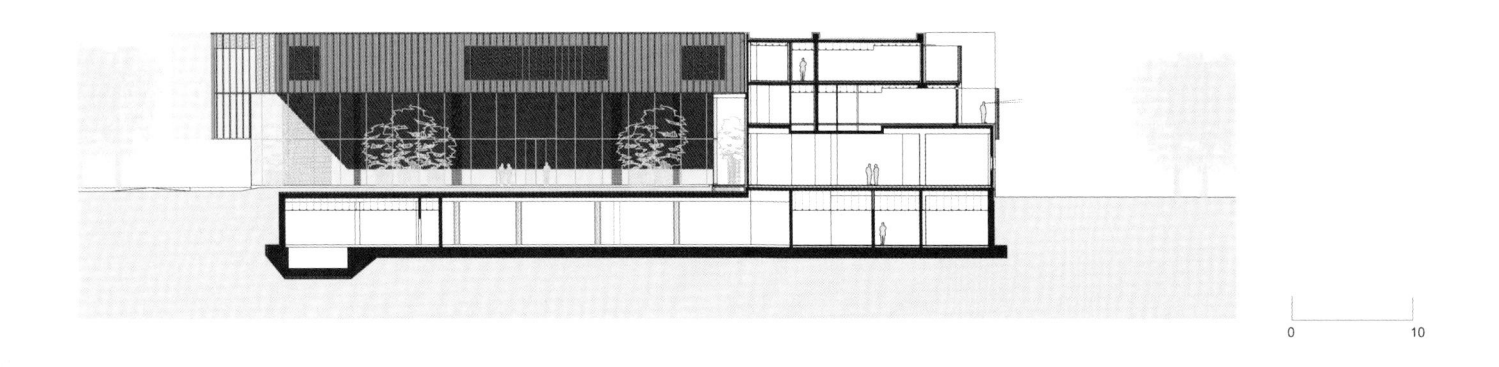

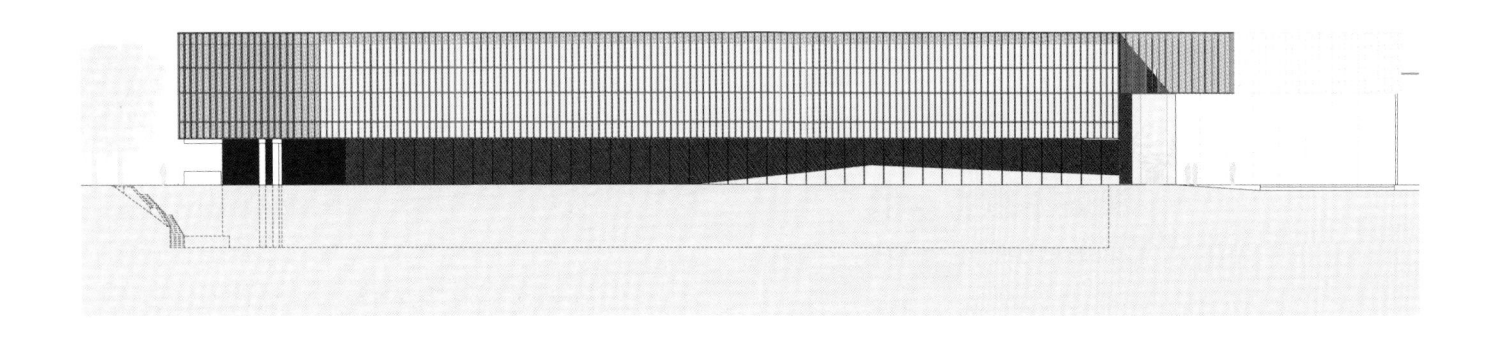

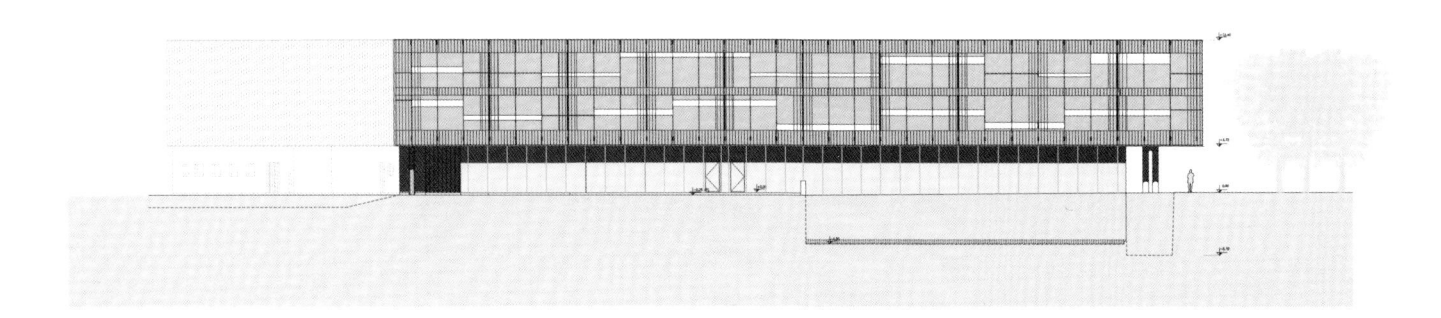

274

ECONOMY

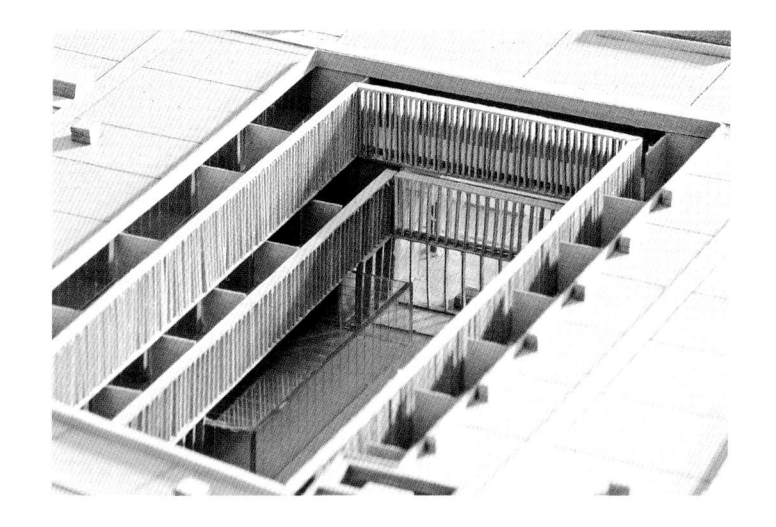

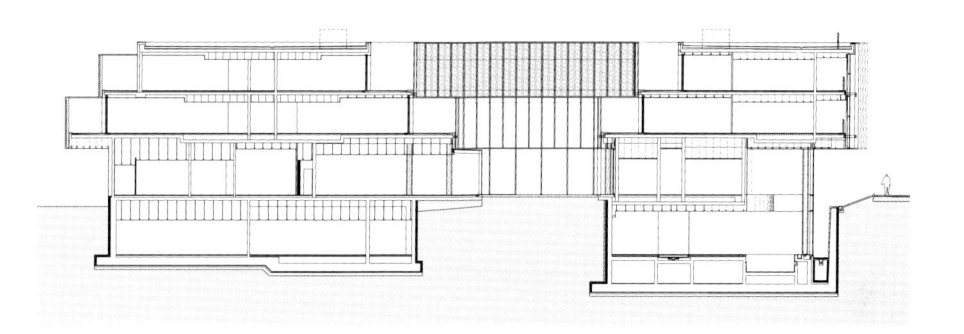

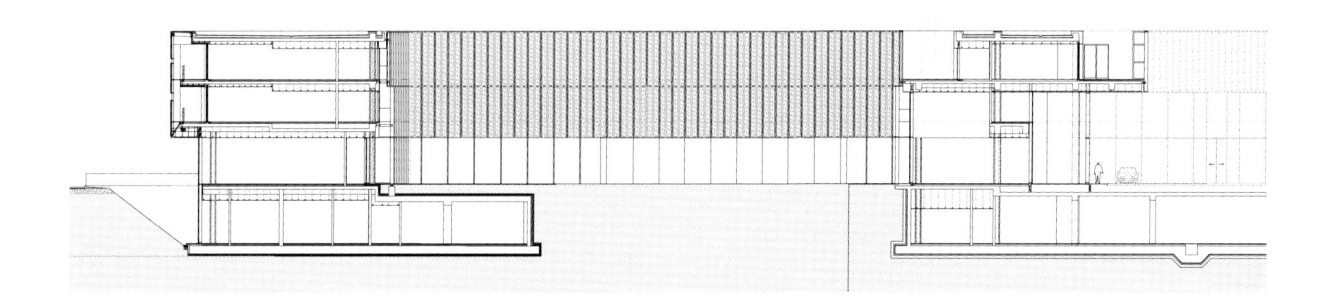

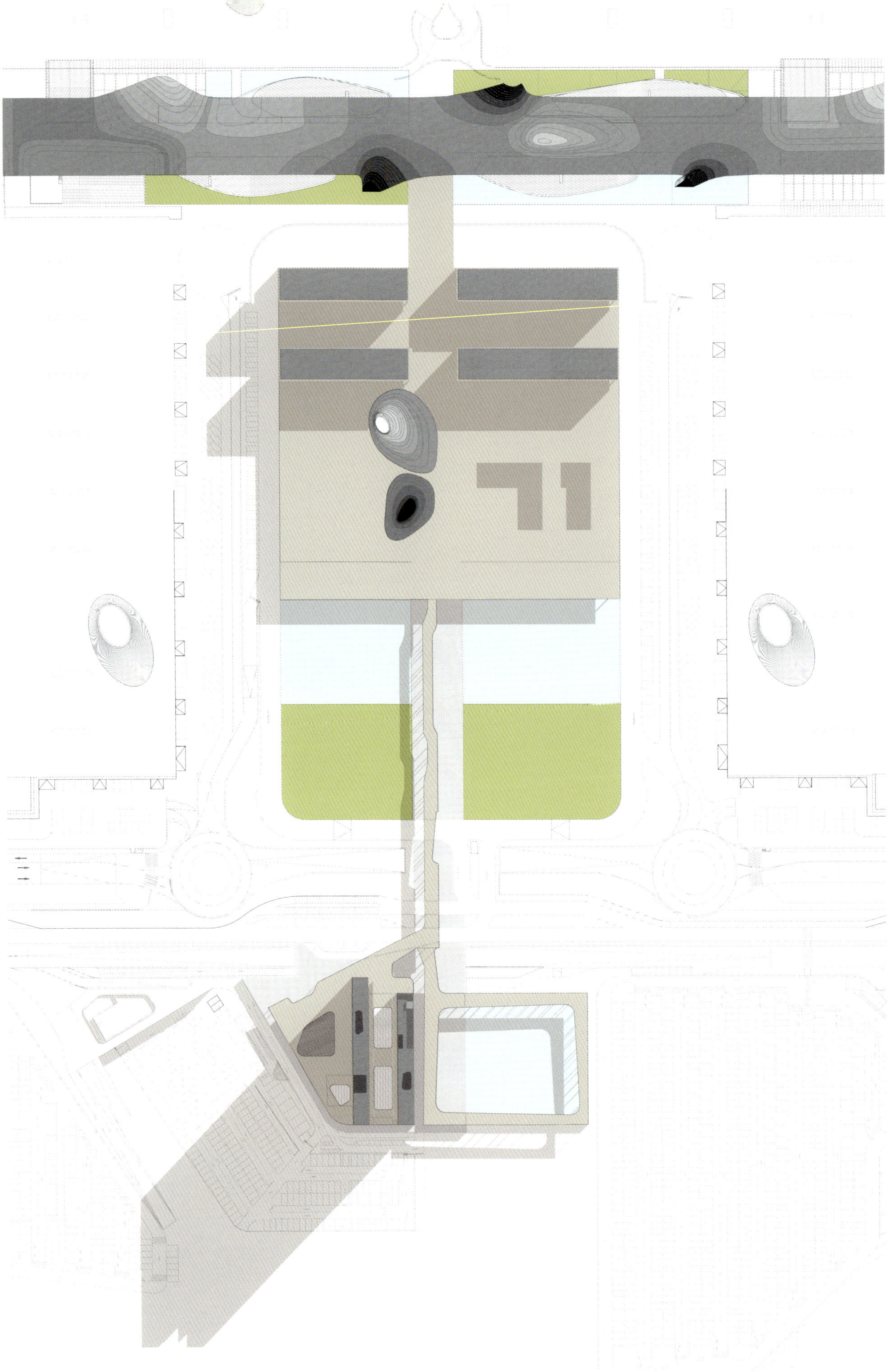

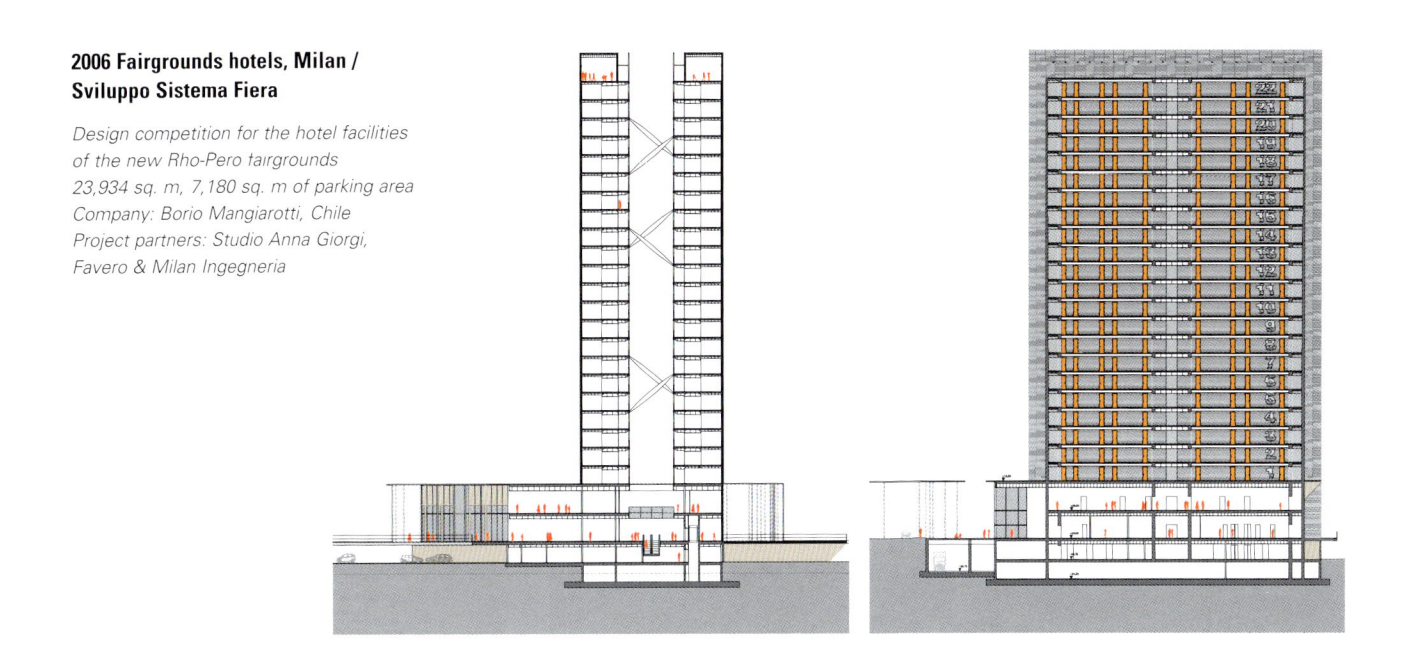

2006 Fairgrounds hotels, Milan / Sviluppo Sistema Fiera

Design competition for the hotel facilities of the new Rho-Pero fairgrounds
23,934 sq. m, 7,180 sq. m of parking area
Company: Borio Mangiarotti, Chile
Project partners: Studio Anna Giorgi, Favero & Milan Ingegneria

ECONOMY

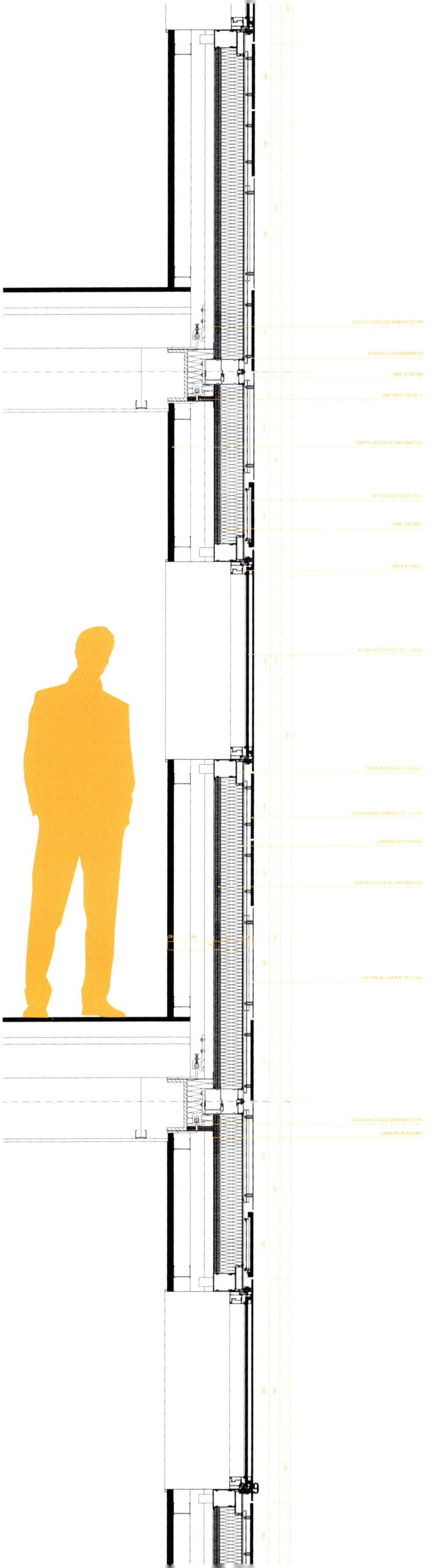

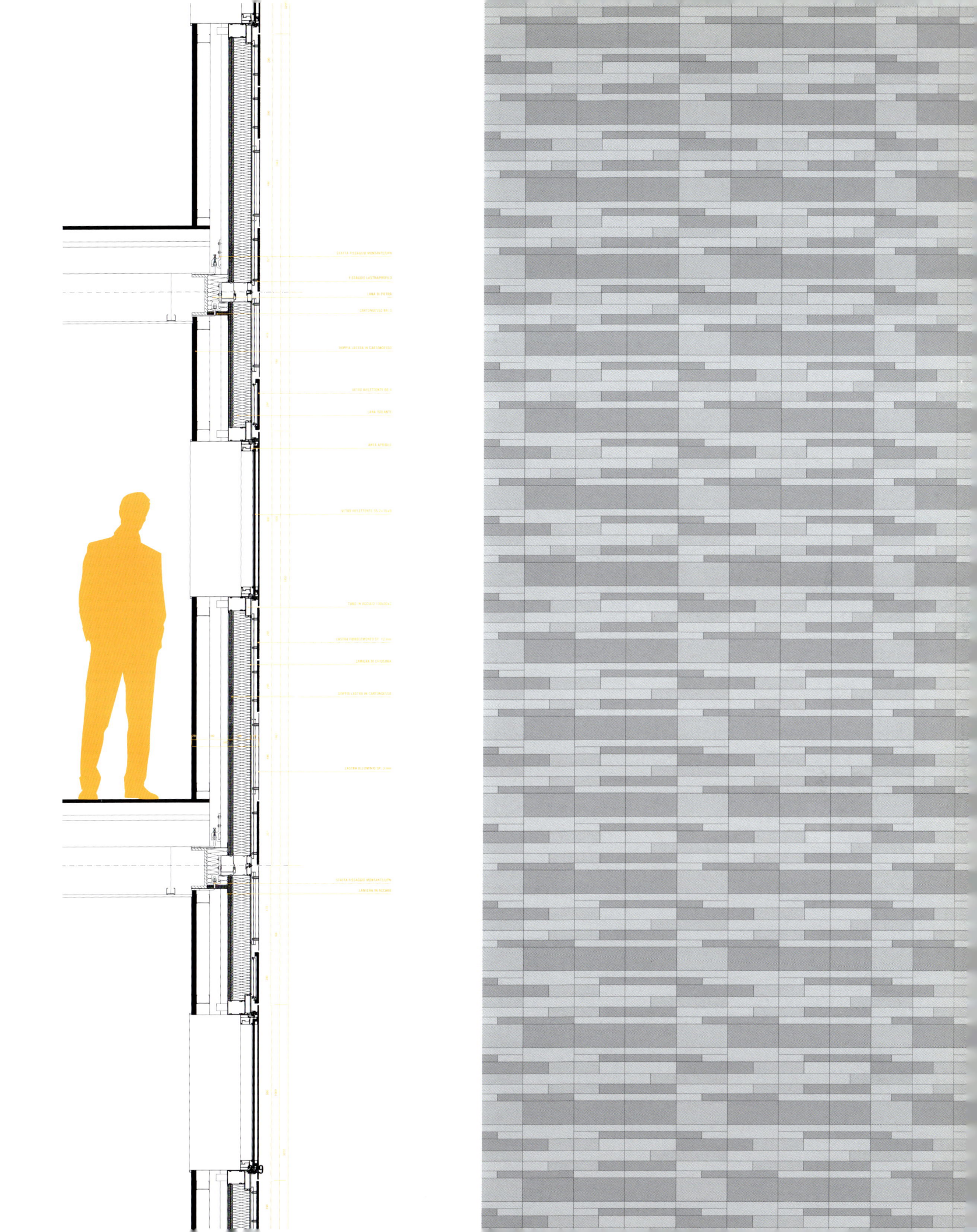

ECONOMY

The residential complex to the south comprises four buildings joined at their base by a sort of socle that encloses an historic courtyard containing the private gardens. The façades slope back slightly to enhance the perspective onto the roadway.
The wall is made of unfaced white cement with a polished look due to the incorporation of white marble. The openings for the doors and windows are cleanly and deeply cut, and the bronze-finish aluminium frames complete a classic design of a façade that can dialogue with the urban plan of the historical city.

2006 Varesine, Milan

*Design competition /
Le Varesine S.r.l. – Hines Italia
Residential complex
11,390 sq. m*

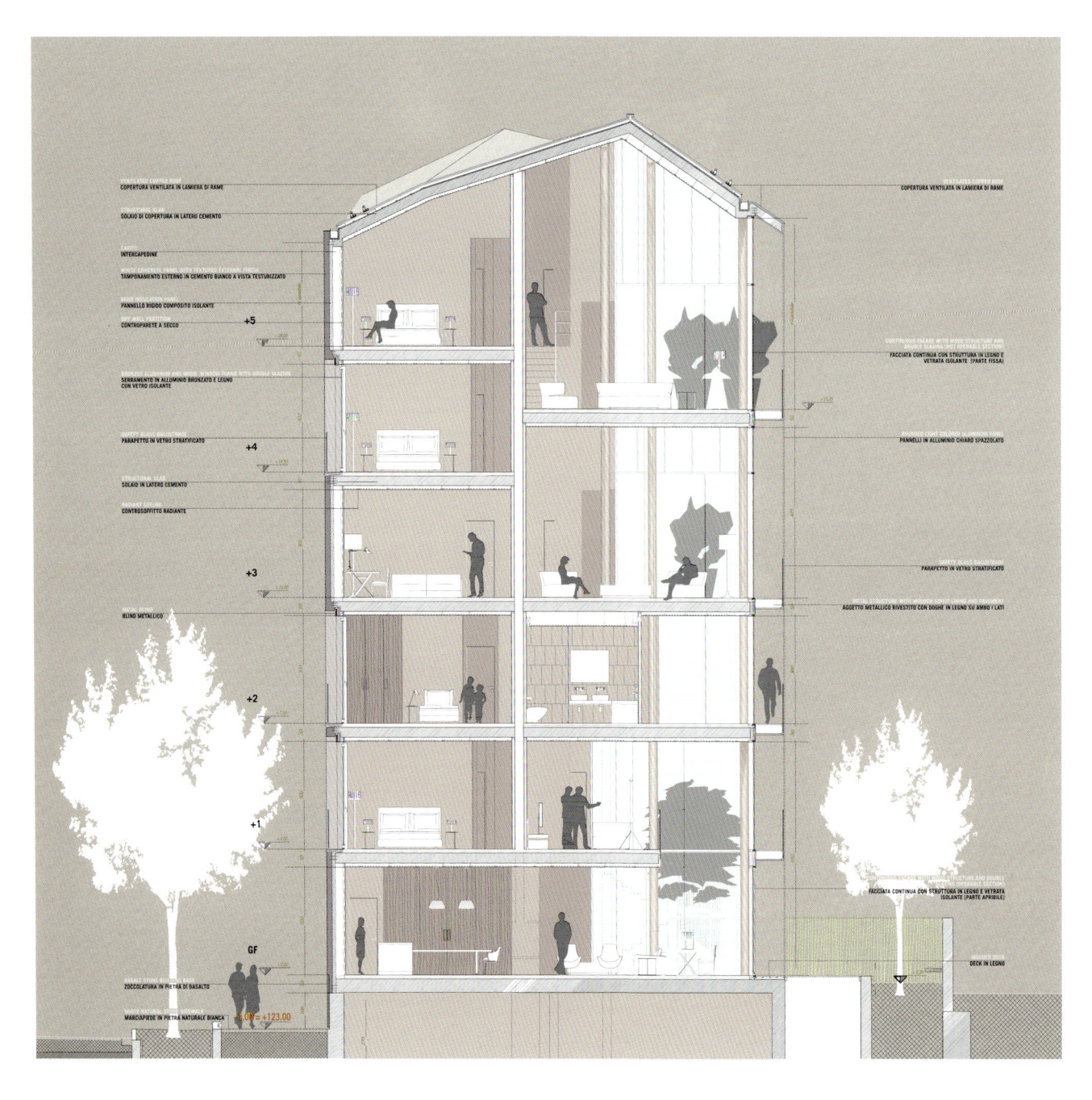

ECONOMY

281

ECONOMY

1996 Fausto Santini, Düsseldorf

Showroom
200 sq. m

"The store projects have been influenced by my experience with residential projects."
Antonio Citterio
From his first stores for Santini in the 1980s to his recent creations for Aspesi and De Beers, his quest to conjugate the methods and processes of fashion with design is evident. Indeed, we hear with increasing regularity the binomial "fashion and design" as a symbol of Italian-ness in the world, characterising a universe of products that as a whole represent the "Made in Italy".

The new boutiques become the testing ground and the common ground for clearly distinct disciplines, which Citterio unites in the coherence and grace of his architectural language. Showing an unusual capacity for foresight, Citterio picks out visual metaphors for his clients that will transmit their image to the customer.

ECONOMY

283

ECONOMY

2005 De Beers, Los Angeles

Jewellery store
400 sq. m

284

ECONOMY

2001–2002 De Beers, London

Jewellery store
500 sq. m

Based on the display of jewellery, the characteristics of this project seek to emphasise the lighting effects of glass and the abstract nature of matter. Glass is used as a backdrop and as the enclosure for the display area and is juxtaposed and contrasted with heavy and opaque materials such as ebony and stone. The jewellery is arranged in a series of crystal boxes that appear to float in space.

ECONOMY

2000 U Beam, Flos

with Glen Oliver Löw

2000 H Beam, Flos

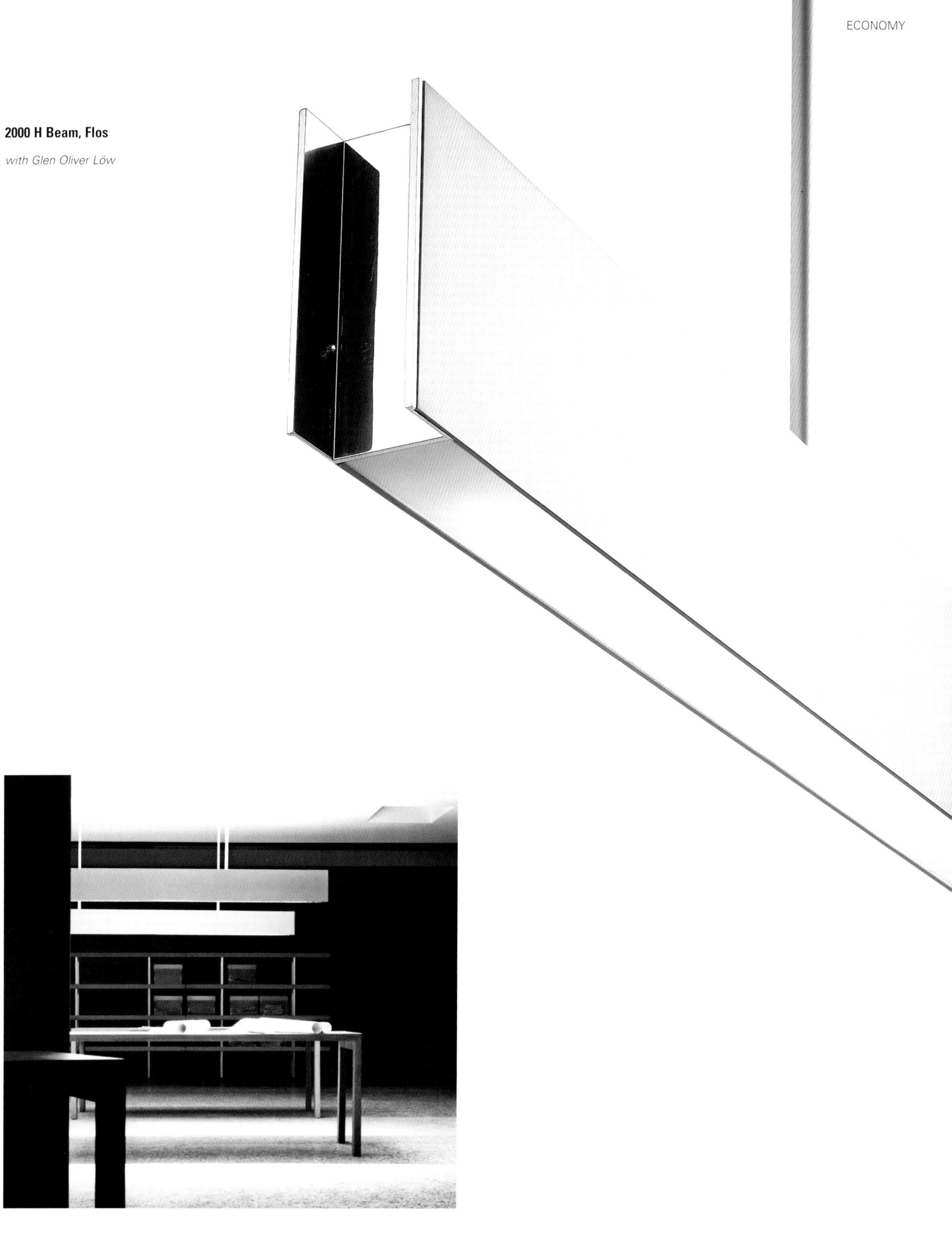

with Glen Oliver Löw

ECONOMY

2005 Shinsaibashi, Osaka

Project for multipurpose building.
Commercial area on ground floor.
Hotel and residences on upper floors.
2,987 sq. m

ECONOMY

ECONOMY

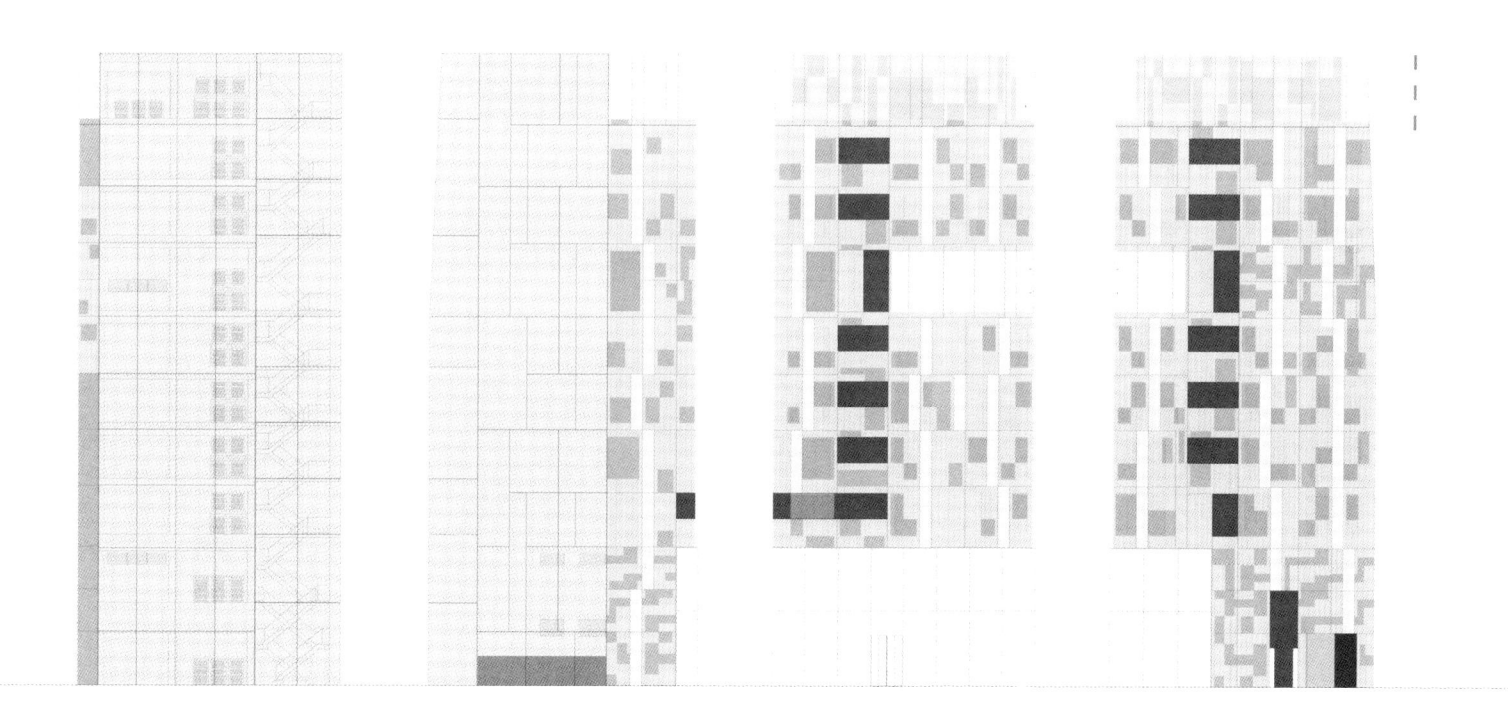

289

ECONOMY

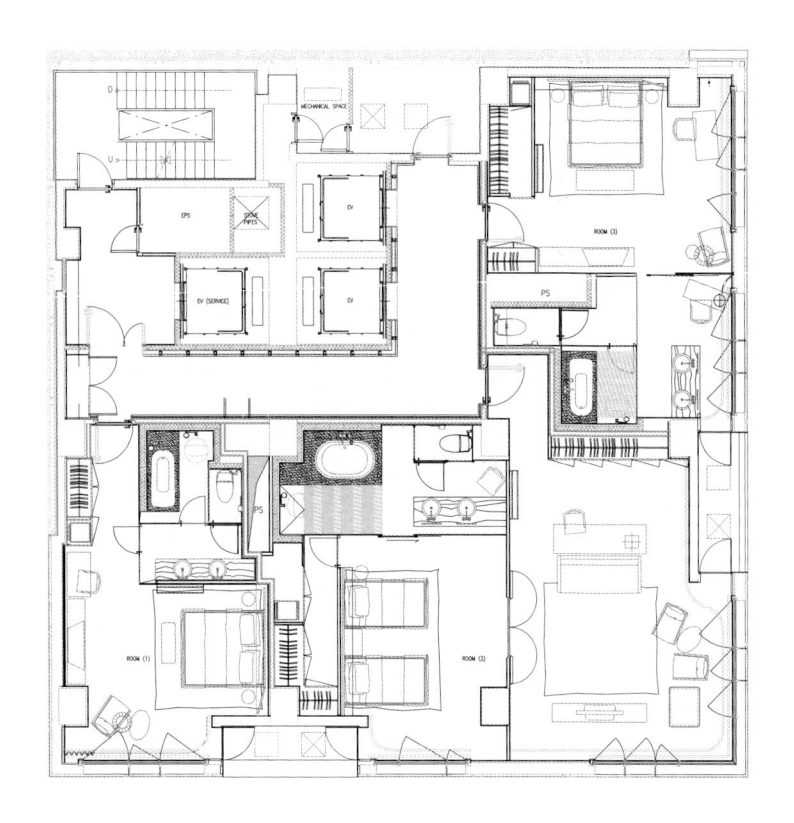

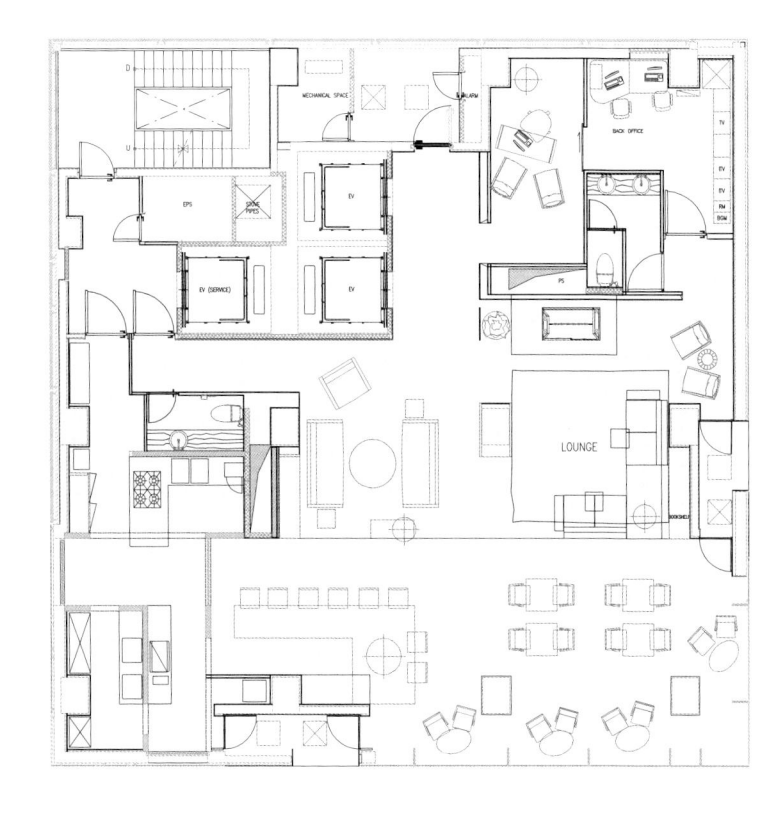

ECONOMY

ECONOMY

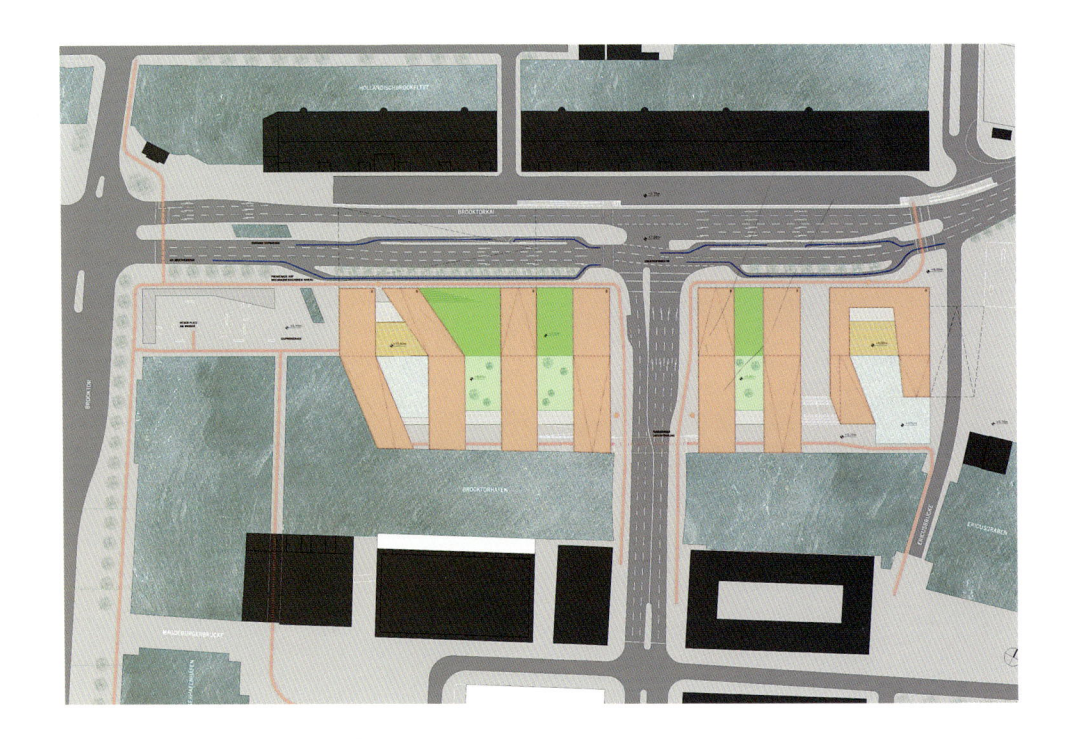

ECONOMY

2004 Brooktorkai Hafencity, Hamburg

Design competition.
Masterplan for Hafencity, in Hamburg,
that includes a system of multipurpose buildings:
offices and accommodations.
Offices 33,000 sq. m, Hotel 8,700 sq. m

The pools of water in the courtyards of the end buildings characterise the project. The water level in the courtyards corresponds to the promenade, whose edges accommodate two restaurants serving the general public.
The buildings are linked internally on the ground floor by a glassed-in walkway that gives onto the shopping arcades fronting the parking facility along the promenade.
The new urban level created behind the arcade offers public and private spaces accessible from the Brooktorkai. The area is completely pedestrian.

2004 Wettbewerb Brooktorkai Hafencity, Hamburg

Design competition for a hotel structure as part of the Hafencity / Quantum Immobilien AG – German Lloyd AG urban requalification project

The hotel adheres to the historical form of the building enclosing a courtyard. The rooms face onto the courtyard, onto the future Poggenmuehle pedestrian area and a few onto the canal, with a view of the bridge and the historical buildings of the Speicherstadt.
The project places an esplanade at the front of the new urban system and thus constitutes a privileged viewpoint for taking in the panorama of characteristic elements of this part of the city: the water, the bridges, Hamburg of the historical red clinker-brick façades and the new architecture.

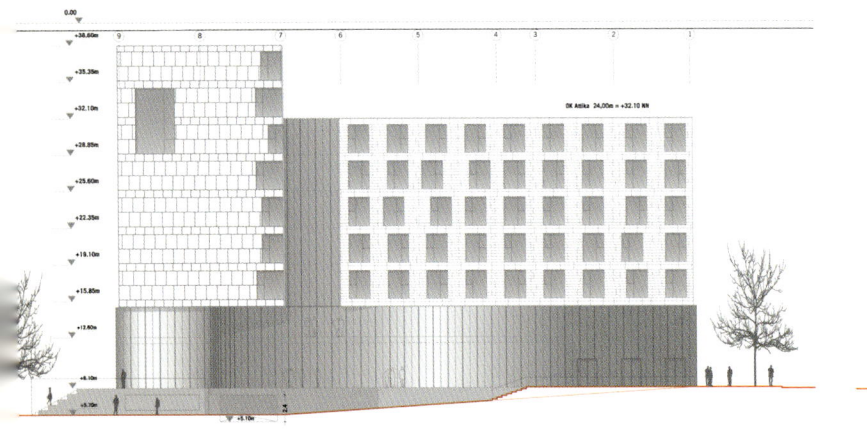

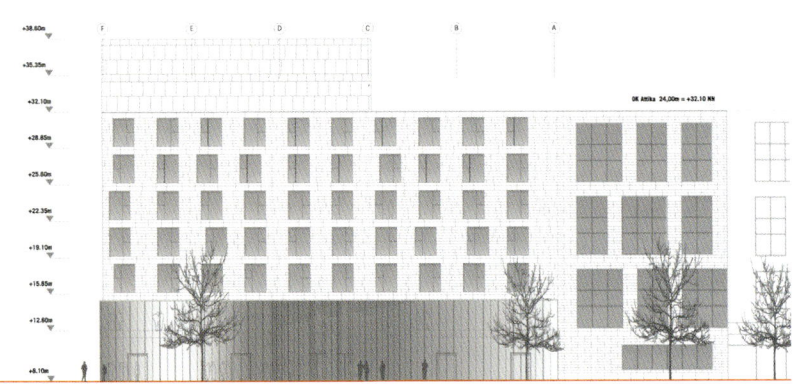

ECONOMY

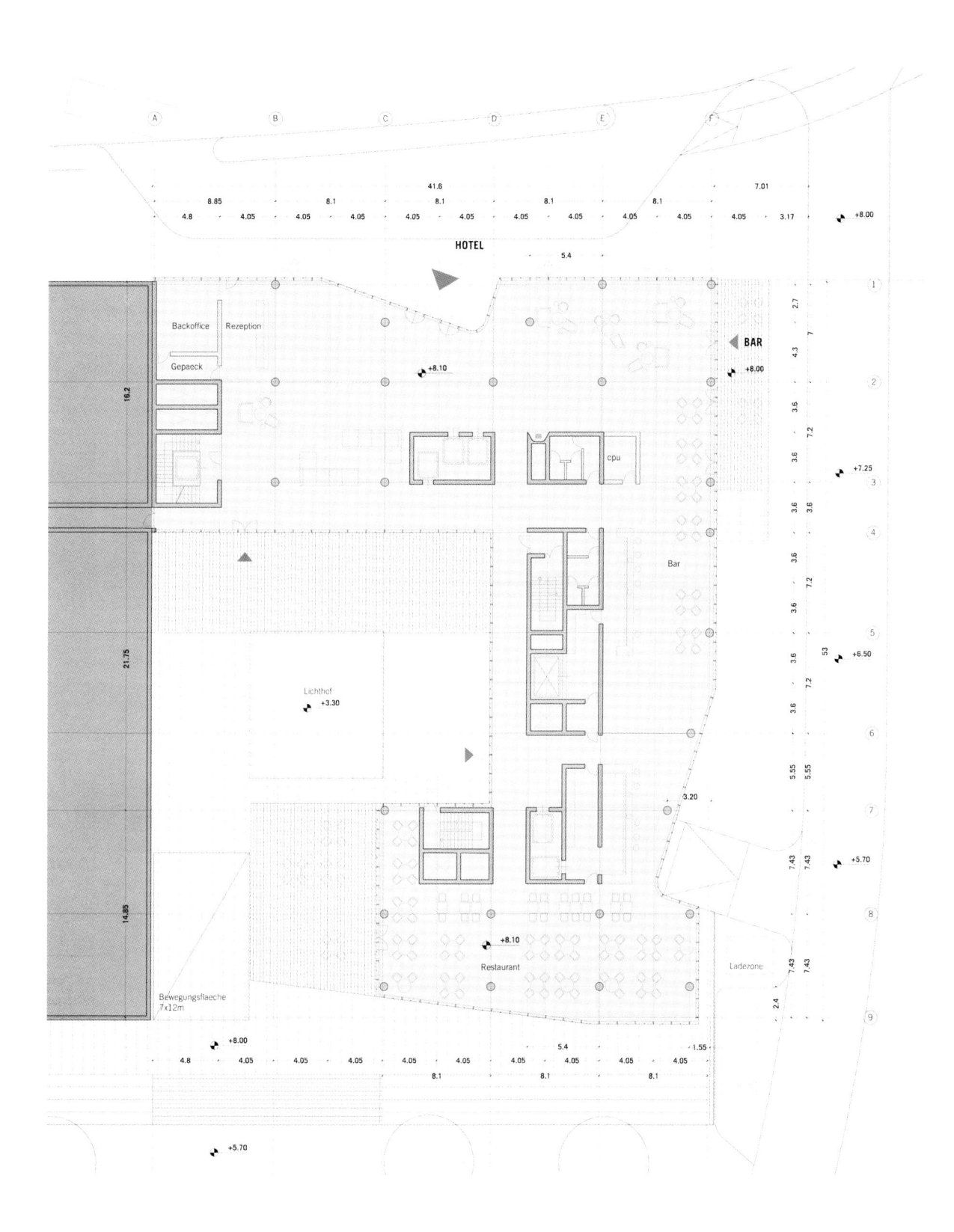

HOTEL

BAR

Backoffice Rezeption
Gepaeck

+8.10

cpu

Bar

Lichthof
+3.30

+8.10
Restaurant

Ladezone

Bewegungsflaeche
7x12m

+5.70

295

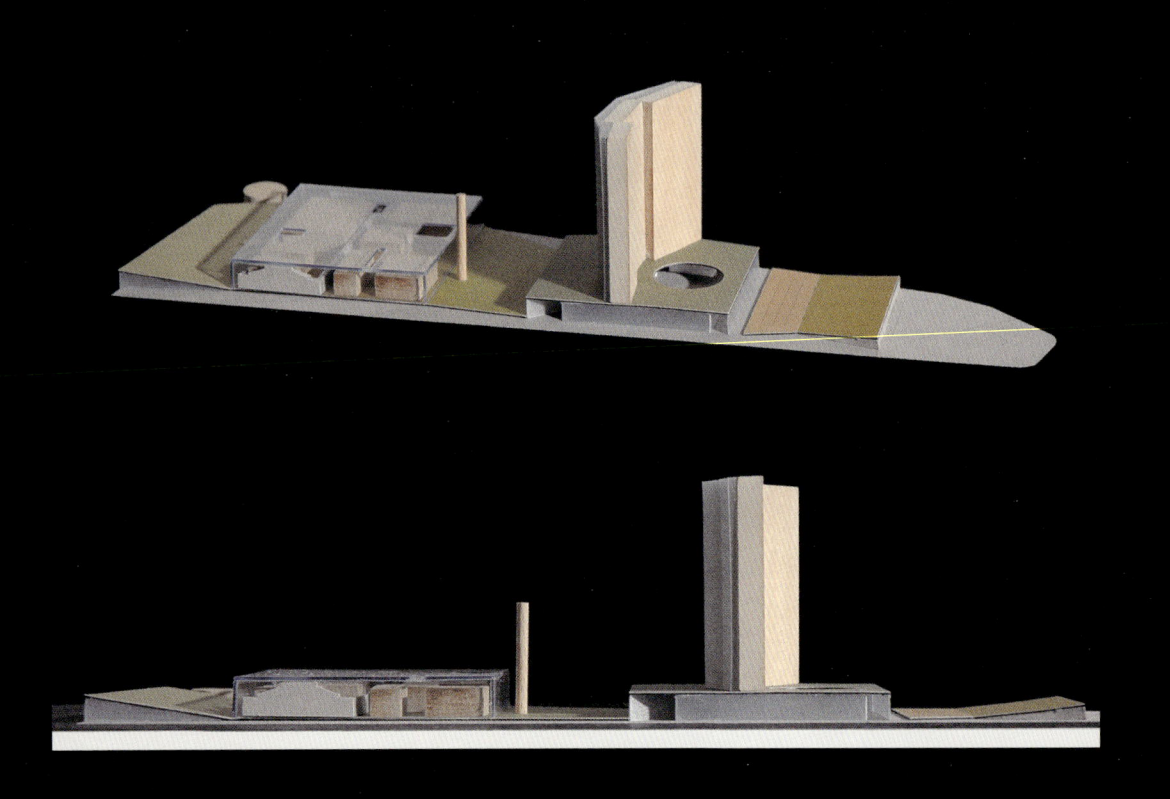

2004 Former Tobacco Works, Verona / Palladium

Private competition
Multipurpose use: tertiary, commercial, accommodations, residential.
31,000 sq. m

In the new tourism and conference centre in Verona designed for the area between the fairgrounds and the railroad, the architect chose to work on two fronts, public and private, internal and external, developing an environment with a wealth of elements connecting it to the historical centre and elegant architectural figurations, such as the grand façade toward the city.

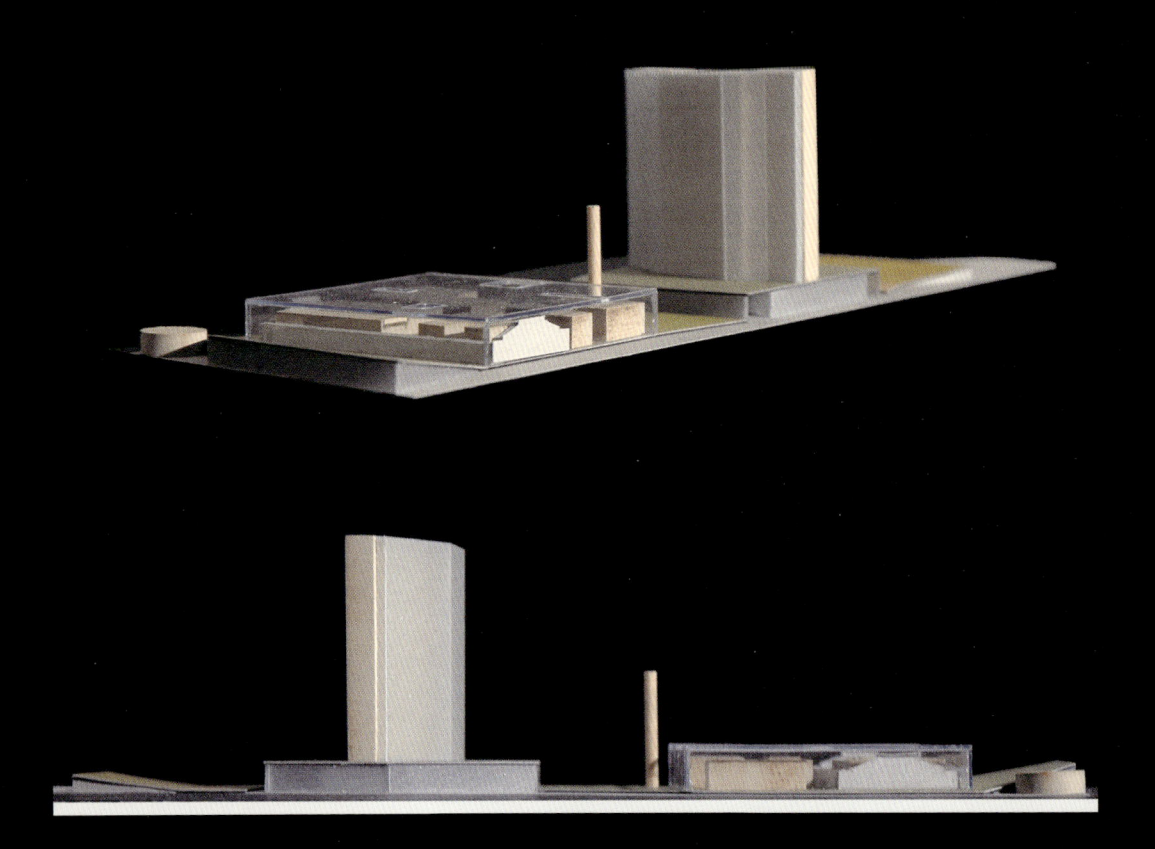

ECONOMY

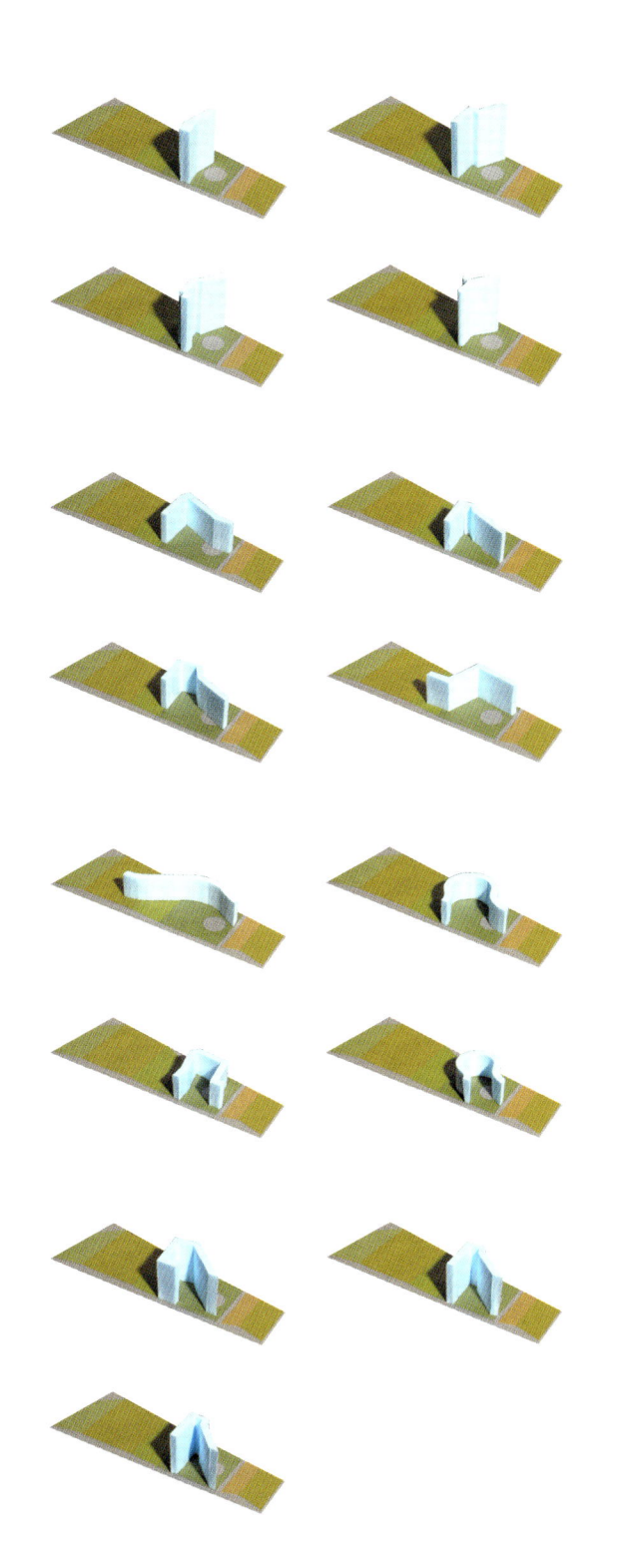

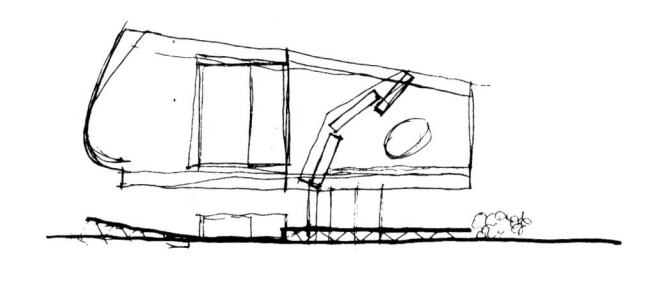

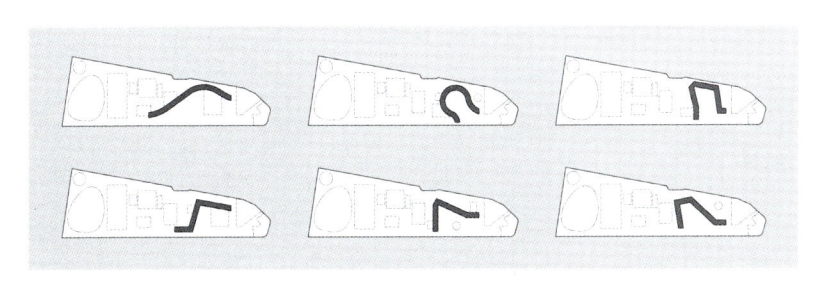

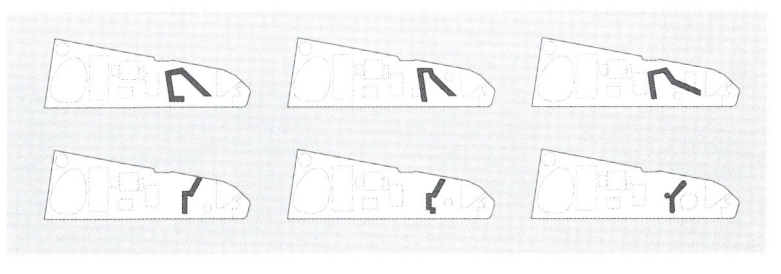

ECONOMY

2003 Mon bijou, Wall

with Toan Nguyen

ECONOMY

ECONOMY

300

ECONOMY

2006 Alba, Aubrilam

with Toan Nguyen

Streetlamps, barriers and benches made of wood slats and steel, characterised by the lightness of the visible structure and by the elegance of the coupling elements.

ECONOMY

2004 Historical Milan fairgrounds / Greenway exposition park

*Design competition for the requalification of the historical fairgrounds of Milan.
Project partners: Jean-Pierre Buffi, Michel Desvigne, Anna Giorgi, Pierluigi Nicolin, Ermanno Ranzani, Italo Rota*

The project group proposed a meditation on habitation in the city centre in line with the new contemporary lifestyles. The dwelling spaces are based on improved environmental quality, something that is now impossible for structures in the historic centres of contemporary metropolises: contact with nature, energy savings, ecologically compatible materials and soft technologies aimed at favouring flexible dwelling conditions both in terms of the variety of social groups in the area and regarding the possibility of integrating home time with free time and professional time.

ECONOMY

Economic reality is what gives architecture its civic content, its role in contemporary society uniting utility and beauty, ethical values and aesthetic striving.

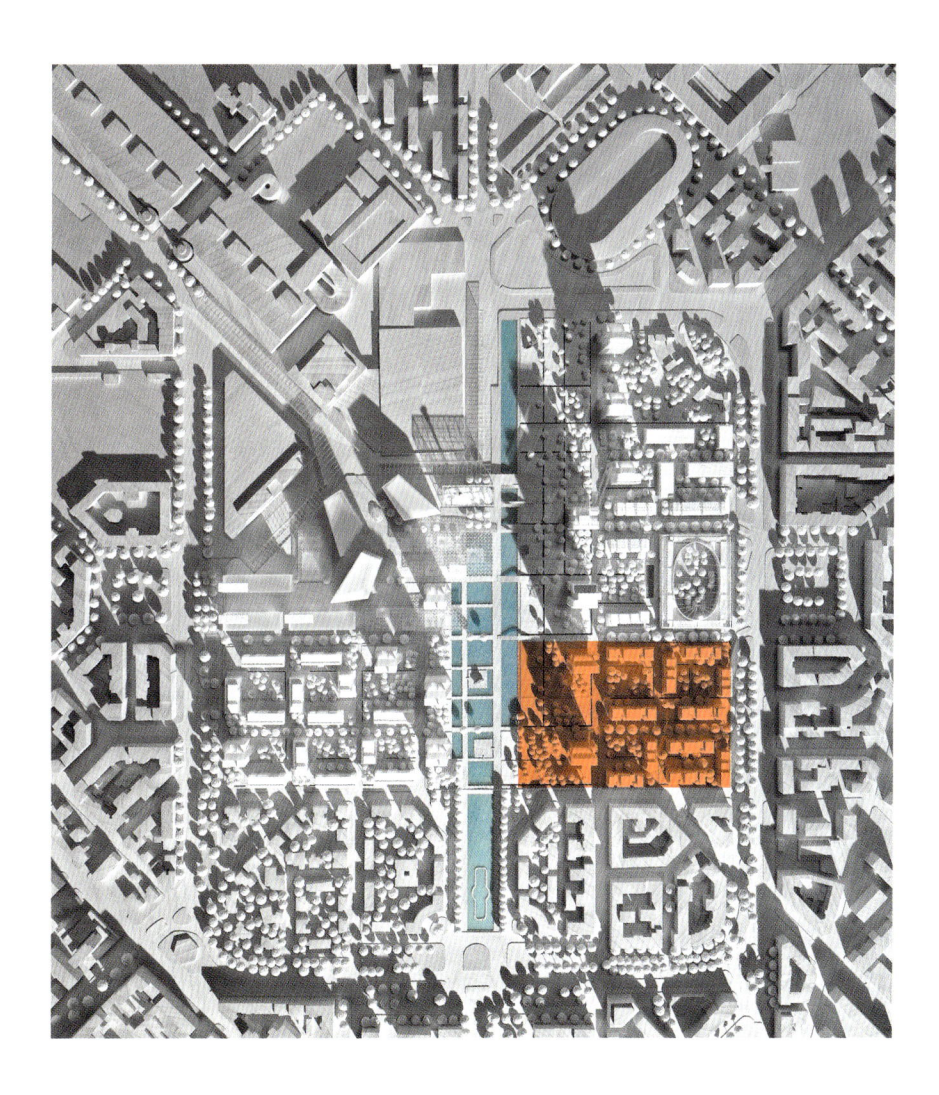

303

ECONOMY

2005 Neubau ABC Strasse / Hochfiel http

Design competition.
Multipurpose building: restaurant, offices

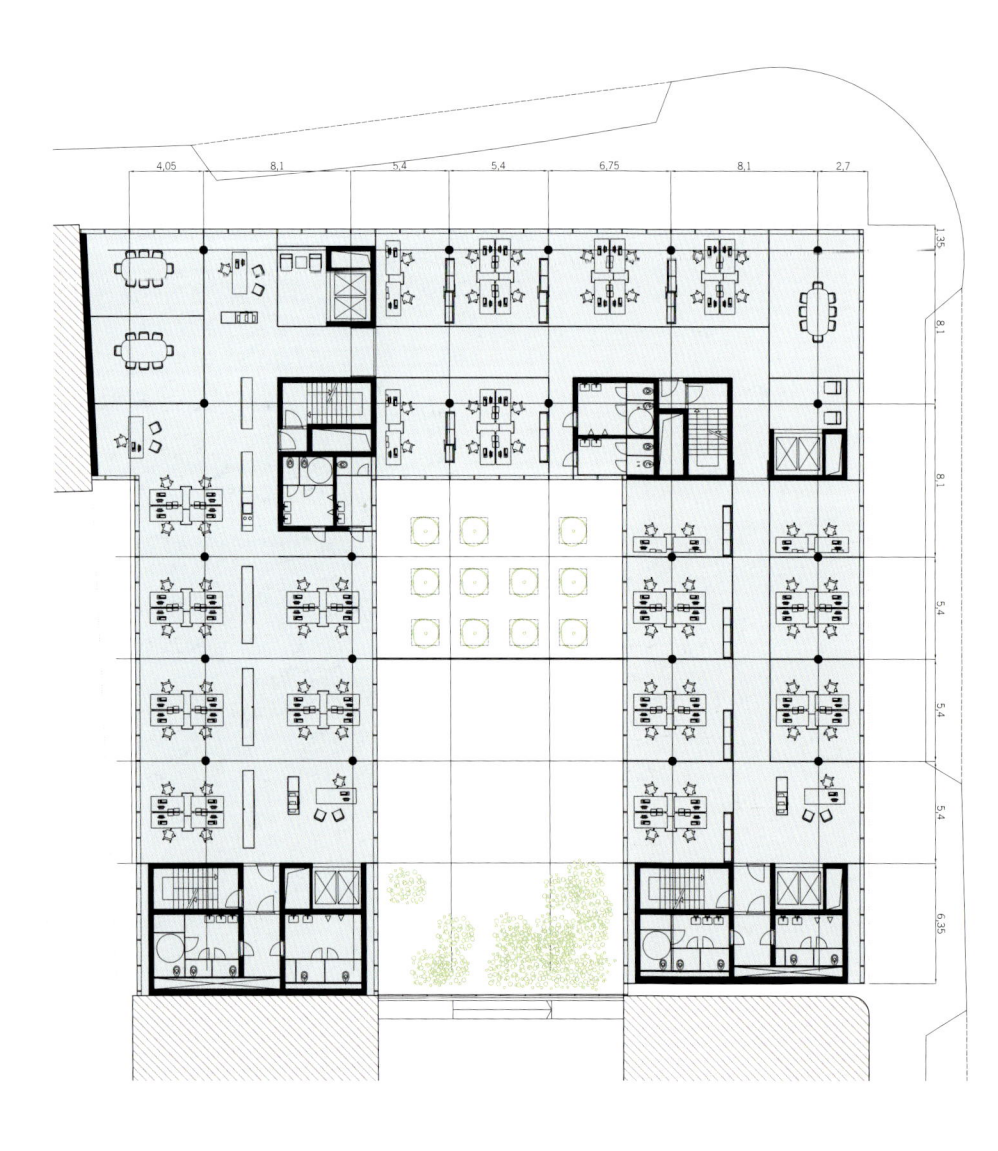

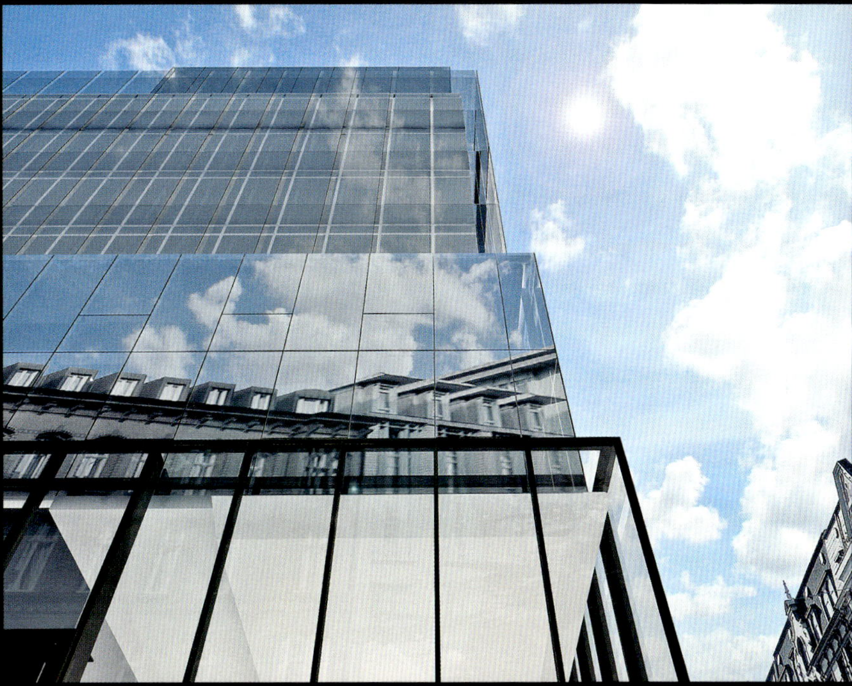

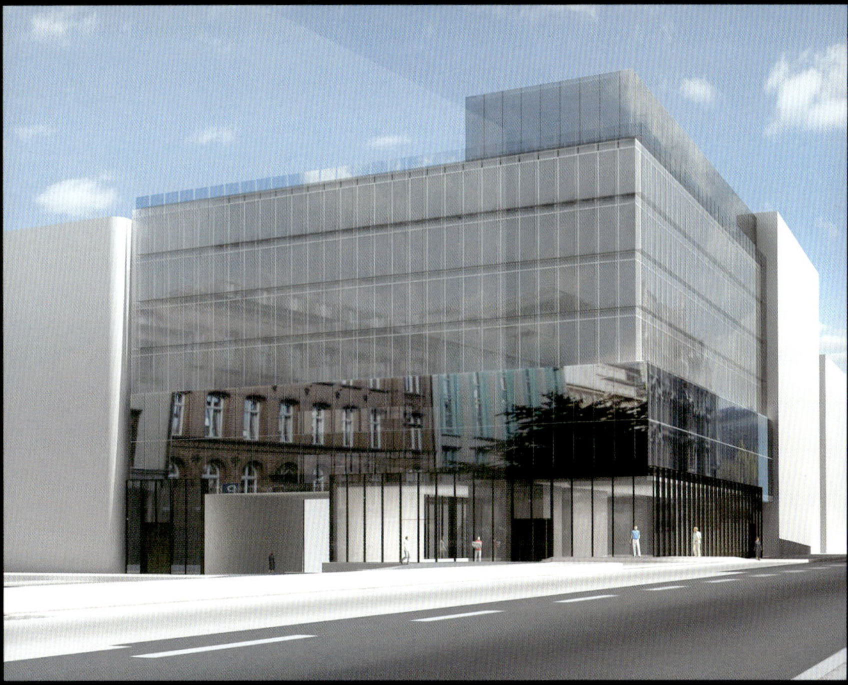

ECONOMY

ECONOMY

2005 Palazzo Toro, Milan / CB Richard Ellis Limited

*Design competition.
Project for the requalification of the historical Toro Assicurazioni palazzo in Piazza San Babila, Milan, for multipurpose use: businesses on ground level, offices and residences on upper levels.*

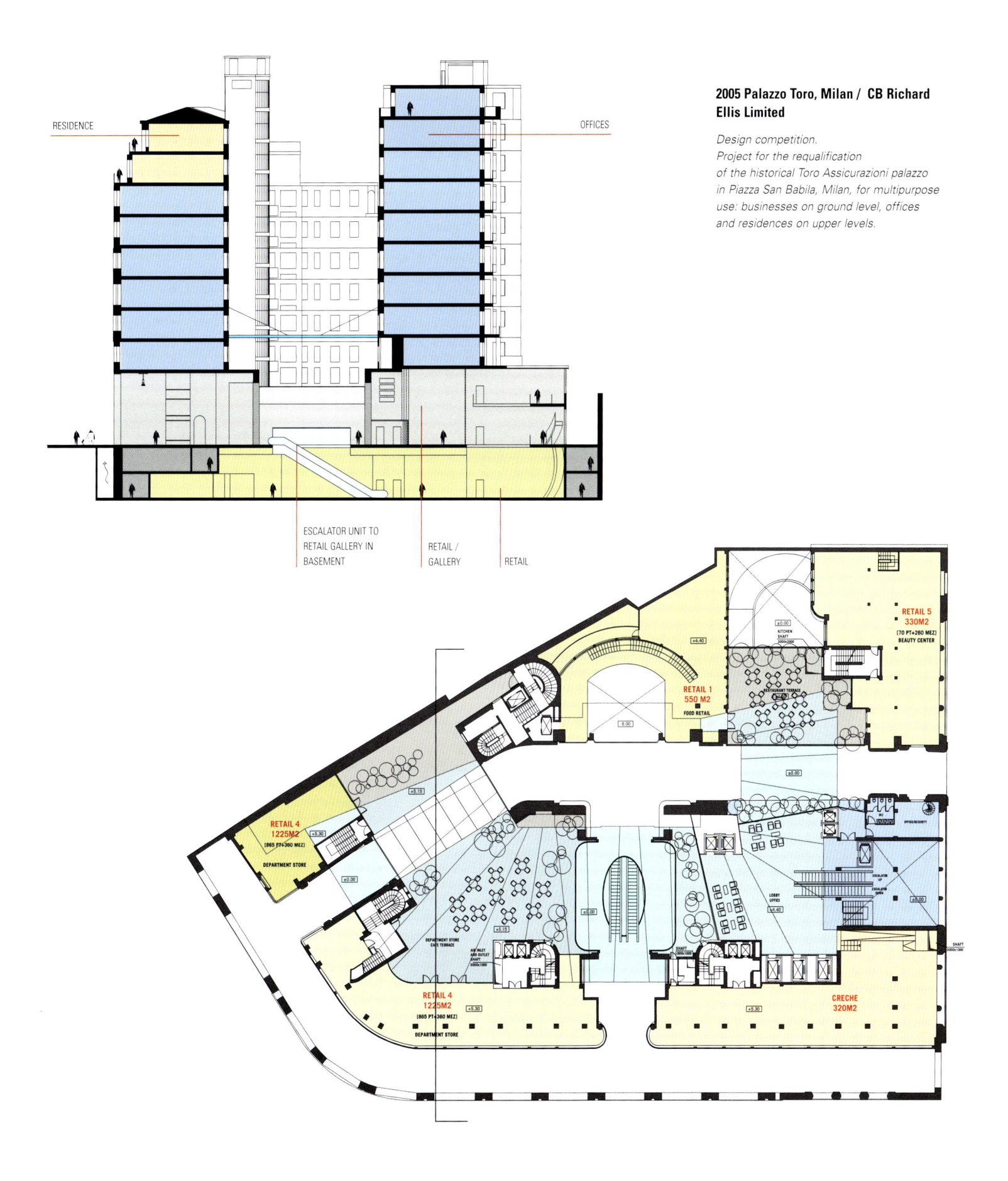

ECONOMY

The project addresses land-use issues and seeks to enhance the historical, architectural and environmental characteristics of Morbegno, a municipality whose geographic position and rich endowment of extra-municipal services rightfully define it as the "gateway to Valtellina".
The Integrated Renewal Plan includes: enhancement of the entire valley floor "backbone" system by means of careful design of building orientation and visual penetrability, the creation of excellent vistas and the construction of buildings of varying heights in order to harmonise with the physiographic characteristics of the Bitto alluvial fan; improvement of the quality of public spaces by means of a complex system of routes and piazzas; the needed revitalisation of the municipality's historical commercial vocation by enhancing the vitality and mobility system of the entire urban fabric; and the design of a residential complex that will dialogue with both the historical centre and with the surrounding natural environment.

ECONOMY

2006 Former Martinelli Morbegno, Sondrio

Integrated intervention programme / Morbegno 2000
19,500 sq. m requalification of public spaces, design of squares and walkways, underground public parking area.
24,673 sq. m built area divided among residences, businesses, direction and accommodations.

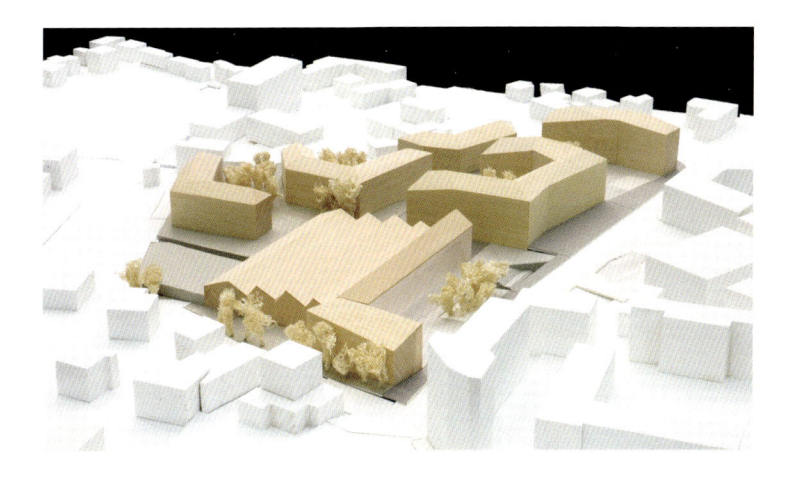

CLIENT.7

CLIENT

Giorgio Busnelli; Piero Gandini; Rolf Fehlbaum; Nerio Alessandri; Anna Zegna

Johnson's admonitions conclude with the client, where he comments that there is another nasty crutch that architects will encounter in their careers: Please listen well. You will not be able to escape criticism by saying, "The client wanted it this way." That is what Hood, one of the greatest American architects, always used to say. He was capable of putting a gothic door in a skyscraper and saying, "Why shouldn't I? The client wanted a gothic door and I gave him one. Why should I have acted on my own volition? Am I not here to do what the client wants?" It needs to be very clear that it's one thing to satisfy the client, and it's another to practice the art of architecture.[1]

With rare exceptions, the architect needs a client in order to express his or her work. It is in the nature of things. Unlike the artist, the architect has to deal with the desires, ambitions, tastes and finances of a client. But this is not sufficient warrant for sacrificing the integrity of the architect's work whenever his or her views do not coincide with those of the client. While an artist has the option of destroying unsuccessful works, "the ivy never grows fast enough" for an architect. The artist does not have a city council to convince, urban planning schemes to adhere to or budgets to negotiate. Paraphrasing Philip Johnson, of the artists, the architect is the one that has the hardest professional life. As Massimiliano Fuksas put it, "we need a courageous governing class, one willing to get into the game and take risks, if we are to build liveable cities and buildings that are not banal. We need architects – but first and foremost, we need clients."[2] His *j'accuse* is only the most recent in a series of barbs by architects aimed at the client class.

"An architect's true fortune is to find exceptional clients. I was lucky."[3] Antonio Citterio does not seek support from the crutch of the client. He does not identify the client as the cross that the designer has to bear, and he does not blame the clients for the stagnation in Italian architecture and design. On the contrary, he considers "industry to be an opportunity and its constraints a stimulus for design."[4] He chooses his clients with care. He shares their values, takes part in their company strategies and attends to them with passion and dedication. It goes without saying that certain professional encounters have developed into friendships that "have had a decisive influence on my professional growth." And if the ordinary client is the one masterfully described by Alessandro Mendini – "the typical client is always quite banal: an administrative organisation, a politician, a cultural institution, a merchant or an industrial structure incapable or poorly suited to expressing idealised needs. They can only think in the short term, within a limited dimension and on a small scale, about minor issues"[5] – then Citterio can truly boast having "exceptional clients". They include Doug Tompkins, Rolf Fehlbaum and the Busnelli

[1] Philip Johnson, "The Seven Crutches of Modern Architecture", *Perspecta 3*, 1955, pp. 40–44, adapted from the Italian translation, "I sette puntelli dell'architettura moderna", in Philip Johnson, *Verso il Postmoderno. Genesi di una deregulation creativa*. Genoa: Costa&Nolan, 1985, p. 102.

[2] Massimiliano Fuksas, "Architetti all'inferno", *L'Espresso*, 25 August 2006, p. 96.

[3] Conversation with the author, June 2006.

[4] Ibid.

[5] Alessandro Mendini, *La poltrona di Proust*. Milan: Tranchida Editori, 1991, p. 40.

[6] Andrea Branzi, *Introduzione al design italiano*. Milan: Baldini e Castoldi, 1999, p. 8.

[7] See F. Zurlo, R. Cagliano, G. Simonelli and R. Verganti, "Innovare con il design", *Il sole 24 ore*, Milan 2002, and in particular, the essay by Paola Bertola, "Design e territori di conoscenza", pp. 25–31.

[8] Richard Normann, *Le condizioni di sviluppo dell'impresa*. Milan: Etas Libri, 1979.

[9] Giancarlo C. Cocco, *Creatività, Ricerca e Innovazione*. Milan: Franco Angeli, 2002, p. 159.

family. With their respective firms, Esprit, Vitra and B&B, they have marked various turning points in Citterio's work. They also represent an example of the harmony between entrepreneur and architect that characterises Italian design. The same is true for Piero Gandini of Flos, Nerio Alessandri of Technogym and Anna Zegna, just to name a few of the entrepreneurs who invest in research and consider design to be both a strategic resource and a road to innovation.

And if Italian design is a phenomenon that is "able to elaborate innovation as a political response to negative cultures and operating conditions",[6] it goes without saying that design-oriented innovation is more than just technological: it is above all aesthetic, performance-oriented and functional. It is founded, in short, on the awareness that the individual product produces no innovative thrust on its own, but is rather to be considered part of a "product system", meaning by this the whole apparatus of advertising, performance and services associated with it.[7] Echoing Richard Normann,[8] Gian Carlo Cocco observes that "within the company structure there is a process of transformation and a process of development. The former transforms inputs into outputs. The latter corresponds to growth and includes the identification of new business opportunities, technological innovation, learning of new methods, etc."[9] Companies have to manage both these variables simultaneously. They have traditionally done so by assigning the development process to top management or to designers like Antonio Citterio who are capable of managing both.

The objective is to "revitalise" a series of values innate to the "Made in Italy": values that are more poetic than technological; values that do not relate to the technical capabilities of the product, but rather to the poetics, lifestyles, consumption patterns and aesthetics typical of Italian culture. This is where the "creativity" of the designer confronts industrial demand for products capable of telling a story in which the typically Italian design culture becomes a visible, recognisable and communicable value.

Because if it is true, as Andrea Branzi has written, that Italian design was born out of an ambiguous situation – Italian industrialists were predominantly artisans whose businesses were growing and could thus afford to make prototypes. They were artisans with the odd trait of being open to experimentation and working together with designers – conditions today are radically different and the learn-by-doing approach that informed Italian design has given way to industrial processes where even the *ex tempore* has no alternative but to be designed in all its details.

"In the 1960s in Italy, the figure of the industrialist who believes in architecture as a component of the industrial ethic crumbled," explains Citterio. "After the season of Adriano Olivetti, a trend towards deindustrialisation and politicisation set in, which had a strong impact on architecture and design. There were certainly few entrepreneurs interested in architecture. Today things are changing. The new generation of Italian industrialists has expanded its horizons, consolidating the position of an industrial middle class that is not entrenched in its positions, but sensitive and open to the external world. I have observed among many of my current clients, especially the younger ones, an interest in architecture that rejects the merely aesthetical. They understand the symbolic and representational – and I would dare say 'monumental' – function of architecture, its political and social role, its ability to shape the territory and incarnate values."[10]

Citterio's analytical rigour united with his extraordinary capacity to identify and resolve critical points are qualities that are recognised and appreciated by his clients. Having to choose between semiartisanal and serial production, Citterio unhesitatingly opts for the latter, integrating industrial processes and methods into the project. And this appeals to industrialists for whom, as Rolf Fehlbaum sums up so effectively, "designing fundamentally means resolving a problem. A designer has to have a good grasp of production processes and an equally good grasp of company identity. Good designers are problem solvers. They work with an aesthetic sensitivity to resolve ergonomic, formal or ecological problems. Citterio is an excellent problem solver."[11] This observation finds indirect confirmation in Citterio's statement: "I have a hard time designing if there are no problems. The main stimulus behind my work is to resolve a problem, whether it is formal, technical, functional, typological or aesthetic. Architecture, for example, always presents some sort of problem." Citterio's collaboration with Vitra, spanning over a quarter century, could be recounted as a tale of problems: many were resolved, some put on hold, a few left unresolved but certainly none were ignored. Because Citterio is a tenacious professional, as his many architecture and design projects created for Vitra demonstrate: from the office systems to the Neuenburg production facility in 1992, the redesign of the offices and the new pedestrian walkway in Weil am Rhein (1993–1994), the Vitrashop Paris showroom and offices in 1991 and the Vitrashop showroom in Weil am Rhein in 1989. More than a professional collaboration, the relationship with Vitra could better be described as a tacit and discreet agreement about founding the concept of architecture and design on an ethical vision of work. It is a vision free of haste and free of tricks, because, as Fehlbaum states, "today, slowness is a precious value. I think that every object has to follow its own evolutionary path. If Charles Eames had said 'we have to finish in a hurry', his chairs would not still be so expressive half a century later. I believe in doing things well and I share this ardent desire with Antonio. At Vitra, you cannot rush things if you want to have good results. Every object has its own soul and our job is to find it, even if at times you have to abandon or radically modify a project. We do not worry about being the first ones because what we do is unique by its very nature. Good design is timeless. For this reason, Antonio Citterio is much more than a good designer. His products for Vitra do

[10] Conversation with the author, February 2006.

[11] Rolf Fehlbaum, conversation with the author, May 2006.

[12] Ibid.

[13] Conversation with the author, February 2006.

[14] Ibid.

not fear the dust of time. In addition to representing a response to new demands – of the contemporary office, for example – they are poetic, pure and emotive."[12]

If Doug Tompkins's Esprit introduced him into the elite of cosmopolitan architectural culture, Rolf Fehlbaum's Vitra elevated Citterio into the empyrean of international design. In keeping with the Eames model, this realm is identified with the needs of businesses and the global project, much in line with the Milanese architect's steadfast pursuit. "Design is an integral part of industrial fertility," says Fehlbaum. "There are no PC designers in Italy because there are no companies that make PCs. Demand creates supply, and we work where the industry is."[13] Business culture has a primary role in Citterio's works, not only in aesthetic terms, but also as the expression of values. The encounter with Doug Tompkins was momentous in this sense. In 1985, he commissioned Citterio to design the building for Esprit Italia. This work marked a fundamental milestone in Antonio's career, giving him recognition as an architect and allowing him to stand face to face with internationally famous architects. As Citterio himself states, "Esprit allowed me to do architecture at a time when much of my work was dedicated to design. I missed dealing with things on a large scale, and then they called me from San Francisco and sent me all around the world, to Hong Kong and Tokyo, to meet the architects who worked with Tadao Ando and Kuramata. It was a fundamental experience both professionally and on the human level. It was a relationship with the client unlike any other. I was fascinated by the Esprit philosophy, where the project was seen in terms of creativity and joie de vivre. Not coincidentally, their image was groomed by Oliviero Toscani, who did an excellent job of translating the company culture."[14]

Fehlbaum comments in this regard with his usual lucidity, "design is not an abstraction, but rather the direct manifestation of company philosophy and culture. For this reason it is very important how a company chooses to translate its values into design. Sure, it can tell lies or break promises, but that's 'bad design'. The bigger the promises, the worse the result. Of course there is also 'good design' and 'great design'. 'Good design' is the honest expression of the values of a company or designer, while 'great design' is something that has something important to say, something that communicates an epochal ideal. 'Great design' is an icon of the times, a metaphor for an attitude, the expression of a soul. The object does not have to call attention to the fact that it is a 'design' object, because it is always conceptually new; it is new forever, like those objects designed fifty years ago that you never get tired of looking at and using. 'Great design' has a strong impact without needing to show off – like Citterio's design. I met Citterio over twenty years ago. Bellini was working for us at the time, but I wanted to have another voice for Vitra. Antonio struck me back then for his unusual capacity to be a problem solver and, at the same time, a form giver. He has a technical and rational approach coupled with an extraordinary passion for his work."¹⁵

Fehlbaum is echoed by Giorgio Busnelli of B&B and Piero Gandini of Flos, representing two important collaborations for Citterio. Gandini says that "Antonio has an absolutely unique level of professionalism, with a keen eye for detail and for all company processes. We often joke with Philippe Starck that if we were going to have someone build a house for us, we would ask Citterio, because we would be sure of the results. For Antonio, it's a sort of mission. His rigour and dedication reveal his ethical attitude towards design. I have always been struck by his precision, which I consider to be a synonym for passion."¹⁶

Giorgio Busnelli takes an analogous position, stating that "Antonio has an enormous passion and an amazing curiosity for the things of the world. He is incredibly focused on the project. I have never seen anyone work like him. He has a total commitment, and a 360 degree perspective. He is not the kind of designer who arrives with the sketch all ready; the project is the fruit of a vision built working together and discussing things with us. He doesn't fall in love with the product like most designers do. He is one of the few who are able to distance themselves from the project and preserve a clearheaded critical stance regarding the product and its relationship to the market."¹⁷

Citterio's attention to the market is something different from the marketing strategies in vogue today among interior design firms. "We are living in a very interesting historical period," states Piero Gandini. "We have finally got beyond the ideological concept of 'right' design and 'wrong' design. Now we have minimalism, neobaroque and a host of other aesthetics. The reality is that everyone wants to do different things even though this plurality of approaches could degenerate into anarchy, to the detriment of quality. I do not believe in 'do-it-all' designers, and I especially do not believe in analyses of trends, scenarios, consumption patterns and so on. In a word, I don't believe in marketing as a tool in the design process. Antonio has an ideal vision of the bond between himself, his product and the client that will be using it. He doesn't think in terms of 'targets', he thinks precisely of who is going to live in his spaces, sit on his chairs or read in the light of his lamps. In our work, we extrapolate the consequences of our being and our thinking."¹⁸

A different sort of opinion is held by Nerio Alessandri, for whom Citterio has worked on a variety of different scales, from the Technogym Village fitness centre to *Kinesis*, a multifunctional piece of equipment. For Alessandri, "the designer not only has to be an industrial designer and an artistic consultant, but also a manager who has to share an intent for customer satisfaction and have a plan for creating value. He has to be able to intuit the needs of the market, be sensitive to trends, know how to instil emotions, respect the client's image and not impose his own design or his own style. He also has to know how to manage costs and develop timelines, as well as how to

[15] Rolf Fehlbaum, conversation with the author, May 2006.

[16] Piero Gandini, conversation with the author, October 2006.

[17] Giorgio Busnelli, conversation with the author, July 2006.

[18] Piero Gandini, conversation with the author, October 2006.

[19] Nerio Alessandri, conversation with the author, July 2006.

[20] Anna Zegna, conversation with the author, July 2006.

[21] Rolf Fehlbaum, adapted from an interview in *Business Week*, 26 January 2004.

[22] Piero Gandini, conversation with the author, January 2006.

[23] Erica Corbellini and Stefania Saviolo, *La scommessa del made in Italy*. Milan: Etas, 2004, p. 154.

collaborate with all the various company functions and be a part of the company system, of an overall team."[19]

Alessandri's designer-manager concept is complemented by an interpretation of the designer as a figure capable of decoding the signals coming from the outside world and reinterpreting them for the company into an ad hoc aesthetic. Anna Zegna stresses Citterio's sensitivity for the context: "His architectural and design projects are always refined down to the smallest detail. Antonio is able to express the sense of tradition in various ways, interpreting it in a modern key through purity of line and research into materials. He mirrors the Zegna culture and philosophy, where tradition and innovation are synonyms for contemporary style."[20]

These words evince Citterio's deep knowledge of the companies he works with, of all of their elements, from their industrial processes to their advertising efforts. This is not always an easy thing to achieve, given that most Italian interior design companies are family-run. At times this limit may be transformed into an advantage, as Fehlbaum observes: "Family businesses have the disadvantage that the boss does whatever he wants in his own house. He does not have to account for his work like managers of public companies have to do. This may be a dangerous thing at times. But on the other hand, being free from certain pressures has its opportunity benefits. You can do things that public companies cannot afford to do, like working on a project for forty years. From this perspective, Vitra is a precapitalist company, where you can try things out that have no immediate purpose or return, where the mix of culture and commercial interests becomes a characteristic of the company."[21]

Piero Gandini also considers family-based management "on the one hand, to be a limit to company growth, while on the other, a potential for innovation. The freedom to make mistakes is what allows one to make immediate decisions, accelerate the choices and decision-making processes. The problem for Italian family-run companies today is not their business model, but generational changes, which have been extremely problematic in Italy."[22]

And family management remains one of the characteristic business models of the "Made in Italy", as is evidenced by the entrepreneurs with whom Citterio works. The strength of family businesses lies in their attachment to the product, their capacity for mediation, their long-term vision and, as has been observed, "onward and upward with family businesses, provided that they know how to separate management of the business from management of the family and that they are able to grow."[23]

Biography Antonio Citterio and Partners

Antonio Citterio was born in Meda (Milan) in 1950. He graduated in Architecture from the Politecnico of Milan and opened his studio in 1972 where he started his architectural and interior design business.

Between 1987 and 1996 he worked in association with Terry Dwan and, together, they created buildings in Europe and Japan.

Among his most significant works: the restyling of a block in the historical centre of Seregno, the Esprit headquarters in Amsterdam, Antwerp and Milan, industrial plants for Vitra, in Germany, and for Antonio Fusco, in Milan.

In 1999, Antonio Citterio and Partners was founded by Citterio and Patricia Viel; it is a multidisciplinary studio for architectural design, industrial design and graphics.

Patricia Viel was born in Milan in 1962. She graduated in Architecture from the Politecnico of Milan in 1987 and started her collaboration with Antonio Citterio in 1986 as project leader.

Head of the architecture section and since 1999 a partner of the firm, she is now actively involved in its management.

Since 2005 she has been a member of the National Institute of Architecture IN/ARCH.

The studio develops projects for residential complexes, apartment buildings, hotels, trade centres and industrial sites, refurbishes public buildings and plans workspaces, offices and showrooms; it also operates in the field of corporate communication – implementing corporate image projects, fittings, graphics – and in the field of industrial design.

Antonio Citterio works for Italian and foreign companies such as Albatros – Sanitec Group, Ansorg, Arclinea, Aubrilam, Axor-Hansgrohe, B&B Italia, Flexform, Flos, Fusital, Guzzini, Iittala, Inda, Kartell, Maxalto, Metalco, Sanitec Group/Pozzi Ginori, Simon Urmet, Skantherm, Tre Più, Vitra, Wall.

In April 2000, the new headquarters opened in Milan, on Via Cerva 4, and in May of that same year, new offices were opened in Hamburg, on 75b Wrangelstrasse.

In 2002, the construction of the building where the headquarters of the Edel Company are located, along the Elba River, was completed as well as an office building in Neuer Wall, two constructions for offices and textile manufacturing in Legnano (Milan) and Lecco and the headquarters of the R&D Centre with showroom and offices for B&B Italia in Novedrate (Como).

Between 2003 and 2004, a corporate image project was implemented for De Beers (London and Tokyo) and, in May 2004, the Bulgari Hotel was inaugurated in Milan, the first of a chain of luxury hotels known as "Bulgari Hotels and Resorts".

In 2005, the restructuring of the historical Town Hall of Clusone, facing Piazza dell'Orologio, the project for the headquarters and day-care centre of the pharmaceutical company GlaxoSmithKline in Verona, the project for a law firm in Sondrio and two projects for private residences – one in Basel, Switzerland, the other in Sardinia, Italy, were all completed.

The Bulgari Hotel in Bali and the Aspesi showroom in the Milanese fashion district on Via Montenapoleone were inaugurated in September 2006. In December of that year, the "Michele Alboreto" pedestrian square in Rozzano (Milan) was opened.

Current projects include: the new "Technogym Village" in Cesena (production site, offices and trade centre), the former Riva Calzoni reconversion as business fashion district, in Milan; a new square in Busto Arsizio (Varese); the refurbishment, furniture and security of the south pier in Ravenna Marina; the renovation of the urban former Martinelli area in Morbegno and various private residences.

Antonio Citterio has taken part in a great number of international competitions. In 2002, a project was presented at a competition for the restyling of the "Jungfernstieg", an area where the tourist boats land on Lake Binnenalster, complete with trade centres, walking areas and an underground stop. In March 2004, a project was presented to change the historical centre of the Fiera di Milano into a new urban centre, in cooperation with other architects. In April 2004, the project for the building of the Brooktorhafen bridge in the new Hafencity district, with docks and pedestrian subways, in Hamburg. In May 2004, a project for the new exhibiting concept for the halls of the Rijksmuseum in Amsterdam. In June 2004, the project to enlarge a new multifunctional school building and a nursery for the Deutsche Schule Mailand. In September 2004, together with other architects, he won the competition for new ideas for the functional arrangement, street furniture and security systems of the Guardiano Sud pier, Ravenna Marina, which was presented on the occasion of the IX. International Architecture Exhibition of the Biennale of Venice, "Towns on Water" section.

Citterio won, in 2005, the competition for a hotel project in the Hafencity district in Hamburg; he has been invited to the design competition for the hotel facilities in the new exhibition grounds of Rho-Pero and for a residential complex in Lezzeno on Lake Como.

Moreover, the Neumühlen project won second prize from the Hamburg Architektur Preis and a special mention from the Deutscher Architektur Preis.

In January 2007, Antonio Citterio and Partners won the international architectural competition for the refurbishment of the Ferrante Aporti building (which formerly housed the Italian post office) in Milan. That same month the project for the GlaxoSmithKline day-care centre in Verona was selected by the Mies van der Rohe Award jury and, together with thirty-two other projects, will be part of the catalogue and exhibition. Beginning in January 2007 the firm is UNI EN ISO 9001:2000 certified.

In 2004, the Italian publishing house Electa issued the monograph *Antonio Citterio. Industrial Design*. The monograph *Antonio Citterio*, written by Luigi Prestinenza Pugliesi and published by Edilstampa, was released one year later.

Since 2006, Antonio Citterio has been a professor at the Accademia di Architettura dell'Università della Svizzera Italiana.

Architecture

2006

- *Bulgari Hotels & Resorts*
Bulgari Hotel in Bali

- *CMB Cooperativa Muratori Braccianti*
New square in Rozzano (Milan) project

2005–2006

- *Luna Co.*
Hotel and commercial building in Osaka. Under project

- *Quantum Immobilien AG*
Hotel and offices complex in Hafencity, Hamburg. Under project

2005

- *Clusone City Council*
Renovation of the city hall of Clusone (Bergamo, Italy)

- *GlaxoSmithKline*
Headquarters and offices and day-care centre on the company campus in Verona (Italy)

- *Private Client*
House in Basel

2004–2006

- *Agnona S.p.A.*
New corporate headquarters of the Ermenegildo Zegna Group, Milan. Under construction

- *Autorità Portuale Ravenna*
Renovation of the Guardiano Sud pier in Ravenna Marina. Under project

- *Immobiliare Berget*
Offices and showrooms complex in Lissone (Milan). Under construction

- *Mercury Trading Company*
Luxury village hotel and spa in Moscow. Under construction

- *Soceba*
New pedestrian square in Busto Arsizio (Varese, Italy). Work in progress

2004–2005

- *Private Client*
Villa project in Sondrio (Italy). Under construction

2004

- *ATM*
Restyling of the MM1 underground mezzanines (Duomo area). Design of the glazed roofing for lifts and escalators, MM1 and MM2 underground lines

- *Bulgari Hotels & Resorts*
Bulgari Hotel in Milan

- *Private Client*
Villa in Villasimius (Sardinia)

2003–2006

- *Private Client*
Apartment and hotel building in Bormio (Sondrio, Italy). Under construction

2003

- *Private Client*
Beach house in Doha (Qatar). Under project

- *Private Client*
House in Nienstedten (Germany)

2002–2006

- *Technogym*
"Technogym Village": production plant, office building and multifunctional centre project in Cesena (Italy). Under construction

2002–2005

- *The Brown Companies*
Private house, Sagaponac, Long Island. Under project

- *Mody&Mody*
European furniture store in Dallas and Houston. Under project

2001–2002

- *Bernd Kortum*
Office building in Neuer Wall, Hamburg

2000–2002

- *B&B Italia*
R&D Centre headquarter and showroom in Novedrate (Como)

- *Gentilann srl*
Textile factory and offices in Lecco (Italy)

2000–2001

- *Alberto Aspesi*
Factory in Legnano (Milan)

- *Edel Music*
Headquarters on the Elbe River in Hamburg

- *Private Client*
Villa project in Nebbiuno (Novara, Italy)

2000

- *Antonio Citterio and Partners*
Offices in Milan, Via Cerva 4

In 2000, another Antonio Citterio and Partners studio was opened in Hamburg by Antonio Citterio, Patricia Viel and Jan Hinrichs.
In 1999, Antonio Citterio and Partners was established by Antonio Citterio and Patricia Viel.

1998

- *Eurojersey*
Offices and showroom in Caronno Pertusella (Varese, Italy)

1997

- *Private Client*
Residence in Hamburg

1995

- *Flexform*
Office building in Meda (Milan)

- *Private Client*
Villa near Bergamo (Italy)

- *Private Client*
Villa near Como

1993

- *Antonio Fusco*
Factory, offices and showroom in Corsico (Milan)

1992

- *Daigo Company*
Headquarters in Tokyo

- *Vitra*
Production plant in Neuenberg (Germany)

1991

- *Ohbayashi*
Office building and showroom in Tokyo, with Toshiyuki Kita

1989

- *Government of Kumamoto*
Experimental housing in Kumamoto (Japan)

1987–1988

- *Esprit Benelux*
Renovation to create a new store, office, showroom and restaurant for the Esprit Benelux headquarters in Amsterdam and Antwerp

In 1987, Terry Dwan became partner in the Antonio Citterio Dwan project, and all the subsequent projects until 1996 were signed Antonio Citterio and Terry Dwan Architects.

1986

- *Private Client*
Commercial and administrative building complex in Seregno (Milan)

1985–1987

- *Esprit de Corp*
Renovation to create a new store, office and showroom complex for the Esprit Italy headquarters in Milan

1984

- *Private Client*
House in Meda (Milan)

Interiors

2006

- *Aspesi*
Concept store for Aspesi showroom, Milan and Rome

- *Bulgari Hotels & Resorts*
Interior design for the Bulgari Hotel in Bali

- *Mercury*
Interior design for a multipurpose hall and auditorium in Barvikha (Moscow). Work in progress

- *Terra Group*
Interior design concept for the apartment building Freedom Tower, Miami. Under project

- *W Hotels*
Interior design for a hotel in St Petersburg. Work in progress

2005 2006

- *Loungesleep*
Interior design for a hotel in New York. Work in progress

- *Peek&Cloppenburg*
Store concepts per the chain in Germany

2005

- *B&B Italia*
B&B Italia Store in Münich

- *Clusone City Council*
Council offices in Clusone (Bergamo, Italy)

- *De Beers*
Concept and interior design for the new jewellery stores in New York and Los Angeles

- *GlaxoSmithKline*
Offices in the headquarters complex in Verona (Italy)

- *Private Client*
Interior design for a house in Lecce (Italy)

- *Trunk Ltd.*
Interior concept for Mitsui Aoyama Housing Project, Ltd. (Japan)

- *Valentino*
Concept and interior design for the new store in Tokyo

2004

- *Bulgari Hotels & Resorts*
Interior design for the new hotel in Milan

2003

- *Private Client*
Penthouse in Milan

2002

- *B&B Italia*
B&B Italia Store in Milan

- *Casa Damiani Jewellery*
Flagship store on Via Montenapoleone, Milan

- *De Beers*
Flagship concept store in London and Tokyo

2001

- *Ab Hotels*
Concept and interior design project for the Broadway Grand Hotel in New York. Project

- *B&B Italia*
B&B Italia and Maxalto showroom on Brompton Road in London (with John Pawson); Maxalto showroom in Paris

- *Bulgari Hotels & Resorts*
Concept and interior design project for the new chain of luxury hotels

- *Edel Music AG*
Offices, restaurant, coffee shop and auditorium in the headquarters building in Hamburg

- *Emanuel Ungaro*
Stores in New York, London, Rome and Paris

- *Valentino*
Flagship store on Via Montenapoleone, Milan

2000–2001

- *ATM*
Restyling of MM1 underground line, Milan

- *Mitsui Real Estate*
Design for six typologies of apartments, with construction of a pilot project on full scale, Tokyo

- *Private Client*
Interior and furniture design for a villa in Bachsul on the lake of Zurich

1999–2000

- *Stefanel*
Flagship concept store in Berlin, Milan, Rome, Naples, Palermo and Bologna

1999

- *Frmenegildo Zegna*
Concept for Zegna Sport clothing stores in Europe, North America and Asia

- *UEFA*
Interior design of the new headquarters of the UEFA in Nyon (Switzerland)

1998

- *Alberto Aspesi*
Showroom in Milan

- *Arclinea*
Showroom in Caldogno (Vicenza, Italy)

- *Daimler Chrysler & MCC*
Concept for the "Smart" car showrooms

- *Enzo degli Angiuoni*
Offices and showroom in Birago (Milan)

1996–1999

- *Cerruti*
Flagship store and showroom in Milan and New York

1996–1997

- *Habitat*
Concept store in London and Paris

1996

- *Commerzbank*
Pilot branches in Frankfurt and Berlin

1993

- *B&B Italia*
Furniture showroom in New York

1992

- *Massimo De Carlo*
Art Gallery in Milan

1990

- *Esprit*
Concept stores in Paris, Madrid, Lisbon and Neuchâtel (Switzerland)

1989

- *Vitrashop*
Showroom in Weil am Rhein (Germany)

- *World Co. Headquarters*
Offices and showroom in Kobe (Japan, with Toshiyuki Kita)

1983–1996

- *Fausto Santini*
Flagship concept stores in Florence, Düsseldorf, Miami, Geneva, Paris, Milan and Rome

1983

- *Pinacoteca di Brera*
Joint project with Gregotti Associates for general refurbishment of the Piero della Francesca and Raphael Halls, Milan

Design Products

Aiko

1999
- Design and coordination of the complete Aiko kitchen collection

Albatros

2005
- Cube**, tubs and shower system

Ansorg

1993
- Cupola*, pendant downlight
- Elettra*, lighting system

1994
- Quadra*, office lighting program

1996
- Camera*, surface mounted spotlights
- Duo-Office*, office lighting program

1998
- Alumina*, floor and wall mounted lamps

2001
- Pizza*, lighting system

2002
- Brick, lighting system

2004
- Vario, variable lighting duct system

Arclinea

1988
- Italia, kitchen programme

1992
- Mediterranea, kitchen programme

1995
- Ginger, kitchen programme

1996
- Artusi, kitchen programme
- Florida, kitchen programme
- Florida Young, kitchen programme

2002
- Convivium, kitchen programme

Artemide

1998
- Enea, wall mounted lamp

2003
- Hal, floor and wall mounted lamps

Aubrilam

2006
- Alba***, street furniture (Innovation & Design Award 2007)

Axor Hansgrohe

2001–2003
- Axor Citterio***, bathroom fittings and accessories (on permanent display at the Museum of Architecture and Design in Chicago)

2006
- Axor Citterio Kitchen***, kitchen fitting (Red Dot Design Award 2006)

B&B Italia

1973
- Modulo 30°, chairs and small armchairs

1975
- Baia°, modular sofas

1979
- Diesis°, sofas, armchairs and small tables (selected for Resources Council Product and Program Award)

1980
- Ialea, chair

1982
- Ottomana, sofas

1986
- Sity, sofas and armchairs (Compasso d'Oro Award 1987)

1989
- Domus, storage units
- Baisity, chairs and small armchairs

1993
- Compagnia delle Filippine, chairs and small armchairs
- Panama, chairs and small armchairs

1994
- Balletto, beds
- Canaletto, beds

1995
- Harry, sofas and armchairs
- Florence, armchair

1996
- Melandra, chairs and small armchairs
- Angiolo, table
- Domusnova, storage units

1997
- Charles, sofas, armchairs, small tables and beds
- Dandy, sofa collection
- Basiko, sofas

1998
- T60, small tables
- Web, chairs and small armchairs

1999
- Cross, storage units
- Dado, sofas and armchairs
- Freetime, sofas and armchairs
- Solo, sofas, armchairs, chairs and small tables
- Tight, sofas and armchairs

2000
- Iuta, chairs and small armchairs

2001
- Domus '00, storage unit
- George, sofas, armchairs and small tables

2002
- Door, wardrobes

2003
- Eileen, tables and small tables
- Marcel, sofas, armchairs and beds
- Mart, armchairs
- P60, complements
- Te 3000, table

2005
- Arne, sofas, armchairs and complements
- J.J., armchair and small armchair

2006
- Otto Chairs***, chairs

2007
- Luis, sofa and armchair

Bieffe

1989
- Draft Line***, drafting table system

Boffi Cucine

1980
- Factory°, kitchen programme

Edilkamin

1994
- Foco, fireplace

Flexform

1978
- Aria°, sofas

1979
- Pasodouble°, sofas and armchairs

1980
- I divani di famiglia°, sofas and armchairs

1982
- Magister°, sofas

1983
- Max, sofas

1985
- Ginger, sofa and chaise lounge

1996
- Carlotta, chair, small armchair and complements

1998
- ABC, armchair
- Brenda, small armchair

2001
- Groundpiece, sofa, ottoman and complements

2002
- Lightpiece, sofa, ottoman and complements

2003
- Wilson, small armchair

2004
- Infinity, bookshelves
- Peter, small armchair
- Timeless, small armchair

2005
- Air, chaise lounge
- Happy, sofas and armchairs
- Kidd, small tables
- Vic, small tables
- Artwood, small tables

2006
- Happyhour, sofa

Flos

1998
- Lastra*, suspended lamp
- Riga*, wall mounted lamp

2000
- U Beam, H Beam*, suspended lighting system
- XXL, floor lamp
- Metropolitan, floor and table lamps
- Plaza, ceiling lamp

2003
- Kelvin***, table, floor and wall lamps (Red Dot Design Award 2004)
- Ontherocks***, wall lamp (Red Dot Design Award 2004)
- U- Beam Connect, suspended lighting system
- F Beam, floor lamp
- XL, L, M and S, floor, suspended and wall lamps

2005
- Mini Beam, suspended lighting system

2006
- Kelvin T5***, suspended lamp

Fusital

1991
- AC Novantuno, door and window handles

1993
- AC Novantatre, door and window handles

1996
- AC Novantacinque, door and window handles
- AC1 Novantacinque, door and window handles
- AC2 Novantacinque, door and window handles

1997
- AC Novantasette, door and window handles

2000
- K2, door and window handles

2004
- AC3***, door and window handles

Guzzini

2005
- My Table***, cutlery and glassware (If Design Yearbook 2006)
- Square***, cutlery

Halifax

1996
- Minni, chair and stools

Herman Miller

1998
- Sumo, executive office system

Iittala

1998
- Tools Citterio 98*, cutlery

2000
- Collective Tools*, kitchen tools (on permanent display at the Museum of Architecture and Design in Chicago)
- Citterio 2000*, cutlery (on permanent display at the Museum of Architecture and Design in Chicago)

2004
- Decanter***, wine carafe (Design Plus Award 2005)

Inda

1999
- H2O**, bathroom furniture and accessories

2001
- H2O Frame**, bathroom furniture and accessories

Industrie Guido Malvestio

1993
- Emme, hospital ward furniture

IP – Company

2004
- ip 55, lock security system (awarded the Red Dot Design Award, "Best of the Best" 2006)

JCDecaux

1999
- Citterio Collection, street furniture

Kartell

1991
- Battista*, folding trolley and small table (on permanent display at the Centre Pompidou in Paris and the Museum of Modern Art in New York)
- Filippo*, folding trolley
- Gastone*, folding trolley (on permanent display at the Centre Pompidou in Paris)
- Leopoldo*, folding table

1992
- Oxo*, cart (on permanent display at the Centre Pompidou in Paris)

1994
- Mobil*, container on wheels (Compasso d'Oro Award 1995, on permanent display at the Museum of Modern Art in New York and the Centre Pompidou in Paris)
- Tris*, small tables

1996
- Dolly*, folding chair (on permanent display at the Centre Pompidou in Paris)

2000
- Glossy*, table

2002
- Spoon***, stool

2005
- Spoon Chair***, swivel armchair

2006
- Flip***, folding trolley

Maxalto

1996
- Apta Collection, furniture collection

2001–2002
- Simplice Collection, furniture collection

2003
- AC Collection, furniture collection

2007
- Maxalto Collection

MaxData

1997
- Artist, PC unit case

Metalco

2005
- Sedis***, street bench (Uli Milan Bench Competition, second prize)

Pozzi Ginori

2000
- 500**, sanitary appliances
- Join**, sanitary appliances

2002
- Join**, bath collection

2003
- Easy**, sanitary appliances

2004
- Q3**, sanitary appliances
- Quinta**, sanitary appliances

2006
- Novecento**, sanitary appliances

Sawaya & Moroni

1996
- Silver cutlery service

Simon Urmet

2007
- Nea***, switch system
- Foglio***, video entry phone (Innovation & Design Award 2007)

Skantherm

2004
- Shaker***, chimney stove (Red Dot Design Award, "Best of the Best" 2006)

Technogym

2006
- Kinesis Personal***, home wellness strength equipment

Tisettanta

1984
- Metropolis, bookcase system

1996
- XL, wardrobe system

1999
- Centopercento, wardrobe system

Tre Più

1998
- Pavilion, sliding door system

1999
- Planus, hinged door system

2000
- Pavilion Light, sliding door system

2004
- Pavilion Frame, sliding door system

2006
- Continuum, boiserie system

Visplay

1990
- Cargo, retail furniture system

1999
- Kado*, retail furniture system
- Pick up*, retail furniture system

Vitra

1990
- AC Program, office chairs collection
- Area, sofa system for public areas

1992
- Axion*, office chair
- Spatio*, conference table and executive office
- Visavis*, visitor chair

1994
- T-Chairs*, office chair
- Ad Hoc*, office furniture system

1996
- Ad Usum*, conference table
- Axess*, office chair
- Monowall*, workstation
- Quattro*, office chair

1998
- Monowall 2*, workstation
- Visasoft*, conference chairs
- Vademecum*, height adjustable workstation

1999
- Storage wall, storage units system

2000
- Ad Wall, equipped wall system
- Bench, executive table system
- Transphere, library and storage system
- Visarolls, visitor chairs

2002
- Ad One***, table system
- Mobile Elements***, mobile storage and accessories
- New Spatio, executive office
- Oson C / Oson S, office chairs
- ToniX***, visitor chair
- Visofa, sofa
- Visacom, armchair
- Visalounge, lounge armchair
- Visatable, low table

2003
- CEO***, executive office
- Ad Wing***, panel system

2004
- Ad Hoc, office furniture system
- Oson CE, office chair
- Visavis 2, visitor chair
- Visastripe***, visitor chair

2006
- ACSU***, storage system

Wall

2003
- Mon bijou***, street furniture

Xilitalia

1981
- Quadrante°, storage system
- Eridiana, chairs and small armchairs

2003
- CEO***, director's office
- Ad Wing***, panel system

(°) design by Antonio Citterio and Paolo Nava
(*) design by Antonio Citterio with Glen Oliver Löw
(**) design by Antonio Citterio with Sergio Brioschi
(***) design by Antonio Citterio with Toan Nguyen

Competitions

2006

International competition for the design of a wellness village in Cesenatico, Forlì

Design competition for the hotel facilities in the new exhibition grounds of Rho-Pero, Milan

Competition for the residential complex in the "Varesine" district, Milan

Competition for office complex in the "Garibaldi-Repubblica" district, Milan

Competition for the design of a hotel in Bremen

Competition for the requalification of the historic building in Milan, Ferrante-Aporti. Winning competition entry

2005

Competition for the design of a new residential complex with facilities and hotel in Lezzeno, Como

Mantova Fornaci Brioni competition for the design of a new residential and commercial complex

Competition for the requalification of the former tobacco works in Verona and the design of a residential, commercial facilities complex and hotel. Winning competition entry

Competition for the design of a new hotel building with facilities in the "Brooktorkai" area, Hafencity, Hamburg. Winning competition entry

International design competition for the residential complex in Assago Milanofiori, Milan

European competition "Pratum Magnum" for the redevelopment of Piazza Trento, Monza (Milan)

2004

International competition for the new convention centre and hotel facilities in Palma de Mallorca

Competition for the Guardiano Sud pier, Ravenna Marina. Winning competition entry

International competition for the Darsena urban requalification in Milan

International competition for the design of a new bridge for the Hafencity district in Hamburg

Competition for the enlargement of the Deutsche Schule Mailand complex

International competition for the redevelopment of the Fiera di Milano's historical exhibition complex

International competition for the design of the New Rijksmuseum exposition, Amsterdam

2002

International competition for the Yungfernstieg urban design in Hamburg, in collaboration with Kiefer Landscape Design, Berlin

International competition for the Mercedes exhibition stands, upon invitation of Daimler Chrysler

2001

European competition "Media City Port" for the planning and design project of an existing dock area of 54,000 square metres in the port of Hamburg

International competition for the design project of a private residence in Hamburg, upon invitation of Mr Paulmann

2000

International planning competition for the Museo del XX secolo in Arengario in Milan. First phase

International competition for a pedestrian bridge, organised by the City of Rome

International competition for the headquarters of the Italian space agency in Rome, organised by the City of Rome in collaboration with Ingenhoven, Overdiek & Partner Germany. First phase

International competition for "Ansaldo - The City of the Cultures", upon invitation of the City of Milan, in collaboration with Cino Zucchi, architect, Milan. Second phase

1999

Corporate design and interior concept for the Lamborghini showroom and exhibition stands, upon invitation of Automobili Lamborghini - Audi AG

Corporate design and interior concept for the Chrysler and Jeep showroom and exhibition stands, upon invitation of Daimler

Interior design for a restaurant in Hamburg. Winning competition entry - project under construction

1998

Restructuring of the tower buildings of the ENEL headquarters in Rome

The Moenchsberg Museum for Modern Art in Salzburg

1997

Interior design for the ACEA headquarters building in Rome

Interior design for the Landesbank headquarters building in Frankfurt

Interior design for the ENI headquarters building in Rome

Restructuring of the existing Line A underground system of Rome, upon invitation of the City of Rome. Winning competition entry

1996

Corporate design of Commerzbank branches in Germany, in collaboration with Michael Schirner for the graphic project. Competition entry and realisation of the pilot branches in Frankfurt and Berlin

nterior concept for Smart centres, Smart building and exhibition stands, upon invitation of Daimler Chrysler AG and MCC smart GmbH. Winning competition entry

Montpellier Public Library in Montpellier with Emmanuel Nebout Architect, upon invitation of Montpellier Town Hall

Restructuring of the existing MM1 underground system of Milan. Winning competition entry

Selected Bibliography: Books

2006

Designer's Design. Tokyo: Gap Japan Co. Ltd.

Pläne Projekte Bauten. Berlin: Verlagshaus Braun.

Matteo Genghini and Pasqualino Solomita, *Attici*. Milan: Motta Architettura.

2005

Italy Builds. Milan: Arca Edizioni.

Sebastiano Brandolini, *Milano. nuova architettura*. Milan: Skira.

Anja Clorella, *New Hotels 2*. New York: Harper Design.

Massimiliano Falsitta, *Showroom 2*. Milan: Federico Motta Editore.

Caroline Klein, *Cool Shops Milan*. Kempen: teNeues.

Hildegard Kösters, *Neumühlen 17*. Hamburg: BDA Hamburg Architektur Preis.

Simone Micheli, *Centri Benessere*. Milan: Federico Motta Editore.

Francesca Oddo, *Architettura in dettaglio – boutique*. Rome: D.E.I.

Luigi Prestinenza Puglisi, *Antonio Citterio*. Rome: Edilstampa.

Martin Rolshoven, *New Furniture Design*. Cologne: Daab.

2004

The Phaidon Atlas of Contemporary World Architecture. London: Phaidon.

Alberto Bassi, *Antonio Citterio. Industrial Design*. Milan: Electa.

Terence Conran and Max Fraser, *Designers on Design*. London: Conran Octopus.

2003

Graziella Leyla Ciagà, *Gli archivi di architettura in Lombardia*. Milan: CASVA.

Elio Di Franco, *Sanitari. Il design della migliore produzione*. Milan: Federico Motta Editore.

Cherubino Gambardella, *Scale. Repertorio contemporaneo*. Milan: Federico Motta Editore.

Arian Mostaedi, *Cool Shops*. Barcelona: Links Publishing Group.

Carlo Vanniccola, *Maniglie. Il design della migliore produzione*. Milan: Federico Motta Editore.

Carlo Vanniccola, *Porte. Il design della migliore produzione*. Milan: Federico Motta Editore.

2002

Vincenzo Pavan, *Nuova architettura di pietra in Italia*. Faenza: Gruppo editoriale Faenza editrice.

2000

Carol Soucek King, ed., *Designing with Spirituality*. New York: PBC International Incorporated (Casa Lanza), pp. 146–149.

Jeremy Myerson and J. Hudson, *International Interiors 7*. London: Laurence King Publications (Aspesi), pp. 120–123.

1999

Laura Andreini, Nicola Flora, Paolo Giardiello and Gennaro Postiglione, eds., *Case d'autore. Interni italiani 1990-1999*. Milan: Federico Motta Editore.

Giuliana Gramigna, *'Dizionario' dei designers dal 1950*. Turin: Allemandi Editore.

Claudia Neumann, *Design Lexikon Italien*. Cologne: Editrice Dumont.

1998

Mario Campi and Pippo Ciorra, *Young Italian Architects*. Basel: Birkäuser.

Arian Mostaedi, *Single Family Houses*. Barcelona: Links International.

Richard Sapper, *The International Design Yearbook 1998*. London: Laurence King Publications.

Lorenzo Soledad, *New European Furniture Design*. Barcelona: Links International.

Penny Sparke, *A Century of Design*. London: Reed Books.

1997

International Design Review 1997. Milan: Action Group Editore.

François Fauconnet, Brigitte Fitoussi and Karin Leopold, *Vitrines d'architecture. Les boutiques à Paris*. Paris: Editions du Pavillon de l'Arsenal, Picard Editeur.

Paola Gallo, *Nuovi negozi in Italia 4*. Milan: Edizioni l'Archivolto.

1995

Luca Basso Peressur, Remo Dorigati and Elisabetta Ginelli, *L'architettura del caffè*. Milan: Editrice Abitare Segesta.

Pippo Ciorra and Vanni Pasca, *Antonio Citterio, Terry Dwan: Ten Years of Architecture and Design*. Basel: Birkhäuser.

Paola Gallo, *Ville in Italia*. Milan: Edizioni l'Archivolto.

Roberto Marcatti, *Parola di designer*. Milan: Editrice Abitare Segesta.

Jeremy Myerson, *International Interiors 5*. Singapore: Laurence King Publications.

Carol Soucek King, *Furniture: Architects and Designers Originals*. New York: PBC International Inc.

John Welsh, *Modern House*. London: Phaidon.

Anatxu Zabalbeascoa, *The House of the Architect*. Barcelona: Editorial Gustavo Gili, SA.

1994

Ron Arad, *The International Design Yearbook 1994*. London: Calmann & King Ltd.

Lucy Bullivant, *International Interiors 4*. Singapore: Laurence King Publications.

Carol Soucek King, *Coming Home – Residential Furniture by Architects & Interior Designers*. New York: PBC International Inc.

Alfredo Zappa, *Intorno al fuoco: il caminetto tra mito, storia e tecnologia*. Milan: Electa.

Selected Bibliography: Periodicals

1993

John Beckmann, *Interior Details: Showrooms*. New York: PBC International Inc.

Marco Casamonti, *Nuove abitazioni in Italia*. Milan: Edizioni l'Archivolto.

Pippo Ciorra, Brigitte Fitoussi and Vanni Pasca, *Antonio Citterio & Terry Dwan. Architecture & Design. 1992–1979*. Zurich: Artemis.

Phil Sayer, *First Thoughts and Original Images*. London: Phaidon.

1992

Andrée Putman, *The International Design Yearbook 1992*. London: Calmann & King Ltd.

1991

Lucy Bullivant, *International Interiors 3*. London: Thames & Hudson.

Franco Zagari, *Sull'abitare – Figura Materialità Densità*. Milan: Edizioni Over.

1990

Anty Pansera, *Il design del mobile italiano dal 1946 ad oggi*. Bari: Editori Laterza.

1989

Enzo Frateili, *Continuità e trasformazione – Una storia del disegno industriale italiano 1928/1988*. Milan: Alberto Greco Editore.

1988

Giampiero Bosoni and Fabrizio G. Confalonieri, *Paesaggio del design italiano 1972-1988*. Milan: Edizioni Comunità.

Juli Capella and Quimm Larrea, *Architekten, Designer der achtziger-jahre*. Stuttgart: Verlag Gerd Hatje.

Silvio San Pietro and Matteo Vercelloni, *Nuovi negozi a Milano*. Milan: Edizioni l'Archivolto.

1987

Fumio Shimizu and Matteo Thun, *Descendants of Leonardo da Vinci. The Italian Design*. Tokyo: Graphic SHA Publishing Co. Ltd.

1982

Mario Mastropietro, *Un'industria per il design*. Milan: Edizioni Lybra Immagine.

1980

Isa Vercelloni, *1970-1980. Dal design al post design*. Milan: Edizioni Condè Nast.

2006

"Visioni Italiane", *Domus* insert, July–August, p. 45.

Antonella Boisi, "Spazi fluidi", *Interni*, May, pp. 32–37.

Nicoletta Del Buono, "Rapsodia equatoriale", *AD Italia*, October, pp. 286–293.

Lia Ferrari, "Tropico dell'anima", *Io Donna*, August, pp. 152–157.

Alexander Hosch, "Citterio al fresco", *AD Germany*, April, pp. 52–56.

Jennifer Kabat, "Master of All Scales", *Metropolis*, February, pp. 92–97.

Laura Leonelli, "La casa di vetro", "Style" *Corriere della Sera* insert, November, pp. 252–264.

Elena Nemkova, "Antonio Citterio", *AD Russia*, June, pp. 42–48.

Luigi Prestinenza Puglisi, "Antonio Citterio and Partners", *The Plan*, April, pp. 21–26.

Pierpaolo Tamburelli, "L'asilo cortile", *Domus*, May, pp. 46–55.

Rosaria Zucconi, "Uno spazio per l'arte", *Elle Decor*, November, pp. 252–263.

2005

François Burkhardt, "La nuova Amburgo", *Ottagono*, April, pp. 166–167.

Alba Cappellieri, "Tra la terra secca e il mare luminoso", *Abitare*, June, pp. 110–117.

Ray Edgar, "Authentic Ingredients", *Monument*, February–March, pp. 96–99.

Luca Molinari, "Bulgari Hotel in Milan", *a+u*, September, pp. 123–129.

Derya Nüket Özer, "Bulgari Oteli", *Yapi*, May, pp. 69–74.

Claudia Russo, "Sanus per aquam in Mailand", *Baumeister*, April, pp. 40–45.

Veronica Russo, *Economy*, February, pp. 62–63.

Annalisa Trentin, "Edel Music AG", *d'Architettura*, September–December, pp. 72–73.

2004

Sara Banti, "Nuove architetture", *Casamica*, 3 April, pp. 174–181.

Aric Chen, "Hip To Be Square", *Interior Design*, January, pp. 93–94.

Alexander Hosch, "Quo Vadis, Citterio?", *AD Architectural Digest, Germany*, April, no. 4, pp. 48–54.

Hirokuni Kanki, "Antonio Citterio", *Axis*, June, no. 6, p. 145.

Elena Plebani, "Axor Citterio Rabinets d'un designer", *Decors*, no. 1, pp. 100–102.

Jacob Schoof, "Inspiration Italien", *AIT*, no. 9, pp. 67–75.

Luigi Spinelli, "Architettura milanese, stile internazionale", *Domus* special, November, pp. 30–41.

Suzanne Stephens, "Hotels – Sleeping in Style", *Architectural Record*, August, no. 8, pp. 148–150.

Meghan Stromberg, "Hansgrohe: Axor Citterio", *Professional Builder*, January, pp. 118–120.

Jan Van Rossem, "Antonio Citterio", *A & W Special*, February, pp. 18–20.

2003

"Le pape du design", *Le figaro magazine*, 15 March, p. 100.

"The Rustic Man", *Intra*, April, pp. 36–38.

Antonella Boisi, "Spazio astratto", *Interni*, April, pp. 242–247.

Stefano Casciani, "L'albergo modello", *Domus* hotel extra, November, pp. 76–81.

Cornelia Krause, "Zwei Ansichten", *Deutsche Bauzeitung*, no. 9, pp. 63–67.

Frank A. Reinhardt, "Von der Armatur zum Raum", *Design Report*, no. 4, pp. 40–43.

Ingrid Sommar, "Fran tunnelbana till vattenkran", *Arkitektur*, September, pp. 62–66.

Aleksandra Stepnikowska, "Design jest odpowiedzia", *Architektura murator*, no. 4, pp. 74–75.

Paola Tamborini, "Ausgangspunkt Raum Antonio Citterio", *Raum und Wohnen*, no. 3, pp. 122–128.

Paul Taylor, "Enduring Style", *The New Zealand Herald*, 23 July, p. 10.

2002

"Highlight", *Architektur Innenarchitektur Technischer Ausbau*, nos. 1–2, pp. 77–85.

Stefano Casciani, "Costruire ad Amburgo", Domus, November, pp. 74–87.

Edie Cohen, "Antonio Citterio", *Interior Design*, December, pp. S12–S16.

Lauren Goldstein, "Staying in Style", *Time*, 16 December, p. 32.

Dane McDowell, "Géométrie dans l'espace Carimate", *Résidences décoration*, June, pp. 60–69.

Petra Trefalt, "Zeitloser Modernist", *Design Report*, July, pp. 50–54.

Rogalski Ulla, "Ein Moderner geht seinen Weg", *Handelszeitung* home special, March, p. 7.

Jan Van Rossem, "Antonio Citterio: erneuerer der moderne", *Architektur & Wohnen*, March, pp. 77–87.

Matteo Vercelloni, "B&B Italia Store: uno spazio per il design", *Interni*, December, pp. 177–191.

Ahrens Von Inge, "Herzstück vom Profi", *Boulevard*, October, p. 8.

Rosaria Zucconi, "Glamour italiano", *Elle Decor*, September, pp. 166–177.

2001

"La factoria Citterio", *Diseno interior*, April, pp. 138–147.

Antonio Citterio, "Villa nel Comense", *Casa d*, April, pp. 58–79.

Edie Cohen, "Studio Central", *Interior Design*, May, pp. 328–331.

Phoebe Greenwood, "Un tunnel di luce", *Domus*, October, pp. 98–107.

Caroline Klein, "Form-findung", *Deutsche bauzeitung*, no. 4, pp. 51–57.

Fabrizio Todeschini, "Antonio Citterio", *Habitat ufficio*, March, pp. 166–173.

2000

"Antonio Citterio, Cino Zucchi, Philippe Délis, Vignelli Ass., Pietro Clemente, Tedesco, Ariatta – Milano: Ansaldo la città delle culture. Concorso internazionale di progettazione", *Abitare* insert, June.

Pamela Buxton, "Family Ties", *Design Week*, 27 October, pp. 16–17.

Antonio Citterio, "Cene Villa Complex", Zlaty Rez, no. 20, pp. 34–37.

1999

Evi Mibelli, "Ritorno alle origini", *Interni*, March, pp. 76–81.

1998

"Bologna, Saiedue 1998 e Milano, Salone del Mobile 1997", *Rassegna*, no. 73, pp. 98–101, 102–105.

"Casa unifamiliare, Cene, Bergamo", *Domus*, February, pp. 28–33.

"Funktionales Vvolumen", *Möbel Interior Design*, July, pp. 50–51.

"Mariella Burani en Milan", *Diseño Interior*, no. 77, pp. 86–87.

"Negozio 2000: una proposta", *Abitare il tempo*, pp. 15–21.

"Pavillon", *Ottagono*, June–August, pp. 146–149.

"Profilen Citterio", *Elle Interiör*, March, pp. 30–35.

"Tiendas Fausto Santini", *Diseño Interior*, January, pp. 120–123.

"Un'ipotesi di lavoro. Il progetto di immagine coordinata della metropolitana milanese linea 1", *Ottagono*, September–November, pp. 48–51.

Cover: "Exklusiv. Die Wohnung des Stardesigners. Antonio Citterio" Article: Regina Decoppet and Franziska Müller, "Reduzierte sprache in Arkitektur und Design", *Ideales Heim*, June, pp. 91–96.

Cover and article: "Vivienda Citterio-Dwan", *Diseño Interior*, no. 76, pp. 36–41.

Luca Aloisi, "ABC – Buchstäblicher Komfort", *Wohnrevue*, pp. 136–138.

Antonella Boisi, "Tra rigore e poesia", *Interni*, May, pp. 90–97.

Stefano Casciani, "Antonio Citterio. Mode e stili", *Abitare*, October, pp. 132–133.

Edie Cohen, "The New Domestic Landscape", *Interior Design*, August, pp. 138–143.

Anne Draeger, "Les pros de la déco chez eux. Antonio Citterio, un designer chaleureux", *Madame Figaro*, March, pp. 76–85.

Michaela Dunworth, "Modern Language", *Belle*, August–September, pp. 72–79.

Daniela Falsitta, "La casa da vivere", *Interni*, January–February, pp. 132–133.

Marco Mulazzani and Michele Reboli, "Giovani Architetti italiani 97-98", *Almanacco di Casabella*, pp. 62–65.

Michelle Ogundehin, "The Italian Job", *Elle Decoration* (UK), December, pp. 74–81.

Maddalena Padovani, "Una scatola di luce", "Interni capitale del design", *Panorama* insert, 5 June, pp. 54–59.

Caroline Roux, "Staying Power", *ID*, January–February, pp. 68–69.

Carla Shumann, "Privatwelt eines Top-Designers. Citterio pur", *Architecture & Whonen*, August–September, pp. 38–45.

1997

"Antonio Citterio pour Cerruti", *Architecture interieure creè*, no. 275, pp. 118–119.

"Citterio & Dwan boutique Cerruti à Milan", *L'Architecture d'Aujourd'hui*, June 1997, p. 102.

"Form und Flexibilität", *Design Report*, February, pp. 30–33.

"Vom neuen poetischen Purismus", *AD*, February–March, pp. 200–204.

Fabrizio Bergamo, "Apta, dal mobile all'ambiente", *Interni*, May, pp. 110–113.

Heike Bering, "Antonio Citterio", *Moebel Interior Design*, December, pp. 70–75.

Lucas Hollweg, "The Design of a Serious Man", *The Independent Review* (the *Independent on Sunday*), 2 February, pp. 52–53.

Gabriele di Matteo, "Nelle nicchie del Made in Italy", "Casa & Design", *La Repubblica* insert, 18 April, p. 11.

Kicca Menoni, "Antonio & Terry", "Interni", *Panorama* insert, December, pp. 69–81.

Michelle Ogundhein, "Citterio Modern Heroes", *Elle Decoration*, February, pp. 86–88.

Annamaria Scevola, "Declinare un'immagine", *Ottagono*, June–August, pp. 106–109.

Federica Tommasi, "Uno scenario Ad Hoc", *Ufficio Stile*, January–February, p. 44.

1996

"Antonio Citterio sull'aria di un progetto coerente", *Interni*, September, pp. 166–169.

"Come un classico ridisegnato.Citterio per Fusital", *Ottagono*, September–November, p. 160.

Albrecht Bangert, "Mailand Meets New York", *Elle Decoration*, May–June, pp. 76–81.

Antonella Boisi, "Lo spazio Cerruti", *Interni*, October, pp. 90–97.

Stefano Casciani, "L'arte nel cuore della luce", *Abitare*, December, pp. 91–101.

Rudolf Novak, "Doppelpaß", *Möbel Raum Design*, December–January, pp. 56–61.

Phil Patton, "A Classic Goes to Europe, Returning Brand New", *Sunday*, 8 September, p. 49.

Elena Plebani, "Un appartement milanais d'Antonio Citterio", *Decors*, September–November, no. 992, pp. 172–179.

Klaus Schmidt-Lorenz, "Erfolg durch Gespür", *Design Report*, January–February, pp. 47–53.

Rosaria Zucconi, "Boutique", *Elle Decor*, September, pp. 35–36.

1995

"Antonio Citterio. The Evolution of the Kitchen Space", *Interni Annual Cucina*, pp. 5–16.

Antonella Boisi, "Ad Hoc per l'ufficio del Duemila", *Interni*, May, pp. 134–139.

Robert Haidinger, "Antonio Citterio: Möbel mit Logik und System", *Der Standard*, album detail, March, pp. 2–6.

Beverly Pearce, "Process Revealed by Design", *Metropolis*, May, p. 64.

1994

"Antonio Citterio and Terry Dwan", *Axis*, summer, pp. 134–137.

"Three Stores for Fausto Santini", *Domus*, September, pp. 60–65.

Antonella Boisi, "Spazi puri", *Interni*, November, pp. 82–91.

Stefano Casciani, "Storage-Drawer System Kartell", *Abitare*, April, pp. 194–195.

Cecilia Fabiani, "Light. Die reduzierten Ladenbauten Antonio Citterios", *Ait*, March, p. 46.

Gino Finizio, "La riduzione del segno", *Ottagono*, September–November, pp. 82–87.

Eleonora Restelli, "Antonio Citterio: Designer per vocazione", *Office Furniture* insert, no. 62, pp. 14–19.

Federica Zanco, "A Family of Lamps", *Domus*, March, pp. 56–59.

1993

"Antonio Citterio & Terry Dwan. Fabbrica di imbottiti a Neuenburg", *Abitare*, September, pp. 182–185.

"Concours pour le mobilier hospitalier", *Intramuros*, May–June, pp. 38–39.

"Il Fortino. Antonio Citterio et Terry Dwan: siège social de l'enterprise, Tokyo", *Architecture Intérieur*, April–May, pp. 86–89.

"Main Man in Milan Antonio Citterio", *Design Week*, October, no. 41.

Ursula Dietz, "Modern von Renaissance behütet", *Häuser*, no. 1, pp. 30–33.

1992

"Il lusso del vuoto", *Gap Casa*, November, pp. 82–85.

"Vom Reiz der Klarheit", *Ait*, May, pp. 54–66.

Brigitte Fitoussi, "Showroom Corrente à Tokyo, Boutique Fausto Santini à Paris", *L'Architecture d'Aujourd'hui*, September, pp. 152–155.

Rita Imwinkelried, "Antonio Citterio aus Meda", *Hoch Parterre*, January, pp. 54–57.

Dada Sanz and Alvaro Varela, "Showroom de Corrente in Tokyo", *Diseño Interior*, no. 11, pp. 40–43.

Aidan Walker, "The Music Megas", *Designers' Journal*, January, p. 28.

1991

"Japan: West-Östliches Würfelspiel", *Häuser*, no. 5, pp. 146–151.

Brigitte Fitoussi, "Virgin Megastore à Milan", *L'Architecture d'Aujourd'hui*, December, pp. 150–152.

Jose Maria Marzo, "Tienda Esprit", *Diseño Interior*, May, pp. 82–87.

Pino Scaglione, "Antonio Citterio", *d'A*, p. 68.

Sophie Tasma Anargyros, "Antonio Citterio", *Intramuros*, September–October, pp. 38–42.

1990

"From the Architect's Account. Antonio Citterio & Terry Dwan: Casa sperimentale, Kumamoto", *Domus*, February, pp. 8–9.

Brigitte Fitoussi, "Antonio Citterio", *L'Architecture d'Aujourd'hui*, July, pp. 202–222.

Hernàn Grafias, "Antonio Citterio entre la arquitectura y el diseño", *Diseño*, September–November, pp. 56–61.

E.M., "Antonio Citterio per Vitra, AC 1 High Tech", *Domus*, September, pp. 112–115.

Karen D. Stein, "Shadow Box", *Architectural Record*, April, pp. 78–83.

Sophie Tasma Anargyros, "Esprit atterrit Place de la Victoires à Paris", *Intramuros*, March–April, pp. 22–26.

1989

Edie Cohen, "Two by Citterio & Dwan", *Interior Design*, April, pp. 284–288.

1988

"Opulenza ma 'scabra ed essenziale'", *Abitare*, December, pp. 128–137.

"Strenge Ästhetic: Esprit Mailand. Die Architektur zwingt zur Konzentration", *Architektur & Wohnen*, February–March, pp. 90–93.

Vernon Mays, "Esprit Amsterdam: Well-chosen Words", *Progressive Architecture*, September, pp. 66–73.

1987

Manolo De Giorgi, "Antonio Citterio – Afrikahuis ad Amsterdam", *Domus*, September, no. 686, pp. 64–73.

1985

"Restructuration du Musée de Brera Milan", *L'Architecture d'Aujourd'hui*, September, no. 240, pp. 22–23.

Cristina Morozzi, "Ritratto di un designer: in viaggio alla ricerca dei maestri", *Modo*, December, no. 85, pp. 30–33.

1984

Alessandro Colbertaldo, "Shop Design", *Interni*, May, pp. 2–5.

1983

"Salle d'exposition Milan", *L'Architecture d'Aujourd'hui*, November, no. 230, pp. 104–105.

1980

Roberto Beretta, "Diesis: un esempio di coerenza. Un progetto di Antonio Citterio e Paolo Nava B&B Italia", *Rassegna*, June, no. 57, pp. 67–71.

Antonio Citterio and Partners
14 March 2007

Antonio Citterio
Patricia Viel

Architecture

Augusto Barichello
Marco Brambilla
Sara Busnelli
Flaviano Capriotti
Francesca Carlino
Guido Cuscianna
Carmine D'amore
Mira De Middeleer
Ella Dinoi
Fabrizio Ferranti
Ilaria Gatto
Lorenzo Laura
Paolo Mazza
Annalisa Menozzi
Joseph Monteleone
Manfredi Nicoletti
Mauro Novazzi
Daniele Raimondi
Claudio Raviolo
Michele Reboli
Chiara Romoli
Emanuele Santini
Lavinia Sciacchitano
Barbara Soro
Florian Thorwart
Giuseppe Vestrucci
Hodaka Yamamoto

Design

Toan Nguyen
Fabio Busnelli
Leonardo Mangiavacchi
Sergio Schito

Graphics

Alessandro Banfi

Public Relations and Communications

Alessandra Noto

Models

Enrico Pellegrini

Secretariat

Sonia Magrì
Flavia Sapia

Administration

Marcello Citterio
Licia Scagliotti
Michela Scarlata

Head of IT

Claudio Sanfelici